Domestic Enemies

Domestic Enemies

Servants & Their Masters in Old Regime France

Cissie Fairchilds

The Johns Hopkins University Press
Baltimore and London

This book has been brought to publication with the generous assistance of the Andrew W. Mellon Foundation.

Printed in the United States of America

The Johns Hopkins University Press, Baltimore, Maryland 21218
The Johns Hopkins Press Ltd, London

Library of Congress Cataloging in Publication Data

Fairchilds, Cissie C.
Domestic enemies.
Bibliography: p. 287
Includes index.
1. Domestics—France—History—18th century. 2. Master and servant—France—History—18th century. I. Title.
HD8039.D52F837 1983 305.4′364 83-48059
ISBN 0-8018-2978-X

Frontispiece: Jean-Baptiste-Simeon Chardin, *The Kitchen Maid*. Reproduced by permission, Samuel H. Kress Collection, National Gallery of Art, Washington.

Contents

Figures

Tables

Preface

Domestic enemies" was the common euphemism for domestic servants in seventeenth and eighteenth-century France. Apparently first popular in Renaissance Italy, it had become by the beginning of the Old Regime a cliché found in countless French comedies and novels.[1] With its suggestions of simultaneous closeness and distance, intimacy and enmity, the phrase epitomized relationships between master and servant during the *ancien régime*. Such relationships form the subject of this book.

I first conceived of this book in 1970 when I was a graduate student. Like most graduate students, I was oppressed by the thought that all the good topics for research had already been done, and domestic servants appealed to me because they were a social group almost completely neglected by historians. There had been no scholarly work on servants in my period, Old Regime France, since the publications of those antiquarian chroniclers of *la vie quotidienne*, Albert Babeau and Alfred Franklin, in the 1890s, and indeed, apart from the maverick work of J. Jean Hecht on eighteenth-century English domestics, there were no serious studies of servants of any place or period.[2]

This neglect was easy to explain. Traditionally the social history of the lower classes was primarily labor history, which focused on the formation of the modern working class and its eventual emergence into class consciousness and political activity. Historians therefore tended to study only artisans, day laborers, and other heroic precursors of the proletariat. Servants simply did not fit this mold. Their work was economically "unproductive"; their social attitudes were disappointingly deferential; and they rarely left the domestic sphere of the household to take part in politics. Also, many of them were women, an automatic disincentive for study at a time when history was still largely "his story."

Nevertheless, domestic servants formed a substantial portion of the society of Old Regime France, and it seemed to me that a modest monograph about them, modeled on the prosopographical studies of social groups in vogue at the time,[3] and dealing with such matters as their social origins, incomes, and marriage and family patterns, would fill an obvious if relatively unimportant gap in my field. That is how this book began.

I was, however, sidetracked by other projects, and when I returned to my study of servants in 1976, it was with a very different sort of book in mind. For by the late 1970's the field of social history had been utterly transformed by the emergence of the *Annales* school, the history of the family, and the history of popular culture and *mentalités*.[4] My interest in these new fields gave me a whole new set of questions about domestic service: about the occupation as "women's work," about the sexual exploitation of female domestics, about the roles of servants in the family lives of their employers, about the mental universe of servants, their attitudes and behavior toward their masters, and their masters' attitudes and behavior toward them. But I soon realized that these questions could not be encompassed within a narrow monograph. So I began to plan a much more ambitious work which would draw on the topics and techniques of the "new social history," a study including masters as well as servants and focusing on the relationships of the two groups within the household.

This book is the result. Eclectic in approach, it cuts across the boundaries of many traditionally separate fields of social history. The book is, first of all, in part the modest prosopography of the servant population which I had first envisioned. As such it deals with questions which must be asked about any social group: the social origins of servants, their incomes, their marriage and family patterns, their career patterns, their possibilities for social mobility, their political activities, and their criminality.

But the book is also an essay in the history of the family and domestic life in sixteenth, seventeenth, and eighteenth-century France. For servants were, at least until the rise of the affectionate nuclear family in the middle of the eighteenth century, considered part of the families of those they served. Their work created the domestic setting in which family life was played out. Often it was they who raised and educated their employers' children and filled their masters' sexual needs. Therefore the history of the family, of attitudes toward children, of sexual relationships, of household organization and management, and consumption patterns among the French elite all form important parts of my story.

Finally this book is also an essay in the history of social relationships in the ancien régime, not only those between masters and servants but also the broader relationships between the ruling elite and the lower classes. For relationships between the "domestic enemies" were conditioned by the general notions of the proper organization of society and the proper demeanor of superior and inferior prevalent in the Old Regime. Indeed, master-servant relationships not only reflected broader social attitudes but also may have helped to form them, for in prerevolutionary France the household may well have been an incubator of class attitudes. It was, after all, the one place where elite and lower classes were in constant contact, a battlefield (if we may expand the military metaphor implicit in the phrase "domestic enemies") where issues of autonomy and control were continually fought out. Servants were the only lower-class social groups their masters knew intimately; therefore it seems inevitable that their relationships with their domestics would color their attitudes toward the lower classes in general. Similarly, servants were the only segment of the lower classes to acquire an intimate knowledge of the manners and mores of the upper classes, and it was they who acquainted their fellow townsmen and their friends and relations in the countryside with the ways of the elite. Thus the relationships between the "domestic enemies" probably shaped as well as reflected social attitudes in the ancien régime, and these too form an important part of my story.

The book is organized to reflect these concerns. The first chapter is essentially introductory. It gives the basic facts about the composition of households during the Old Regime and explores the attitudes and assumptions that underlay the employment of servants. It also shows how both these attitudes and the households themselves changed dramatically in the last decades before the French Revolution.

Part 1 is devoted to the servants themselves. One chapter deals with their lives within their employers' households: their work, their living conditions, their socializing and leisure-time activities. A second examines their private lives: their social origins, marriage and family patterns, their moneymaking, and their criminality. And a third explores their relationships with and attitudes toward their masters.

In Part 2 the focus shifts to an examination of master-servant relationships from the masters' point of view. The first chapter deals with master-servant relationships in general, and discusses the factors that determined how employers treated their domestics. The second and third chapters explore two "special cases" of relationships within the household which had great psychological influence on masters: their sexual relationships with their servants and their relationships with the servants who cared for them in childhood. The final chapter of the book is an epilogue which traces the impact of the French Revolution on domestic service and on the servants themselves, and sketches some of the changes in the household that would come in the nineteenth century.

The two main parts of the book rely on two very different types of sources. Servants are one of those social groups which used to be called "inarticulate." They left behind few letters or memoirs (although I was lucky enough to find in the Archives Nationales a large cache of letters written by a Parisian cook in the 1780s). Therefore the bulk of my information about servants came from indirect sources, most of which required quantitative analysis: tax rolls, marriage contracts, household account books or *livres de raison; déclarations de grossesse* (statements required by law of unwed mothers in the ancient régime); wills; and police records. These sources were drawn from three main areas, chosen to exemplify the three most important patterns of servant employment in the Old Regime: Toulouse, a typical provincial town, an economically stagnant administrative center dominated by a provincial nobility and a professional and office-holding bourgeoisie; the booming port of Bordeaux, with its dynamic commercial middle class; and Paris, a case unto itself, a mecca for servants because of its high salaries and enormous households of the court nobility. Admittedly these choices show a bias toward southwestern France regrettable in a book that pretends to be national in scope. But this was an unavoidable byproduct of the peculiarities of Old Regime customary law. Only in the southwest were the provisions of the laws on property such as to encourage almost everyone to make marriage contracts and wills, two types of documents indispensable for my study. However there is no evidence that domestic service or servants in the rest of France differed greatly from my Toulousan and Bordelais examples. Also regrettable is the paucity of information on farm servants, whom I treat only tangentially. But their story is so bound up with the agricultural history of France's various regions that it would require another—and very different—sort of book to do them justice.[5]

Because of my source material, servants appear all too often in these pages as statistical averages rather than as individual human beings. Their masters are luckier, because they left abundant letters and memoirs which allow them to speak in their own words. This sort of material is my second major source. Supplemented by household manuals, cookbooks, architectural handbooks, and religious treatises on family life, these memoirs form the basis for those sections dealing with masters and their domestic life.[6] Lacking a good bibliography of such works, I decided to make up my own by working through the printed catalog of the Bibliothèque Nationale—a time-consuming and monumentally boring task I never quite completed, but which nonetheless produced an abundance of useful references. Like the statistically analyzable documents that form my other major source, this material too has its biases. It is heavily weighted with examples from the immediate prerevolutionary decades and from the high nobility: almost every noble of distinguished lineage who survived the Revolution intact seems to have immediately sat down to compose his or her memoirs. Memoirs from the seventeenth century, and from the provincial nobility and the bourgeoisie, are much less abundant. This bias is less serious than it might appear, for, as we shall see, great noble households employed a sizable proportion of the servant population and provided the model for lesser establishments. Nevertheless, I have tried, though doubtless not always successfully, to distinguish among household types, and to refrain from using examples derived from great noble households when they were not applicable.

Acknowledgments

This book has been long in the making and I have incurred many debts in the course of its gestation. The University of California Regents' Research Fund and a summer fellowship from the National Endowment for the Humanities partially supported my research, done mostly in France in the summers of 1977, 1978, 1979, and 1980. A fellowship from the American Council of Learned Societies, funded by the National Endowment for the Humanities, and a generous leave from Syracuse University allowed me to take the year off in 1980–81 to write. My research was made immeasurably easier by the help of the staffs of the departmental and municipal archives and municipal libraries in Toulouse and Bordeaux, of the Archives Nationales and the Bibliothèque Nationale in Paris, and of the Library of Congress, the Van Pelt Library of the University of Pennsylvania and the State Library of Pennsylvania. Two of these people deserve special mention. M. Nadel in the Archives Départementales de la Haute Garonne in Toulouse and the woman whose name I never learned in the municipal archives of that city were, of all the French archivists and librarians I have ever encountered, the most patient, good-natured, and prompt in dealing with the sometimes odd and overwhelming requests of "*l'Américaine.*" It is not surprising that so many good local and regional studies have come out of Toulouse!

Thanks are also due to all those friends and acquaintances whose companionship sustained me through my research and writing. Probably no one who has not done it can imagine either the loneliness of living for months in a cheap hotel room in a provincial French town or the tedium of going through seemingly endless series of boringly similar tax rolls, wills, and marriage contracts. In such circumstances the presence of other historians to talk to (in English!) is an immeasurable boon. Therefore I would like to thank Jack Thomas, Robbie Schneider, and Tim Tackett, companions in Toulouse; Julius Ruff, whose presence relieved the gloom of Bordeaux; and those I call the "B.N. crew": the Americans who flock to Paris each summer to work in the reading room of the Bibliothèque Nationale and who are always willing to go to lunch with someone starved for company after months in the provinces. During my summers of research I enjoyed and appreciated the company of, among others, Theresa

McBride, John Merriman, Louise Tilly, Sharon Kettering, Keith Baker, Bill Weber, Jeremy Popkin, Marjorie Ferrar, Michael Hanagan, Natalie Davis, Lynn Hunt, Robert Paxton, David Bien, John Baldwin, Richard Golden, George Sussman, Bill Cohen, and Alan Spitzer.

I must also thank a number of close friends without whom this book would never have been completed. Jack and Jane Censer put me up on my forays into the Library of Congress. Linda Clark and Lenny Berlanstein not only brought books back for me from Paris, but also endured many despairing phone calls, and patiently doled out encouragement and advice. Conversations with Carole Shammas helped clarify my ideas about the domestic sphere, and her cheerful cynicism about our profession kept me from taking the whole thing too seriously. Nonhistorians Sarah and Alice Heintzelman and Marynelle, Philip, and Betsy Spear provided the distractions of "real life" when I needed them. And as always, my mentor, Robert Forster, gave the inspiration of his example.

Finally, I owe more than I can ever express to my mother, who not only typed the manuscript twice but also put up with me during my year of writing, enduring patiently a dining room table covered with notes and a daughter in the agonies of composition. It is only fitting that a book so concerned with domesticity and domestic relationships be dedicated to the person who has devoted herself to making a comfortable and happy home for me.

Domestic Enemies

1

Introduction: Domestic Service in the Old Regime

The history of servants is a vital topic in this [the eighteenth] century.
—Jules Michelet, *Histoire de France au dix-huitième siècle*

To visitors to Paris on the eve of the French Revolution the domestic servants of the city, said to number close to 100,000, were one of its major sights, on a par with Notre Dame, the fair of St. Germain, and those new-fangled amusements, the balloon ascension and the public restaurant.[1] A traveling Englishwoman, Mrs. Fanny Cradock, who in April 1784 watched *tout Paris* enjoying its traditional Easter week diversion of driving up and down the fashionable boulevards, noted that the "lackeys in superb liveries" as much as the fine carriages and the fashionable clothes of their occupants gave the scene its glamour. Again a month later, when she attended a military review on the plain of Sablons, she was more impressed by the "extraordinarily beautiful liveries" of the numerous lackeys in attendance on the fashionable audience than she was by the maneuvering of the troops.[2] Mrs. Cradock was not alone in her admiration of and fascination with the domestics of Paris. Guidebooks for visitors were full of tips on where to view them and how to treat them, and other tourists commented extensively on their looks, manners, and savoir-faire.[3] French servants were generally conceded to be the most fashionable and knowledgeable—if not the most faithful and obedient—in the world, and they were, like the French language, French fashions, and the works of the philosophes, a major export to the *haut monde* of other countries. Every English duke and German princeling with any pretensions to taste and culture employed a French *valet de chambre* or *chef*.[4]

All this points up a fact that we, who live in a very different society, are liable to forget: servants formed a sizable and important social group in eighteenth-century Europe. They were most likely to be found in cities. Like fashionable clothes, fine china and furniture, and a taste for coffee, tea, and cocoa, their employment was one of the marks of the growing affluence of eighteenth-century urban elites. In France they were of course most numerous in Paris, that center of luxurious living. On the eve of the Revolution around 15 percent of the population of Paris were domestics, and in fashionable districts like the faubourg St. Germain the figure was much higher.[5] The factors that determined the proportion of servants in the population of a given town were, first, the presence of nobles and officeholders, who tended to maintain large households of domestics, and, second, the existence of alternative employment opportunities for the lower classes. Therefore provincial administration centers like Rennes, Toulouse and Aix-en-Provence, with their many nobles and officeholders and lack of commerce and manufacturing, tended to have large numbers of servants among their denizens. In Aix-en-Provence 16 percent of the population in 1695 and 12 to 13 percent in 1750 were servants; in Toulouse figures for the same years were 10 and 8 percent.[6] By contrast, servants were fewer in commercial cities like Lyons, Marseilles, and Bordeaux, where the smaller households of the dominant mercantile elites and the existence of alternative job opportunities for the *menu peuple* diluted their numbers. In the late eighteenth century only 8 percent of the people of Bordeaux and 4 percent of the people of Marseilles were domestics.[7]

Servants were less likely to be found in rural areas. Yet even the most minor country town had a few *notables*—the mayor, the leading grain trader—wealthy enough to employ a maid-of-all-work.[8] And the farmland around cities abounded in *maîtres-valets* and *jardiniers*, tenant farmers considered servants in the eighteenth century, who worked the plots of absentee urban landlords, while landowners in the countryside proper hired numerous farm servants for the season or the year to plant and harvest crops, care for the livestock, and do whatever household chores needed doing. In rural France the percentage of servants in the population probably varied from a low of 2 percent to a high of 12 percent.[9]

Clearly servants formed an important part of the society of the Old Regime. Domestic service was a major employer of lower-class labor. Probably only agriculture and crafts employed more male workers than service did, and service was probably second only to agriculture as an employment opportunity for lower-class women.[10] On the eve of the Revolution in 1789 there were about two million servants in France; therefore one out of every twelve French men and women earned his or her living as a domestic.[11] This proportion was probably as high as it had ever been before or ever would be again.[12]

Types of Servants and Definitions of Servanthood

One reason why there were so many servants in prerevolutionary France is that they formed a social group whose boundaries were very loosely drawn. *Domestique* and *serviteur* (the most common words for servants in the Old

Regime) were umbrella terms that covered people with a wide variety of social backgrounds, incomes, and occupations. Servants included teamsters, musicians, gardeners, silk weavers, shop clerks, and even lawyers as well as people who cooked, cleaned, raised the children, and carried the messages of their employers. Some were as rich and grand as members of the king's household like Charles-François-Joseph L'Escureul de la Touche, *Intendant et controlleur-général de l'argenterie, menus plaisirs et affaires de la chambre du Roi*, who enjoyed a fortune of over 600,000 livres and married his daughter to a noble intendant. Others were as poor and wretched as eighteen-year-old Jeanne Leconte, waitress in a seedy harborside cafe in Bordeaux called the Reine de France, who received no salary but instead lived off her tips and the proceeds from occasional prostitution.[13]

This wide range of servants resulted from the broad definition of the group. Today domestics, like all other occupational groups, are defined primarily by the sort of work they do. Webster's Third Unabridged Dictionary defines a servant as "a person who performs household or menial chores for an employer."[14] But in Old Regime France domestic service was considered an *état* rather than a *métier*: dictionaries defined a *domestique* not by the sort of work he did but instead by the fact that he lived in a household not his own in a state of dependency on its master. For example, Furetière's *Dictionnaire universel*, published in 1701, stated that a servant was "a member of a household, under a household head," a definition echoed by the great *Encyclopédie*, which characterized a *domestique* as "someone who lives in another's household and shares his house."[15] It was this tendency to define servants by their membership in a household which made the boundaries of the group so broad.

This definition of a servant dated back to the Middle Ages, when the household or *domus* (hence the word *domestique*) was the basic unit of society, performing many important functions which it later lost.[16] The household, in the person of the lord administering justice, was the basic unit of local government. It was also the basic unit of economic production. And it provided for the education and defense of its members, as well as serving as a setting for their domestic family life. Given this wide range of functions, it is not surprising that the households of great lords were enormous establishments numbering two or even three hundred people. All the members of the household, from the lord's family and his gentlemen-in-waiting through his troubadors and men-at-arms to the cobblers and blacksmiths in the workshop and the lowly potboys in the kitchen, were members of his *domus*, his *domestiques*, his servants. Indeed, the concept of service extended even beyond the boundaries of the household to permeate all medieval society. For anyone who was dependent upon and owed respect, loyalty, and "service" to a social superior was by medieval definitions a servant.[17] Thus in the Middle Ages serfs, who owed labor to their lord, knights, who owed him fealty, and even kings, who might be vassals of another ruler for part of their domain, could legitimately be classified as servants.

The later history of domestic service is a story of the gradual shrinkage of this broad definition of service and servants as political, economic, and social change robbed the household of many of its functions. In the sixteenth century "service" was permanently confined within the household, and the household itself contracted in size. With the increasing sophistication of the economy, households did not have to produce all they consumed; therefore the late sixteenth century was the last time that a great noble household included craftsmen like goldsmiths and furriers.[18] And with the growing power of the state, nobles no longer regularly fielded private armies; the late sixteenth century was therefore also the last time that a great lord referred to his armed soldiers as his servants.[19] The late sixteenth century was also the last time that well-born youngsters entered a household to receive an education in "courteous" behavior and, it was hoped, the protection and patronage of a great lord. By 1700 young nobles were educated in schools, and young men of gentle birth but small fortune who hoped to rise in the world entered the bureaucracy or the professions rather than domestic service.[20]

Thus by the beginning of the Old Regime the status of servant was increasingly confined to those lower-class types who performed menial domestic labor for their employers, "servants" by our definition as well as theirs. They included the maid-of-all-work in lower-and middle-class households (she was called a *fille de service* or *servante*; the nineteenth-century term *bonne* had not yet come into use); her male counterpart, usually called a *laquais* or *domestique*; and the more specialized domestics who staffed large noble households: personal body servants like *femmes* and *valets de chambre*; the *maîtres d'hôtel, cuisiniers, officiers* and *aides de cuisine* of the kitchen staff; the coachmen (*cochers*), grooms (*palefreniers*), and postilions in the stables; the nursemaid (*gouvernante*) and tutor (*précepteur*) in the nursery; and the lackeys (*laquais*) who wore the household's livery and ran its errands. These were supplemented on country estates by gamekeepers (*gardes-chasse*) and *servantes de basse-cour*, who cared for the household's cows and chickens. The laws of the Old Regime defined these types as servants: it was they for whom their masters paid the special *capitation* tax on servants, and it was they who were subject to the *police des domestiques* by which towns tried to regulate servant behavior.[21]

But apart from these incontestable servants, a number of more doubtful cases claimed servant status on the basis of their membership in a household.[22] Examples are gardeners (*jardiniers*), sedan-chair carriers (*porteurs de chaise*), and wet nurses (*nourrices*), who during the Old Regime were considered servants if they lived in their employer's household and worked exclusively for it and wage laborers if they did not. This same distinction was applied to agricultural laborers. If they were hired on a long-term (usually yearly) contract and shared their master's home, they were servants; if they lived in their own cottage and hired themselves out on a piecework basis they were mere day laborers. In the households of urban craftsmen, apprentices were usually not considered servants, but "hired hands" like bakers' boys or the women weavers in a Lyons silk workshop, if they "lived in," usually were. Also still within the ranks of servanthood were the meager remnants of once numerous gentlemanly attendants of medieval households: secretairies, tutors, musicians, lady companions, and the like.

A final, and most important, category of those considered servants by virtue of their membership in a household were family members. During most of the Old Regime it was customary for prosperous families who needed extra labor to take in poor relations—unmarried brothers, widowed sisters-in-law, orphaned cousins—as servants, who in return for food and board did the housework and labored in the family enterprise. And in addition to these types who actually did servants' work, even members of the immediate nuclear family, wives and children, were considered servants by Old Regime definitions. For during the most of the ancien régime "household" (*ménage*) and "family" (*famille*) were synonymous terms, and little distinction was made between family members and outsiders in the household. Thus in 1690 Furetière's *Dictionnaire* defined *famille* as "a household composed of a head and his *domestiques*, be they wives, children, or servants (*serviteurs*)."[23] Wives and children were in a sense servants of their husbands and fathers (one dutiful seventeenth-century son always signed himself "Vostre très humble, très obéissant et très obligé fils et serviteur" in letters to his father), while servants were in a sense members of a family (one domestic manual of the period called them "adopted children whom parents must care for like children of their own").[24]

This identification of servants as family members is important, for it had implications for domestic service that went beyond mere questions of definition. It gave the domestic service of the Old Regime one of its salient characteristics: its patriarchalism. Families in the sixteenth, seventeenth, and early eighteenth centuries were above all patriarchal.[25] In that harsh world husband and wife, parents and children were bound together by ties of duty and obedience rather than love. Wife and child owed respect and submission to their patriarchal husband/father; in return he provided for their material needs and watched over their moral and spiritual welfare. Such was the natural organization of society ordained by God. The same sort of ties bound the "adopted children" to their patriarchal fathers. Servants owed respect and obedience to their masters; in return, their employers were to care for them as a father would, providing, as one domestic manual put it, "not only temporal subsistence, but [also] instruction, good morality, and spiritual benefits."[26]

As we shall see, this patriarchal vision of domestic service shaped the working conditions of the occupation, the behavior of master and servant, and public perceptions of servants and service in myriad ways during the Old Regime.[27] It was a vision natural to a society in which the basic social unit was still (despite its losses) the household rather than the individual, in which ties between men were personal rather than monetary, and in which the God-ordained form of social organization was thought to be a hierarchy of superior and inferior. Indeed, the concept of patriarchy pervaded the society of the sixteenth, seventeenth, and early eighteenth centuries just as the concept of "service" had pervaded the society of the Middle Ages. Its metaphors of caring father and submissive child shaped all relationships between superior and inferior, not only those of master and servant but also those of king and subject, magistrate and citizen.[28] Thus through most of the Old Regime domestic service was a characteristic product and, with its daily manifestations of the proper demeanor of superior and inferior, master and servant, also an important prop of the traditional hierarchical society in which it flourished.

Patterns of Servant Employment

Another salient characteristic of domestic service in the Old Regime—and one that further marked it as a product and prop of a traditional hierarchical society—was its public nature. Today we employ domestics, if at all, to do those household chores we are unable or unwilling to perform ourselves; in other words, to contribute to our private domestic comfort. But in the Old Regime this was only one, rather minor, reason to hire a servant. Servants were also employed to do productive labor in shops and on farms. And above all they were employed for reasons of status. In the rigidly hierarchical society of the ancien régime, servants were simply a status necessity for all those above a certain social level. For as one seventeenth-century domestic manual stated, it was unsuitable that "a *grand seigneur* walk the streets of a town alone on foot like a bourgeois, or that a rich bourgeois carry a heavy parcel on his shoulders."[29] The employment of servants not only saved one from performing undignified and ignoble tasks, but also served as a public proclamation of one's social rank. In fact, so necessary were servants to social status and so rigid were the customs governing their employment that it was possible to tell the precise social rank and aspirations of a man of the Old Regime simply from the size and makeup of his household.

We can see how strongly status influenced the employment of domestics by examining the patterns of servant-keeping in a typical city. Toulouse, an administrative center with little commerce or industry, was precisely the sort of town where servants were most likely to be widely employed.[30] It is possible to learn a great deal about the size and composition of households in Old Regime France in the year 1695 and after, because the *capitation* tax passed in that year required that employers pay, in addition to their own tax (whose level varied by income), a small extra sum for each servant employed. Thus the rolls of the *capitation* list (in theory at least) all domestics employed in every household.

The pattern of servant employment in Toulouse in 1695, as shown in its *capitation* rolls, is summarized in table 1.[31] It indicates that the employment of servants was quite widespread. Almost a third of the town's households in-

TABLE 1

Employment of Servants in Toulouse, 1695

Employer	Households					Servants		
	N	% of Total		% with Servants		N	% of Total	
Nobility[a]	501	8.8		90.6		1461	45.7	
Professionals, bourgeoise[b]	760	13.4		55.4		564	17.6	
Merchants	276	4.9		64.9		216	6.8	
Minor professionals[c], officials	323	5.7	28.6	44.0	52.3	156	4.9	32.9
Shopkeepers	260	4.6		40.4		114	3.6	
Artisans, textile workers	1961	34.6		12.4		207	6.5	
Food, lodging, transportation workers	390	6.9	54.8	25.4	14.8	133	4.2	11.3
Wage laborers[d]	757	13.3		2.4		19	0.6	
Clergy	93	1.6		88.2		191	6.0	
Other[e]	354	6.2		7.1		136	4.3	
Total	5675			31.5		3197		

Source: ADHG, C 1082, Rolle de la capitation de la ville de Toulouse, 1695.

[a]Includes titled nobles, *écuyers, secrétaires du roi, parlementaires,* judges in other major courts (some of whom are admittedly technically bourgeois) and *capitouls.*

[b]Includes *médecins, avocats, procureurs,* architects, teachers, those labeled *bourgeois,* and those listed only by the respectable titles of Sieur and Dlle.

[c]Minor officeholders and the lower levels of the professions: notaries and surgeons.

[d]Includes those labeled peddlers, beggars, and poor.

[e]Includes servants listed as having their own household and a small number of unknowns.

cluded a domestic. But these servants were distributed unequally among the various social groups that composed the town's population. Nobles accounted for only 8.8 percent of the households in Toulouse, yet they employed almost half of the town's servants. Conversely, over 40 percent of the town's households belonged to members of the lower classes, yet they employed only 11 percent of Toulouse's domestics.

The lower classes—artisans, wage laborers, and the like—were the only social group whose decision to employ a servant was not influenced by status considerations. It was instead determined by two other factors: cost and need. Keeping a servant was surprisingly inexpensive in the late seventeenth century, because servants were often unpaid; the patriarchal concept of the household carried with it the implication that work was a duty a servant owed to the master rather than a commodity to be exchanged for cash.[32] But domestics did have to be fed, and this cost a minimum of 150–200 livres per year—a sum too great for most of Toulouse's shoemakers, textile workers, and the like.[33] Table 2, which summarizes the distribution of households in Toulouse by income level, shows that most lower-class households were so poor that

TABLE 2

Distribution of Households by *Capitation* Level, Toulouse, 1695 (in %)

	Livres					
	0–2	3–10	11–50	51–100	101+	Not Given[a]
Nobility	0.01%	15.6%	23.8%	20.5%	19.2%	19.9%
Professionals, bourgeois	20.8	42.6	30.3	5.0	1.2	—
Merchants	7.9	26.4	54.6	5.3	5.7	—
Minor professionals, officials	23.7	45.5	29.9	0.9	—	—
Shopkeepers	24.0	39.5	35.7	0.1	—	—
Artisans, textile workers	50.9	32.8	16.2	0.1	—	—
Food, lodging, transportation workers	32.9	43.9	23.2	—	—	—
Wage laborers	87.1	11.6	1.4	—	—	—

Source: ADHG C 1082, Rolle de la capitation de la ville de Toulouse, 1695.
[a]Parlementaires and members of other courts were assessed separately from the rest of the town. Therefore, their assessment was often not recorded on the town's *capitation* rolls.

they paid only the minimum *capitation*; their total yearly income was probably only around 500 livres.[34] On such an income it was difficult to keep a servant.

Those few servants found in lower-class homes were often family members, poor relations taken into the household of a slightly more prosperous relative to work in return for food and board. The *capitation* roll for the district of Toulouse known as Dalbade, a poor neighborhood with a high concentration of artisans, is unusually explicit about the familial relationships of master and servant. It shows that eighteen of the eighty-nine domestics in Dalbade were relatives of their employers, and that all but four of the households that contained such servants were lower class (the exceptions were a notary, a minor official, and two priests). Typical were the tailor whose sister-in-law "had the place of a *servante*" and the innkeeper who employed his niece as a waitress.[35]

Whether family members or strangers, servants were employed in lower-class households when extra labor was needed in the family enterprise beyond that which a man, his wife, and children could provide. Table 1 shows that among the lower classes servants were most likely to be found in the households of artisans and textile workers, who might well find another pair of hands useful for tending the counter or working the loom, and in the food, lodging, and transport sectors, whose enterprises—stables, inns, bakeshops and the like—were clearly labor-intensive. Wage laborers, who had no need of extra help, were unlikely to employ domestics.

In the middle ranks of Old Regime society status considerations generally outweighed cost and need in the decision to employ a servant. The shopkeepers, merchants, lawyers, and *rentiers* who composed the middle classes in towns like Toulouse employed a domestic if they could possibly afford one. Usually this person was just a maid-of-all work, or *servante*, hired to help the lady of the house with her domestic chores. Sixty-eight percent of the middle-class households with domestics in Toulouse had just the one *servante*. Especially affluent members of the middle classes might take on an extra maid, but only rarely did they employ any specialized upper servants like *femmes de chambre* or cooks. They were also extremely reluctant to employ male domestics. This was not for reasons of cost, although skilled upper servants and male servants in general did command higher salaries than mere *servantes* (see chapter 2), but instead for reasons of status. Large households and male servants were hallmarks of the nobility, and had been since the Middle Ages, when great lords boasted of huge and almost totally male establishments (the household of a medieval Earl of Northumberland, for example, numbered 175, of whom only 9 were women).[36] Because of their traditional association with the nobility, few members of the bourgeoisie dared to employ male or skilled domestics.

This is illustrated in table 3, which analyzes the households with male servants in Toulouse in 1695. Few petty bourgeois households contained male domestics. What menservants there were among Toulouse's middle classes were concentrated in the households of professionals like doctors and lawyers, and of those who were "bourgeois" in the eighteenth-century meaning of the term, rentiers who lived off their incomes without working. Few were found in merchants' households. The difference between the mercantile and professional bourgeoisie clearly indicates the role of social status in the employment

TABLE 3

Employment of Male Servants by Household in Toulouse, 1695

	Male Servants				
Employer	N	% of Total		% of all Servants in Household	
Nobility	782	63.4		53.5	
Professionals, bourgeois	116	9.4	13.0	20.6	15.2
Merchants	21	1.7		9.7	
Minor officials	12	1.0		7.7	
Shopkeepers	11	0.9		9.6	
Artisans, textile workers	14	1.1	4.1	6.8	14.2
Food, lodging, transportation workers	34	2.8		25.6	
Wage laborers	3	0.2		15.8	
Clergy	137	11.1		71.7	
Other	103	8.3		75.5	
Total	1233				

Source: ADHG C 1082, Rolle de la capitation de la ville de Toulouse, 1695.

of servants. Merchants could well afford male domestics; as table 2 shows, they were in general wealthier than members of the professions. But merchants lacked prestige in the society of the ancien régime because their wealth derived from sordid commerce. Therefore they did not dare to imitate the life style of the nobility. But types like lawyers, with their more genteel incomes and their hopes of purchasing an office that would bring them nobility, and bourgeois, who already "lived nobly" in preparation for the transition to noble status, were much less diffident about aping the nobility. As table 4 shows, at almost every income level professionals had larger households than merchants, and as table 3 shows, they employed many more male domestics. Indeed, so powerful were the taboos surrounding servant-keeping that it is possible to trace the exact boundary separating those who could legitimately aspire to multi-servant households and male domestics and those who could not. This boundary ran right down the middle of the professions, dividing the gentlemanly upper ranks of law and medicine from their less prestigious lower reaches. Thus gentlemanly *avocats* (barristers) employed an average of 1.12 servants per household, and 24.6 percent of these servants were men. But the less respectable *procureurs* (solicitors) averaged only 0.87 servants per household, and only 9.1 percent were men. Male servants composed 17.9 percent of the average 0.54 servants per household of gentlemanly *médecins* (doctors), while lowly *chirurgiens* (surgeons) contented themselves with 0.53 servants per household, of whom only 9.7 percent were men.[37]

These figures suggest two distinct patterns of servant employment in the middle ranks of Old Regime society. Among the mercantile middle classes the single *servante* household was the rule; even the wealthiest merchants rarely

TABLE 4

Servants per Household by *Capitation* Level, Toulouse, 1695

	Livres					
	0–2	3–10	11–50	51–100	101+	Not Given[a]
Nobility	1.25	1.05	2.01	2.61	6.27	6.27
Professionals, bourgeois	0.04	0.43	1.20	1.72	2.57	2.00
Merchants	0.00	0.30	0.93	1.75	1.31	—
Minor professionals	0.00	0.38	1.04	1.00	—	—
Shopkeepers	0.05	0.26	0.87	2.00	—	—
Artisans, textile workers	0.07	0.14	0.38	1.00	—	—
Food, lodging, transportation workers	0.03	0.38	0.83	—	—	—
Wage laborers	0.01	0.12	0.78	—	—	—

Source: ADHG C 1082, Rolle de la capitation de la ville de Toulouse, 1695.

[a]Parlementaires and members of other courts were assessed separately from the rest of the town. Therefore, their assessment was often not recorded on the town's capitation rolls.

had large establishments or male servants. This was true not only in administrative centers like Toulouse, but also in commercial cities like Bordeaux, which had much less diffident and more dynamic mercantile elites.[38] Professionals and true "bourgeois," on the other hand, were more likely to have multi-servant households, and to employ menservants. But even they rarely aspired to more than one or two maids and a male *domestique*. Large households and long trains of lackeys were clearly reserved for the nobility.

Nobles, ranging from modest *écuyers* and *secrétaires du roi* to the courtiers whose family names fill the pages of history books, were the servant employers par excellence in Old Regime France. As table 1 shows, although they formed only a small percentage of Toulouse's population in 1695, they employed almost half of its servants. This forms a striking contrast to patterns of servant-keeping in later periods: in nineteenth-century France the majority of servants were found in bourgeois households.[39] In the ancien régime the employment of at least one domestic was a bare minimum for those with any claim to noble status. Servants were so essential to the status pretensions of the nobility that, so Pierre-Jean-Baptiste Nougaret, a chronicler of eighteenth-century Parisian life, tells us, an elderly miser who begrudged paying a servant's wages bought a coat of livery and paraded in it in front of his windows so that his neighbors would think he kept a domestic![40] In Toulouse in 1695 over 90 percent of noble households contained a servant, and, as table 4 shows, often even the poorest of nobles, those who paid the minimum 0-2 livres of *capitation*, somehow managed to scrape together enough to feed and house—though rarely pay—a domestic.

Most nobles of course were not content with a single-servant household. As table 4 shows, at every income level they employed more servants than any other social group. Noble households in Toulouse averaged 2.92 servants each. Many were considerably larger, for the larger the household the more prestige reflected on its master. An eighteenth-century German traveler, J. C. Nemeitz, noted that French noblewomen regularly boasted of the number of servants they kept, just as they did of "the price of their coiffure, the style of their clothes, and the behavior of their children."[41] The employment of men servants also contributed to a master's standing, as did the employment of skilled upper servants like *femmes de chambre*, coachmen, and cooks. An early eighteenth-century treatise on manners advised flattering one's friends and acquaintances by giving their *servantes* the more prestigious title of *femmes de chambre* and referring to their *domestiques* as *valets*.[42]

The association of large and elaborate households with social prestige encouraged an endless proliferation of domestics in the households of the upper ranks of the nobility, a proliferation that nonetheless followed exactly the complex gradations of rank in the highly status-conscious society of the ancien régime. Titled nobles had larger households and more male and skilled upper servants than did mere *écuyers; parlementaires* employed more domestics than did judges in the lesser courts. Even within Parlements rank determined servant-keeping. *Présidents à mortier* employed more servants than did mere *conseillers*, and *premier présidents* had the most of all.[43] In a town like Toulouse, an administrative center dominated by its Parlement, it was the *premier président* of that court's Grande Chambre who had the largest household in the city. He employed sixteen domestics: a chef; a *femme de chambre* and a lady companion for his wife; a *valet de chambre* for himself; a nursery maid and tutor for his children; two coachmen; a groom; a *suisse* (a guard for the door); four lackeys and two *servantes*.[44]

This may have impressed a provincial town like Toulouse, but if *M. le premier président's* household had been transported to Paris or Versailles it would have seemed meager and mean compared with the establishments of the court nobility—*les grands*, as they were known in the seventeenth century. For them twenty or thirty servants were a bare minimum: the Comtesse de Rochefort, living modestly in the country, nonetheless employed thirty-odd domestics.[45] A well-known seventeenth-century domestic manual maintained that any truly *grand seigneur* needed a household of at least fifty-three.[46] Many noble establishments of the period numbered considerably more. The Duc and Duchesse de Gramont employed 106 servants, the Pontchartrains 113; the Duc de Nevers, though laden with debts, had a household of 146; Cardinal Richelieu employed 180 domestics. Largest of all was of course the household of the king, which numbered over 4,000 in the middle of the seventeenth century.[47]

These gargantuan establishments, swollen by enormous trains of liveried lackeys who wore their masters' colors and accompanied them when they appeared in public, were obviously much larger than was necessary to keep even the biggest *hôtel* or *château* running smoothly. But this was not their primary purpose. Throughout most of the Old Regime, in the sixteenth, seventeenth, and early eighteenth centuries, the nobility was little interested in domesticity and in the private joys of family life.[48] Their marriages were arranged for reasons of financial and familial advantage, and relationships between spouses were distant, formal, and unloving. So too were relationships between parents and children. Noble ladies spent their lives as court attendants or *salonnières*, not as wives and mothers; child-raising was left to servants. Children were brought up in an atmosphere of both neglect and fear of the patriarchal father-figure. In these circumstances the emotional focus of the nobility was rarely the private joys of family life.

Old Regime nobles were instead "public men" as sociologist Richard Sennett has characterized them.[49] They were as emotionally involved in their public encounters with strangers as they were in their private relationships with family and friends. And in such encounters they used dress, speech, bearing, and gestures to elicit a proper recognition and response. No social group was more adept at these public relationships than the nobility. All aspects of their style of life—their extravagant dress, their lavish hospitality, their enormous houses with their entrances, staircases, and rooms arranged to overawe visitors—functioned as public proclamations of their place at the apex of the social hierarchy. And no element of the noble life style was more vital for this than their long trains of servants. Servants not only provided opportunities, with their rich liveries and their sheer profusion, for further displays of wealth; they also created what E. P. Thompson has called a "theater of rule," demonstrating constantly to the world the obedience and deference they—and, by implication, everyone else—owed to their masters.[50] Thus one major function of domestic servants was to provide a public demonstration of the nobility's right to rule.

The essentially public nature of domestic service persisted during most of the Old Regime. In the sixteenth, seventeenth, and early eighteenth centuries family ties were cold and distant and the pleasures of domesticity were not highly valued. Servants were therefore hired less for the private tasks of providing domestic comfort than they were for public display. This was especially true of the nobility, who employed the majority of servants and set the tone for the occupation as a whole. But it was also true to a lesser extent of the bourgeoisie, who carefully adjusted their households to what was appropriate for their precise social rank. This use of servants for public display made domestic service in the seventeenth and early eighteenth centuries very different from what it would be in later periods. The public nature of domestic service, like its patriarchalism, marked it as both a product and a prop of the traditional hierarchal society of the Old Regime.

Changes in Domestic Service in the Last Half of the Eighteenth Century

Domestic service was so closely tied to the traditional society of the Old Regime that when, in the 1760s, 1770s, and 1780s, society began to change domestic service inevitably changed too. Historians are beginning to realize that the years from around 1760 to 1789 form a major turning point in French history, a break in continuity perhaps even more important than the period of the French Revolution, for it was the economic, social, and political changes of the last decades of the Old Regime that prepared the way for revolution in 1789.[51] Economic growth; demographic growth; changes in the definition of the family and the emotional climate of family life; new attitudes toward life and death, religion and the natural world; changes in the composition of society and in basic social attitudes; new notions about the purposes of government and about its relationship with its citizens: all these transformed French society in the years immediately preceding the Revolution. And at least some of these factors—the spread of a market economy and its values, changing definitions of the family and of sex roles, changing notions about social organization and the prerequisites of status—had a great impact on that mirror of traditional society, domestic service.

Their impact becomes obvious from a comparison of patterns of servant employment in 1789 to those of the late eighteenth century. The employment of servants in eighteenth-century Toulouse, as revealed in the *capitation* rolls for 1750 and 1789, is summarized in table 5.[52] These figures compared to those in table 1 indicate that during the eighteenth century employing a servant became less common: in 1695 almost a third of all households in Toulouse contained a domestic, but by 1789 the proportion was only 23.3 percent. And an increasing proportion of households that employed servants were bourgeois. The middle classes employed 32.9 percent of Toulouse's servants in 1695, 34.9 percent in 1750, and 47.7 percent in 1789.[53] In 1695 the nobility had employed almost half of Toulouse's servants, and the middle classes almost one-third, but by 1789 these proportions were reversed. Thus by the eve of the Revolution there was a clear trend toward what we might call the "bourgeoisification" of domestic service.

In part this trend resulted from a decline in the lower classes' role as servant-holders. Hard hit by population growth and a rising cost-of-living, by 1789 the lower classes could no longer afford to keep a domestic. Although Toulouse had more lower-class households in 1789 than in 1695, they employed a much smaller share of the town's servants (7.7 percent vs. 11.3 percent). The average number of servants per lower-class household declined in the course of the eighteenth century (from 0.12 in 1695 to 0.06 in 1789), and so did the percentage of lower-class households that employed domestics.

Although many of the bourgeoisie's gains came at the expense of the lower classes, the nobility's share of domestics also declined in the late eighteenth

TABLE 5

Employment of Servants in Toulouse, 1750 and 1789

	1750			1789		
	% of Total Households	% of Total Servants	% of Households with Servants	% of Total Households	% of Total Servants	% of Households with Servants
Nobility	9.2	43.0	89.4	4.6	35.5	91.5
Middle class	27.9	34.9	51.5	29.1	47.7	45.6
Lower class	47.5	10.4	11.7	52.8	7.7	5.5
Clergy	1.3	4.8	87.7	1.3	7.4	95.1
Other	14.1	6.9	14.8	12.1	7.7	53.6
Total			30.5			23.3

Sources: Archives Municipales, Toulouse, *Capitation* rolls CC 1004, 1008, 1014, 1041, 1046, 105 1062, 1069, 1086, 1116, 1120.

century. While most nobles continued to employ servants if at all possible (the percentage of noble households with domestics actually rose slightly from 1695 to 1789), these establishments were often smaller than they had been in the seventeenth century. This was less likely to be true of the households of provincial nobles in towns like Toulouse, which were small (at least by noble standards) to begin with, than of the households of *les grands* in Paris and Versailles. By 1789 the enormous noble household numbering over 100 was clearly a thing of the past. In her memoirs the Marquise de Villeneuve-Arifat described the household of her father, a robe noble who was first *président* of the Cour des Comptes in Paris and moved in the most fashionable circles of the Parisian *haut monde* in the 1780s. Along with a staff of five in the kitchen he employed:

> at the door, a tall and true *Suisse*, complete with cross-belt and halberd . . . two coachmen and a postilion; my father had a *valet de chambre* and three lackeys; my mother, two lackeys and a *valet de chambre*; my oldest brother, one *domestique*; the three others and their tutor, one *domestique*; a *femme de charge*, who had another woman to help her; my mother, two *femmes de chambre*; and us one *femme de chambre*.[54]

These twenty-three servants were typical of the world in which the Marquise's father moved. Even the court nobility of late eighteenth-century Paris had households that numbered only in the twenties. The Maréchal de Mirepoix employed twenty-one domestics; the Prince de Lambesc twenty-nine; the Comte Dufort de Cheverny began married life with a mere fifteen.[55] These establishments were sizable, but still far from the fifty-three servants deemed a bare minimum for a *grand seigneur* in the seventeenth century. Thus a contraction in size of the households of the high nobility also contributed to the "bourgeoisification" of servant employment in the late eighteenth century.

Accompanying this "bourgeoisification" was another shift in patterns of servant employment, which might be labeled a "feminization" of the occupation. In the last decades of the Old Regime the proportion of servants who were women started to grow, beginning a process that led eventually, by the middle of the nineteenth century, to a predominantly female work force in domestic service and a labeling of the occupation as "women's work." In the 1770s and 1780s this process had barely begun, yet it is detectable in the changing sex ratios of the servants of Toulouse. In 1695, 38.6 percent of the town's domestics were men. In 1750 the figure was down to 34.3 percent, and in 1789 it was 35.3 percent. In part this trend toward feminization was a simple outgrowth of the increasingly middle-class nature of servant employment: the middle classes had always favored female domestics, and they continued to do so in the late eighteenth century. But other factors were also at work. The shrinking of noble households obviously cut into the ranks of male domestics, as did a growing tendency among nobles to hire women to do work formerly done by men servants—cooking, for example. Toulouse's *capitation* roll of

1695 list 70 cooks, all but 2 of whom were men. But in 1789, 225 cooks were listed, and of these 173 were women.

A final characteristic of the new patterns of servant-holding, and one that tended to slow the trend toward feminization and keep numbers of male servants high, was an increased disregard of the traditional rules which tied household size and type to social status. In Toulouse, socially conservative and economically stagnant, this trend was not very evident. Although nobles were beginning to substitute women for men in some areas, their households were still largely male; 57.9 percent of the nobility's servants in 1789 were men. And the mercantile bourgeoisie remained more reluctant than professionals and officeholders to employ male servants. In 1787, 20.6 percent of the domestics of professionals/officeholders were men (the same proportion as in 1695), while only 8.1 percent of the domestics of merchants were male. But in towns like the booming port of Bordeaux, with a more economically aggressive and self-confident bourgeoisie, a shift in pattern is evident. In the years 1717–29, 72 percent of the male servants who made marriage contracts in Bordeaux were employed by the nobility, while the bourgeoisie employed only 16 percent. But in 1787–89 the nobility's share was down to 49 percent, while that of the middle classes rose to 39 percent.[56] Another sign of the eagerness of the Bordelais merchant community to employ male servants was the popularity of the peculiar figure of the *jakez* or *jockei*—not a horseback rider, as an amused English visitor noted, but instead a boy who performed all the functions of a male domestic.

> Everybody last year . . . had to wait upon them, what they called a *Jackay*, a little boy with straight, lank, unpowdered hair, wearing a round hat—and this groom-like thing waited upon them at dinner. . . . It was in vain for me to assert that "jockey" meant riding-groom in a running-horse stable, and that no grooms ever waited upon us. . . . They answered it must then be a new fashion, for it was *tout-à-fait à l'anglaise et comme on se fait à Londres*.[57]

Bordeaux's newspaper, the *Journal de Guienne*, carried in the 1770s and 1780s innumerable advertisements for *jockeis*, most placed by merchants and other members of the middle classes. Clearly the *jockei* was a cheap shortcut to the employment of a prestigious male domestic.

Thus by 1789 the patterns of servant employment in France were beginning to change. The rigid rules about household size and type were weakening, women servants were beginning to replace men, and the middle classes were overtaking the nobility as the chief employers of servants. These changes were only the most visible manifestations of the deep-seated transformations brought about in domestic service by the new economic and social forces of the late eighteenth century.

In the years from 1750 to 1789, domestic service lost the two characteristics that had shaped it in earlier periods: it ceased to be public and it ceased to be patriarchal. The major blow to the public character of domestic service came with the emergence among the nobility and the office-holding bourgeoisie of a new style of family life, as the traditional patriarchal family was replaced by a more modern, more affectionate, more egalitarian, and more child-centered one.[58] Spouses began to marry for love, or at least to treat each other with affection and respect after they were married. And they began to work together to raise their children in an atmosphere of security and indulgence. For the nobility the joys of this newly close and affectionate family life came to be more important than their public relationships. This transformed the very purpose of their servant-keeping. For with the new style of family life came new notions of domesticity and a new emphasis on domestic comfort. The nobility began to have servants primarily for housework rather than "public" functions. Consequently smaller and more feminine households characterized noble servant-keeping in the last decades of the Old Regime.

This shift from a public to a "private" domestic service was reinforced by new notions about the nature and perquisites of social status. The social thought of the Enlightenment challenged the traditional, rigidly hierarchichal society and sought to replace it with a more egalitarian one. In this new society prestige derived less from inherited rank than from social usefulness and individual worth, qualities which were more difficult to exemplify by outward signs of social status. Therefore these signs—the size and type of one's household, for example—began to lose their importance. This probably lay behind the growing disregard of the traditional rules about household size and the employment of male servants visible in the last years of the Old Regime.

Thus by the eve of the French Revolution domestic service had lost much of its traditional public character. It also lost much of its patriarchalism. Here again the major culprit was the emergence of the modern affectionate family. This new type of family life brought with it a new definition of the family. No longer was "family" synonomous with "household"; instead it was defined as only the nuclear unit of parents and children.[59] Thus in the last decades of the Old Regime the servant was expelled from the family circle. He ceased to be the "adopted child" of a patriarchal family and became instead a stranger, someone hired to do housework or personal service in return for a wage.

Behind this redefinition of the servant as stranger and wage laborer lay not only the new notions about the family but also the spread of the market economy and its values. During spectacular economic growth of the last half of the eighteenth century these values engulfed even the last occupation in which the ties between employer and employee were still personal rather than monetary: domestic service. By 1789 domestic service had at long last ceased to be an *état* and became instead a *métier*. A servant's work was no longer a duty he owed to his master; instead it was a commodity of his own which he could exchange for cash. Servants ceased to be members of patriarchal households and took their place in the ranks of the working classes.

This redefinition of the servant as wage earner also had an impact on the size and makeup of households. In the late eighteenth century servants became wage earners in fact as well as in theory. It was no longer possible to hire servants simply for their food and board; instead they had to be paid money wages.[60] This monetization of servants' work naturally raised the cost of servant-keeping, and this in turn affected patterns of servant employment. Rising costs eliminated servants from lower-class households and encouraged the trend toward smaller establishments and more women servants among the nobility.

The most important effect of the new definition of the servant as wage earner, however, was that it changed the way people thought about domestic service. The last years of the Old Regime were, like the sixteenth century, a period when the occupation was redefined and the ranks of servanthood were narrowed. This was when our modern definition of the servant as someone hired to perform menial domestic labor finally emerged. Therefore all those whose status as servants depended solely on their membership in a household were no longer considered servants. The poor relations and "hired hands" who were taken into lower-class households when extra labor was needed did not entirely disappear; indeed, Balzac's murderess Thérèse Raquin is a nineteenth-century example of the classic poor relation taken in by better-off relatives to do domestic chores. But after 1750 these types were no longer labeled servants.

The new definition of domestic service as wage labor also eliminated from the ranks of servitude gentlemanly upper servants—secretaries, tutors, musicians, and the like. In this case the departure was voluntary. Such people found the new definition of servanthood insulting. Not only did it imply that servants were wage laborers and therefore drawn from the lowest ranks of society, but also that the tasks they performed were menial and therefore degrading. Indeed, the very condition of being a servant was considered degrading in the late eighteenth century. Classically-minded commentators of the period tended to trace the origins of domestic service not to the great households of the Middle Ages where gentlemen performed acts of service with no loss of status but instead to the household slavery of ancient Greece and Rome.[61] This suggested that servanthood was essentially servile in nature and therefore an occupation unworthy of a free man. Being a servant inevitably involved surrendering one's freedom of choice, and this was increasingly seen as unacceptable in a society in which the philosophes were beginning to define freedom as freedom of the will, as being one's own master.[62] By the 1770s the conviction that domestic service was an occupation unworthy of a free man was so widespread that it was found even in government edicts. The preamble to a Parisian police ordinance of 1778 said of servants: "Born free, like all other citizens, but however obliged by the occupation they embraced to sacrifice their repose to the need, the taste, sometimes even to the caprice of those to whom they devote themselves . . . they live in a state of veritable slavery."[63]

In these circumstances it is not surprising that gentlemanly secretaries, tutors, and the like refused to accept the label of servant and used linguistic niceties to distinguish themselves from the rank and file of servanthood. It was customary in the last decades of the Old Regime to draw a distinction between *domestique*, a term that harked back to the traditional definition of servants as household members, and *serviteur*, which carried connotations of the new servility. The *Dictionnaire des Trévoux* explained the difference in 1762: "*Domestique*: includes all those who act under a man, who compose a household, who live in his house . . . like intendants, secretaries, clerks, men of affairs. . . . *Serviteur* signifies only those who serve for wages, like valets, lackeys, porters, etc."[64] Gentlemanly servants admitted to being *domestiques* but not *serviteurs*. One gentlemanly attendant who firmly insisted on this distinction was Jean-Jacques Rousseau, who had been secretary to the French ambassador to Venice but who greatly resented the imputation that he had ever been a servant: "It is true [he wrote] that I have been a *domestique* of M. de Montagu . . . and that I ate his bread, as his gentlemen were his *domestiques* and ate his bread. . . . But while they and I were his *domestiques*, it does not at all follow that we were his valets."[65]

Other gentlemenly servants found this distinction too flimsy, and solved their status problem by taking themselves out of the ranks of servitude altogether. In the late eighteenth century clerks, tutors, and estate agents successfully laid claim to professional rather than servile status, and musicians abandoned the status of servant for that of artist—and indeed genius.[66] Even male cooks tried to do the same. In 1654 the famous chef La Varenne described himself in the preface to his cookbook as the humble servant of his master, but by 1755 the equally famous Menon argued in the preface of *his* cookbook that cooking was a profession, and in 1822 the great Carême stated emphatically that cooks no longer belonged in "the class of domestics."[67] Chefs never did succeed in convincing society that they were not servants: their work was too clearly housework—"servants' work" by the new definition. But their attempt to escape the stigma of servitude shows how differently domestic service was viewed in the late eighteenth century from the way it had been in the past.

The great nineteenth-century historian Jules Michelet argued that domestic service was a vital topic in the history of eighteenth-century France. This has more than a touch of the hyperbole characteristic of the man, but it does contain a grain of truth. Domestic service is an important topic in the history of eighteenth-century France, and not just because servants and servant-holding were so widespread. The occupation fulfilled many important social functions and was a mirror of the society's basic values. Therefore when French society was transformed by the many new forces of the late eighteenth century, domestic service inevitably changed too. For domestic service was not only vital to the history of the eighteenth century; the history of the eighteenth century was also vital to domestic service. It was a key period of transition for the occupation. In the last half of the century domestic service changed from public to private, noble to bourgeois, masculine to feminine, patriarchal to egalitarian: in short, it lost the characteristics that had marked it since the late Middle Ages and began to take on instead the form it would have in the nineteenth and twentieth centuries. These transformations affected not only the types of servants people hired and the way they thought about the occupation but also every aspect of life within the household. Servants' work, their living conditions, their pay, their private lives, and their possibilities for social mobility all were affected, and they began to feel differently about themselves and their masters. Masters too found their lives changing in the late eighteenth century. They developed a new image of the servant, one that prompted them to reorganize their households and to change the ways they treated their domestics in all situations from the most casual daily contacts to the most intimate sexual relationships. This book is the story of these changes.

I

SERVANTS

2

The Servants' World: Household and Housework

It is necessary to overcome the repugnance and to dissipate the boredom which the reading of these writings [about the household and its organization] inspires. One must descend to details so ignoble that my pen would have fallen from my hand, had I not felt that the result would justify the undertaking.

—Abbé Grégoire, *De la Domesticité chez les peuples anciens et modernes*

What was it like to be a domestic servant in seventeenth and eighteenth-century France? What attracted so many people to the occupation? We ourselves would, I think, find servanthood so distasteful that we find it hard to believe that anyone given another choice, would willingly have become a domestic. But the *menu peuple* of Old Regime France saw the occupation in a very different light. To them it was, in terms of its work, living conditions, and financial rewards one of the more desirable employment opportunities.

Servants' Work

During the Old Regime, servants' work had three basic characteristics. It was, first of all, in comparison with other occupations, extremely unspecialized. Tanners cured leather and cobblers made shoes, but servants were expected to be what one sixteenth-century poet called them: "varlets à tout faire" and "chambrières à tout faire,"[1] jacks and jills of all trades, ready to turn their hands to a wide variety of tasks if the need arose.

Secondly, the rhythm of servants' work was extremely erratic. Usually short bursts of frantic activity punctuated long stretches of comparative idleness. Of course, uneven work rhythms were characteristic of all labor in the preindustrial period, before the Industrial Revolution made workers adapt to the discipline of machines. In the eighteenth century, even in so specialized and mechanized a trade as printing, the workday was an erratic mixture of "work" and "play."[2] But the rhythms of servants' work were even more discontinuous than those of other preindustrial occupations, and servants, especially lackeys, enjoyed long periods of idleness envied by the rest of the *menu peuple*.

The third characteristic of servants' work was that little of it was what we would call housework. As we have seen, among the reasons for employing servants in the Old Regime the creation of a comfortable domestic environment was, at least until the last decades before the Revolution, low on the list. Therefore much of the servants' time was taken up with tasks very different from the cooking and cleaning which the nineteenth-century has taught us to think of as servants' work.

The unspecialized nature of servants' work is especially obvious in the small households of the bourgeoisie and artisanate. Their single servant—or more often *servante*—had to do literally everything necessary to keep the household functioning. The immense variety of tasks that made up her working day is described in a seventeenth-century household manual, Audiger's *La Maison réglée*, published in 1695. According to Audiger, every morning the *servante* must rise at dawn, make a fire in the kitchen and set her *pot-au-feu* to simmering. She then should do the marketing, keeping careful accounts of money spent and not wasting time in idle gossip. When she returns home she must make the beds and clean the bedchambers. If the household includes children, she must wake them, feed them, dress them, and see that they get off to school. The rest of her day is spent in cleaning, and in preparing and serving the *déjeuner* (the main meal of the day, served at noon) and the *souper* (the evening meal). But she must always be prepared to drop whatever she is doing and run errands for her master and mistress.[3] We might add, although Audiger does not, that in the households of artisans and shopkeepers *servantes* were expected to perform industrial labor as well as household chores. The maid of a *boulanger* might serve customers behind the counter; a *couturière's* servant would sew when she was not doing housework; and a *tisserand*'s would spend most of her time weaving alongside the master's wife and daughters.

Male domestics in one- or two-servant households also performed a variety of tasks, although simply because they were male servants their duties were more likely to involve public display to enhance the dignity of their employers. *Domestiques* too marketed, cooked, and cleaned; they shaved their masters and cared for their clothes; they helped out in the stables or shop. But when they stepped across the threshhold they were often required to don livery and behave as though they were a great lord's lackeys, for this would reflect prestige upon their employers.

In the large households of the nobility a much greater specialization of labor among servants was possible. These establishments displayed, although only in a rudimentary form, the elaborate servant hierarchy and strict division of labor that would characterize great households in the nineteenth century. At the summit of this incipient servant hierarchy were the respectable gentlemen servants: the chaplain, the intendant or *homme de confiance*, the secretary, the tutor. Their prestige derived both from the dignity of their tasks and from their direct descent from the gentlemen servants of the Middle Ages. They did not have to wear livery, and often did not even have to reside in the households of their masters. Thirteen percent of such servants listed on the *capitation* roll in Toulouse in 1695 were heads of their own households. When they did "live in," they were set off from the lesser servants by special marks of status: a newspaper advertisement for a tutor specified that he "would be lodged, shod, lit, fed, and supplied with linen like the master of the house."[4] The prestige of these positions allowed bourgeois to occupy them with no loss of status. Even in the late eighteenth century, when the bourgeoisie increasingly shunned the occupation of servant,[5] they continued to fill such posts. For example, in 1788, Sr. Jérôme Réal, son of a Toulousan *négociant*, was secretary to a *seigneur*. This sort of servant made respectable marriages—Sr. Réal wed the daughter of a *sieur* who had a dowry of 4,000 livres—and lived in respectable bourgeois style. Forty-two percent of the secretaries and *hommes de confiance* listed on Toulouse's *capitation* rolls in 1695, 1750, and 1789 employed servants of their own.

The tasks of such servants were fairly straightforward: tutors taught, chaplains cared for the spiritual welfare of the household. But in addition to these functions gentlemenly domestics also often had a rather amorphous set of duties perhaps best labeled as financial management. That is, they did for their employers what hordes of accountants, stockbrokers, investment counselors, and tax lawyers do for the wealthy today: they managed their money with an eye to the greatest profit for their employers—and for themselves. Many great lords apparently simply handed over all their money to their secretaries or (aptly named) *hommes de confiance*, who were expected to dole it out when needed. The apocryphal but nonetheless true-to-life memoirs of the "Comte de Bonneval" (supposedly a French general who changed allegiances, fought in the Austrian army, and ended his career as an adviser to the sultan of Turkey) include a character named Dominique, described by the "Comte" as "my *homme de confiance*, who governs my purse and warns me when it is empty."[6] A real life equivalent of Dominique was Goujon, *maître d'hôtel* to Monseigneur de Belsunce, archbishop of Marseilles during the plague of the 1720s. Goujon recorded in his *livre de raison* in December 1722: "I have given to the Monseigneur 120 *louis d'or*, which makes 5,400 livres, for his trip to Paris."[7] Obviously Goujon controlled the purse strings in that household.

Even when servants were not given complete charge of their masters' finances, they often had extensive responsibility for purchasing items needed in the household. Indeed such purchasing (usually done with their own money, for which they were later reimbursed by their employers) was one of the major duties of all types of servants, not just secretaries. The *maître d'hôtel* bought the household's food, as the following description of his duites in Audiger's *La Maison réglée* shows:

> The duty of the *maître d'hôtel* consists of the general spending done daily in a great household. . . . It is he who bargains with a good baker, for bread for the master's table. . . . He must know meat and bargain with the butcher. . . . He must . . . sometimes go to the country to learn the current prices of everything in season. . . . He must bargain with an *épicier* for sugar and with a candlemaker for candles.[8]

Even in modest bourgeois households the *servante* did the marketing for her mistress. Other types of servants also made purchases for their employers. The household accounts of a late eighteenth-century Maréchal de Mirepoix contain a demand for reimbursement of expenses submitted by the *femme de chambre*, Mlle. Bellisent, listing three livres, eighteen sous, in tips to various messengers and delivery boys, one livre, four sous, for paper and ink, and twelve sous for toys for Mme. La Maréchale's cat.[9] Similarly, the household accounts of the Duc and Duchesse de Fitz-James include requests for reimbursement from the groom (for eleven livres of unspecified stable supplies), the *valet de chambre des enfants* (he apparently bought all the children's clothes, and his accounts include 181 livres 10 sous spent on twenty-nine pairs of shoes for young Mlle. de Fitz-James in the period from November 1782 to July 1784), and the tutor (he sought reimbursement for pens, an inkwell, a volume of Caesar's *Commentaries*, and four tickets in the public coach to Versailles, in which he took the duke's sons to watch the opening of the Estates-General in 1789).[10]

The privilege of purchasing was important to servants, for it constituted a lucrative supplement to their salaries, as did their other accepted perquisites—the gifts of food at Easter and New Year's, the "baker's dozen" (the *maître d'hôtel* received one free loaf of bread from the baker for every twelve he ordered), and the cook's right to sell all the grease rendered in cooking.[11] Obviously a servant's opportunities to feather his own nest, or *ferrer la mule*, as it was called in the ancien régime, were extensive. The technique is described in a bit of seventeenth-century poetry, *La Maltôte des cuisinières, ou la manière de bien ferrer la mule*.[12] This is a supposed dialogue between an elderly cook and her neophyte colleague, whom she instructs in the fine art of defrauding her masters. Always buy the fattest meat, so that there will be lots of grease to sell, she suggests. Always pad your marketing accounts; collect kickbacks from merchants; and don't forget to "lose" your marketing money every few months. If you play your cards right, my girl, she says, you can end up like me, with fine furniture in your room and 1,000 *écus* worth of *rentes* on the Cinq Grosses Fermes. This fictional picture of servant profiteering was only slightly exaggerated. In the early nineteenth century the Abbé Grégoire estimated that at least 4 percent of all money spent on food ended up in the pockets of the domestics, and one eighteenth-century chef, M. L'Amireau, wrote to his fiancée that they could marry earlier than they had originally planned because his "*petits profits de cuisine* [were] coming along so well."[13]

We may wonder why employers tolerated such costly practices. Didn't they realize they were being cheated? Of course they did. The young Comte Dufort de Cheverny once bribed his tutor to turn a blind eye to his misbehavior with an offer to let him handle his financial affairs: "You will keep my books, you will pay my bills, and that will set you up for life."[14] Employers regarded this as the price they had to pay to preserve their dignity. It would not do for aristocrats, who should disdain mere money-grubbing, to haggle with common tradesmen. Thus the system had advantages for both master and servant: masters kept their dignity, and servants derived not only profits but prestige from the patronage they could dispense through the trust of their masters.

The enjoyment of their master's confidence and trust also gave prestige to the next highest group in the servant hierarchy of large noble households: the *femmes* and *valets de chambre*, the personal attendants of the master and mistress. They had few other claims to respect. Their tasks, described in one revolutionary pamphlet as "dressing, waking up, putting to bed, leading around, and indulging" a grown person as though he or she "were a child of three," were generally regarded as "lowly, wearisome, and humiliating."[15] They required little specialized skill or knowledge. Body servants' most difficult duties were caring for their employers' clothes, which involved knowing how to "iron, work in linen, whiten silk stockings, dye ribbons, and clean satins and taffetas" (as one *femme de chambre* advertised her accomplishments in Bordeaux's newspaper, the *Journal de Guienne*),[16] and dressing their hair. Even the daily powdering and curling of a gentleman's wig was difficult and time-consuming, while the creation of a woman's coiffure, which in the 1770s might tower several feet above her head and be crowned with pictures of public figures and events, and favorite horses, dogs, and loved ones, was a task of awesome complexity.[17] Admittedly most court ladies were coiffed by hairdressers who came to the house every day; teen-aged Laurette de Malboissière, the daughter of a tax-farmer, faithfully recorded the daily arrival of her coiffeur Garçon in her letters.[18] But *femmes de chambre* had to know how to touch up their creations, dismantle them, and deal with them in emergencies. One enterprising hairdresser in Bordeaux advertised lessons for ladies' maids in this difficult art.[19]

Such skills brought little respect in the eyes of the world. What gave the *femmes* and *valets de chambre* their power and prestige, both within the household and without, was the fact that they lived on terms of intimacy and confidence with their masters and mistresses. Let us take the life of that young lady of fashion Laurette de Malboissière. Her *femme de chambre*, one Mlle.

Jaillié, was with her constantly, reading to her, walking with her, gossiping with her, caring for her *toilette* and her pet goldfinch. Mlle. Jaillié appeared in almost every one of Laurette's letters; she was certainly mentioned more frequently than the girl's parents or friends.[20] *Femmes* and *valets de chambre* knew virtually everything there was to know about their employers. They often handled their finances and correspondence, especially in households where no secretary or *homme de confiance* was employed. Voltaire, Mme. de Genlis, and Napoleon's mother, Madame Mère, were among those who used their body servants as secretaries.[21] They helped their employers to receive guests, joining in the conversation and games, and they were privy to their love affairs.[22] Obviously no fellow servant—and indeed no friend, lover, or favor-seeker—could afford to offend these powerful domestics, who could with a word turn Madame or Monsieur against them. *Femmes* and *valets de chambre* of the rich and powerful were assiduously cultivated with presents and flattery by their employers' potential lovers and petitioners. The English tourist Fanny Cradock recorded a visit of an admirer, a German baron, thusly: "Baron Callenberg came in the morning; he offered me a very pretty little box of perfumed bonbons and to my *femme de chambre* a ribbon."[23] And Mme. de Pompadour's *femme de chambre*, Mme. du Hausset, became rich from the gifts of those eager for the favor of her influential employer.[24] The intimacy with their employers which gave such servants their prestige and power is well suggested in paintings like Boucher's *La Toilette* (see figure 1). Note here the elegant appearance of this lady's maid: only her unpowdered hair differentiates her from her mistress. *Femmes* and *valets de chambre* often imitated the dress and manners of their employers. Their fine clothes, *savoir-faire*, and knowledge of the *haut monde* further contributed to their prestige within the household.

The prestige of the kitchen staff, or *gens de bouche*, had a very different foundation. It rested on their acknowledged skill and talent, factors on which they based their unsuccessful attempt to escape from the stigma of servitude in the late eighteenth century. And indeed extraordinary skill and talent were required to produce the quantities and types of food consumed in the noble *hôtels* of the seventeenth and eighteenth centuries. During the Old Regime as in the Middle Ages food was still a major status symbol, something to be displayed as much as consumed by those who could afford it. Staggering amounts of food emerged from the kitchens of noble *hôtels* every day. In eighteenth-century France there were two main meals, the *diner*, served in fashionable circles at two or three in the afternoon, and the *souper*, which began anywhere from nine to eleven and continued well into the night.[25] The *souper* was in theory the more formal meal: women were formally dressed and coiffed for it, while for the *diner* they were formally coiffed but wore "morning dress."[26] Similar food was served at each meal. In 1746 the cookbook writer Menon suggested for a dinner for twelve a first course consisting of two soups,

FIGURE 1 François Boucher, *La Toilette*. Reproduced by permission of the Thyssen-Bornemisza Collection, Lugano, Switzerland.

A lady of fashion and her equally elegant *femme-de-chambre.*

a roast beef, and two hors d'oeuvres; a second course of more beef, veal with truffles, lamb chops, duck and chicken; a third service of two more roasts, three *pâtés* and two salads; and a dessert course of apples, pears, walnuts, *crêpes*, and jellies.[27] This was for a simple bourgeois household. In noble establishments eight course meals were usual, with each course involving several more dishes, or *plats*, than those listed by Menon.[28] Special feasts and entertainments were even more lavish. When Archbishop Lomenie de Brienne entertained the Parlement of Toulouse at dinner, it took his large kitchen staff six days to wash all the dirty china and cutlery.[29]

All this food was served, or rather presented, in a manner that enhanced its visual impact of opulent extravagance. Until the 1860s, when the passing of dishes from diner to diner (called *service à la russe*) became the norm, food was served *à la française*. All the dishes of each course were put on the table, with the largest and most impressive roast in the center, the others arranged symmetrically around it according to size, and the many small hors d'oeuvres comprising the outer ring. The diners sat around the edges of the table, and began by helping themselves to the nearest food, gradually working their way toward the prize in the center.[30] Even the food itself was chosen to make a visual impression. Although French cuisine had by the eighteenth century taken its classic form, with relatively simple dishes that preserved the natural look and flavor of their ingredients, the medieval penchant for exotic and expensive ingredients and food that looked better than it tasted still lingered.[31] Desserts, for example, were usually ices and jellies. They were prized for their costliness and their carefully molded shapes and jewel-like colors (blue and violet, created with costly indigo dyes) rather than for their taste, which was usually nonexistent.[32]

Producing this sumptuous visual parade of food was the responsibility of the *gens de bouche* who labored in the kitchens of the nobility. The plural is used deliberately, for most noble *hôtels* had at least two kitchens, the kitchen proper, where the *maître d'hôtel* and the *cuisinier*, assisted by numerous *aides* and *garçons de cuisine*, reigned supreme, and the *office*, domain of the *officier* who had charge of the household's bread, wine, silver, and linen and created its preserves, candies, liqueurs, and desserts. The *office* was necessary because the preparation of desserts and preserves involved sugar, which absorbs moisture readily from the air and is then useless in many recipes. Such preparations therefore had to be done away from the moist and steamy air of the main kitchen.[33] The main feature of the *office* was an *étuve*, a storage space for sugar, candy, and the like, heated with a charcoal brazier to insure a constant flow of warm dry air. Because of its pleasant atmosphere, the *office* was the place where the households' servants ate their meals and spent their free time.[34]

The bulk of the cooking was done by the *cuisinier* in the main kitchen, which usually had at least two fireplaces, lined with tiles and cast iron heat reflectors to send the heat back toward the fireplace mouth. At their mouths were hooks to hold pots and a flat iron bar to hold skillets and sauce pans. There were also several spits for roasting, usually turned by hand by the *garçons de cuisine*, although in the most up-to-date eighteenth-century kitchens mechanical spits powered by dogs were used. Most of the cooking was done in the hearth, although there was also often a free-standing charcoal stove where the most delicate sauces were prepared.[35]

The techniques of classic French cuisine, difficult to master today, were even more difficult to carry out in the eighteenth century, when all cooking was done over the unregulated heat of a stove or open hearth. It is not surprising then that cooks made high claims for their skill and had a reputation for being nervous and temperamental. Cooks were notorious drunkards, not just because their work made them hot and thirsty and they had easy access to the household liquor supply but also because drink offered relief from the psychological pressures of their profession.[36] Great cooks could claim to be artists, with all the burdens of the artistic temperament. The famous seventeenth-century chef Vatel committed suicide when the eel he planned to serve at a supper for Louis XIV did not arrive in time; contemporaries like Mme. de Sévigné found this unfortunate but understandable.[37] Their talents gave the *cuisinier* and *officier* their prestige within the household and at least a modicum of respect from society at large.

Secretaries, personal body servants, and the *gens de bouche* formed the aristocracy of the servant world in large noble households. They were separated not only by higher wages and the privilege of eating at a separate table in the *office*[38] but also often by their literacy, savoir-faire, and more respectable social backgrounds from the proletarians of the world below stairs, the *gens de livrée* and *servantes*. The *gens de livrée* were defined in a royal edict of 1717 as "*portiers* (doorkeepers), *laquais* (lackeys), *porteurs de chaise* (sedan chair carriers), *cochers* (coachmen), *postillons* (they rode either clinging behind or on the lead horse of a gentleman's coach), and *palefreniers* (grooms)."[39] They were distinguished by the livery they wore, which marked them as descendants of the armed retainers of the great lords of the Middle Ages. Such retainers had literally worn livery, that is, badges displaying their lords' coat-of-arms. But by the Old Regime the badge of livery had evolved into a knot of colored ribbons or, more commonly, a piece of gold braid worn on the right shoulder; only the color, cut, and trimming of the coat identified the household to which a liveried servant belonged.[40] This knot of gold braid was the identifying mark of a servant. Royal ordinances required domestics to wear gold braid so that in their fine clothes they would not be mistaken for gentlemen, and foreign visitors were urged to leave their braided coats at home, lest they be taken for lackeys.[41]

The duties of the liveried lackey frequently took him outside the household, and therefore he was a symbol of its splendor in the eyes of the public at large. This made it tempting to turn his livery into a display of wealth. During the Old Regime liveries became increasingly extravagant and expensive. In the mid-eighteenth century the Comte Dufort de Cheverny spent 10,000 livres over a period of eighteen months just on the gold braid for his servants' coats, although his pursuit of the lovely young wife of his *passementier* may have prompted part of this outlay.[42] The rising cost of liveries inspired countless royal ordinances against extravagance.[43] It also caused prudent employers to pass along the same expensive suit of livery to servant after servant, and to seek lackeys who would fit the livery rather than vice versa. In 1776 a former mayor of Caen wrote to his brother-in-law, apropos of hiring a lackey: "My wife sends you a thousand compliments and thanks for the trouble you have taken in writing her about the lackey who is available. She has not yet decided. His very small stature works against him; he would not fit the livery. When she has decided if she will take him, she will write to you."[44] Men looking for work as lackeys often listed their height in their advertisements, so that potential employers would know what size they wore: "A man, age thirty-two, height 5 foot 6, knows how to serve, clean rooms, curry horses, drive a carriage and garden, desires a position suitable to his talents."[45]

Good looks as well as the right height could help a lackey find a position. The richest of livery, after all, would appear mean if its wearer was hunchbacked, bow-legged, or pockmarked. Therefore employers deliberately sought out men with fine figures and attractive faces. Such assets were also frequently listed in the advertisements of male servants looking for work: "A Swiss *garçon*, age twenty-three, very tall and with an attractive figure, knowing how to carry the post and serve, wants to find a position as domestic."[46]

A lackey's appearance was so important because one of the primary functions of the *gens de livrée* was to act as living status symbols, as representatives of the wealth and might of their households in the eyes of society at large. Their other major function was to protect the household from invasion and insult. Like the bands of medieval armed retainers from whom they were descended, the *gens de livrée* were in a sense the outriders of the household, the filter through which it made contact with the outside world.[47] They carried its messages, ran its errands, and made its purchases. They accompanied, transported, and protected its members when they ventured out, and they regulated the flow of visitors within its walls.

These roles are reflected in the duties of the various types of *gens de livrée*. The *portier* or *suisse* (the latter name came originally from the foreign mercenaries who filled the bands of armed retainers in the late Middle Ages) guarded the door, admitting visitors and taking deliveries from tradesmen. The coachman drove his master's carriage, often badly (coachmen, like cooks, were notorious drunkards, although with less reason; almost every noble memoir of the ancien régime includes a harrowing account of a carriage accident caused by a drunken coachman).[48] The postilion, standing on blocks at the back of the carriage, provided protection. Mme. de la Tour du Pin considered his job the worst of all; during long trips she always felt sorry for the postilions clinging to the back of the carriage with aching arms for hours at a stretch.[49] The *palefreniers* lived in the stables and cared for the horses, carriages, and tack.

As for lackeys, they ran errands, accompanied their masters on calls, and regulated the flow of visitors within the household. During the Old Regime it was almost unheard of for a noble, at least a court noble or *parlementaire*, to venture outside his front door without a minimum of one liveried lackey tagging along. When the Duc de Croy paid a condolence visit to a bereaved relative with his family but "without our people," it was unusual enough to merit a mention in his memoirs.[50] A revolutionary pamphlet, *Avis à la livrée par un homme qui la porte*, gives us a glimpse of lives of lackeys as they followed their masters on their daily social rounds:

> Monsieur makes calls in the morning. This does not tire him, seated in his *cabriolet*. *We* are the ones exposed to the weather. . . . Dinner hour arrives. . . . For us, who have been on our feet since morning, it is a chance to sit down until dessert. . . . Quickly, quickly, someone is calling us! We must take monsieur to the theater. Here we stand on the pavement for three hours. . . . When he comes out, he goes to a *souper* or *chez des femmes*, or to gamble. This time we do not stand in the street, but we must stay in the antechamber.[51]

When their masters remained at home and received calls instead of making them, lackeys spent most of their time in the antechamber, stationed, often in matched pairs, in the doorway to regulate the flow of callers. The rite of calling was central to the social life of *les grands* in the ancien régime. Like the king at Versailles, *les grands* in their *hôtels* and *châteaux* spent almost every moment of their waking lives on public view; even their most intimate actions, like dressing and undressing, were occassions for the ritualized receptions of friends and favor-seekers. The very proper and *bien élévée* Laurette de Malboissière, for example, entertained her suitor while she dressed: "From eight o'clock on he was with me, assisting at my *toilette*, powdering me, putting on my shoes, attaching my bracelets, fastening my necklace. . . . At night, when Mlle. Jaillié [her *femme de chambre*] came to look for me to put me to bed, he went up with me, undoing everything that he had put on in the morning, and when my hair was fixed for the night he went away."[52]

The setting for these social rites was the so-called axis of honor,[53] a series of rooms, *antichambre, chambre,* and *cabinet*, found, in that order, in virtually every noble *hôtel* and *château* and in many more modest households in the seventeenth and early eighteenth centuries (see figure 3). The *chambre* was, as its name suggests, a bedchamber, but it was also much more than that. It was the room in which petitioners were received, friends entertained, gossip exchanged, games played, and informal meals served. But not all visitors were worthy of admission to these intimacies. The unchosen were confined, along with the waiting lackeys of the chosen, in the *antichambre*, which was just what its name suggests: a waiting room for those denied entrance to the *chambre*. The final room in the series, the *cabinet*, had an opposite function. It was a private refuge from the public socializing of the *chambre*, a place where a nobleman could retreat to read, to think, to pray, in solitude.[54] To be allowed into a nobleman's *antichambre* was prestigious, to be invited into the *chambre* was even more of an honor, and to share the intimacy of the *cabinet* was the most sought-after privilege of all.

Essential to this system of socializing were the lackeys. Posted outside the doorways of each of these rooms, they controlled access to them and decided which desperate petitioners in the *antichambre* (defined in an eighteenth century comic dictionary as "the place where servitude consoles itself through insolence and misleads through malignity")[55] would be allowed to enter the *chambre*, and of these which select few would gain the privilege of the *cabinet*.

For lackeys this duty was both pleasurable, as the quote suggests, and profitable. In theory French servants did not accept the tips, called vails, which were so much a part of life in the English country house, and which could double, triple, or even quadruple an English servant's wages.[56] But in fact they were not above taking bribes to allow eager favor-seekers to gain access to the inner sanctum. The Baron Pollnitz reported that John Law's servants made fortunes that way: "Towards the Close, there was no coming to the Speech of him [Law] without Money. The Swiss must be fed for Entrance at his Gate, the Lackeys for Admittance into his Antechamber, and the *Valets de Chambre*, for the Privilege of access to his Presence—Chamber or Closet [the *cabinet*]."[57] Ordinances forbade the *gens de livrée* of public officials from taking such bribes, and domestic manuals condemned the practice, but both did so in tones that suggest it was deeply entrenched.[58]

A lackey's life was largely one of idleness: lounging around outside a shop or theater as he waited for his employer, standing guard in the *antichambre* when his master received callers. Boredom and sore feet, rather than overwork, were its occupational hazards. Domestic manuals overflowed with advice to masters on filling their lackeys' all too abundant leisure hours. Toussaint de St. Luc suggested that they be taught to read, so that they could peruse edifying religious works as they sat in their antechambers; Claude Fleury suggested that they be taught to knit or do needlework.[59] The extremely public and visible idleness of lackeys gave all domestic servants a reputation for laziness—a reputation that not only created resentment and envy among the lower classes but also prompted many attacks by economists and *philosophes* on the unproductivity of male domestics in the last decades of the *ancien régime*.

In fact, however, the lounging lackey performed a valued function for his master. By his very presence at his master's side or in his antechamber he signified that his employer was a man of rank who should be treated with respect and deference. And if these were not automatically forthcoming, the lackey was there to act as a protective shield to deflect the insults and blows aimed at his master and to punish the disrespectful. The police records of the Old Regime suggest that the *menu peuple* were extremely resentful of the wealth and power of the aristocracy. But they were understandably wary of assaulting or even insulting a powerful noble directly. The noble's servants, however, were accessible surrogates for their masters and, with their fine clothes and proud bearing, tempting targets for abuse in their own right. Therefore assaults on servants were common. When the Parisian banker, Sr. Agasse, went debt collecting, he took his lackey along; it was of course the lackey and not Sr. Agasse who was beaten by irate debtors. And when the humble neighbors of the Duc de Luynes wished to express their resentment of his wealth and power, they doused his liveried lackey with the contents of their chamber pots—treatment they did not dare to give to the Duc himself.[60]

Servants dealt out blows and insults in their masters' stead as well as received them. For it was the duty of a servant to defend his master's honor and to punish those who impugned it—activities a noble himself could not do without lowering his dignity. Voltaire was not the only bourgeois to be beaten by powerful nobles' lackeys for a supposed insult against their masters. In Paris in 1721, for example, the lackeys of the Portuguese ambassador to France set upon the wife of Jean Le Brun, master wheelwright; her husband had had the temerity to try to collect a debt of 460 livres owed by His Excellency.[61] Tradesmen who dunned their noble clients, coachmen who were not quick enough in yielding the right-of-way to a nobleman's carriage, sedan-chair carriers who failed to take a noble passenger where he wanted to go—all might experience the violence of lackeys avenging insults to their masters' honor. Night after night the streets of French cities and towns rang with arguments and blows as noble carriage confronted noble carriage at street corners and the *gens de livrée* fought over who should yield to whom (see figure 2). Altercations were so frequent that they make the reports of M. de Marville, the hapless *lieutenant-général de police* of Paris in the mid-eighteenth century, dull reading. On January 8, 1745, he reported a battle outside the Comédie Italienne between the coachmen of the Mme. de Bauffremont and the Duc de Fleury over whose carriage should have first place in line. On March 17 the same place was the scene of a similar fight between the coachmen of M. de Villeprieux and the Comtesse de la Marck. On November 3 yet another coachmen's argument occurred on the same contested spot.[62] Such battles often involved large crowds of people, for beleaguered lackeys would call on fellow members of their households and the servants of friends and clients of their masters for assistance. One famous melee of the 1720s, a fight between the lackeys of Archbishops Noailles and Dubois over whose master took precedence, left scores injured.[63] The royal government attempted to curb this violence through innumerable edicts prohibiting the *gens de livrée* from carrying swords, sticks, canes, batons, or anything else that might be used as a weapon.[64] But these laws were ineffectual, since this violence was encouraged tacitly and often openly by masters (see figure 2), and for good reason. It guaranteed them deference and respect, and so preserved their position at the apex of the social hierarchy. In a society in which power was still personal and exercised in face-to-face encounters, the lackey, both symbol and instrument of the prestige of the nobility, was essential to its survival. For their masters these laziest servants did the most important "work" of all.

The final group of servants in great noble households, those who formed the bottom of the servant hierarchy, were the unskilled female servants, the *femmes de charge* and the *servantes*.[65] They were the only ones, apart from the cooks, whose tasks comprised what we have come to consider servant's work, that is, housework. Domestic comfort and cleanliness simply were not valued

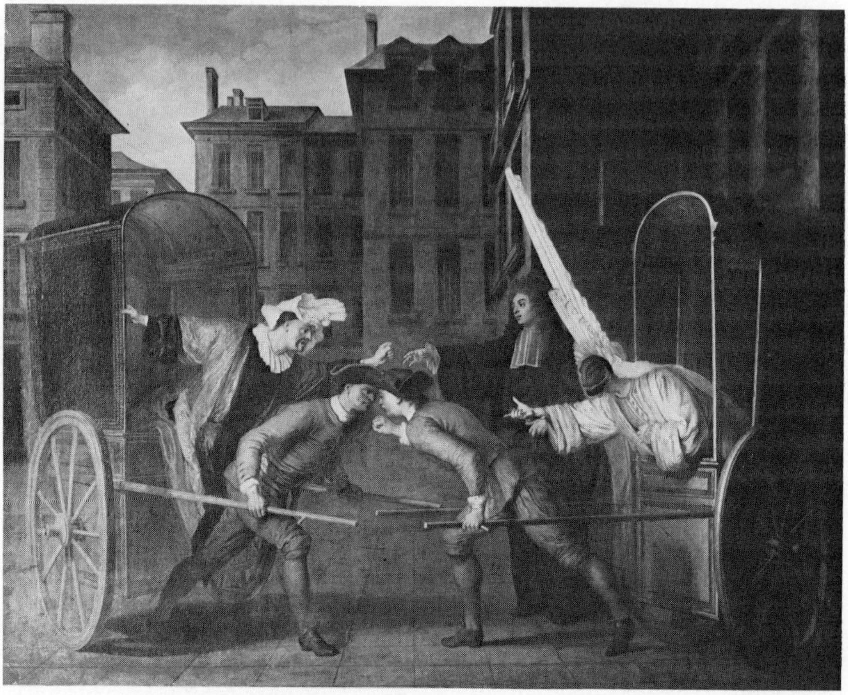

FIGURE 2. Claude Gillot, *La Scène dite des deux carrosses*. Reproduced by permission of the Louvre.

The public role of servants. Two sedan-chair carriers argue over whose employer has precedence. The woman at right, in mask and towering headdress, is probably on her way to a ball.

in the noble households of the seventeenth and early eighteenth centuries. Few servants spent their time cleaning and scrubbing. A great household of the late seventeenth century usually had only one *femme de charge*, who kept track of the linen (the washing itself was done by hired laudresses), and at most two or three *servantes* to do the cleaning.[66] Their work was not considered important. Domestic manuals gave copious and detailed instructions about all other aspects of servants' work, but they were almost totally silent about the *servante* and her duties. In Audiger's *La Maison réglée*, for example, the only reference to housecleaning is a suggestion that the *servante de cuisine* scrub the kitchen each morning; this could be done by "throwing water everywhere."[67]

Foreign travelers in France, especially the English with their advanced standards of domestic comfort, were appalled at the filthy appearance of even the greatest of noble *hôtels*. Philip Thicknesse wrote: "The Frenchman is always attentive to his person, and scarce ever appears but clean and well dressed; while his house and private apartments are perhaps covered with litter and dirt, and in the utmost confusion; the Englishman, on the other hand, often neglects his external appearance, but his house is always exquisitely clean."[68] Conversely, French travelers abroad were astonished at the cleanliness of private homes in England and Holland, and especially by the Dutch habit of thoroughly cleaning every inch of their houses once a week.[69] In the ancien régime the French invested their servants' time in public display, not private domestic comfort.

From gentlemanly secretary to lowly *servante*: this then was the servant hierarchy in seventeenth- and early eighteenth-century households. But we should not take either the status distinctions or the division of labor it implied too seriously. For Old Regime French households were not like English country houses of the nineteenth century, where each servant's task was strictly delimited (at Hatfield House servants' duties were spelled out in printed regulations),[70] and the lady's maid would have felt insulted had she been asked to clean the parlor. Instead, memoirs show that even specialized servants often stepped outside their usual roles. *Valets de chambre* cooked for their employers when the need arose; cooks were summoned from the kitchen to run errands when no one else was available; a mere lackey who caught his master's fancy might be asked to play the role of *valet de chambre* and read to his employer or amuse his guests.[71]

Old Regime households also differed from those of the nineteenth century, in that a high rank in the servant hierarchy did not give its holder the right to discipline the lower servants. In seventeenth- and eighteenth-century households the butler did not tyrannize over the footmen nor the housekeeper over the parlormaids, as was true in later establishments. Instead, what little disciplining there was—and it was not much—was done by the masters themselves, who seem to have dealt with each servant individually.[72] This approach of course could have its disadvantages. A domestic who dropped a dish within sight of his mistress received not a scolding eventually delivered through channels but instead an immediate cuff across the ear from the fair hand of Madame herself.[73] But in general the system worked to a servant's advantage, for when he was not directly under his employer's eye he could more or less do as he pleased.

This easygoing discipline, combined with the relatively undemanding nature of servants' work, tended to make domestic service (in noble households, at least) an attractive employment option for the lower classes in the seventeenth and early eighteenth centuries. The lone *servante* in a bourgeois or artisan household might be overworked and bullied, but the domestics of the nobility enjoyed less taxing work and more relaxed discipline than did either the artisans and peasants of the Old Regime or servants of later periods. Also attractive was the fact that domestics derived vicarious status and ego gratification—not to mention lucrative tips and bribes—from their roles as mediators between their masters and society at large. The chance to dole out the household patronage to fawning tradesmen, to put self-important callers in their place, to take out their aggressions in violence toward innocent passers-by doubtless helped compensate for the inevitable indignities involved in servanthood: the dependency it entailed and the ignoble nature of many of its tasks. In noble households of the patriarchal period the work itself was one of the most attractive aspects of domestic service.

The World below Stairs

Another attractive aspect of domestic service, and another way in which households of the Old Regime differed from their nineteenth-century successors, concerned servants' living conditions. Although Paris boasted a surprisingly large number of servants who "lived out"—married couples with apartments of their own; lackeys whose masters did not have room to house them and instead arranged for their board in a nearby apartment and their meals in a nearby cabaret; men servants who hired themselves out to foreign visitors by the day, week, or month[74]—most servants in prerevolutionary France shared a home with their masters. Being a part of someone else's household was, after all, what defined a servant in the ancien régime. For that period the phrase "sharing a home" should be taken literally, since one of the most obvious ways in which servanthood in the Old Regime differed from that of later periods is that servants did not spend their off-duty hours in that separate and often uncomfortable world "below stairs" which was a standard feature of all large (and many small) nineteenth-century households. In the seventeenth and early eighteenth centuries households had not yet developed that separate world of the servants' hall which isolated domestics both from their masters and from the other, greater world outside.

This was of course especially true of the small households of the bourgeoisie and the artisanate which employed one or at most two domestics. Such servants spent almost every moment of every day in the company of their masters. The *servante* of a *couturière*, for example, worked all day side by side with her mistress and the daughters of the house in the home and shop; she ate the same food, which she and her mistress usually prepared jointly, as the rest of the family.

Even at the end of the day she did not retire to a separate area of the house. For the small cramped quarters of farmhouses and the modest apartments of the urban bourgeoisie had no separate rooms for servants. They slept wherever they could. Farm servants usually bedded down in the barn or stables; the latter often also housed male *domestiques*.[75] Female servants were more likely to sleep in the house. In the seventeenth and eighteenth centuries *servantes* usually slept on a distinct type of bed called a *lit de domestique*, a camp bed with a wooden frame and a crisscrossing of ropes (hence its other name, *lit de sangle*) which supported a straw-filled mattress. Such beds could be set up in any odd corner. Often they were put in kitchens. Marie Eleanor Davisard, daughter of a Toulousan noble, willed to Françoise Courtard, her *fille de service*, "the bed which is in my kitchen and on which she sleeps." The will of a *procureur* in the Parlement of Toulouse contained a similar provision.[76] Servants also slept in entry foyers, in the *cabinets* off their masters' *chambres* (in Toulouse in 1729, a priest, Durand Pujos, left to his *servante* 200 livres and "the bed where she ordinarily sleeps which is in the *cabinet* joining the *chambre* in my house") and even in the toilet (*fille de service* Jeanne Perez inherited from her mistress her "bed which is actually in the toilet" in a shed at the back of the house; the bed may simply have been stored there.)[77]

For *servantes* such arrangements clearly had their disadvantages. Not only were they cramped and unpleasant, but they also left the women extremely vulnerable to the sexual advances of the men of the household. *Servantes* had no privacy, no room to retreat to, no place to call their own. Such living conditions, however, were probably no worse than those they had experienced at home in the crowded hovels of the peasantry, and in one important way they were much better: servants, unlike peasants, always got enough to eat. In fact, the living conditions of servants in small households were not much worse than those of their employers. The farmsteads of the peasantry and the two- or three-room apartments of the urban bourgeoisie were small and cramped; employers did not give their servants privacy because they did not value it for themselves. *Servantes* of the Old Regime were therefore at least spared the psychological humiliation that was the lot of the nineteenth-century *bonnes*: the deliberately painful contrast between the solid comfort of the family areas of the house and the Spartan discomfort of their own rooms, usually unheated, unlit, poorly ventilated, lacking running water and other amenities.[78] Such stark contrasts were impossible in the small households of the patriarchal period, when domestic life and its discomforts were intimately shared by master and servant.

This was also true even in the large households of the court nobility. Admittedly the plans of chateaux and of the great hôtels built by the nobility in the Marais and other fashionable urban districts in the seventeenth and early eighteenth centuries seem to show a strict division between the areas of the house that were the preserve of the master and his family and those where the servants worked and slept. This division is obvious in figure 3, which shows the floor plan of a noble hôtel built in Paris early in the eighteenth century. The area between the master's space and that of the servants was obviously the great courtyard, which functioned both as a *cour d'honneur*, where the carriages of important visitors were greeted, and a *basse-cour*, which contained the toilets, the laundry, and numerous chickens and pigs waiting to be slaughtered.[79] Nobles of the seventeenth and early eighteenth centuries saw nothing odd about subjecting their guests to such sights and smells. On the far side of the courtyard lay the master's domain, the main block of the house with its seemingly endless series of interconnected *antichambres, chambres*, and *cabinets*. On the other side of the court lay the servants' world: the stables and *remises*, where the carriages were stored; the kitchen; the *office*, where the servants ate their meals and spent their leisure time; and, on the second floor, the long dormitory-like *chambres des domestiques*, where they slept.

In great noble households skilled upper servants might have rooms of their own, which they were allowed to furnish with their own possessions. Many seem to have developed a taste for luxurious furnishings. The inventory of the room of an eighteenth-century *officier* of the Maréchal de Mirepoix reveals, among the thirty-five items listed, a feather bed, a gilded armchair, a mirror, and two silver candlesticks.[80] Those who lived in such rooms certainly could not complain of their living conditions—they enjoyed a luxury unmatched by all but the richest of the *menu peuple*.[81]

Most servants in great noble households, however, did not have rooms of their own but instead slept in the *chambres des domestiques*. There were usually at least two of these dormitories, one for men and one for women, and often they contained separate beds for each servant. Writers of domestic manuals insisted that masters had a patriarchal duty to oversee the sexual behavior of their domestics, and that the cause of morality was best served by separating the sexes and making sure each servant slept alone.[82] The *chambres des domestiques* rarely contained much more than beds, however; the room of the *postillons* in the household of the Maréchal de Mirepoix, for example, was furnished with two *lits de sangle*, two mattresses, two blankets, one bolster, two chairs, and a folding table.[83] This may seem Spartan, but it was extremely comfortable by the standards of the *menu peuple* of the eighteenth century. For most servants fresh from a peasant's cottage simply having a bed of their own was an undreamed-of luxury.

The *office* and the *chambres des domestiques*, in theory at least, made up the servants' world in the great noble households of the patriarchal period. In practice, however, the division between the worlds of master and servant evaporated, and the two lived together almost as intimately in great hôtels as they did in the cramped quarters of the petty bourgeoisie. Most servants spent most of their time not in "their" part of the house, but instead in the masters', specifically in the *antichambres*, regulating the traffic of callers and waiting to be summoned by their employers. There they whiled away the hours in card games and conversation, not only with their own kind but also with their master and his guests. A traveling Englishwoman, Mrs. Hester Lynch Piozzi, accustomed to the more subdued manners of her native land, where notions of domestic privacy and decorum were already highly developed, left a bemused description of what went on in the antechambers of late-eighteenth-century

Italian palazzos. It could easily have been written about French hôtels of a slightly earlier period:

> It is expected that two or three of them [lackeys] at least sit in the antechamber, as it is called, to answer the bell . . . for the stairs, high and wide as those of Windsor Palace, all stone too, run up from the door immediately to that apartment, which is very large and very cold, with bricks [to set their feet on] only, and a brazier filled with warm wood ashes, to keep their fingers from freezing, which in summer they employ with cards, and seem but little inclined to lay them down when ladies pass through the receiving room. The strange familiarity this class of people think proper to assume, half joining in the conversation and crying *oibò* [oh, dear!], when the master affirms something they do not quite assent to, is apt to shock one at the beginning . . . the footman if not very seriously admonished indeed, yawns, spits, and displays what one of our travel-writers emphatically terms his flag of abomination behind the chair of a woman of quality, without the slightest sensation of its impropriety.[84]

Other sources confirm Mrs. Piozzi's description. A French etiquette book published in 1731 prescribed the proper behavior for servants in the *antichambre*: they should not interrupt their masters' conversations; they should not constantly get up and walk about, passing in front of the guests; and they should not shout out greetings to friends in the courtyard below.[85] But such familiarity was only natural when master and servant spent almost every waking hour in each other's company.

Even at night servants were not necessarily banished to "their" section of the household. Despite the existence of *chambres des domestiques*, many servants in great noble households, especially personal body servants, slept in *antichambres* or *cabinets* near their masters. The *valet de chambre* of the seventeenth-century Comte Bussy de Rabutin slept in his master's *cabinet*, as did the *femme de chambre* of the eighteenth-century teen-ager Laurette de Malboissière.[86] The Empress Josephine was another employer who always kept her *femme de chambre* within earshot. When one of the splendid palazzos that housed the victorious Bonaparte and his new bride during the Italian campaign had no *chambre* with *cabinet* attached, workmen were summoned to wall off a section of the terrace next to Josephine's bedchamber so that her maid would have a place to sleep.[87] In these circumstances the spatial division of dwellings into "upstairs" and "downstairs," "master's space" and "servants' space" had little significance.

If the existence of a separate world below stairs did not necessarily isolate servants from their masters, neither did it isolate them from society at large. In nineteenth-century households the servants' hall was a social world unto itself. Masters and other outsiders rarely penetrated its confines; delivery boys and policemen stopping in for refreshment as they walked their beats were almost the only visitors. Servants rarely had any social contacts outside the servants' hall, for their free time was severely limited (one free Sunday afternoon a month was the standard holiday for maids in Victorian England) and masters discouraged as much as possible ventures into the corrupting world of the industrial city. Therefore social life in the servants' hall had a claustrophobic intensity. Petty jealousies and slights grew in its hothouse atmosphere into major grievances. Epic feuds—and love affairs—periodically swept through the world below stairs, leaving devastation in their wake.

In seventeenth- and early-eighteenth-century households, however, the servants' social world was not nearly so insulated and its passions were not nearly so intense. For one thing, Old Regime servants were much more likely than their successors to venture outside the household. A major part of their duties, after all, consisted of being publicly visible, providing public evidence of the status and dignity of the household. Old Regime servants were also more likely to spend their leisure hours outside the household. Apart from farm servants, who traditionally received the week between Christmas and New Year's as a holiday, seventeenth- and early-eighteenth-century domestics apparently had no institutionalized time off.[88] But the easy work rhythms of Old Regime households gave them abundant leisure, and masters appear to have made little attempt to restrict their movements. Police records of the ancien régime give the impression that servants spent most of their time on the streets or in taverns.

If it was easy for servants to venture out of the household, it was also easy for outsiders to venture in. Households of the patriarchal period were infinitely penetrable. Friends, relatives, and lovers of servants; tradesmen, delivery boys, *colporteurs*; artisans looking for work and beggars looking for handouts swarmed through the courtyards and kitchens in endless processions. *Servante* Victoire Durand was seduced by a *colporteur* who stopped by the kitchen where she worked; *servante* Marie Bonefay received daily visits from her suitor; and *servante* Janeton Jourdan regularly shared her *lit de domestique* with her lover, an actor in the *comédie* in Aix-en-Provence.[89]

Consequently social life below stairs was much less claustrophobic than it would become in later establishments. Of course a certain amount of socializing within the household was inevitable. Domestic servants were apparently a gregarious lot. They spent much of their leisure time together, in the kitchen or *office*, gossiping about their masters, drinking (that servants were overly fond of the bottle was not just one of their masters' prejudices; when the *fille de service* of a *président* of the Parlement of Bordeaux, sent to fetch wood from the cellar, fell down the stairs and died, her fellow domestics told the police that "Janeton often took a little too much wine"),[90] dancing (the English tourist Fanny Cradock was invited by the proprietor of her hotel in Paris to go down to the *office* and watch the servants dance,)[91] and playing endless games of cards. Card-playing, for money or simply for fun, was apparently the favorite pastime of domestics. Laure Junot noted in her memoirs that the servants in her mother's household regularly stayed up all night playing cards and dominoes, and visitors to Russia observed that Catherine the Great's servants were often so absorbed in their games that they ignored her angry calls.[92] Servants could not hold themselves aloof from these communal recreations: *L'Auteur laquais* wrote that a *domestique* who sat reading by himself instead of joining in the conversation and card games of the *antichambre* would be called a "cold pisser" and shunned by all the other servants in the household.[93]

Given this enforced sociability, love affairs, rivalries, and feuds were inevitable. The letters written by one L'Amireau, chef in a fashionable Parisian household in the 1780s, to his fiancée Rose Farcy, governess in a similar establishment, offer a glimpse of tumultuous passions of life below stairs. They show that all too often what L'Amireau called the "spirit of discord" blew its "devouring breath" over the servants' world. At one point no one in L'Amireau's household would speak to the *valet* Néron, because he was a talebearer who curried favor with his employers by informing on the other servants. At another time the *femme de charge* was similarly shunned because she made a show of religious devotion to please her pious mistress, "letting herself be discovered four or five times a day on her knees no doubt reciting all the funeral orations of His Grace the Archbishop of Bourges," as L'Amireau noted in disgust. Once L'Amireau himself was cold-shouldered when the other domestics became jealous of the fact that the local *curé* had invited him—and him alone—to dine with him on terms of equality. L'Amireau wrote that during this period he spent his forced solitude taking long walks and thinking about his Rose.[94] The memoirs of Mlle. Avrillon, *première femme de chambre* of the Empress Josephine, paint a similar picture of backstairs jealousies and intrigues. After describing her epic battle with another maid ("the most malicious woman that one could imagine") for the coveted position of *première femme de chambre* to Josephine, Avrillon stated that being a servant was "like walking across a volcano" and that "there is no less diplomacy in domestic service . . . no fewer intrigues, no less hypocrisy and base jealousies than in the *salon d'honneur*."[95]

In general, however, such backstairs brouhahas were less serious in Old Regime establishments than they would be in those of the nineteenth century. Their ferocity was diluted by the fact that servants spent much of their leisure time and made many of their friendships outside the household. In the seventeenth and eighteenth centuries much if not most of a servant's social life was carried on in public. Domestics pursued their favorite leisure-time activities—drinking, dancing, and card-playing—in public taverns and cabarets as well as in the privacy of the kitchen.

Another favorite pastime was dressing up in their best clothes and promenading in the streets and public parks in fashionable areas of the city. In theory access to public parks was reserved to the well-to-do. In Paris liveried lackeys were forbidden by law to enter the Tuileries and other public gardens because the authorities feared their violence and disliked their habit of accosting with obscene invitations any unprotected noble ladies who passed by.[96] But if they were respectably dressed and behaved well, servants could penetrate even these precincts of privilege. In fact most of the courtship of our chef L'Amireau and his Rose took place in the public gardens of Paris. L'Amireau's letters to his love are full of missed meetings in parks and plans for future rendezvous there: "I hope to have the pleasure of seeing you in the Tuileries at 6. I will remain there until 11," and "today Wednesday, June 7, 1786, I was in the Luxembourg in the Grand Allée before 6 o'clock. I do not know what happened to you, but I stayed there until 7 waiting for the pleasure of seeing you" are typical passages.[97]

Servants mingled with the respectable in other places as well. Indeed, they adopted many of their leisure-time activities in imitation of their employers. Like their masters, lackeys frequently attended the theater, where they made a habit of commenting loudly and unfavorably on the actors portraying domestics in the productions.[98] And like their masters, they played billiards and gambled; Restif de la Bretonne's *Les Nuits de Paris* has a marvelous description of a billiard parlor *cum* gambling den frequented by domestics.[99]

But servants' acquired taste for the sophisticated pleasures of their employers did not prevent them from also enjoying the simpler pleasures traditional to the *menu peuple*. Farm servants danced the traditional dances and sang the traditional songs at *veillées*, harvest festivals, and hiring fairs.[100] Their urban counterparts, for all their assumed sophistication, were not above taking a glass of wine or a hand at cards at a working-class cabaret in the company of artisans and *gagne-deniers*. They too danced at carnivals and attended fairs, laughing at the bawdy comedians and puppet shows, and gaping in wonder at the tumblers and acrobats, the tightrope walkers and the women who danced barefoot on hot coals, the exotic animals and the freak shows.[101] And servants were always prominent in the crowds at any public spectacles, *Te Deums*, hangings, fireworks, and the balloon ascensions which dazzled the people of Paris and other major cities in the eighteenth century.[102]

The fact that servants shared so many of the recreations of the *menu peuple* raises some important questions about the degree to which they were integrated into the social milieus of the towns and villages in which they lived. Did urban servants seek out the company of the artisans and day laborers who made up the bulk of the population in towns like Toulouse and Bordeaux? How did such people regard domestic servants, those people who were similar to them in background but whose lives and tastes often were different from their own?

Such questions are difficult to answer. On the one hand, there is much to suggest that servants were not well integrated into the social world of the urban lower classes. The social universe of the eighteenth-century cities was, after all, highly compartmentalized. Social life was carried on in the small, cohesive units of neighborhood and gild, which did not welcome strangers. It is certainly possible that servants held themselves aloof from the rest of the lower classes. Their tendency to imitate their masters—in dress, speech, mannerisms, and attitudes as well as in recreations—gave them tastes not shared by artisans and wage laborers.[103] Servants tended to believe themselves better than the rest of the *menu peuple* because of their sophistication and their association with *les grands.* However humble their own social background and however lowly the tasks they performed, they felt themselves superior to mere artisans and day laborers who worked with their hands to support themselves. An incident recorded by the famous seventeenth-century letter-writer Mme. de Sévigné illustrates this attitude. Once at harvest time she sent her household servants to help the farm laborers trim the trees on her country estate. The servants found this insulting. One of them, Picard, refused to go. He told his mistress "that he had not left Brittany for that, that he absolutely was not a worker [qu'il n'étoit point un ouvrier], and that he preferred to go to Paris."[104]

Attitudes like that naturally did not endear servants to the other members of the lower classes. The latter widely disliked servants, who, as surrogates for their noble masters, were often targets of popular resentments and hatreds otherwise too dangerous to express. The lower classes resented domestics for the violence they so often exercised on behalf of their masters, and for the power their control of their masters' purse gave them over tradesmen and shopkeepers. And they disliked them for their own sake as well. They resented their fine clothes and superior manners, their relatively high salaries, their abundant leisure time, and the security they enjoyed of having their food and lodging always provided for them. But above all they resented their arrogance, their bland assumption that their association with *les grands* and their knowledge of the ways of the fashionable world made them superior to a mere artisan or laborer. The latter, by contrast, believed that servants had absolutely no justification for feelings of superiority. Servants were, after all, mere lackeys who had surrendered the independence that was the birthright of a free man to put themselves under the yoke of a master.

These differing attitudes frequently inspired clashes between servants and other members of the lower classes. In Bordeaux in 1741, for example, a surgeon sent his two *domestiques* to place an order with a ship's carpenter. Their arrogant behavior annoyed the carpenter's apprentices, who called them "fiches laquays"; the servants responded that the apprentices were themselves subordinate to the will of a master, just as they were. A fist-fight ensued, with serious injuries on both sides.[105] Such incidents were all too common in the police records of the Old Regime. Their fellow townsmen punished servant arrogance with verbal and physical insults; servants responded with the violence so central to their social role.

Yet it would be a mistake to paint the relationships between domestics and the rest of the *menu peuple* solely in terms of violent confrontation. Servants, after all, came from the same social milieu as other members of the lower classes;[106] often they had relatives who were artisans and day laborers, and of course such people often had relatives who were domestics. And the penetrability of the average ancien régime household gave servants many opportunities to meet and form friendships with their fellow townsmen. The memoirs of Jacques-Louis Ménétra, an eighteenth-century Parisian glassworker, allow us glimpses of such relationships. Ménétra himself once indignantly refused an offer of employment as a servant, announcing, "Monsieur, I have never worn livery and I never hope to wear it," but he counted among his best friends a *maître d'hôtel* and an *officier*, and while working in great households, he "made friends with the *maître d'hôtel* and the *valets de chambre*, who entertained me in the *office* and, since I was a fellow countryman, invited me along in all their pleasures."[107] Police records yield similar vignettes: a Parisian *sergent de guet* goes drinking and picks up girls with his best friend, a lackey; a young *servante* entrusts all her belongings to an artisan and his wife when she is forced to return to her family in the country.[108] But our best evidence of the friendships between servants and the *menu peuple* comes from marriage contracts. These not only show that servants frequently married into the artisanate, but also that they often asked artisans to act as witnesses at the signing of their marriage contracts. Of servants' marriage contracts signed in Toulouse in 1727–29 and 1787–89, 67 percent had witnesses other than relations or the employers of the couple, and of these 51 percent were artisans, shopkeepers, or day laborers; only 8 percent were fellow servants.[109] Thus when Guillaume Faure, *domestique*, signed his marriage contract with the daughter of a *brassier* in 1789, he invited a mason, presumably a friend of his, to act as witness. Two cobblers, also presumably friends, witnessed the signing of the contract between François Pons, *cocher*, and Jeanne Lamourelle, *servante*.[110]

These social contacts suggest that while antagonisms did exist between domestics and the rest of the *menu peuple*, relations between them could also be friendly. In the ancien régime the social lives of servants were clearly not confined to the world below stairs. They might be most comfortable in the company of fellow domestics, whether those of their own households or those of other establishments in the neighborhood whom they met in cafes to share drinks and cards and to boast about their good looks, fine clothes, and the grandeur and importance of their employers. But servants also inhabited the world of their masters, with whom they lived on terms of intimacy unthinkable in a later age. And they were, despite inevitable antagonisms, surprisingly well integrated into the social world of the urban *menu peuple*. In prerevolutionary France being a servant was not the isolating experience it would become in the nineteenth century.

The Rise of Domesticity and Its Effects on Servants

On May 31, 1781, the Marquise de Bombelles, lady-in-waiting to Madame Elizabeth, great-aunt of King Louis XVI, wrote to her husband, the French ambassador to the Holy Roman Empire:

> The court is a dog of a place. I shall long regret the sweet and tranquil life I led at Ratisbon [Regensburg, where her husband was stationed], and I feel certain that my lot should have been to be a good wife [*une bonne femme*] occupied solely with her husband, her children, and her household. For the pleasures of the court, of what is called good taste [*le bon ton*] have no attraction for me, and I have too bourgeois a way of thinking for that place.[111]

The Marquise was not alone in her dislike for the court and her preference for the simple joys of family life. The 1770s and 1780s were the years when the French *haut monde* turned away from public socializing and display to focus their emotional energies on the more private pleasures of family life. Richard Sennett might have labeled the period the "fall of public man" or at least of the public noble.

Two generations of the ducal family of de Croy illuminate this development. The first Duc de Croy, born in 1718, was a noble of the traditional pattern.[112] His private family life was almost nonexistent. He mentions his wife, whom he married in a match arranged by their families in 1741, in only two paragraphs of the four volumes of memoirs he wrote about his life, and these dealt largely with her ancestry and the fact that the king and queen had deigned to sign the couple's marriage contract. The Duc's children got equally short shrift—he obviously viewed them simply as means of perpetuating the family name. The emotional focus of his life was his public career, especially his intrigues at court, which he detailed at inordinate length. But the second Duc, born in 1743, was (at least as described by his puzzled father) a different sort of person. He too had a marriage arranged for him, but he astounded his father by promptly falling in love with his bride. She returned his affection, and the young couple devoted themselves to each other and to their children, shunning the court in favor of private domestic bliss.

This pattern was repeated in scores of noble families as the Old Regime drew to its close. Noble girls like Laurette de Malboissière dreamed of marrying for love: "I would wish, if I were married, that my husband occupied himself only with me, that he loved only me . . . that he lived with me forever more like a lover than a husband."[113] Court beauties like the Marquise de Bombelles turned themselves into *bonnes femmes*, devoting their lives to raising their children and running their households. And noblemen like the sec-

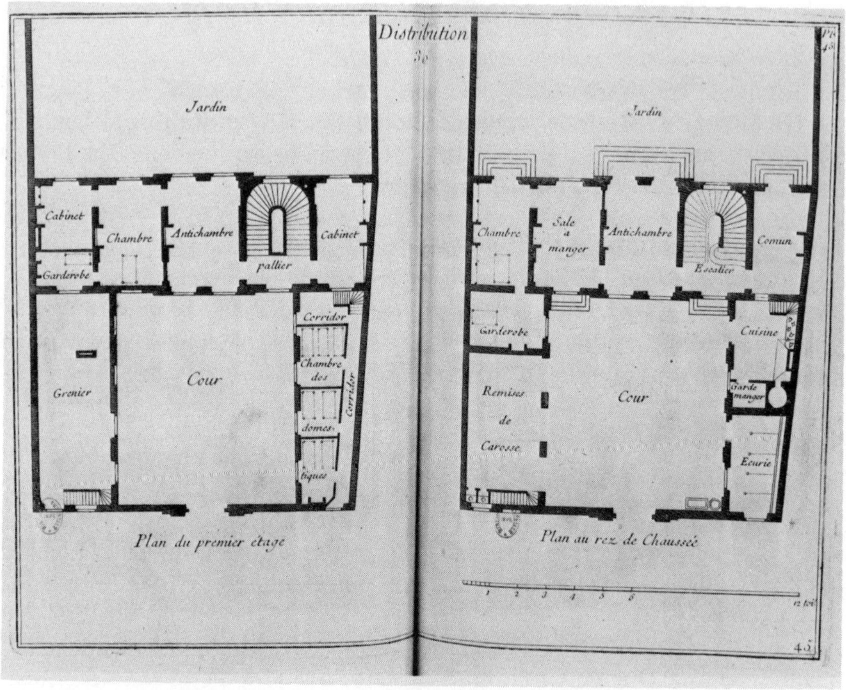

FIGURE 3. House Plan, Plate 45 from Charles Antoine Jombert, *Architecture moderne, ou L'Art de bien bâtir pour toutes sortes de personnes* (Paris, 1764). Reproduced by permission of the Bibliothèque Nationale, Paris.

The first floor (*right*) and second floor (*left*) of a typical Parisian *hôtel* of the early eighteenth century. Note the rooms arranged along the axis of honor (*antichambre*, *chambre*, and *cabinet*), and the dormitorylike *chambres des domestiques* over the stable.

ond Duc de Croy abandoned political careers for the pleasures of private life.

The nobility's discovery of domesticity necessarily had great impact on their households and servants. The very purpose of the household changed. Hôtels ceased to be backdrops for the public socializing and display that had characterized the noble life style in the previous century; they became instead comfortable settings for the private pleasures of family life. This change was reflected in the arrangement of rooms within the household. Noble hôtels built in the years immediately preceding the French Revolution showed a much clearer separation of public and private space within the household than was usual in earlier buildings. Figure 3 is the plan of an early eighteenth-century hôtel, taken from Charles Antoine Jombert's *Architecture moderne, ou L'Art de bien bâtir pour toutes sortes de personnes*, published in 1764.

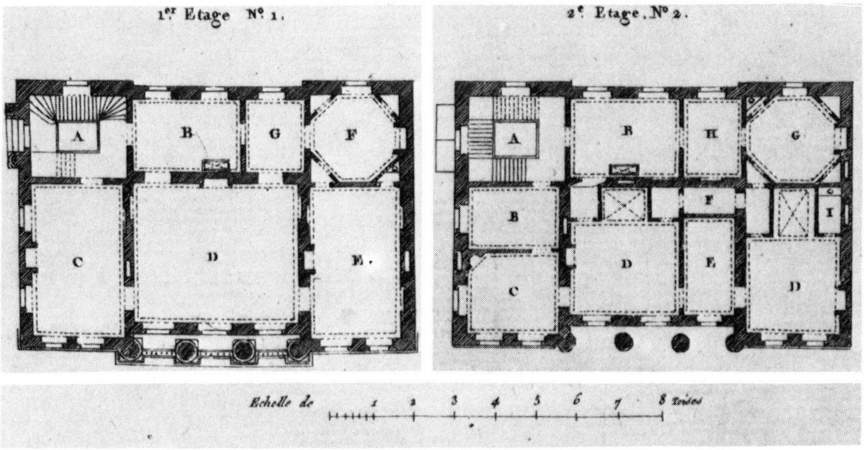

FIGURE 4. House Plan, detail of Plate 2 from Johann Karl Krafft and Pierre Nicolas Ransonette, *Plans, coups, élévations de plus belles maisons et des hôtels construits à Paris et dans les environs, 1771–1802* (facsimile ed., Paris, 1902). Reproduced by permission of the Library of Congress.

First floor (*left*)

A = *escalier*
(stairs)
B = *antichambre*
(antechamber)
C = *salle à manger*
(dining room)
D = *salon de compagnie*
E = *chambre à coucher*
(bedroom)
F = *boudoir*
G = *cabinet de toilette*
(dressing room)

Second floor (*right*)

A = *escalier*
B = *antichambre*
C = *cabinet de travaille*
(study)
D = *chambre à coucher*
E = *cabinet de toilette*
G = *boudoir*
H = *cabinet*
I = *lieux d'aisance*
(toilet)

The first and second floors of the house of the Marquis d'Argenson, built on the Champs Elysées in 1780. By then the axis of honor, so notable in earlier houses, had disappeared; in its place were single-purpose rooms like the *salon de compagnie* and the *cabinet de travaille.*

Figure 4 shows the house of the minister d'Argenson, built in 1780 on the Champs Elysées, and published in Johann Karl Krafft and Pierre Nicolas Ransonette's *Plans, coupes, élévations de plus belles maisons et des hôtels* construitsà *Paris* . . . in 1802.[114] The earlier plan shows the traditional mingling of public and private space. On the ground floor the *salle à manger* opens into an *antichambre* and *chambre*, and on the first floor these rooms, used for both the private functions of dressing, sleeping, and contemplation and the public function of receiving visitors, retain their traditional arrangement along the "axis of honor." But in the later house the public spaces of *salle à manger* and *salon de compagnie* (note this new label for the *salon*, which emphasized the public nature of the room) are more distinctly separated from the private space of *boudoir, chambre à coucher*, and *cabinet de toilette* or *de travaille*. This new group of private rooms, arranged more informally than before, is clearly not intended for the social ritual of calling. The *chambre* has become unequivocally a *chambre à coucher*; the *cabinet* is clearly labeled a dressing room or study.

An atmosphere of informal though luxurious comfort characterized both the public and private spaces of these newly divided houses. In the public space entertaining became much more relaxed and informal. By the 1780s the ritual of calling was on the decline and its essential room, the *antichambre*, was on the verge of extinction (almost none appear in the later house plans published in Krafft and Ransonette). It was replaced by rooms suitable for more informal entertaining—card rooms, billiard rooms, picture galleries—arranged so that guests could circulate freely among them without liveried lackeys to bar the way.[115] The other main social ritual of the ancien régime, the formal banquet, was also on the decline by the 1780s. It was replaced by the smaller and more informal and intimate *souper*, popularized by fashionable hostesses like the portraitist Mme. Elizabeth Vigée-Lebrun. In her memoirs she described one of her popular *soupers à la grecque*. The guests wore informal clothes designed to imitate classical draperies. The food was informal too, much less costly and abundant than that served at traditional banquets. Mme. Vigée-Lebrun gave her guests only chicken and fish, a plate of vegetables and a salad, plus honey cakes and grapes for dessert; all of which, she noted triumphantly, cost less than fifteen livres.[116] This was a far cry from the profusion of dishes and emphasis on expensive ingredients at earlier noble tables.

A similar emphasis on informal and comfortable luxury marked the private rooms of the new hôtels. In their *chambres* and *boudoirs* light pastel colors replaced the deeper shades of an earlier era; printed cottons and *toiles de Jouy* replaced brocades and damasks. Lighter and simpler neoclassical furniture, straight-lined but comfortable, replaced the overstuffed curves of rococo. For the first time bedrooms were adequately heated, by means of complicated ventilating systems and free-standing stoves. And for the first time bathrooms and indoor flush toilets were an integral part of the private spaces of the household (see figure 4).[117] The latter convenience was often called the *lieux à l'anglaise* in a backhanded compliment to the country that had pioneered modern affectionate family life and its comfortable domestic setting. *A l'anglaise* was the fashion in the Parisian beau monde of the 1780s in everything from dresses to horse-racing to the liberal politics of the Duc d'Orleans.[118] *A l'anglaise*, too, was the nobility's new-found devotion to domesticity and their determintion to turn their hôtels into comfortable settings for the joys of family life.

The reorientation of noble life styles from public display to private domesticity and the new emphasis on comfort within the household had profound effects on servants' work. Servants like lackeys whose main tasks involved the public "display" aspects of noble life found themselves growing obsolete. In the last years of the Old Regime the lackey's role as public representative of his household was limited first, by a new code of noble behavior which emphasized civility rather than the violence that lackeys had traditionally exercised on behalf of their masters, and second, by their employers' determination to keep their newly important private lives private. Noble families no longer wanted the sort of publicity that liveried lackeys provided. Mme. Vigée-Lebrun complained in her memoirs that when a female friend borrowed her carriage and liveried coachman to keep a rendezvous with her lover, the finance minister Calonne; Mme. Lebrun was afraid everyone would see the livery and conclude it was she who was Calonne's mistress.[119] A noblewoman of an earlier era would not have been so concerned about public revelations of her private life. Also, the decline of the ritual of calling and the disappearance of the *antichambre* robbed lackeys of their major duty within the household, that of regulating traffic along the axis of honor. Therefore it is not surprising that the number of lackeys employed in great households gradually declined during the Revolution and throughout the nineteenth century.[120]

The work of chefs, too, was affected by the changes in the life style of the nobility. As the formal banquet gradually gave way to the more informal *souper*, the tasks of cooks became simpler. Not only were fewer dishes served at these meals, but the food itself was less elaborate. The last decades of the Old Regime saw the development of the first "nouvelle cuisine," a cuisine that emphasized simple rather than costly ingredients and the natural flavors of food rather than elaborate sauces.[121] The new emphasis on naturalness and simplicity led to a new appreciation of the simple cooking traditionally done in modest French homes—what was coming to be called in this period "cuisine bourgeoise." This cooking was the creation of women, housewives and their *servantes*, as the title of Menon's famous cookbook, *La Cuisinière bourgeoise*, suggests. Published initially in 1746, this was the first cookbook to give recipes for the simple traditional dishes prepared in bourgeois and peasant homes, and it was also the first cookbook designed specifically for *female* cooks.[122] Thus the new simplicity in French cuisine encourged the replacement of male chefs by female *cuisinières*, a process that by the 1780s put women in the kitchens of most French households except those of the highest court nobility.

Thus the new domesticity changed the composition of great noble households. It also probably changed servants' patterns of work. It seems likely that in the last years of the Old Regime servants spent more of their time doing housework, especially cleaning, than they had ever done before, and that they worked harder than servants had in the past. For the nobility's new-found notions of domestic comfort postulated a serene backdrop for family life: a house exquisitely clean and run to perfection, with everyone's slightest wish anticipated and provided for. All this was impossible without much hard work on the part of servants. This is reflected in the domestic manuals of the period. An example is Jean-Charles Bailleul's *Moyens de former un bon domestique*, published in 1812.[123] In sharp contrast to the domestic manuals of the seventeenth century, Bailleul's book emphasized the private rather than the public role of servants (it was subtitled *La Manière de faire le service de l'intérieure d'une maison*). For Bailleul servants' work was housework pure and simple. His book is full of the sort of household hints that one would expect in such a publication but were so conspicuous by their absence in earlier domestic manuals: advice on how to beat carpets, how to lay fires so that they do not smoke, how to make beds so that the sheets will not wrinkle.[124] His is also the first French domestic manual that I know of to give a detailed, hour-by-hour schedule of a servant's working day. The schedule stretched from dawn to well after midnight, and would have appalled the domestics of the easygoing households of an earlier era. Bailleul constantly emphasized that servants must work hard and not waste time on the job; to do so was to rob a master as surely as by stealing his pocketwatch. In the domestic manuals of the patriarchal period the qualities most desirable in a servant were loyalty and obedience. But for Bailleul a good servant was one who had the skills necessary for his job and never wasted a minute.[125]

The rise of domesticity also had a great impact on servants' nonworking hours. It created that separate world below stairs where servants spent their lives in the nineteenth century. For a key element of the new noble life style was privacy. Their desire to keep their private lives private meant that they had to conduct them out of the sight of curious servants. This inspired the efforts to keep domestics at a distance which were such a novel and significant feature of late eighteenth-century households.

The techniques for keeping servants apart from the private life of their employers were many and various. One involved the creation, for the first time, of a genuinely separate servants' space within the household. In the new houses built in the 1770s and 1780s the areas in which servants worked—the *cuisine* and the *office*—were placed as far away as possible from the family quarters. Even in earlier buildings these areas had usually been detached from the main body of the house and relegated to separate wings across the *cour*, along with the stables, the toilets, and other unsightly—and smelly—necessities (see figure 3). But by the end of the eighteenth century the kitchen and *office* were distanced still farther: they were often buried in the cellars of the house.[126] Similarly, the servants' sleeping quarters were separated as far as possible from the family living areas, often in the attic or cellar. And now servants were actually expected to sleep there, instead of on a *lit de domes-*

tique in their employers' *garde-robe* or *cabinet*.[127] Another change indicating the new value placed on privacy was the substitution of separate rooms for each servant for the traditional dormitory arrangement of the servants' quarters.[128]

Yet another aspect of the new concern for privacy was an effort to limit the occasions when family members would come face to face with the servants going about their work. This was done by means of the backstairs or servants' stairs, which allowed domestics to enter bedrooms of their employers without passing through the main staircase and corridors used by the family and its guests. The backstairs were a late eighteenth-century invention. The first *escalier de service* clearly labeled as such appeared in a house designed by the great architect Ledoux in 1770. It ran from the basement kitchen and *office* to the dining room on the *rez-de-chaussée*, thence to the bedroom corridor on the second floor, and finally to the attics where the servants themselves slept.[129] Thus servants could go about all their work and go from their work areas to their bedrooms without ever intruding in the "family areas" of the house.

Another change in the layout of houses that helped to banish servants from the family quarters was the elimination of the *antichambre*. No longer did crowds of noisy lackeys lounge around gossiping and playing cards as they awaited a shouted summons from their employers. Now they had to keep to the *entresol* (a special story built between the main floors of the house as a refuge for domestics) or to the *cuisine* and *office* until another late-eighteenth-century invention, the bell, indicated that they were wanted.[130] Still other new inventions helped eliminate the occasions when servants had to be summoned. For example, the *athénienne* allowed the mistress of the house to brew her tea herself, on a sort of tripod over an open fire, and the dumbwaiter enabled a master to dine without the presence of servants. Louis XV even had installed in his private rooms at Versailles a "flying table" which rose from the basement completely set for dinner.[131]

A final method of keeping servants at a distance was to make certain that during the few times when they were allowed to venture into their masters' presence they remained as inconspicuous as possible. Late-eighteenth-century domestic manuals like Bailleul's emphasized, for the first time, that servants must behave prudently when in the company of their masters. They should not join in their masters' conversations, as had been usual in earlier periods; instead, they should speak only when spoken to. They should keep a poker face, and not laugh at the jokes or cry at the sad stories they overhear. They should even make every attempt to minimize the physical traces of their presence, handling wineglasses by the stem so that they leave no fingerprints, wearing gloves to avoid sweaty palm prints on the furniture, and changing clothes after working in the stables to prevent offensive body odors. Servants should also constantly strive to be even-tempered, and not inflict changes of mood or personal problems on their masters. And finally, servants should above all be discreet. As Bailleul noted, it was unavoidable that they know a great deal about the private lives of their employers, for they "have access to our most secret places." But they should try to curb their natural curiosity about their masters' doings, and never, never reveal the secrets of the household to outsiders.[132]

For proponents of the new domesticity servants were a necessary evil. It was impossible to create the comfortable domestic environment necessary for a happy family life without them, yet their presence inevitably intruded on the privacy that was a prerequisite for familial happiness. Therefore the ideal servant was efficient, hard-working, and above all inconspicuous, if not completely invisible—as one early-nineteenth-century domestic manual put it, "an intelligent and obedient machine costing 200 francs per year."[133] This image of the servant as a machine to do housework is striking, both for its repudiation of the close and personal master-servant relationships of the past and for its anticipation of the future, when actual machines for housework would finally guarantee the inviolability of domestic space and doom the servant to extinction.

The Rewards of Service

Domestic service was in many ways a less attractive employment option in the last half of the eighteenth century than it had been in earlier periods. The changes engendered by the rise of domesticity—the longer hours, the stricter discipline, the sharper separation between master and servant—made the occupation both more laborious and more humiliating. But for most servants these unattractive features of domestic service were probably offset by another important change: a spectacular rise in servants' wages.

In the sixteenth, seventeenth, and early eighteenth century servants' wages were in general so low as to be almost nonexistent. Indeed, many servants did not receive cash wages at all. Instead they were hired *à récompense*: they received for their work their food and board and some sort of gift—an apprenticeship, a dowry, a legacy—at the end of their labors. Such practices were natural to a patriarchal society which viewed domestic labor of servants not as a commodity to be exchanged for cash but instead as a duty a servant owed to his master. Hiring *à récompense* was almost universal for farm servants, and was also widespread for house servants in provincial cities like Toulouse and Bordeaux, at every social level from artisan to noble households. The wills of the period indicate how prevalent it was. In Toulouse and Bordeaux in the years from 1727 to 1729, 173 employers left legacies for their domestics, and in 21 of these cases the gift was specifically stated to be in lieu of wages.[134] Typical were the wills of Dlle. Jacquette de Pezan, daughter of a Toulousan noble, who left to Marguerite Payre, "her servant who has no fixed wages," the bed she slept in and an annual pension of forty livres, and that of Dlle. Toinette de

Lugis, widow of a *marchand droguiste* in the same city, who left a bed, household goods, and ten livres to Anne "who is near the testatrix and serves her without any retribution or wages but only for her expenses."[135]

The alternative to hiring *à récompense* was hiring *à gages*, for a yearly wage. But even this was far from modern wage labor. For one thing, servants' wages were quite often paid partly in kind; François Louradour was hired in 1705 as a farm servant by the Chevalier de la Renaudie, a minor Toulousan noble, for what was recorded in the Chevalier's *livre de raison* as a yearly wage of "eighteen livres, two shirts, and one of my old hats."[136] Servants' wages often went unpaid for long periods of time. Again the experience of François Louradour provides an illustration. He was hired in 1705 for eighteen livres, but he received no cash until six years later, when he left his job to marry. Until then François was paid only in kind and in petty sums for pocket money: in May 1705 his master bought him a pair of shoes costing three livres, and five lengths of rough cloth for five livres; in August he received thirty *sous* to spend at the fair of St. Jean; in September he got another sixteen *sous* and one *liard* to buy a hide to make a pair of breeches, and so forth.[137] This pattern of providing for servants' immediate needs but allowing their wages to fall into arrears was prevalent before 1750 in all types of households, even great noble establishments in Paris, and at all levels of the servant hierarchy. Guillaume Escaffié, a country *curé*, paid his maidservants in this manner, and so did the noble Sentou Dumont. The latter even paid his son's tutor, a respectable bourgeois, in this way.[138]

In practice, therefore, the wages for which a servant was theoretically hired bore little relationship to what he actually received. Figure 5 shows the theoretical wages of four different types of servants from 1591 to 1820.[139] This shows, first of all, that servants' wages tended to vary by sex. Male servants always received more than women, even if they did the same kind of work. In the mid-eighteenth-century household of Marquis de Barneval, for example, male cooks earned 120 livres per year, while *cuisinières* got exactly half that.[140] This differential, incidentally, apparently annoyed at least one female servant. Nougaret's *Tableau mouvant de Paris* tells the story of a *servante* who dressed in men's clothes and got a job as a groom. Forced to disclose her sex when accused of fathering a fellow servant's child, she explained to the magistrate that, "since women servants earned less than men, and since she was strong enough to do men's work, a natural self-interest prompted her to dress in men's clothes."[141] Wages also varied by skill: skilled upper servants like *maîtres d'hôtel* and *femmes de chambre* always earned more than mere *domestiques* and *servantes*. Wages tended to vary too by location. Of the three cities studied, servants' salaries were lowest in economically stagnant Toulouse, higher in booming Bordeaux, and highest of all in Paris, where the munificent salaries paid in great noble households set the wage level for the occupation as a whole. In the 1770s a stable boy earned around 60 livres in Toulouse, 72 in Bordeaux, and anywhere from 120 to 450 livres in Paris.[142]

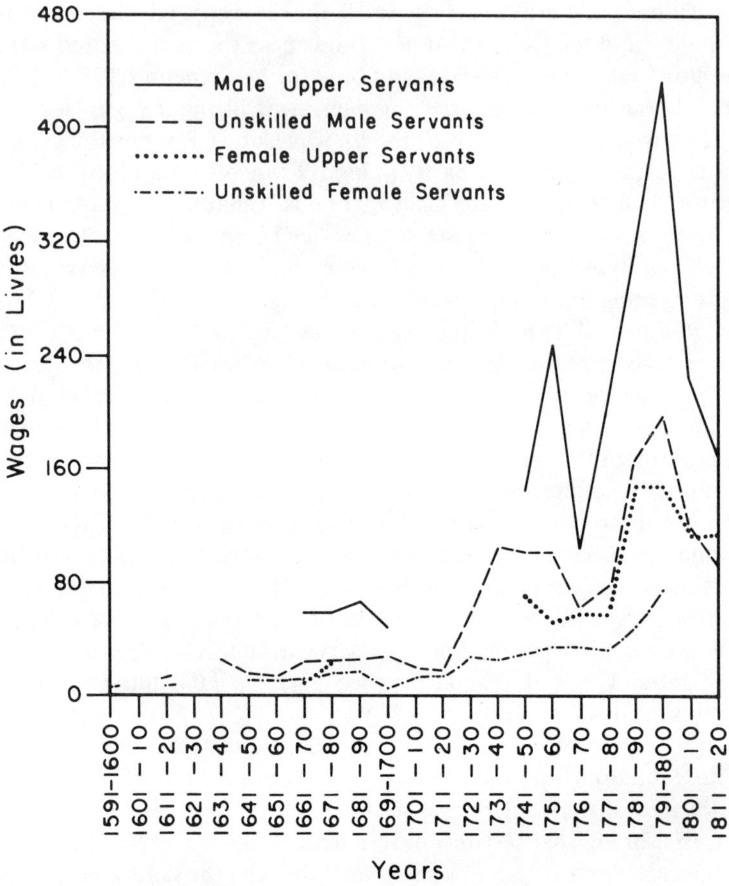

Sources: See Bibliography, section I, D.

FIGURE 5. Servants' wages, 1591–1820.

But in practice these variations mattered little in the sixteenth, seventeenth, and early eighteenth centuries. Except for skilled male upper servants, wages were uniformly extremely low, much lower than those of any other occupation. The real compensation for servants was not their cash wages, which so often went unpaid, but the food and shelter they received in return for their labor. These items were the largest elements in all lower-class budgets of the period. But even if the cash value of this food and shelter is added, servants' wages remained meager. Figure 6 shows a comparison of the wages of an unskilled male servant, and his wages with food and shelter added, to the

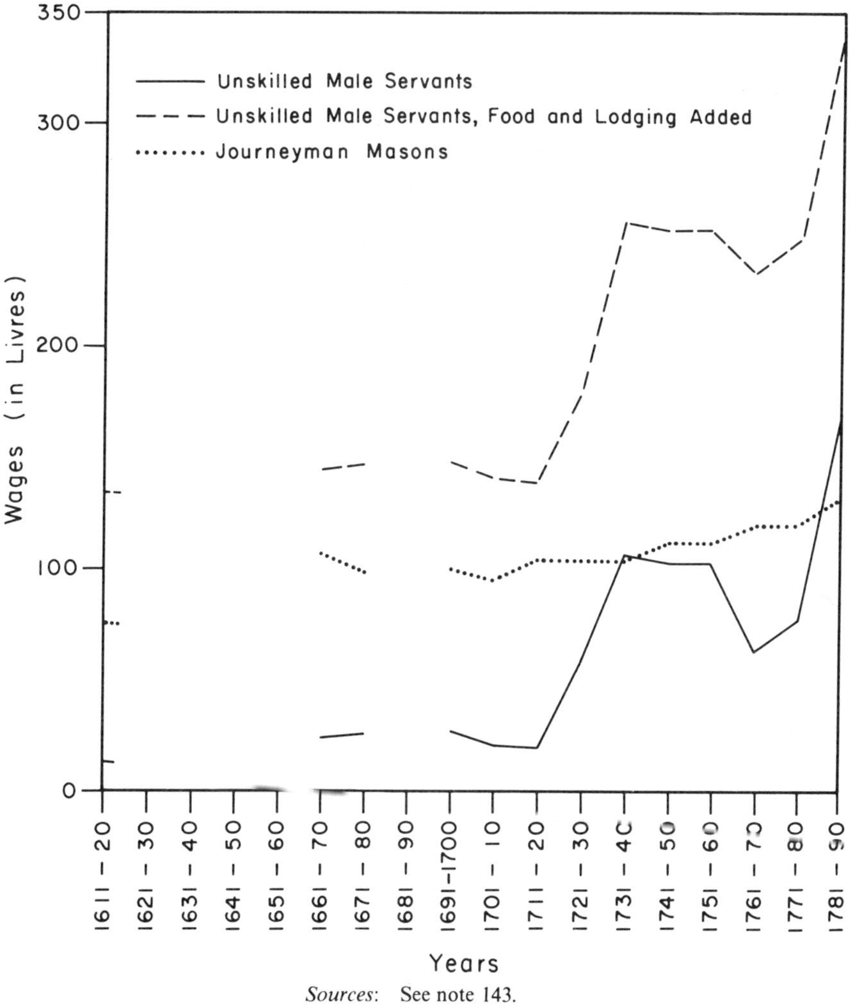

Sources: See note 143.

FIGURE 6. A comparison of wages for lower-class occupations.

salary of a journeyman laborer.[143] Throughout the seventeenth century servants' salaries were regularly lower than those of journeymen, and even with the value of food and shelter added they were only slightly higher than those of other occupations. Therefore in terms of financial rewards domestic service was not an especially attractive occupation in the seventeenth century.

In the eighteenth century, however, this situation changed dramatically. As figure 5 shows, servants' wages rose over the course of the century, showing a mild rise in the years from 1730 to 1750, a slight check in the 1750s and 1760s, and then a spectacular rise in the 1770s and 1780s. Of course, wages in general rose in the eighteenth century. As C. E. Labrousse's famous calculations have shown, they were 11 percent higher in the period from 1771 to 1789 than they were in his base years of 1726–41, and from 1785 to 1789 they were 22 percent higher than the base.[144] But servants' wages rose even more than those of other occupations. Those of unskilled female servants were around 40 percent higher in 1771–89 than they had been in 1726–41, and for 1785–89 the figure is over 100 percent. Wages for unskilled male servants show even greater rises: 46.7 percent for 1771–89 and 109 percent for 1785–89.

Furthermore, by the last decades of the Old Regime these wages were actually paid to servants. From around 1750 on domestic service was wage labor in fact as well as definition. The practice of hiring servants *à récompense* died out in the course of the eighteenth century. Legacies in lieu of wages almost completely disappear from wills by the 1780s; of the wills I read from Toulouse and Bordeaux for the years 1787 to 1789, only two had such provisions. In the course of the eighteenth century the practice of allowing servants' wages to fall into arrears also disappeared. *Livres de raison* from the last decades of the century show a consistent pattern of regular cash payments to domestics.[145]

The reasons for these changes are hard to pinpoint. The wage rise may simply reflect the fact that salaries in this newly monetized occupation were finding their true level. Or they may reflect the scarcity of skilled male upper servants, those symbols of nobility, as the growing scorn accorded to servants in the last decades of the Old Regime kept men of respectable backgrounds from entering the occupation. The high salaries paid these sought-after domestics may have raised the wage levels of the occupation as a whole. As for the monetization of servants' work, the economic growth during the eighteenth century, with the spread of the market economy and its values, was probably the main factor at work.

Whatever their causes, the monetization of servants' work and the rise in servants' salaries combined to make domestic service a financially attractive occupation for the lower classes by the end of the eighteenth century. As figure 6 shows, servants' salaries were by then approaching those of other occupations, and when the value of food and shelter, increasingly expensive over the course of the century, is added, servants' salaries were strikingly superior. By 1789 journeymen, squeezed between stagnant salaries and a rapidly rising cost of living, were finding it difficult to make ends meet. But servants were increasingly prosperous, and moreover, since their food and shelter were provided, they could save most of their salaries to invest in their future. This prosperity probably was what continued to attract people to the occupation despite increasingly unattractive working conditions and the growing public scorn of servants. Domestic service was the one occupation that gave a member of the lower classes some hopes of realizing his or her dreams of a better future.

3

Servants' Private Lives

No matter what profession they are in, the French have a passion for making their fortunes. . . . Even les petits gens, *those who elsewhere content themselves with having enough to survive on, here [in France] are possessed with a mania for bettering themselves; and someone has rightly remarked that it is France that furnishes Europe with* valets de chambre *and cooks, employments that made the fortunes of the people.*

—De Muralt, *Lettres sur les anglois et les françois et sur les voiages*

Domestic service! It's a losing game.

—Martine, a *servante*, in Molière, *The Learned Ladies*

In her study of the portrayal of domestic servants in the French comedies of the eighteenth century, Maria Demers points out the increasing tendency, as the century wore on, to picture servants, especially men servants, as ambitious and eager to get ahead. "Around 1650," she notes, "a valet is nothing, has nothing, and wants nothing," but by the eve of the Revolution he is Figaro, whose pride, self-confidence, and ambitions are virtually unlimited.[1] In portraying the growing ambitions of servants in the course of the eighteenth century, writers were only mirroring what was happening in real life. For, ironically enough, it was this least modern and "capitalistic" employment that attracted some of the most ambitious members of the lower classes. And it fostered in them some of the most modern attitudes: a passion for social mobility, a devotion to making money, and a willingness to take risks to make their fortunes. All of these were different from the attitudes of the typical peasant or artisan of the Old Regime.

They were different from the attitudes of earlier generations of servants as well. To be sure, domestic service had always been a pathway of social mobility for a certain type of servant: the well-born but penniless young man who entered the household of a great lord in expectation of protection and advancement. One thinks of the career of Guilio Mazarin, or on a lesser level, that of M. de Gourville, born in 1625 into the petty bourgeoisie of Angoulême.

At seventeen he became a *valet de chambre* in the Rochefoucault household and eventually rose to become its chief *homme de confiance*, meanwhile garnering enough in gifts and commissions to end his days as a modest country squire, with land, a carriage, and servants of his own, and a fortune sufficient to provide for his ninety-six nieces and nephews and endow a *maison de charité* besides.[2] But in the sixteenth and seventeenth centuries such success was confined to gentlemanly upper servants; the vast majority of domestics seem to have been content to have their food and lodging provided and did not dream of having anything more.[3]

By the eighteenth century, however, the monetization of servants' work appears to have given domestics a new vision of themselves. Their labor was no longer a duty they owed to their masters; instead it was a commodity to be exchanged for cash, a resource of their own to be sold to the highest bidder. As C. B. MacPherson argued in his classic exposition of the value system of a market economy, this new view of labor fostered an individualistic outlook, a sense of pride and ambition, a determination to make the best possible bargain with life.[4] And on a more mundane level, the rise in servants' pay in the course of the century enabled them to accumulate the wherewithal to make their dreams come true.

At any rate, in the last decades of the Old Regime servants seem to have become more ambitious and independent of their masters. They changed jobs more frequently than formerly. They saved more money, and they were more "capitalistic" in its management. They were less apt to look on their service as a temporary occupation that would enable them eventually to return home to their native villages, and more apt to become permanent settlers in the towns to which they had migrated. And they made much more ambitious marriages. All of this suggests a determination to rise as high as they possibly could.

The ultimate ambitions of servants varied, of course, in relation to their sex, background, personalities, and experiences in life. For many female domestics a respectable marriage was a major goal. Male servants, by contrast, were usually more interested in moneymaking than marriage, and they often dreamed rather impractically of leaving service for new careers in commerce. Many higher servants—secretaries, tutors, and cooks, for example—even hoped for social recognition as respectable members of the bourgeoisie.

Unfortunately most of these dreams were doomed to failure. Domestic service probably provided the best road to social mobility open to the lower classes during the Old Regime, but it was a road strewn with pitfalls for the unwary. An illegitimate pregnancy, an unfortunate marriage, a long period of illness or unemployment which ate up years of savings, even a stingy employer who withheld wages or an unfair one who refused to give a reference—all these could spell ruin for a servant's hopes and dreams. The monetization of domestic service may have encouraged in servants the ambitious attitudes inherent in a market economy, but it also left them victims of its vagaries. Using domestic service as a pathway to social mobility was at best a gamble, and for all too many the gamble was what Molière's Martine called it: "A losing game." This chapter will explore the private lives of domestic servants—their social origins, their career patterns, their moneymaking, their sex lives and marriages, their survival in old age—to see how they fared in their quest for a better future.

The Decision to Enter Service

Picturing domestic service as a road to social mobility implies that people specifically chose to enter the occupation with that in mind. In fact this was not necessarily so. Most servants seem to have entered service at such a young age that it is likely they did not choose the occupation for themselves, but instead had the choice made for them by their parents or other relatives. Most servants came from such poor backgrounds that it seems likely that the immediate attraction of relieving the family of the burden of feeding and sheltering one of its members weighed more heavily in the decision to place a child in service than did prospects of future advancement.

The best source for the family backgrounds of domestic servants is their marriage contracts, which usually give the servant's birthplace and his or her father's occupation. I have analyzed all the marriage contracts of servants registered in Toulouse and Bordeaux in the years 1727–29 and 1787–89, periods chosen to illuminate changes over the course of the eighteenth century. For Paris, the great number of marriage contracts and the limited daily allowance of documents permitted to researchers in the Minutier Central (five per day) made a similarly thorough investigation impossible; there I relied on a small sample drawn from the years 1787–89.[5] Marriage contracts are of course a source biased in favor of the more successful and prosperous servants, for only they could afford to marry. Therefore the evidence they provide of the poverty and deprivation of servants' backgrounds is all the more striking.

Marriage contracts reveal that servants were usually the sons and daughters of poor peasants, who left home and family to come to a town or city in search of work. As table 6 shows, the overwhelming majority were born in rural villages. This was especially true of female domestics; in all cities and in all periods men servants were more likely to be urban born than women were.

Men were also more likely to migrate to the towns of their employment from long distances, as table 7 shows. Toulouse and Bordeaux show striking similarities in the recruitment patterns of servants. Female domestics were usually drawn from the towns and villages of a city's immediate hinterland. As table 7 shows, over 50 percent of the women servants of Toulouse and over 70 percent of those of Bordeaux came from what I have labeled the "surrounding district," that is, the dioceses of Toulouse and Bordeaux and those dioceses

TABLE 6

Origins of Servants (in %)

Origin	Toulouse 1727–29	Toulouse 1787–89	Bordeaux 1727–29	Bordeaux 1787–89	Paris 1787–89
Rural					
Male servants	86.8%	89.9%	90.9%	91.7%	88.4%
Female servants	94.4	94.1	93.3	96.6	90.9
Urban[a]					
Male servants	5.3	5.8	3.0	5.2	9.3
Female servants	1.9	0.0	0.0	0.9	0.0
Native to city[b]					
Male servants	7.9	4.3	6.0	3.1	2.3
Female servants	3.7	5.8	6.7	2.6	9.1
N					
Male servants	40	70	33	97	43
Female servants	110	103	75	120	11

Sources: See Bibliography, section, I, B.

[a]Born in an urban area (town of over 4,000) other than the one in which they worked and married.

[b]Born in the city in which they worked and married.

immediately adjacent to them.[6] (The difference between the figures for the two cities results primarily from the fact that the dioceses surrounding Toulouse are much smaller than those around Bordeaux.) Toulouse's *servantes* came mostly from the wheat-producing plains of the Garonne valley, while those of Bordeaux came from the vine-growing villages that now make up Bordeaux's *appellation controllée*. The names of their birthplaces—Entre Deux Mers, St. Emilion, Fronsac, Médoc—would warm any wine-lover's heart. Both the Garonne valley and the Bordelais were relatively prosperous during the eighteenth century. Male children of peasant families could therefore find work at home, or as agricultural laborers or *vignerons*; only girls were likely to be sent away to support themselves as servants in the nearby cities.

Male servants, by contrast, tended to migrate from farther afield. A large proportion came from what I have labeled "feeding areas," regions so poverty-stricken that male as well as female children were forced to leave at young ages to relieve their families of the burden of their support. For Toulouse the feeding area was the region to the south and southwest[7] stretching to the foothills of the Basses-Pyrénées, where the land was rocky and difficult to farm, and where migration to Spain, often for years at a time, was the only alternative employment. For Bordeaux the feeding area was similarly hilly and impoverished.[8] The city was a magnet for the peasants' sons from the Bas-Limousin, a picturesque but unproductive region of green hills and valleys curving to the east and northeast of the city. Here too small rocky unproductive farms exported their men in regular cycles of migration.[9] Male servants also came from

TABLE 7

Birthplaces of Servants (in %)

Birthplace	Toulouse 1727–29	Toulouse 1787–89	Bordeaux 1727–29	Bordeaux 1787–89	Paris 1787–89
City					
Male servants	12.5%	4.5%	7.4%	3.3%	2.7%
Female servants	4.8	6.3	7.9	2.8	11.1
Surrounding district[a]					
Male servants	32.5	49.2	37.0	22.2	13.5
Female servants	58.3	56.9	79.3	72.9	22.2
Feeding area[a]					
Male servants	32.5	16.4	14.8	35.6	51.3
Female servants	21.4	22.1	6.3	14.0	33.3
Elsewhere in France					
Male servants	17.5	26.9	37.0	33.3	32.4
Female servants	13.0	14.7	6.3	8.4	33.3
Foreign					
Male servants	5.0	3.0	3.7	5.6	0.0
Female servants	2.3	0.0	0.0	1.9	0.0
N					
Male servants	40	67	27	90	37
Female servants	84	95	63	107	9

Sources: See Bibliography, section I, B.
[a]For an explanation of these terms, see text.

other, more distant areas of France, or from foreign countries, more often than women servants did, as the columns labeled "Rest of France" and "Foreign" suggest.

Recruitment patterns of Parisian servants differed slightly from those of Toulouse and Bordeaux, for the simple reason that the capital was a mecca for domestics: its high salaries and prestigious households drew ambitious servants of both sexes from all parts of the country. To "make it" as a servant sooner or later one had to go to Paris, just as to make it as an actor in America today one has sooner or later to go to Hollywood or New York. Therefore both male and female servants traveled longer distances to Paris than to Toulouse or Bordeaux (although Bordeaux too attracted the ambitious, since it was the gateway to the riches of the Indies). In other ways Parisian migration patterns matched those of the other cities.[10] *Servantes* were more likely than male domestics to come from the Paris immediate hinterland, the Seine basin, and they often came by water because, as Richard Cobb has shown us, river barges were a favorite means of travel to Paris in the eighteenth century.[11] Male servants came largely from a "feeding area," which for Paris included the whole northern third of France: Normandy, Picardy, and Artois, the Val du

Loire, Champagne, Burgundy, the Franche-Comté, and Lorraine. Much of this feeding area differed from the others in that it was not poor and mountainous but instead a rich fertile plain. But here too it was poverty that triggered migration, for these plains were divided into large estates farmed by landless agricultural laborers, *brassiers*, whose families sent their surplus sons to Paris to become domestics.

The patterns of migration of servants to the three cities differed little from those of other migrants to the same towns.[12] Artisans and wage laborers newly come to these cities showed the same patterns of short hops for women and longer displacements, from the same poverty-stricken feeding areas, for men. They also showed the same tendency, seen in table 7, toward increasing longer distance migration as the eighteenth century progressed. As the price rise and overpopulation made conditions in the countryside worse, migration of all sorts increased, and immigrants to towns tended to come from farther and farther afield.[13] All this suggests that the initial decision to enter domestic service was probably primarily a matter of "push" instead of "pull." Poverty rather than hope for the future drove men and women from home, and domestic service was only one of several employments to choose from in the city.

Further evidence that it was poverty that drove people into domestic service comes from an analysis of servants' social backgrounds. Most domestics came not only from poor sections of the country but also from the lowest levels of rural society: they were the sons and daughters of poor agricultural day laborers. This was especially likely to be true of female servants. As table 8

TABLE 8

Occupations of Fathers of Women Servants (in %)

	Toulouse		Bordeaux		Paris[a]
	1727–29	1787–89	1727–29	1787–89	1787–89
Domestic servant	3.0	2.5	0.0	1.6	0.0
Agricultural laborer	63.4	58.5	63.6	50.0	30.0
Craftsman	19.4	22.8	18.2	17.7	10.0
Textile worker, wage laborer	5.9	3.8	9.1	16.1	30.0
Food, lodging, transportation worker	3.0	3.8	0.0	0.0	20.0
Soldier, sailor, minor public servant	1.0	0.0	2.3	3.2	0.0
Petit bourgeois	0.0	3.8	4.5	6.4	10.0
Unknown[b]	4.0	3.8	2.3	4.8	0.0
N	84	79	44	62	10

Sources: See Bibliography, section I, B.

[a]This sample is too small to be statistically valid; it was included because it is the only information I have for Parisian female servants.

[b]Occupation unknown because identity of father unknown.

shows, the majority of *servantes* were the daughters of agricultural laborers: *journaliers, manouvriers, brassiers, vignerons* in the wine country of Bordeaux. Agricultural laborers formed the largest single category of fathers of female servants in all three cities. Other female servants were the daughters of petty rural craftsmen; those few who were urban-born were usually the daughters of textile workers or wage laborers. Only a small minority came from the respectable petty bourgeoisie. Not surprisingly this category was largest in Paris, which attracted the most ambitious and socially respectable servants.

The social background of male domestics was slightly different (see table 9). Although here too most came from families of agricultural laborers, men servants were more likely than women to have parents who had been in service themselves. They were also more likely to come from families of craftsmen (not surprisingly, since more of them were born in cities) and of minor public servants—*huissiers* and the like. Above all, they were more likely to have fathers who were members of the petty bourgeoisie: schoolmasters, notaries, surgeons. Again such respectably born servants were especially concentrated in Paris. Fully a quarter of the male servants in Daumard and Furet's sample of marriage contracts for 1749 came from the petty bourgeoisie. But Toulouse also had a sizable number of men servants from such backgrounds in the 1720s (12.8 percent of all male domestics). In both cities the proportion of men servants from respectable backgrounds decreased in the course of the eighteenth century, probably because of the declining prestige of domestic service. The repectably born increasingly shunned an occupation labeled vile and degrading. They were replaced by young men whose poverty did not allow them

TABLE 9

Occupations of Fathers of Men Servants (in %)

	Toulouse		Bordeaux		Paris	
	1727–29	1787–89	1727–29	1787–89	1749[a]	1787–89
Domestic servant	20.5	7.1	7.7	9.5	5.2	6.7
Agricultural laborer	35.9	70.0	30.8	48.9	44.6	53.3
Craftsman	23.1	2.9	30.8	21.3	15.2	11.1
Textile worker, wage laborer	2.6	5.7	7.7	8.5	4.5	6.7
Food, lodging, transportation worker	0.0	1.4	7.7	0.0	—	8.8
Soldier, sailor, minor public servant	0.0	1.4	7.7	6.4	4.8	6.7
Petit bourgeois	12.8	5.7	0.0	2.1	25.7	6.7
Unknown[b]	5.1	1.4	7.7	4.3	0.0	0.0
N	40	70	13	47	287	45

Sources: See Bibliography, section I, B.
[a]Derived from Daumard and Furet, *Structures et relations sociales à Paris.*
[b]Occupation unknown because identity of father unknown.

such scruples. A clear "proletarianization" in the social backgrounds of male domestic servants occurred over the course of the eighteenth century. The percentage of those whose fathers were petty bourgeois and independent craftsmen declined, while those whose fathers were textile workers, wage laborers, and peasants rose. From the rural sector, fewer were sons of relatively well-off *laboureurs* and more were the sons of penniless *journaliers* and *vignerons*. In sum, the pattern of recruitment of male domestics drew closer to that of the less prestigious female servants in the last decades of the Old Regime. By then domestic service was, for both sexes, an occupation that attracted primarily the children of the poor whom their families could not support.

Finding a Job—and Keeping It

Domestic service was clearly what we would today call an entry-level occupation, a first job. People became servants at a young age and later often moved on to something else. There were certain exceptions to this, to be sure. Many tutors had been seminarians or law students before they entered a household; secretaries were often ex-law students or even lawyers. And the post of *garde-chasse* attracted army veterans, as the following advertisement attests: "Two cannoneers, one aged thirty-two and the other thirty-five, invalids of the Grimaldi Company, garrisoned at the Château Trompette, knowing how to write and hunt, want to become *gardes-chasse*. Address yourself to the château, to their captain, who will vouch for them" (*Journal de Guienne*, June 27, 1785).[14] But apart from these cases, domestic service was an occupation for the young and inexperienced. The vogue for *jockeys* in the last half of the eighteenth century meant that boys could become servants at very young ages indeed. Advertisements for *jockeys* usually specified their ages as twelve or thirteen; one eleven-year-old advertising for the post in the *Journal de Guienne* stated that he had "already been in service."[15] Girls started their careers as domestics slightly later. Twelve to fifteen were the ages usually specified for beginning *servantes* and *filles d'enfants* in advertisements, and evidence from marriage contracts suggests that most female servants got their first jobs in their mid-to-late teens.

Just how these young people left their native villages and found their first jobs in strange cities is not clear. Doubtless many were placed by parents or relatives. When the Chevalier de la Rénaudie hired fifteen-year-old Jean Germane as a farm servant, he noted in his *livre de raison* that the arrangment had been made with the boy's father.[16] Often young people were placed by older siblings already in service. Restif tells of a young man from Normandy who goes to Paris, gets a position as a secretary, and then finds a job for his younger sister and sends for her.[17] Sometimes whole families migrated to the city in that way. One Parisian court case involved three sisters, all domestics; they had probaby come to Paris one at a time, the elder one finding a job for the next, and she in turn paving the way for the youngest.[18] In such circumstances, with job and lodging guaranteed and a familiar face to greet you at the end of the road, leaving home was not too painful.

But if a young servant had to go off to the city alone, he or she was likely to have a difficult time of it. The journey itself could be frightening. Restif has a marvelous description of the trip of a young girl setting out from Normandy to go to Paris to become a servant. She traveled by public coach, wedged in among soldiers and prostitutes whose rough talk and manners frightened her, and three enormous peasant women who crowded her off her seat.[19] Many young people seeking posts as domestics could not afford even such conveyances and went to the city on foot. This too could have its dangers. Marie Guillermine, daughter of a mason in the small Provençal village of Salon, left her home in 1765 to look for work in the larger town of St. Rémy. On the road she met a man who said, what a coincidence: he lived in St. Rémy and he was looking for a maid! Marie eagerly accepted his offer of work, only to be dragged off into the woods and raped along a deserted stretch of the road.[20]

The journey's end could hold perils as well. Restif tells us, "There were always at the arrival of the public coaches [in Paris] unscrupulous men, employees of criminal haunts, shipping off into prostitution the newly arrived girls who have come to enter service."[21] If they avoided that trap, newcomers still had to find a place to sleep, and to learn the ropes of job-hunting in the city; they had to discover the location of the *bureaux d'addresse*, both legal and illegal, where jobs were listed, the names of *cabaratiers* who would be willing to take messages from prospective employers for a small fee, and the spots, like the *petite porte* of the Palais Royal in Paris, where out-of-work domestics congregated to be looked over by those seeking servants and to exchange tips on available openings.[22] Such tips were probably a newcomer's best hopes for finding a position, but even they could hold pitfalls for the inexperienced. Renée Letalu came to Paris from Brittany in 1750 "with the design of serving there as a *femme de chambre*." She met a certain Mme. Beaufrère, who said that she had heard that *La nommée* Riquet knew someone who needed a maid. That someone, a Mme. Alléon, offered Renée a job as *servante*, which she took "while waiting for a better position." But after three weeks Mme. Alléon told her she was no longer needed; however, she offered to introduce the girl to "a gallant gentleman" whose acquaintance might prove profitable to her. Renée at first refused, but after some discouraging job hunting she agreed to meet the man. He raped her, then set her up as his mistress, and eventually left her pregnant and syphilitic, her career as a servant over before it had really begun.[23] Doubtless such occurrences were all too common. Failure to find a first job or settling for the wrong sort of position could mean a quick descent into criminality, with girls turning to prostitution to survive, and boys taking up that combination of scrounging, begging, and outright thievery which characterized male juvenile delinquency in eighteenty-century cities.[24]

Finding the right first job was important for another reason as well. The first job seems more or less to have determined the level at which a servant would remain through his or her career. In Old Regime France domestics had little scope for advancement either within their original household or through changing positions. Their advancement within a household was limited by the lack of a strictly defined servant hierarchy which, as we have seen, characterized large establishments in this period.[25] The noble households of prerevolutionary France did not offer the automatic progression from bootboy to butler, from skivvy to parlormaid to lady's maid, which marked servants' careers in Victorian England. Usually servants in great houses remained at the level at which they began. Nor was changing jobs a way to better one's position. The goal of most servants was employment in a prestigious noble household. Yet it was almost impossible for, say, a woman who started her career as an inn servant to end up as a *femme de chambre* to the wife of a *parlementaire*. In general servants spent their careers in households of the same social level as the one where they first worked. An example is the career of Jeanne Duchamps, a *servante* who married in Bordeaux in 1788. When she made her marriage contract she had been with her current master, a merchant, for only three weeks; before that she had spent two months in a different household, three months in a second, and a year in a third. All but one of these previous employers were also merchants.[26] Servants might sink on the social scale, for the bourgeoisie apparently derived some snobbish satisfaction from employing former members of noble households (for example, Marguerite Siari, former chambermaid of a marquise, was employed by a Toulousan *avocat* when she married,)[27] but they rarely rose.

Despite this discouraging situation servants changed jobs frequently, especially in the latter half of the eighteenth century. This suggests that while servants did not necessarily enter the occupation out of ambition, they often developed that quality in the course of their careers. Of course, servants had other reasons for changing jobs as well. Much of their movement was involuntary, when they were fired for incompetence or for some misdemeanor. And sometimes they left their jobs because that was the only way to escape from an intolerable situation—beatings, sexual abuse, and the like. Servants also changed jobs because that was often the only way they could get paid or get a raise. In the seventeenth and early eighteenth centuries, as we have seen, servants remained unpaid for long periods, and leaving a position was frequently the only way a servant could make his master actually hand over his wages. Even in the late eighteenth century, when payment was more regular, leaving a job was often the only way to get a raise, since employers tended to pay a servant his entry level salary throughout his career, although the general level of servants' wages might have risen in the meantime. For example, one Marion, last name not recorded, was hired as a maid-of-all-work by the Marquis de Barneval in 1754 for the then fairly high salary of forty-eight livres per year. But she continued to receive this amount throughout the twenty-eight years she remained in the Marquis's household. Meanwhile, wages had risen, of course; Marion's successor was hired at a starting salary of sixty livres.[28] Thus there were very practical reasons why a servant might quit his or her job. Nonetheless one gets the impression that many domestics left perfectly satisfactory positions because they imagined something better might lay just over the horizon. Many seem to have had an image in their minds of the ideal job: a post in a prestigious noble household, where the master was easygoing and liberal, the pay good, the work light, and the company below stairs congenial. And many spent their lives pursuing this chimera.

Before 1750 servant movement was inhibited by the fact that they were not paid and therefore could not save to tide them over a period of job-hunting. Lack of self-confidence and excessive deference to their masters may also have dampened their impulse to leave. But in the late eighteenth century the more regular payment of servants' wages and the resulting boost to their self-image removed these inhibitions. In the *livres de raison* which I examined dating from 1600 to 1750, the average stay in a household for servants was four years; in those from 1750 to 1820 the average stay was only one and one-half years.[29] In some households of the late eighteenth century the turnover was staggering. The Marquis de Barneval, a Toulousan noble, employed no less than 149 different servants between 1769 and 1783; three-quarters of these stayed less than one year, and of these three-quarters stayed less than six months.[30]

In the last decades of the Old Regime the career pattern of the typical servant showed a few relatively long stays at congenial households, interspersed with many short sojourns in less pleasing surroundings. A good example is the career of Marguerite Tallandier, a forty-six-year-old woman who had worked as a *servante* in Paris for twenty-two years. She stayed at her first job, with a *marchand de vin*, for three years, then moved on to the home of a *marchande lingerie*, where she stayed for four. Next came her apparently favorite post, with a clerk; she stayed there eleven years. But after he died she began a period of unhappy searching for a household she could like as well, remaining in one job for six months, another for three weeks, and so forth. She spent almost four years drifting from place to place.[31] Most domestics held many jobs in their lives: between five and ten was probably the average, although some, like Damiens, the would-be assassin of Louis XV, served over thirty different masters.[32] For such restless spirits, changing employment was a way of life: the ideal job always lay just over the hill.

Unemployment and Downward Mobility

Changing jobs could have its rewards, of course, but it had its dangers as well. Unless a servant lined up a new position (either through his own contacts with friends of his master or through the offices of a friendly servant in a household adding to its staff)[33] before he quit his old one, job-changing carried with it the threat of a long period of unemployment—*chomage* in the French term. Nothing was more dangerous for servants' ambitions, for even a few weeks' unemployment could eat up the savings of a lifetime.

Some unemployment among servants was of course involuntary and therefore unavoidable. This tended to peak in the summer months, when nobles in cities and towns shut up their hôtels and adjourned to their country châteaux during the hot weather, often taking only a small core of household staff with them and firing the rest.[34] Unemployment among servants probably also rose with the price of bread,[35] because high bread prices usually created commercial depressions in the preindustrial economy of the eighteenth century, prompting hard-hit artisan and mercantile employers to fire their servants. Thus domestics were often thrown on the job market just when the cost of the food they needed for survival was at its highest and when competition for what few jobs there were was sharpest because the cities were flooded with hordes of immigrants looking for work.

Servants with some savings could survive up to a month of unemployment with relative ease. Of course they had to adjust their life style to their new circumstances. They pawned their fine clothes, ate the black bread of the poor instead of the leavings of *haut cuisine*, and abandoned the fashionable districts of the city to seek lodging in the cheapest and most disreputable *chambres garnies*. Marc Botlan was fortunate enough to find the registers of some Parisian lodging houses in the 1770s. These show that unemployed servants were most often found in the seedy establishments of the rue du Pelican and the rue des Vieux-Augustins; they were much less likely to stay in the more respectable houses on the rue de Grenelle.[36] With such adjustments, a servant could usually manage to survive for a few weeks. When Pierre Jallet, an unemployed *valet de chambre*, was asked at the Châtelet how he survived without a job "he replied that he did not work, that he waited for a position [to be obtained] through the protection of M. DuBarry or other employed servants, and that he lived on the interest from his loans, the belongings he had sold, and a few small *rentes*." He neglected to mention that his wife worked as a *femme de chambre*, at least until she was fired because her mistress found her constant crying about her husband's unemployment too depressing.[37]

Most servants could manage to keep themselves fed and housed for a month of unemployment on about 15 livres, one-tenth of the yearly salary of a *cocher*—though more like one-third of that of a *servante*.[38] But any more prolonged *chomage* could make serious inroads on their resources. Therefore after a month or so of joblessness, most unemployed servants bundled up their remaining belongings, left them with a trusted friend, and began to live a nomadic life, changing lodgings every few days to avoid paying the rent and turning their hands to any work available. Unemployed *servantes* often worked temporarily as laundresses or *gardes-malades*. But male servants, always more conscious of the gulf between themselves and the rest of the *menu peuple*, apparently refused to become day laborers and instead tried to survive by hanging around the fashionable districts and running errands for tips.[39] If these expedients failed, servants would take to the road in earnest, trying their luck in another city, or going back home to throw themselves on the mercy of their families. When Françoise Maugras, a Parisian *servante*, was fired from her job in 1747, she packed up her remaining belongings, "*nippes et hardes*" consisting of a skirt, two chemises, an apron, twelve headkerchiefs, three *fichus*, and a pair of stockings, left them with her friend Lefebvre and his wife, and went back home for a stay which would last three years. When she returned to Paris she discovered that the Lefebvres, having had no word from her and thinking that she had died, had long ago sold all her possessions.[40]

Servant Criminality

A final option for the unemployed and desperate servant was to turn to crime—to beggary, theft, or prostitution. And this brings us to one of the most misunderstood aspects of servants' lives: their criminality. Most employers during the Old Regime were convinced that their servants were basically criminal at heart, and that their characteristic crime was *vol domestique*, the theft of money or goods by a servant from his master. And most officials of the royal and municipal governments believed that the dishonest servant was responsible for the great increase in theft which plagued French cities and towns in the last decades of the Old Regime. These notions were embodied in police ordinances, and they have been accepted uncritically by many modern historians.[41] But these notions reveal more about the attitudes of the master class toward its domestics than they do about servant criminality. They reflect the subconscious fear and worry masters felt about the strangers who shared the intimacies of their households, a worry that grew to hysterical proportions with the more rapid turnover among servants in the last decades of the eighteenth century. But they do not reflect the realities of servant crime. For analyses of actual police and court records from the ancien régime show that in fact servants were probably less criminally inclined than other members of the lower classes; that when they did commit crimes they were more likely to be crimes of violence than theft; and that their thefts were usually not *vol domestique* but instead cases in which an unemployed servant robbed a friend, landlord, or casual passer-by.

Court records reveal that servants in general committed far fewer crimes than might be expected, given the size of their presence in urban populations. In Paris in the last decades of the eighteenth century, approximately 15 percent of the population were servants, but they contributed only 7.6 percent of those accused of crimes.[42] Similarly, servants formed approximately 8 percent of the population of Bordeaux, but only 4 percent of all accused felons.[43] Nor did servant criminality increase as the century progressed—in fact, the opposite occurred. In Toulouse, for example, the Parlement condemned to death for theft and other serious crimes an average of 1.09 persons per year between 1633 and 1728; 12.5 percent of these were servants. But between 1750 and 1778, the average condemnations per year rose to 7.79, but only 10.1 percent of these were domestics.[44] Paris showed a similar trend. Servants were one of the few occupational groups whose proportional contribution to criminality declined over the last half of the eighteenth century, and this decline continued through the years of the Revolution.[45] The only area of criminal statistics in which servants appear to have been over, rather than under, represented is that of violent crimes. The Châtelet records for the last decades of the Old Regime show that only 7 percent of all crimes involved violence, but almost 13 percent of those of servants did so.[46] This tendency toward violence may reflect the rural backgrounds of most domestics: in early modern Europe violence was the characteristic crime of the countryside, while crimes against property typified urban criminality.[47] Or it may have grown out of the high level of violence traditionally allowed to servants, since one of their duties—and privileges—was to chastise physically anyone who offended their masters. But whatever its cause, the penchant of servants for crimes of violence throws further doubt on traditionally accepted notions of servant larceny centering around *vol domestique*.

Defenders of the traditional view of servant criminality might argue that criminal statistics of the Old Regime are not convincing, given the wide gap between crimes committed and those reported and prosecuted, and that these statistics are especially unreliable for cases of *vol domestique*. For it has been suggested that masters became increasingly reluctant to report and prosecute the thefts by their domestics during the course of the eighteenth century.[48] Their reluctance is said to have stemmed from the ferocious punishment accorded such crimes. *Vol domestique* was considered worse than ordinary theft because it involved a betrayal of trust. A servant owed his primary loyalty to his master; his primary duty was the protection of his master's property. Therefore a servant who robbed his master was doubly guilty: he was a disloyal servant as well as a thief. Given the familial rhetoric that surrounded the patriarchal household of the Old Regime, the act was almost equivalent to patricide. Thus it is not surprising that the crime was harshly punished. In all law codes of the Old Regime, *vol domestique* carried the death sentence, usually death by hanging. The *coutume* of Paris mandated that the guilty servant be executed on the doorstep of the master whom he had betrayed. This punishment is said to have been a major factor in dissuading masters from reporting domestic thefts. Their growing humanitarianism, so the argument goes, made them reluctant to exact the death penalty for petty pilfering, and their new notions of domestic comfort made the thought of a rotting corpse suspended in their doorway understandably distasteful.[49]

Doubtless there is something to this argument. Employers' memoirs of the period do show a humanitarian reluctance to prosecute servants for petty thefts. For example, the famous artist Elizabeth Vigée-Lebrun was robbed by one of her servants while in exile in St. Petersburg during the Revolution. She was unable to prevent the reporting of the crime, but she moved heaven and earth ("I cannot tell you what it cost me in prayers and solicitations," she wrote) to see that the thief was pardoned. The young man's parents had once been in her employ, and she did not want to inflict on them the grief of having their son hanged.[50] But while such cases did occur I find it hard to believe that they were prevalent enough to alter substantially the statistics of servant criminality. Instead these statistics seem to me an accurate reflection of what we know of servants' lives and attitudes. The generally low crime rate of servants could easily have stemmed from their passion for "respectability," and their relatively high rate of violent crimes could reflect the license for violent behavior traditionally allowed male domestics.

Another way in which the criminal statistics seem to reflect the reality of servants' lives is the fact that among at least the *reported* instances of servant thievery unemployed servants predominated. Statistics of servant larceny suggest that the typical servant thief was not the employed *servante* who filched her mistress's handkerchief, but instead the out-of-work domestic who shoplifted, picked pockets, or robbed his landlord and fellow lodgers simply to stay alive. Such is the pattern revealed in thefts of servants prosecuted in the Châtelet in the last decades of the Old Regime, summarized in table 10, below. Clearly *chomage* drove the majority of servants to stealing.[51]

TABLE 10

Victims of Theft Perpetrated by Servants, Paris, 1750–89

Victim	Employed Servants	Unemployed Servants
Master or former master	49	12
Other servants	7	12
Fellow lodgers	0	21
Shopkeepers, passers-by, etc.	30	71
N	86	116

Source: Botlan, "Domesticité et domestiques," 300.

Theft was simply the most desperate expedient by which unemployed servants stayed alive. Most thieving servants were not habitual criminals; instead, they were trying to survive as best they could. Unfortunately, however, the committing of just one theft could easily draw a servant from the paths of respectability, and plunge him—or, much less frequently, her[52]—permanently into the criminal underworld which existed in all French cities and towns. This was especially likely to happen if a servant stole clothing or table linen, favorite targets of servant larceny. Stolen money was easily spent, and stolen food was simply eaten, but stolen clothing or linen had to be disposed of through a fence. Frequently these were *revendeuses*, women who wandered the streets peddling patched and faded sheets, and skirts and stockings which had already passed through the hands of fifteen or twenty owners.[53] *Revendeuses* were often wives of servants and former servants themselves, like Anne Baudière, *ditte* La Mangonette, wife of Jean Semèze, *cocher*, arrested for trafficking in stolen goods in Toulouse in 1689, and *La nommée* Faur, described by one of her criminal contacts as a former domestic and "married to a man who remains in the service of some *gros Monsieur*."[54] For *revendeuse,* was, like laundress, a logical occupation for a female servant forced to give up her job upon marriage. Servants were therefore often acquainted with these women, and they in turn often put the domestics who brought them goods to fence into contact with bands of robbers on the lookout for accomplices who might leave a window open or a door ajar for the convenience of thieves.[55] Thus servants might be drawn into a permanent life of crime. This happened to Gabriel Larrisière, who began his career as the respected and well-paid cook of Cardinal Bonzi of Toulouse and ended it on a scaffold. Unemployment apparently drove Larrisière into petty thievery, and through this he discovered a criminal underworld which appealed to him more than the kitchens of *les grands*. He left domestic service, adopted a *nom de guerre*, Laforgue, and embarked on a career of crime, eventually joining a gang which stole the plate from church altars and fenced it through a shady goldsmith in Montauban. Larrisière was executed for *vols avec effraction* and sacrilege in 1717.[56]

Stories like Larrisière's point up the dangers of *chomage* for servants. Long-term unemployment could not only wipe out the savings from decades of work; it could also set a servant on a downward spiral to disaster. The same also holds true for that special criminal opportunity for women: prostitution. The extent of servant prostitution, like servant thievery, has been greatly exaggerated by historians. And like thievery, prostitution is best understood in the context of servant unemployment and the desperation it induced.

Ever since Parent-Duchâtelet's famous survey of Parisian prostitutes of the 1830s revealed that almost one-third of them had once been servants (thus making domestic service the most heavily represented former occupation among them), historians have assumed that servants were especially likely to join the ranks of the world's oldest profession.[57] For them the classic prostitute is the female servant seduced and then abandoned by her employer or swain and forced to sell herself to survive. Olwen Hufton, for example, emphasizes this type in her discussion of prostitution among the eighteenth-century poor.[58]

The notion that servants contributed heavily to the ranks of prostitutes fits well with employers' perceptions of the immorality of domestics, but it does not accord with what we know about at least *professional* prostitution in the ancien régime. Unfortunately our knowledge is sparse, because lists of professional prostitutes rarely give anything besides their name and crime. Yet what information there is suggests that servants were in fact rather unlikely to become prostitutes. For example, in the lists of women condemned for prostitution to the Hôpital La Grave in Toulouse from 1729 to 1739, former occupations were given for fourteen. Only one was a former *servante*, although two others were, respectively, the wife of a *cocher* and the widow of a *cuisinier*.[59] In Bordeaux, where prostitution flourished as befitted a great port, 150 professional prostitutes were listed on the *capitation* roll of 1784. But most of these were former *lingères* and *couturières*; the former servants among them were mostly ex-slaves from the West Indies, like Marie La Negresse and La Martiniquaise.[60] In the records of arrest for prostitution in Bordeaux's municipal archives, the only servant mentioned is a male *domestique* condemned for patronizing a *fille de joie*.[61] Even in Paris, which had the most widespread, organized, and professionalized prostitution of any city in France, servants were surprisingly underrepresented among the inhabitants of brothels.[62] And new studies of prostitution in the nineteenth century show that even in that era of Parent-Duchâtelet servants were not especially likely to take to the streets. Instead the needle trades were the largest contributors to the ranks of the *filles de noce*.[63]

Thus the traditional conception of the servant prostitute, like that of the servant thief, needs some revision. Nevertheless there were two types of female domestics who often became prostitutes: inn servants and the unemployed *servante*. That the serving women of inns, taverns, and cabarets would offer more than drinks to their customers was a longstanding tradition in European society. As M. Fournel, an eighteenth-century jurist, pointed out, in the laws of ancient Rome inn servants were classified as prostitutes. This tradition lingered in the law codes of the ancien régime: because of their equivocal reputation inn servants were denied the legal right to sue their seducers for damages if they became pregnant, a right that all other women, including all other types of domestic servants, enjoyed.[64] This provision reflected the realities of their situation. Even in the eighteenth century, when most servants' work had become monetized, inn servants apparently did not receive regular wages and lived solely on their tips. In one court case Jeanne Leconte, *servante* in the Reine de France in Bordeaux, was "interrogated how long she had been a servant in the aforesaid cabaret and how much she earned as wages. Responded that she had been a servant for two months and that she got no wages, only sharing gifts and tips with another *servante.*"[65] Therefore it is not surprising, given the traditions of the occupation, that inn servants supplemented their meager earnings with casual prostitution. Those who made *déclarations de grossesse,* statements required by law of unwed mothers in the ancien régime, were quite frank about their activities. Marthe Peyrig, *servante* at the Bras d'Or in the Provençal town of Lambesc, stated that her pregnancy was the work of one of the inn's overnight guests, an army officer; she had carried his bags to his room, and after what she described as "certain discourses," they had sex.[66] Rose Michel became pregnant by a frequent guest at the inn where she worked, a carter whose name she did not know; and Jeanne Marie Lamere, employed in a cabaret in Orgon, could not identify the author of her pregnancy; she confessed to "having been known abandonedly by various men."[67]

The other type of female domestic likely to engage in prostitution was the unemployed *servante*. Whether out of work because she had been seduced and abandoned, or simply the victim of bad luck in the job market, the unemployed *servante* might easily turn to casual, short-term prostitution to survive. Such casual prostitution by normally respectable women was in fact the characteristic type of prostitution in the late eighteenth century and was far more widespread than the "professional" kind practiced by women who made prostitution their sole support. Part-time prostitution was not automatically considered disgraceful among the poor, who well understood the exigencies of survival. Nor did it necessarily represent a first step on the road to ruin. Many a woman who sold herself in time of need returned to respectability in better times and even eventually married.[68] On the other hand, prostitution could also easily be the first step on a downward path to the criminal underworld. For prostitutes risked, besides the two obvious hazards of their calling, pregnancy and venereal disease (both of which could make a *servante* unfit for further respectable employment) contacts with the criminal world of shady cabarets and backstreet gambling; like servant thieves, servant prostitutes could therefore easily be drawn into a lifetime of crime.

These then were the risks of job-changing and unemployment: loss of savings and of hopes for the future, a hand-to-mouth existence of temporary jobs and shelters, an ignominious return to home and family, and an opening to criminal temptations which could draw a servant deep into the underworld of illegality. How many domestics succumbed to these dangers is impossible to say. In her study of nineteenth-century servants Theresa McBride estimated that about one-third were downwardly mobile.[69] This is probably a good guess for the Old Regime as well.

Moneymaking and Upward Mobility

The majority of servants, however, appear to have survived occasional spells of unemployment with little difficulty, and marched steadily onward toward their goals in life. Paramount among these was making money. Many servants were surpringly successful at this. As mentioned earlier, this least "capitalistic" of occupations ironically produced some of the shrewdest businessmen—and -women—and the largest fortunes among the working classes.

As we have seen, domestic service, with its high salaries and its wide variety of perks and perquisites, was at least after 1750, one of the more lucrative occupations open to the lower classes.[70] And since their food and shelter were usually provided for them, servants could save almost every *sou* they earned. Therefore it is not surprising that they were among the wealthiest members of the lower classes.

It is difficult to compare the fortunes of servants with those other members of the lower classes because domestics were not listed under their own income level on *capitation* rolls. The best source for comparison is therefore marriage contracts, although admittedly these are biased in favor of the more prosperous types who could afford to marry. Analysis of marriage contracts reveals a striking pattern. In town after town of the Old Regime servants regularly commanded more wealth at marriage than did agricultural workers, wage laborers, or even artisans, and in many cases their fortunes matched those of the lower levels of the bourgeoisie.

The value of servant dowries in Toulouse, Bordeaux, and Paris are summarized in table 11. The patterns discernible here are not surprising. Male servants, as befitted their superior salaries and prestige, generally commanded greater wealth at marriage than did their female colleagues. Dowries were greater in commercial Bordeaux, with its higher wages, than in Toulouse, and they were greatest of all in Paris, that Promised Land of eighteenth-century servitude. And in each town and for each sex dowries rose dramatically with the rise in servants' wages during the course of the eighteenth century.

Perhaps the most striking feature of this table is the wide range of wealth it reveals. Even in the late eighteenth century there were servants whose total possessions at marriage were less than 100 livres. For example, the entire dowry of Jeanne Joffres, *servante* of Toulouse, is described as "a bit of linen," so poor that the notary put no monetary value on it; and Magdeleine, an illegitimate farm servant, married solely on the strength of a forty-livre charitable donation from Toulouse's Hôpital La Grave.[71] Yet a substantial and growing segment of the servant population was well-off; an example is Gabriel Lachasse, Parisian *cocher,* who started life as the son of a poor farm laborer in

TABLE 11

Dowries of Servants at Marriage

	Livres				Average Value of Dowry (in Livres)	Median Value of Dowry (in Livres)
	Less than 100	100–499	500–999	1000+		
Dowries of female servants (in %)						
Toulouse						
1727–29	53.4%	46.0%	0.5%	0.0%	142.3	100
1787–89	39.6	45.6	12.1	2.7	296.4	150
Bordeaux						
1727–29	30.1	51.7	17.2	0.9	249.7	150
1787–89	10.5	36.8	25.3	27.4	653.7	500
Paris, 1787–89	7.7	23.1	15.4	53.8	1404.7	1025
Dowries of brides of male servants (in %)						
Toulouse						
1727–29	74.4	23.3	0.0	2.3	115.8	60
1787–89	22.7	44.3	21.6	11.3	342.9	300
Bordeaux						
1727–29	31.0	54.8	9.5	4.8	323.5	200
1787–89	10.9	30.4	21.7	37.0	789.7	536
Paris, 1787–89	8.2	18.4	20.4	53.1	1457.1	1000

Sources: See Bibliography, section I, B.

Brie but, by the time he married, had accumulated 2,000 livres cash and numerous clothes and household goods, and his bride, widow of a master-shoemaker, owned property worth almost 4,000 livres.[72] Such wealth was rarely found in other working-class occupations. In Bordeaux in the 1780s servants had more than double the proportion of dowries of over 800 livres than did masons; in Toulouse in the same period the average dowry of a servant was 100 livres more than that of an artisan and over 200 livres more than that of an agricultural laborer.[73] And in mid-eighteenth-century Paris the percentage of servants with dowries of over 1,000 livres almost approached that of the bourgeois *roturiers sans profession.*[74]

Why were servants often so much wealthier than other lower class types? The answer lies in part in their large salaries and the opportunity for saving that their occupation afforded. But it also lies in the fact that their role as purchasers of household supplies for their employers gave them experience in the techniques of handling large sums of money denied to other members of the lower classes. Domestic service exposed them to the ways of wealth as well as the ways of the wealthy; they gained a sophisticated knowledge of financial practices which often encouraged them to try their luck at commerce. For example, many servants who learned about the wholesale food trade through buying provisions for their households eventually began to trade on their own account. Philippe Briquet, a *maître d'hôtel* to a baron in Toulouse, made sizable investments in wholesale wheat, financing them by loans from friends as well as his own savings.[75] And while servants were especially active in the provisioning trades, these were not their only commercial activities. The notarial records of the ancien régime reveal servants who trafficked in everything from cotton stockings to mulberry leaves for the silk industry.[76]

But the favorite investment of servants was undoubtedly the *rente,* or personal loan at interest. In the Parisian estate inventories studied by Daniel Roche, almost 50 percent of the assets of servants who died intestate from 1695 to 1715 and over 50 percent of the assets of those who died intestate from 1775 to 1790 were in *rentes.* (Comparable figures for salaried workers were only 19 percent and 45 percent.)[77] Servants were among the major buyers of the small *rentes* sold by charitable institutions.[78] They also made many loans to private individuals. Servants were probably the major moneylenders to the *menu peuple*; loan transactions like that between Joseph Pidoux, *suisse* of Mme. La Maréchale de Broglie, and one Romedon, a secondhand dealer, who borrowed 48 livres from him, abound in the police and notarial records of the ancien régime.[79] Even their social superiors were not above borrowing from domestics. A Toulousan *avocat* owed 300 livres to chef Louis Vintrou; a Jewish trader borrowed more than 6,800 livres from Parisian *domestique* Nicolas Cornette *dit* Champagne at a hefty 20 percent interest.[80] Especially common were loans by servants to their employers. Costerine Patou, *fille de service* of the Dlle. de Vitry, was asked by her mistress if she had saved any of her wages from earlier jobs; she replied, yes, she had 200 livres. Madame promptly borrowed that to pay the household expenses. François Pages, a merchant in Toulouse, borrowed 550 livres at 5 percent interest from his *servante*; Dominique Trilhon, a priest, borrowed 200 livres from his. And a Bordelais maidservant, Jeanne Jonc, loaned her mistress, the widow of a noble, a total of 1,453 livres in the course of the twenty-five years she worked for her; this money probably kept the household going.[81] So accustomed were servants to making loans that one gets the impression that many of them thought of money primarily in terms of the interest it could earn. Maidservant Marianne Fabruel, urged by her mistress to buy some new clothes, gave her employer 121 livres to purchase the garments. When her mistress refused to hand them over, Fabruel complained to the police: not only had she lost the 121 livres, she pointed out, but she had also lost the 5 percent interest she could have earned by loaning out the money.[82]

Their experience in handling money inspired many domestics to dream of leaving service and going into business. *Femmes de chambre* often hoped to set up shop as dressmakers; Anne Lavigne, for example, lady's maid to the

Marquise Denointelle, paid 200 livres to a *marchande de modes* for a two-year apprenticeship in that trade.[83] The traditional ambition of male domestics was to go into the provisioning trades, following in the footsteps of Audiger, a seventeenth-century *maître d'hôtel* and author of *La Maison réglée*, who after failing to get monopolies on all the peas and roses (both great luxuries in the seventeenth century) sold in Paris, made a fortune selling lemonade and iced drinks in his shop near the Palais-Royal.[84] By the 1780s, however, many male servants were interested in other forms of commerce as well, especially in the booming commercial cities like Bordeaux. Bordeaux's newspaper, the *Journal de Guienne,* often carried advertisements placed by *maîtres d'hôtel* who wanted to become respectable clerks "in an office or shop" and cooks who wanted to set sail for the West Indies to make their fortune.[85] Indeed, the sugar islands seem to have been the focus of the hopes and dreams of many ambitious servants in the eighteenth century. *Femmes de chambre* in Bordeaux offered to serve free of charge during the voyage employers who would pay for their passage to the Indies, and Parisian *domestique* Antoine Gonthier was cheated out of his savings by a man who promised to take him to Martinique, give him a slave, and set him up as a sugar planter.[86]

Servants' grandiose dreams of becoming West Indian sugar planters were doubtless doomed to failure. Although there were a few spectacular examples of servants who made fortunes—Gourville, Audiger—most of them lived in the seventeenth century and owed a great deal to the generosity of noble patrons. The notion propagated by Montesquieu that many financiers of the Regency had once been domestics has recently been proven a myth.[87] But servants' more modest hopes of becoming shop clerks or *marchandes de modes* probably were realizable, although we have no way of knowing how many men and women deserted domestic service for such ventures or how well they fared.

What attracted servants into the lower levels of commerce was not simply a desire for gain, for the financial rewards of such positions were rarely greater than those of domestic service. It was instead the bourgeois respectability such positions conferred. By the last decades of the eighteenth century the spread of the notion that domestic service was degrading made many servants desire to leave their occupation and join the ranks of the respectable. The Parisian chef L'Amireau provides a good example. His letters show that, although financially successful and proud of his skill at his craft, L'Amireau was self-conscious about and resentful of his position as a servant. He once apologized for a present he gave to his fiancée: it was not much, he wrote bitterly, but it was "sufficient and even very proper for a person obliged to servitude," as he was. And one of his proudest moments came when he alone of all the household was asked to dine on terms of equality by a country *curé*.[88] It was ambitious and touchy servants like L'Amireau who were most apt to desert the occupation for the sake of bourgeois respectability.

Love, Sex, and Marriage

A major goal for most servants, and one inextricably bound with their other goals of leaving service and moving up in the world, was marriage. Marriage was especially important for the female servant. Only in marriage could she legitimately seek sexual fulfillment and find real economic security. And only when she married could she cease to be a servant and become instead mistress of a household of her own.

Marriage was less crucial for male domestics, both because their financial situation was more secure and because they faced fewer penalties if they sought sexual fulfillment outside the bonds of matrimony. Nonetheless most men servants also wanted to marry, and not only for the personal happiness it might bring. In early modern Europe marriage was an economic as well as a social rite of passage. Since the lower classes rarely married without some sort of economic stake, marriage symbolized the attainment of at least a modest financial success. It also marked the period when dependency ceased and a man became a true adult, when he left his father's or his master's household to found a household of his own and take upon himself the economic responsibilities of an adult member of the community. This symbolic aspect of marriage appealed to male servants, so conscious of their dependency. Marriage was a part of their dreams of achieving economic success and of being recognized as independent and respectable citizens by society. Again the correspondence of Parisian chef L'Amireau illustrates this feeling. In his letters to his fiancée he dwells as lovingly on the joys of being a respectable master of his own household, with a good bourgeois *bonne ménagère* for a wife, as he does on the pleasures of sharing their lives together.[89]

But servants who wished to marry faced a number of formidable obstacles, the most important of which was their employers' prejudice against married domestics. Household manuals of the Old Regime were adamant on this point: married servants should be avoided at all costs. The problem with marriage was that it created divided loyalties. Married domestics could not devote themselves totally to their masters' interests, as good servants should. Instead they would always be tempted to put the interests of their own families first. Married servants would be distracted from their duties by family worries; they would be tempted to insinuate their dependents into the household, to sneak away to visit their spouses, and to rob their masters to feed their hungry children.[90] This preference for celibate servants is important, for masters had the means to enforce it. Not only could they refuse to hire married servants, but they could also prevent the marriages of those already employed, for by a law of 1567 employed domestics were required to obtain their masters' permission before marrying.[91] That masters did indeed prevent their servants from marrying is suggested by the fact that seventeenth-century confessionals listed a master's denying his servants permission to marry for purely selfish reasons as a mortal sin.[92]

The prejudice against married servants never completely prevented their employment—in 1714, for example, the Sieur de Lamourous, Bordelais landowner, hired Pierre Dupersson and his wife as "*valet* and *servante* in the house" at a combined wage of fifty-seven *écus* per year.[93] And signs suggest that by the last decades of the eighteenth century employers were less inclined to exercise patriarchal controls over the private lives of their servants. The newspapers of the 1780s are full of advertisements of married domestics seeking employment in the same household: "A husband and wife, aged twenty-eight, want to be placed in a household, the one as *domestique,* the other as *femme de chambre.* Both know how to read, write, iron, and work in linen."[94] But the prejudice never completely disappeared. Even during the Revolution married servants feared dismissal, as the following anecdote, recounted by the Duc de Bourbon in a letter written in 1798, illustrates:

> A very interesting event . . . is a secret marriage: that of my *servante*, named Riche . . . and my intrepid *marmiton* Ursin. Fear of my whip prevented the disclosure while it was not strictly necessary, that is, not forced by any symptom of the appearance of any little Ursins. But they were afraid of an indiscretion and took the great decision to come and throw themselves at my feet to confess the mutual fault. . . . It was hard not to burst out laughing at the mixture of tears, sadness, happiness and worry of the new household which waited to be fired.[95]

The prejudice against married servants did not mean that servants had to forswear marriage completely. Their rates of celibacy were probably only slightly higher than those of the rest of the lower classes.[96] But it did mean that their marriage patterns differed from those of artisans and wage laborers. Servants were more likely than any other lower-class group to indulge in premarital sex. They married later than artisans or wage laborers, and they married much more exogamously. They were, as we have seen, generally wealthier at marriage than other members of the lower classes, but marriage was for them often an economic setback instead of a benefit. All of these oddities in servants' marriage patterns are directly traceable to the prejudice against married domestics.

We can see how the prejudice against married domestics shaped servants' private lives as we follow them on their long road to the altar. Let us begin with the sex to whom marriage was most important: women. Most women servants began their careers in their mid-teens, but they generally did not marry until their late twenties or early thirties.[97] The ten or fifteen years between their starting to work and their marriage was devoted to two objectives: first, accumulating a dowry large enough to snare a respectable husband, and second, avoiding an illegitimate pregnancy which might ruin their marriage prospects.

Of the two, accumulating a dowry was infinitely easier. It was almost impossible for a lower-class woman to marry without a dowry, if only a modest *lit garni* (bed and linens) worth ten or twenty livres. In the south of France almost every couple made a marriage contract—91 percent of all servants marrying in eighteenth-century Toulouse did so, for example[98]—and almost every contract specified at least a small dowry. Usually the bride's parents provided her dowry, but female servants came from backgrounds so poverty-stricken that they often had to provide their own. In my sample of marriage contracts from Toulouse and Bordeaux, only 10.8 percent of the women servants had their dowries given to them by their families, their master, or a charitable foundation, while 63.5 percent furnished their own dowries out of their own "salary and loans."[99] Luckily it was fairly easy for a servant to save a substantial sum, since she did not have to spend her salary on food and lodging. Indeed probably many women were attracted to domestic service in the first place because of the unparalleled opportunity it provided to save for a dowry.

As shown in table 11, the size of the dowries of female servants varied widely. Two factors influenced this: the length of time women worked before marriage and the type of job they held. Obviously the longer a woman worked the more she could earn and save. In Toulouse marriage contracts often specified the length of time a woman spent in service before marriage: it averaged 5.3 years in the 1720s and 4.8 in the 1780s.[100] In Toulouse in the 1720s, women who worked for less than a year before they married had dowries that averaged only 47.3 livres, while those who worked from one to five years had dowries averaging 141.3 livres and those who worked for over five years had dowries averaging 219.3 livres. Equally important in determining dowry size was the type of job a woman held. Specialized upper servants usually earned higher salaries and therefore accumulated bigger dowries than mere *servantes*. In Toulouse in the 1780s, for example, the average dowry for *servantes* was only 210 livres but cooks, *femmes de chambre,* and *gouvernantes* commanded dowries averaging 452 livres, 700 livres, and 1,400 livres respectively. Also, women who worked in noble and bourgeois households, where salaries were more likely to be high—and to be regularly paid—generally found it easier to accumulate a large dowry than did farm servants or those employed in lower-class households.[101]

The size of a servant's dowry was important, for it helped determine the sort of husband she could win, although obviously it was not the sole factor affecting the choice of a spouse. *Servantes* who kept up their ties to their family often returned home to marry a peasant suitor approved by their parents. Others married young men they met while in service: male servants in the same household (although masters' prejudices against married domestics made such matches rarer than might be expected); artisans and clerks whose stores they visited; shopboys who came to the kitchen on errands; day laborers whom they met dancing at carnival time. But the size of dowries definitely affected a woman servant's range of choice. As table 12 shows, servants and artisans who married female domestics generally demanded bigger dowries than did mere peasants or wage laborers. Male servants, after all, were fairly well-off and socially ambitious, and they needed a large fortune at marriage in case they had to leave service and set themselves up in some other occupation. And artisans could afford to be choosy, for they had much to offer a wife: they were among the most prosperous and prestigious members of the lower classes. Also, they tended to marry endogamously, wedding the sisters and daughters of fellow craftsmen; such alliances brought useful contacts within their crafts. A servant girl needed a large dowry to compete with such brides.

The marriage patterns of female servants have been classified in table 13. Two trends immediately stand out. The first is the low rate of endogamy—that is, marriage between servants. This trend is especially striking in the first half of the eighteenth century, when employers' prejudices against married servants were strongest. In the latter half of the century the prejudice lessened, and the number of servant-servant marriages rose. But never (except in Paris, where married domestics could easily hire themselves out as servants by the day) did it approach the levels of endogamy usual among the *menu peuple*. In most eighteenth-century towns, after all, at least 40 percent and usually 50 percent of artisans married within their social group; among daily laborers the figure often rose to 60 or 70 percent.[102]

The second trend which table 13 reveals is a turn toward more adventurous and ambitious marriages as the century progressed. In both Toulouse and Bordeaux fewer servants returned to the villages of their birth to marry peasants and agricultural laborers in the last half of the eighteenth century; instead they increasingly cut themselves off from their families and early roots and established themselves permanently in town.[103] And among townsmen they increasingly chose as husbands not the relatively "undemanding" textile workers and wage laborers, but instead domestics, artisans, and shopkeepers, who required substantial dowries from their brides. An apparent exception to this is Bordeaux, where the percentage of artisan husbands decreases and that of wage laborers increases from 1727–29 to 1787–89. But this is the exception

TABLE 12

Average Dowry of Female Servants, Classified According to Husbands' Occupations (in Livres)

	Toulouse		Bordeaux	
	1727–29	1787–89	1727–29	1787–89
Agricultural laborer	100.4	249.9	140.7	300.5
Textile worker, wage laborer	126.9	32.0	178.1	613.9
Servant	88.0	267.7	200.9	312.0
Shopkeeper, artisan	199.4	356.4	358.4	445.7

Sources: See Bibliography, section I, B.

TABLE 13

Occupations of Husbands of Female Servants (in %)

	Toulouse		Bordeaux		Paris
	1727–29	1787–89	1727–29	1787–89	1787–89
Agricultural laborer	42.4%	26.4%	21.3%	14.0%	0.0%
Shopkeeper, artisan	22.4	24.5	40.2	23.3	15.4
Servant	15.2	37.3	17.2	27.3	53.8
Textile worker, wage laborer	10.4	6.3	5.7	24.7	15.4
Food, lodging, transportation worker	8.0	4.5	5.7	2.7	0.0
Soldier, sailor, public servant	1.6	0.9	4.9	5.5	0.0
Other	0.0	0.0	7.9	2.6	15.9
N	125	110	122	150	13

Sources: See Bibliography, section I, B.

that proves the rule. For in Bordeaux crafts became increasingly modernized and monetized in the last decades of the eighteenth century: instead of hiring apprentice journeymen who hoped to gain the *maîtrise* one day, masters increasingly employed laborers who worked for a daily wage. It is these *tonneliers à la journée* and *garçons platiers à la journée* who form the bulk of the "wage-laborer" category in Bordeaux in the 1780s. Because of the high wages in Bordeaux, they were relatively prosperous, and they could demand the substantial dowries traditional to craftsmen, as table 12 shows.

This turn toward more ambitious marriages on the part of the female servants obviously owed a great deal to the monetization of servants' work and the rise in servants' wages over the course of the eighteenth century. Higher wages allowed servants to accumulate large dowries and therefore to compete successfully with the daughters of artisans and shopkeepers for city-bred spouses. But the mere fact that servants could accumulate large dowries was not solely responsible for their turn toward more ambitious marriages in the late eighteenth century. Opportunity, after all, means little without the will to take advantage of it. It was probably the new self-confidence of female servants, bred of their participation in a market economy, which made them determined to strike the best possible bargain with life. For them this meant becoming the wife of a respectable and prosperous artisan or shopkeeper.

Attaining this goal was not, however, simply a matter of saving for a dowry and looking around for a prospective husband on whom to bestow it. Husband-hunting was for female servants a perilous business. From the moment they began to work and save for a dowry until they arrived safely at the altar, they faced a danger that could ruin not only their marriage plans but all their hopes for the future: the bearing of an illegitimate child.

We know a great deal about the women who bore illegitimate children in Old Regime France because of the existence of *déclarations de grossesse*, statements required by French law of unwed mothers which are full of details about their seducers and the circumstances surrounding their pregnancies.[104] Unfortunately no *déclarations* survive for either Paris or Toulouse, and only a spotty sample, three half-burned registers covering the years 1772 to 1784, exists for Bordeaux.[105] I have analyzed these and also used an informative sample of over 2,000 *déclarations* covering almost all of the eighteenth century and drawn mostly from Aix-en-Provence, a parlementary city very like Toulouse in its economic and social makeup.[106]

In both, and indeed in every sample of *déclarations* that I know of, domestic servants formed the largest single category of women who became pregnant out of wedlock. In Aix they formed 58 percent of the total; in Bordeaux almost 20 percent, figures far greater than the proportion of servants in the female working population of the two towns. This suggests that there were aspects of domestic service that posed special threats to a woman's virtue. And this was indeed the case. *Déclarations* show that all lower-class women, no matter what their occupation, ran a high risk of an illegitimate pregnancy during the months when they were courting. Sex between an engaged couple was apparently acceptable during the ancien régime, because of the popular tradition, dating back to before the Council of Trent, which regarded a betrothal as equivalent to marriage.[107] If the woman became pregnant and eventually married, the result was a prebridal pregnancy, fairly widespread and easily tolerated by the society of the Old Regime. But if something—lack of money, family objections, or the man's simply getting cold feet—prevented the marriage, the woman suffered through an illegitimate pregnancy and became part of the illegitimacy statistics. Domestic servants, however, faced a sort of double jeopardy. For in addition to the normal risks of pregnancy during courtship, servants ran the risk of being seduced during their long years of waiting and saving, before they could really start courtship in earnest, by either their masters or by the male servants in the households in which they worked.

This danger is illustrated in tables 14 and 15. Table 14 shows the sexual partners of the servants who made *déclarations* in Provence and Bordeaux. The largest categories of seducers were, first of all, male servants and second, masters and other men of the upper classes.[108] Table 15 gives the ages of the servants at the time of their *déclarations*. This shows that while female servants involved in relationships with artisans and other lower-class potential suitors were usually in their late twenties and early thirties, years when they could legitimately begin to think about courting, those involved in relationships with their masters and other upper-class men were usually in their teens and early twenties, new to town and to their jobs and just beginning the long slow process of saving for a dowry.

TABLE 14

Sexual Partners of Female Servants, Provence and Bordeaux (in %)

	Provence				Bordeaux	
	1727–49		1750–89		1773–76	
Master	12.8%		16.1%		12.5%	
Other upper-class man	20.0		10.8		15.0	
Agricultural laborer	3.8	(0.6)[a]	9.5	(13.1)	4.2	(5.7)
Craftsman	9.3	(13.8)	12.2	(16.7)	29.2	(40.2)
Servant	45.5	(67.7)	32.2	(44.1)	22.5	(31.0)
Textile worker, wage laborer	0.7	(1.0)	2.3	(3.1)	3.3	(4.6)
Food, lodging, transportation worker	2.8	(4.1)	6.3	(8.5)	2.5	(3.4)
Soldier, sailor, minor public servant	3.8	(5.6)	3.3	(4.5)	10.0	(13.8)
Other	1.4	(2.1)	7.2	(9.1)	0.8	(1.1)
N	290	(195)	304	(222)	120	(87)

Sources: See Bibliography, section I, C.
[a]Numbers in parentheses indicate lower-class seducers only.

TABLE 15

Ages of Seduced Female Servants, Provence, 1727–89, and Bordeaux, 1773–76 (in %)

	19 or under	20–24	25–29	30 and over
	Seduced by Master			
Provence	14.0	59.1	19.4	7.5
Bordeaux	15.4	61.5	15.4	7.7
	Seduced by Other Upper-Class Man			
Provence	13.3	61.7	10.0	15.0
Bordeaux	30.8	53.8	7.7	7.7
	Seduced by Male Servant			
Provence	6.4	38.1	39.0	16.5
Bordeaux	17.4	39.1	26.1	17.4
	Seduced by Other Lower-Class Man			
Provence	6.2	47.6	29.0	17.2
Bordeaux	20.3	35.6	27.1	16.9

Sources: See Bibliography, section I, C.

Doubtless these factors lay behind many of the sexual relationships between servant and master. The sheer loneliness of many maids, newcomers to the city, away from home and family for the first time, afraid or unable to make new friends in the city, must have driven them into their masters' arms. For such women their masters' advances were a sign that at least someone knew and cared about their existence. The sexual frustration involved in the long years of waiting until they could start courting doubtless also made many servants enter into relationships with their masters. So too did the temptations to cut these years short by accumulating a dowry through "gifts" bestowed by enamored employers, for upper-class men often promised to "take care of" their lower-class paramours, and offered them gifts of money, clothing, and jewelry in exchange for their favors. Such promises were made in 26 percent of the master-servant cases in my sample from Provence. A few servants may have even fallen in love with their employers, who with their fine clothes and manners might be more attractive than the rough cobblers and carters who came courting. After all, domestic service exposed its practitioners to a dazzling new world of wealth and luxury, and it is not surprising that at least some of them found this world—and its inhabitants—more alluring than their own.

The *déclarations* suggest, however, that the majority of servants accepted their masters' advances not out of loneliness, desire, or love, but simply because they felt they had no other choice. A servant, after all, shared a house with her master; she had nowhere to hide if he was bent on her seduction. She was all too easily approached as she slept on the kitchen hearth or outside her master's door, all too easily cornered as she went on her daily rounds. Employers did not scruple to use physical force against their servants. Thérèse Cavaillon, twenty-two-year-old *servante* of the *receveur des gabelles* at Berre, was raped at knifepoint by the son of the house on carnival day when he knew that no one else would be at home to hear her screams.[109] But usually force was unnecessary; in most cases economic threats sufficed. Marguerite Angellin slept with her master, although, she stated, he "was married and even a grandfather," because "he said that if she didn't he wouldn't pay her wages."[110] A final factor at work was the long tradition of the sexual exploitation of servant by master, which doubtless made many maids give in with a sense of resigning themselves to the inevitable.[111] Farm servant Thérèse Roux expressed this in her *déclaration* when she said that she had at first resisted the advances of her employer, Louis Seste, "but since he was her master she was obliged to consent."[112]

Many of the same factors were involved in the seduction of *servantes* by their male fellow domestics. Like masters, fellow workers too could offer relief from the loneliness and frustrations of the years of waiting; like masters, they too could take advantage of sharing the same household to force themselves on reluctant women. And if they lacked the economic threats which masters could make, they had an equally potent weapon in the promise of marriage.

Déclarations suggest that sexual relationships between servants in the same household could take three forms. Some were clearly exploitative: male servants taking advantage of living under the same roof to trap their prey. *Servante* Magdeleine Comte was raped on the dining room table by the *domestique* of the household while she was folding linen.[113] Often servants were attacked as they made the bed, not only for reasons of comfort, but also because of the suggestive overtones of the task.[114] Not all servant-servant relationships were exploitative, however; in the two other types the female servants were willing and even eager victims. One type was the "courtship gone wrong"—relationship in which two servants fell in love and planned to marry but were prevented from doing so, usually by money problems. This was especially likely to happen in the seventeenth and early eighteenth centuries, when the prejudice against married domestics meant that both of the potential partners often had to find new careers if they married. In fact marriage was so difficult for domestics in this period that it seems probable that any female servant in earnest about getting married would not become serious about a servant suitor. She would instead indulge in a servant-servant relationship—the other type—a love affair with no thought of marriage. Doubtless many cooks and maids found that such affairs enlivened their long years of waiting with flirtation and romance. *Déclarations* show that such relationships often began during the summer months when households adjourned to the country. It is easy to imagine how the fine weather and the relaxation of household discipline turned servants' thoughts to love.[115]

In the last half of the eighteenth century the dissipation of the prejudice against married domestics seems to have changed romance within the household. Servant could now court servant in earnest. Therefore it seems likely that in the last half of the eighteenth century fewer servant-servant relationships were "waiting games" and more were genuine courtships, and that more servant-servant relationships ended in marriage rather than in an illegitimate pregnancy, as was the case earlier. Evidence for this comes from a comparison of tables 13 and 14, showing the husbands and seducers of female servants. In the last decade of the Old Regime the proportion of servant-servant illegitimacies declined dramatically, while the proportion of servant-servant marriages rose.[116]

Masters and fellow servants were of course not the only sexual partners of female domestics. As table 14 shows, they also slept with artisans, day laborers, soldiers, sailors, and other members of the lower classes. The advanced ages of the female servants in such cases (see table 15) suggest that they entered these relationships with marriage in mind—that these were either cases of genuine "courtship gone wrong" or cases in which the servant slept with a man in hopes of receiving a marriage proposal. During their courting years female servants were probably more likely to end up seduced and abandoned than other women of the lower classes, both because they had much greater freedom of action than girls living with their families and because, uprooted as they were, they could not bring to bear the pressures of parents and community on their suitors to make them do their duty. For despite the premises of patriarchy, masters did not act *in loco parentis* in this matter. In Old Regime households servants could come and go more or less as they pleased, and they could entertain their suitors in the kitchen or their rooms more or less at will. Eighteenth-century police records are full of complaints like that of Sr. Jean Duré, master tailor in Paris, who employed a servant named Nanette who had always behaved "with dignity." But one day Duré entered the kitchen unexpectedly and surprised Nanette in the arms of a young man named Gaillard, who during the ensuing shouting match fled naked except for his shirt.[117] *Déclarations* show that the majority of sexual relationships between female servants and lower-class suitors were consummated not in the man's lodgings but in the household where the servant worked. Given their freedom of action and their lack of protection it is not surprising that many *servantes* were taken advantage of by unscrupulous suitors; instead it seems amazing that any managed to marry at all.

Servants who were seduced and abandoned faced a bleak future. To be sure, an illegitimate pregnancy did not inevitably ruin a servant's life. In my samples of wills I found two made by women servants who acknowledged bearing bastard children; they had left their babies with peasant nurses and gone on working.[118] An illegitimate pregnancy did not even necessarily ruin a servant's prospects for marriage. But on the other hand, it took an enormous dowry to wipe out such a stain on one's character. This is shown by the case of Marie Pradel, a twenty-eight-year-old *servante* who gave birth to a bastard in 1721. The next year she robbed her master of over 2,000 livres, most of which she handed over to Louis Bonamy as part of the substantial dowry he had demanded before he agreed to marry her.

Marie's act is a measure of the desperation an illegitimate pregnancy could induce. Most servants found it difficult to survive one. They usually lost their jobs when their condition became apparent, especially if their mistress thought the husband or son of the house might be responsible for their pregnancy. They could not go home for fear of bringing disgrace upon their families. Therefore they took to the road, sleeping in the open and supporting themselves by beggary, theft, and/or prostitution. The interrogations of servants arrested for infanticide offer glimpses of this life on the road. For example, Anne Coignet gave birth to her baby in the open, by a river bank, and left the child behind a tree stump, although when arrested she maintained that she had given it to a passer-by to take to a hospital. Bertrande Fouquelle bore her child in an abandoned hut. After it was born she simply reached up through a hole in the thatch and left it on the roof. She too denied her guilt and maintained that the baby had been born dead.[119] Such unconvincing lies are frequently found in infanticide interrogations; they represent, I think, what the woman desperately wished was the truth.

Disgrace, dismissal, descent into vagabondage, theft, and prostitution, perhaps even the killing of one's child on one's conscience: the price female servants paid for their sexual indiscretions could be heavy. Young girls who entered servitude in order to marry were therefore taking a risky gamble. The circumstances of the occupation made it easy for them to save for a dowry, but it also exposed them to heightened risks of seduction, illicit pregnancy, and all the problems they entailed. Those *servantes* who managed to marry were not only very clever—they were also very lucky.

For male servants marriage was neither so vital nor so difficult as it was for their female counterparts. Obviously men could relieve the sexual frustrations of the long years of waiting for marriage without the disastrous consequences that befell their female colleagues. Menservants appear to have taken full advantage of this fact. In most samples of *déclarations* male servants formed the largest single occupational category of accused seducers (see table 14). After all, they had certain advantages which their rival craftsmen and artisans lacked. First of all, menservants were usually handsome, because they were hired to look well in livery, and their fine clothes and sophisticated manner, adopted in imitation of their masters, might well turn a woman's head. Second, unlike most other workers, they had a lot of free time from their not very arduous duties to spend in the pursuit of women. Third, they often inhabited a special servant subculture which encouraged both exploiting women and boasting about it. Traces of this subculture appear in police records. The reports of the Parisian *commissaires de police*, for example, memorialize one twenty-year-old lackey, Jean Jacques Toussaint, who bragged in a cabaret to two male friends, both also servants, about his seduction of a seventeen-year-old laundress, Marie-Jeanne Dubuisson. He said that Marie was his mistress, that he had had her maidenhead, that he had made her reach climax three times the previous night, and that he was sure he had made her a baby.[120] Fourth, male domestics had virtually unlimited access to a captive group of women—the female servants in their household. And finally, male domestics found it easier than other young men to abandon rather than marry their victims, not only because the households in which they worked traveled frequently, but also because they themselves changed jobs so often.

All these factors facilitated their careers as lady-killers. As table 16 shows, male servants most often bestowed their sexual attentions on their fellow servants, but they also seduced laundresses, peddlers, and textile workers. They were also attracted to *couturières*, whose fine clothes and lady-like demeanor, adopted in imitation of their customers, appealed to men who themselves imitated the appearance and adopted the manners of their upper-class masters.

Yet despite the ease with which male servants found sexual companionship, most wanted to marry. Marriage was for male domestics a badge of the success and respectability they craved. Their choice of wives reflected this. Table

TABLE 16

Women Seduced by Male Servants, Provence and Bordeaux (in %)

	Provence		Bordeaux
	1727–49	1750–89	1773–76
Servant	88.4	86.7	87.1
Widow	6.9	2.2	0.0
Laundress	1.5	0.0	0.0
Peddler	1.7	0.0	0.0
Textile worker	0.0	3.3	3.2
Couturière	0.0	0.0	9.7
Other	1.5	7.7	0.0
Total given	130	90	31
Total cases	224	204	31

Sources: See Bibliography, section I, C.
Note: This table is incomplete, since women's occupations, apart from domestic service, are not often given in the *déclarations*.

17 gives the family backgrounds (derived from the occupations of their fathers) of the brides of men servants in our sample of towns and periods. This shows that male domestics had a strong tendency to "marry up" on the social scale, especially in the last half of the eighteenth century. It was a popular truism in the ancien régime that respectable young women shunned male servants because of their bad sexual reputation; in an anonymous *Misère des domestiques* a lackey complained: "Mais bien plus qu'une fille ait en soit peu d'honneur/ D'un habit de livrée elle aura de l'horreur."[121] Yet their marriage contracts show that male servants successfully wooed the daughters of respectable artisans and shopkeepers and even members of the petite bourgeoisie, like surgeons and schoolmasters, and sometimes even the daughters of *marchands* and *négociants*. In 1787 in Bordeaux, for example, Pierre Georges, cook of a *président à mortier* in the Parlement, married Dlle. Jeanne-Claudine Groy, the daughter of a small-scale *negociant* with a respectable dowry of 7,000 livres.[122] Male servants favored the daughters of artisans and shopkeepers not only because of their respectability, but also because their fathers might help them leave service and make a new start in a shop or craft. The same reasons made the daughters or widows of *cabaratiers*, bakers, and other members of the food and lodging trades attractive to domestics; such businesses were logical places for ex-servants to put their skills to work. And the daughters of *marchands* and *négociants* of course offered a chance to go into commerce. This tendency of menservants to make ambitious, hardheaded marriages which offered both respectability and new careers increased noticeably in the course of the eighteenth century. By the last decades of the Old Regime most male domestics were themselves the sons of the poorest agricultural laborers, but their brides were increasingly drawn from the artisanate, the

TABLE 17

Family Backgrounds of Wives of Male Servants (in %)

	Toulouse		Bordeaux		Paris
	1727–29	1787–89	1727–29	1787–89	1787–89
Agricultural worker	45.5	35.3	53.3	28.8	17.0
Shopkeeper, artisan	21.2	29.4	6.7	17.3	39.0
Servant	9.1	4.4	0.0	1.9	2.4
Textile worker, wage laborer	3.0	5.8	6.7	1.9	4.9
Food, lodging, transportation worker	9.1	13.2	13.3	21.2	22.0
Soldier, sailor, public servant	3.0	1.5	13.3	7.7	0.0
Petit bourgeois	0.0	5.0	0.0	15.4	14.6
Unknown	9.1	4.4	6.7	5.8	0.0
N	33	68	15	52	41

Sources: See Bibliography, section I, B.

food and lodging trades, and the bourgeoisie. For male servants, as for their female counterparts, marriage was intimately bound up with their hopes for the future.

The Obscure Later Years

Given the importance that most servants attached to marriage, it is sad to report that for many of them their wedding day marked the beginning of a period of financial and personal problems. Little is known about the middle and old age of servants—or indeed about that of the lower classes in general. But what we do know suggests that for domestics marriage often marked the beginning of financial setbacks that would darken their later years and heighten the tensions between spouses that seem to have marked the marriages of servants.

The evidence that many servant marriages were unhappy comes mainly from police records—admittedly a biased source, since only couples who fought called in the police or were reported by the neighbors. But the marital problems recorded in police records appear to have been widespread; when divorce was legalized during the Revolution servants were in the forefront of those taking advantage of the new laws.[123]

Why were servant marriages so often troubled? In part their problems seem to have stemmed from the fact that they married so late. By their early thirties, both bride and groom were usually set in their ways, and it was difficult for them to adjust to the give and take of married life. Late marriages also meant that often servant couples did not have the children who might have held together a bad marriage. Jean-Pierre Gutton has reconstructed the families of servants who married in the parish of Saint-Nizier in Lyons in every tenth year from 1710 to 1790. He found that only 22.7 percent of all married servant couples had children, and that of these more than one-third had only one child.[124]

The prejudice of employers against married servants was another source of tension. For this meant that a servant couple either had to quit their jobs and find new ones when they married, or live apart. In the former case the financial problems of making a new start often put strains on the union. In his complaint to the police Anglebert Théodore Berg, a former Parisian *valet de chambre*, stated that the trouble between him and his wife, a ladies-maid, stemmed from their decision to leave service and set up in business as *marchands de vin*. His wife became a drunkard and drank up all the profits. The couple fought and finally separated, each eventually going back into domestic service.[125]

Remaining in service could lead to problems as well. The prejudice against married servants meant that the couple could rarely find work in the same household and therefore had to live apart. If both stayed in service, they lived in their separate households, like our chef L'Amireau and his Rose, who, despite L'Amireau's dreams of having his own home and turning his wife into a proper bourgeoise *ménagère*, refused to give up her job when she married.[126] More often, however, only the husband continued in service. The wife became a laundress, *ouvrière en linge*, *marchande de bière*, or the like, and was established in rented rooms, where her husband visited her whenever he could get away from his duties. Such was the arrangement adopted by Jean Le Doux, *domestique* of the Marquise de St. Sulpice. In a complaint to the police he was described as living in the Marquise's household on the rue des Vieilles Huileries, while his wife, Marie-Magdeleine Fosinier, a *revendeuse de bas*, lived in a nearby apartment on the rue Sts. Pères.[127] Either way, the couple saw each other only at infrequent and irregular intervals. L'Amireau and his wife, for example, met mostly for walks in the public gardens of Paris, just as they had during their courtship.[128]

In these circumstances relationships were easily corroded by misunderstandings and suspicions, especially about sexual fidelity. This is shown in police records. In complaints to Parisian *commissaires de police*, both Françoise Guillet and Marie Quidou, wives of the *cocher* of the Comte de Guehry and the *valet de chambre* of the Comte de Vaugrenon, respectively, were accused of taking lovers during their husbands' frequent absences, and Françoise Baudouin, married to Nicolas Poivre, *cocher* of M. de Berque, suspected her husband of carrying on an affair with the wife of his employer, whose household he of course shared.[129] Even when there were no such suspicions servant marriages were often precarious; separated for so much of the time, the spouses often simply drifted apart. One such couple was François Tournier, *domestique* of the Comtesse de Bonnevaille, and his wife Françoise Braty, a *marchande de linge*. Braty complained to the police that over the years her husband had gradually grown indifferent toward her and no longer took an interest in their children.[130]

The marriage of L'Amireau and his wife Rose shows a similar history of love turning to indifference and finally hatred. During their courtship L'Amireau idolized his bride-to-be; he wrote a poem to her and stood in the rain for hours waiting for their rendezvous.[131] But after they were wed in 1786, they argued over Rose's reluctance to give up her job and turn herself into a *ménagère*, and despite the birth of a daughter, Caroline, whom they both seem to have loved, they grew apart. The relationship between them became so bad that in 1791 L'Amireau refused to attend a farewell party given for his father-in-law, Pierre Farcy, a *valet de chambre*, who was emigrating to Switzerland with his employer. He explained that he wished to avoid meeting his wife there. In a letter of apology to his father-in-law he wrote: "Now I still love my wife enough, in spite of all the trouble she has caused me, not to give her the discomfort of finding herself face to face with me."[132] The L'Amireau marriage was probably unique only in being so well documented. Its problems were common enough.

If marital tensions cast a shadow over the later years of many domestics, so too did financial difficulties. As we have seen, when they made their marriage contracts servants were in general wealthier than other members of the lower classes. But by their death they had lost this advantage, and were often worse off than artisans and even agricultural laborers. In Toulouse for example, in the late 1780s, servant marriage contracts averaged 434 livres, while those of petty craftsmen averaged 291 livres, and those of agricultural laborers a mere 228 livres. But *inventaires après décès*, the official evaluation of estates of people who died without leaving a will, paint a different picture. The average estate of an intestate domestic was only 912 livres, while that of petty craftsmen was 1,841 livres.[133] This pattern was common in most cities and towns. Only in Paris, home of the highest salaries and most ambitious domestics, did servants manage to retain their financial superiority over other members of the lower classes into their old age. There, in 1790, the median of servant *inventaires* was 3,000 livres, and many female servants left estates of 10,000 to 15,000 livres, while those of men servants could rise as high as 55,000 livres. But the median estate of a day laborer was only 500 livres.[134]

Except for the prosperous Parisians, servants clearly lost ground financially in the years between their marriages and their deaths. Why did this happen? A number of factors seem to have been at work. If a husband or wife—or both—changed jobs when they married, they were faced with the financial difficulties of starting out on a new job or launching a new business, and often, especially for female servants, their new career—laundress, *revendeuse*—was much less lucrative than the one they had left behind. And if the couple set up their own household, they lost the great financial advantage of having their food and shelter provided for them. A *valet de chambre*'s 250-300-livre annual salary did not seem nearly so princely when, instead of being saved and invested in loans and *rentes*, it had to be spent on the basic necessities of life.

Another factor which contributed to the relatively precarious financial situation of older servants was the expensive tastes many acquired during their service in wealthy households. Servants were much more likely than other members of the lower classes to spend their money on fine clothes and furnishings, on pocket watches and other marks of social status. Daniel Roche has analyzed *inventaires après décès* from eighteenth-century Paris, and he found that servants spent more than twice as much on their beds and bedding—fine woolen coverlets, feather pillows—than did artisans, and that *femmes de chambre* usually had clothes worth four to six times as much as those of the humble wives of *compagnons*.[135] Obviously a taste for the little luxuries of life could have a disastrous effect on a servant's financial situation.

The other spending habit that servants acquired from their employers—investing in *rentes* and other sophisticated liquid assets, rather than in land and shops as artisans and peasants did—also seems to have contributed to their gradual decline in fortune. For while such investments could provide larger immediate returns than land or a shop, they were also much more risky. Debtors could all too easily run away without repaying their loans. But investments in land or a business usually retained their value—and could be passed on to children.

A final factor in the relative penury of older servants was their unique family pattern. In the seventeenth and eighteenth centuries the care of those too old or infirm to work was generally a family responsibility. Sons and daughters, grandchildren, and even nieces and nephews accepted, albeit grudgingly, their duties toward the elderly.[136] Servants, however, were often deprived of the security of having someone to care for them in old age. As we have seen, they were more likely to remain unmarried than were other members of the lower classes. They were also less likely to have children. And their relationships with more distant relatives, with their nieces and nephews, the children of the brothers and sisters who remained behind in their native villages, were often remote. The following letter, sent to Nicolas Petit, *officier* in the Parisian household of the Duc de Villeroy, by his brother, also named Nicolas Petit, a farm laborer back home in their native village of Mennecy, near Corbeil, and probably written by the village letter-writer, shows this:

> My dear brother and my sister, it is to have the honor of writing you, it is to inform myself of the state of your health [and] at the same time to assure you of my respects and hopes for a happy New Year for you and my dear sister [that I write]. I wish you health like mine; by the grace of God I am well; I hope by the grace of God that your health is similar, my brother and my sis-

ter. I have nothing else to say except to extend the compliments of M. Romaine and his wife and similarly M. Appez and his wife.

I am with respect and submission your humble servant Nicolas Petit.[137]

Servants seem to have returned to their native villages only rarely. When they did they made a show of their prosperity, parading their fine clothes and city manners before their relatives, whom they treated as country bumpkins.[138] And their relatives appear to have accepted this role. They apparently regarded servants as the successes of the family, sources of financial help and advice in the ways of the world. Among the papers of Pierre Farcy, *valet de chambre* in fashionable Parisian households, are letters from his brother, an itinerant wine peddler, begging for loans to pay his debts, and among Nicolas Petit's papers is a letter from his wife's brother, a peasant in Bercy, describing a fire which wiped out the family homestead. "I and my children are without clothing and linen; we have no other resource than your humanity," he wrote.[139] It was difficult for elderly servants to return home and throw themselves on the mercy of the distant relations whom they had patronized all their lives—and who were often even worse off than they were.

Thus their lack of normal family ties left most servants to face old age alone. In theory they might expect help from their employers, for it was one of the premises of patriarchalism that masters should continue to care for their domestics when they became too old or infirm to work.[140] But in practice employers do not seem to have taken this obligation very seriously. To be sure, a few, mostly nobles, made careful provision that a favored servant be cared for in old age. For example, Toulousan noble Dlle. Marie de Boussac, charged her heir, her brother, to house her *servante*, Guillamette, during her lifetime and provided a yearly pension of five *setiers* of wheat, one *barrique* of good wine and one-half *chauveau* of *demi-vin* for her nourishment.[141] Other employers bought their elderly servants a bed in a charitable hospital, or left them yearly pensions so that they could make provision for themselves.[142] But such generous employers were the exception. Most masters refused to pay or feed a servant who could no longer work. Lucie Debat, *servante* of a notary, made her will from a bed in the hôtel-Dieu in Toulouse after having been fired from her job "because of her illness."[143] The provisions of the testament of Anne Lacan, widow of a *faiseur de chapeaux*, suggest that firing servants when they were ill was common. She stated that she had "much affection" for Catherine Maigne, her servant for over thirty years, and left her a substantial pension of 500 livres, but only on the condition that she was still in her service at her death. However, if Maigne was "put out of the house because of illness or infirmity," the legacy would still stand.[144] The wills of most elderly and infirm servants show that they were living out their lives not in their masters' households or even in the care of their children but instead in cheap rented lodgings, like the third-floor room with a window over the courtyard of a house in the unsavory neighborhood of the Porte St. Martin in Paris where former cook Marguerite Claude ended her days.[145] They were looked after by a hired *garde-malade*, if they could afford the few *sous* for her wages; otherwise they were dependent on the kind hearts of their landlady and neighbors for whatever care they received.[146]

Abandoned by their employers and lacking a family to sustain them, most servants found that old age was like an unending period of *chomage*: a time when the carefully husbanded savings of a lifetime could disappear in a matter of months. Joseph St. Laurans, a former cook in Bordeaux, rather bitterly described the process in his will. He apologized for having so little to leave. He had once owned a piece of land, part of his wife's dowry, worth a thousand livres, and much fine furniture and clothing. But he had "sold in the past and little by little all the surplus to pay for our food and other needs." Now he had nothing, and he "would have been greatly embarrassed without the help of my daughter and son-in-law."[147]

St. Laurans's experience was probably typical of many elderly servants. On the one hand their plight should not be exaggerated. Even those like St. Laurans who lost almost all their property were still better off than elderly farm laborers or *gagne-deniers*, who, if their families could not support them, were reduced to beggary or public charity in order to stay alive. Most servants at least avoided the fate so dreaded by the poor of the Old Regime: dying in a public hospital.[148] In the eighteenth century, unlike the nineteenth, servants were the one lower-class group underrepresented among the inmates of public hospitals and other charitable institutions. In Aix-en-Provence, for example, only 11.6 percent of the inmates of the town's *hôpital-général* were servants, although the group formed over 30 percent of the town's *menu peuple*.[149]

But if dying alone in a rented room was preferable to a deathbed in a charity ward, it was nevertheless a sad end for all the high hopes most servants cherished. For most domestics the possibilities for social mobility were strictly limited: their dreams of attaining bourgeois respectability, of becoming prosperous grain dealers or West Indian planters, were destined to remain unfulfilled. The best the majority could realistically hope for was to transplant themselves successfully to the city and enjoy a modest prosperity equivalent to that of the lower levels of the urban artisanate. That this was so is indicated not only by the modest estates servants left at their deaths, but also by the social position of their children. Most sons and daughters of servants seem to have either become artisans themselves or married artisans. Among my samples of marriage contracts I found nine that involved children of domestic servants. In every case but one of the six from Toulouse and Bordeaux these children were either artisans themselves or wives of artisans: *tailleurs de pierre, doreurs, maçons*, and the like. The exception is an alliance even lower on the social scale: the daughter of a Bordelais cook who married a sailor. Only in Paris did the children of domestics apparently have a chance to marry higher up on the social scale. One of the Parisian contracts followed the standard pattern: it involved the son of a cook who was himself an apprentice carpenter. But the other two were extremely respectable matches: a cook's daughter who married a haberdasher and the daughter of a secretary who married an architect.[150] Servants' wills reveal the same pattern: the children mentioned either are overwhelmingly artisans themselves or married to artisans. Thus many servants successfully transplanted their families from country to town, but few were able to make the difficult leap into bourgeois respectability for either themselves or their children. Servants could easily attain what one eighteenth-century observer called "the front ranks of the poor,"[151] but real social mobility eluded them.

Two themes stand out in the private lives of the domestic servants of the Old Regime. The first is that of ambition. Servants seem to have had, as de Muralt noted in the passage quoted at the beginning of this chapter, a mania for bettering themselves and making their fortunes. In the last decades of the eighteenth century rising salaries and a sense of self-worth derived from the spreading values of a market economy fed their growing ambitions. These were manifested in many aspects of servants' lives: in their passion for changing jobs, in their increasingly ambitious marriages, in their financial maneuvers, and in their dreams of commercial careers and bourgeois respectability.

But such dreams were, as we have seen, all too often doomed to failure. And this forms the other theme that runs through servants' lives. The road to success was fraught with perils. A prolonged spell of unemployment, an illegitimate pregnancy, a financially unfortunate marriage, a prolonged and penurious old age—all were hazards built into the occupation, and all could spell doom to a servant's high hopes for "a happy future of jobs and money in abundance," as the chef L'Amireau once characterized his dreams in a letter to his fiancée.[152] Domestic service was probably the best pathway to social mobility open to the lower classes, but by the very nature of the occupation opportunities for a permanent, long-term improvement of one's fortunes were strictly limited. Yet they did at least exist. And it was this, I think, which attracted men and women to the occupation despite the bad public reputation of domestic servants and despite the indignities and humiliations involved in the master-servant relationship.

4

The Psychology of Servanthood: Servants' Attitudes toward Their Masters

It is a general belief that those whom necessity subjects to servanthood consider their masters as so many enemies.
—BN Manuscrits FF 21800, Collection Delamare, Serviteurs et manouvriers, C76, Proposition d'un règlement pour les cochers, laquais, et servantes

No aspect of the lives of servants is more difficult for the modern historian to reconstruct than their attitudes toward their masters. In part the problem lies in the simple lack of sources. Servants left even fewer traces of their inner psychology—of what they thought and felt about their jobs, their masters, themselves than they did of the outer aspects of their lives: their births and marriages, their wages and employment patterns.

Even when servants do appear in court records and the like, it is hard to tell whether the opinions and sentiments they express are in any way authentic. For servants were of necessity skilled actors and actresses, constantly engaged in and extremely adept at hiding their true feelings from their masters. Of course everyone in eighteenth-century France was an actor to at least some extent. As one historian of the theater has written: "In eighteenth-century France, the competition between life in actuality and life on the stage had reached the point where no one could say which was more theatrical. In both there were pompous, overstudied phrases, a mannered refinement of bows, smiles and gestures; in both, showy costumes . . . powder, rouge, beauty spots, monocles, and very little of one's "natural" face."[1] The men of eighteenth-century France were, in Richard Sennett's phrase, "public men," never alone with themselves, instead always striking attitudes for the beholder whose inevitable presence, as Michael Fried has shown us, obsessed the visual artists and art critics of the period.[2] But this was especially true of domestic servants, whose very livelihood depended on their ability to conceal grumblings and discontents and to present an always cheerful countenance to their employers. For them role-playing was a way of life. It is no coincidence that both Talma, the pioneer of naturalism on the stage, and Rousseau, the chief advocate of emotional authenticity in real life, had been servants in their youth.[3] But servants' skills in role-playing hide their true feelings from us as well as from their masters.

The greatest barrier to our understanding of servants' attitudes is, however, the simple fact that the attitudes themselves were extremely ambiguous and complex. Perhaps the cliché of a love-hate relationship sums them up best. Servants displayed neither the unquestioning devotion to their master and his interests expected of them by patriarchal theory nor the perpetual rebellion and discontent too often attributed to them by modern social historians, who are accustomed to searching for class-consciousness among the proletariat and who would themselves find domestic service so distasteful.[4] Instead they displayed a strange combination of both these reactions. Domestics manipulated their masters, gossiped about them, laughed at them, insulted them, hit them, robbed them, and occasionally even murdered them. But they also fought for them, served them devotedly, admired them, imitated them, and occasionally even loved them. For every Samuel Coffy, the black servant who robbed his master, a Bordelais merchant, of 138 *louis d'or* "in reprisal for the blows he had frequently received," there was a Le Tellier, the *valet de chambre* of the Marquis de Barthélemy, who during the Directory volunteered to accompany his master into exile in the hellhole of French Guiana, a gesture of devotion which eventually cost him his life.[5]

In this chapter we will attempt to see through the role-playing of servants, and to disentangle their complex and contradictory attitudes toward their masters. We will examine the psychological experiences which shaped these attitudes and the means through which servants expressed both their devotion and discontent.

The Psychological Experience of Being a Servant

Whether docile or rebellious, most servants seem to have shared two psychological traits. They displayed, first of all, an extremely shaky sense of their personal identity, as their penchant for role-playing suggests. Second, they showed a deep sense of inferiority vis-à-vis their employers. These traits seem to have been the sources of both their admiration and their resentment of their masters. And they also seem to have been the inevitable psychological byproducts of servanthood. For domestic service was what sociologists have come to call a "total institution." It controlled every aspect of servants' lives and stripped them of many elements necessary for a sense of identity, while at the same time exposing them to a new and by definition superior culture which they found strange, frightening, and hard to master.

Domestic service could be an intensely depersonalizing experience. Old Regime peasants had a strong sense of personal identity, derived from their village and their place in its traditions. Artisans too felt a sense of identity which grew from the traditions of their craft. But servants were often uprooted from their village and stripped of their contacts with their home and family when they moved to town to enter service. When they entered a household, they were often not only forced to assume many elements of a new identity, but also treated by their masters as if they had no identity at all.

Take, for example, the matter of that recognized badge of selfhood, one's name. Often servants were given a new name when they entered a household. There appear to have been many masters in Old Regime France like that Edwardian Scottish laird, Christian Miller's father, who never bothered to call his servants by their rightful names: "All our footmen were called John, irrespective of what name the parson had bestowed on them at baptism. My father announced firmly that he couldn't be bothered to learn a new name every time the footman changed."[6] One French master with a similar attitude was the father of Alexandrine des Echerolles. He found the name of his Italian manservant Saapa too difficult to remember; Saapa was St. Pierre for the duration of his stay in that household.[7] Nicknames, whether self-bestowed, the gift of admiring friends, or the legacy of indifferent masters, were common among servants. Especially frequent was St. Jean, which seems to have been used almost as a generic name for lackeys during thc Old Regime. One Toulousan household, that of the Marquis de Barneval, appears to have employed no less than seventeen different St. Jeans as lackeys between 1769 and 1783.[8] Nicknames usually reduced the personality of servants to one trait which caught the eye: appearance (Julien Brunet dit Le Brun; Jacques dit La Grandeur); smooth manners or the lack of them (Joseph Burfoy dit Courtois); an accent which betrayed a birthplace (Jean Branche dit Dumaine; Nazaire Brocard dit Champagne—the latter a common servant nickname in Paris where many lackeys came from the Champenois).[9]

Doubtless even more demoralizing was a master's refusal to address his servants by name at all. Many called them "cocher," "laquais," or even "l'homme," or simply shouted "hey" whenever they wanted them. This was considered extremely uncouth—Mme. de Maintenon warned her pupils at St. Cyr not to do it—but the practice was apparently widespread.[10] Servants clearly resented these insulting forms of address, as the following anecdote illustrates. One day an *abbé* addressed his coachman as "l'homme." The servant replied by calling his master "l'abbé": "*Vous êtes un insolent*! Does the word Monsieur hurt your mouth?" "Well, you called me 'l'homme!' I can call you 'l'abbé.' "[11] But of course he could not.

The ultimate weapon for the depersonalization of domestics was, however, the wearing of livery. When they entered a household servants usually had to put on new clothes as well as a new name, dressing themselves in their masters' castoffs or donning livery. Either way, they had to abandon their own garments, reflections of their personality, for something chosen by another. Admittedly servants, like the rest of the lower classes, rarely if ever could afford *new* clothes of their own. But as Richard Cobb has shown, they treasured their second-, third-, and fourth-hand garments, choosing bright colors and luxurious touches to mark them out from the crowd.[12] In service they were robbed of this means of expression. Their clothes were fine, to be sure—often too fine to be comfortable in—but they were not their own. Especially galling was the wearing of livery, that badge of servitude which inescapably marked a man as a domestic. The wearing of livery not only often humiliated a servant, it also depersonalized him and objectified him. As Alison Lurie has written, "Fashion is free speech, and to put on livery is in some sense to be (willingly or reluctantly) censored, to be reduced from a person to a thing."[13] When they donned their gold-laced coats, lackeys became a part of the decorative background of their masters' lives; a liveried domestic was all too often in the eyes of his employer just one more fancy *object d'art* adorning the *antichambre*. In a sense, livery made servants invisible to their masters: their masters saw them, to be sure, but they did not recognize them as individual human beings. It was this "blindness" to their domestics that enabled employers to live out the most intimate moments of their private lives in the constant presence of swarming hordes of retainers.

It should be noted that this did not always work to a servant's disadvantage. A young coachman was once fired by the Prince de Condé for drunkenness. He compounded his fault by announcing:

> "Well! Monseigneur, if I cannot drive you today, I will never again drive you in my ______ life." . . . When the vapors of wine had dissipated, the young man felt all the enormity of his fault; his family had long been employed in the household of the prince; his father and mother came to throw themselves at the feet of His Highness to demand his pardon; Mlle. de Condé and Mme. de Monaco [the prince's sisters] wished to intercede for him . . . all was useless; the prince was inexorable. It was only a short while later that the young man, who had not ceased to show his repentance, took his job again: his first name was changed and the prince appeared not to recognize him.[14]

Nonetheless, the psychic damage inflicted by this sort of treatment usually far outweighed any advantages it might bring. Much servant "misbehavior," especially "insolence" toward their masters, had its roots in a desperate desire to make their employers notice and acknowledge that they actually existed. Even the most horrific of servants' crimes, Damiens's attempted assassination of that most powerful master, the king, seems to have been inspired by a desire to be noticed and recognized as a human being. Damiens told his interrogators that he had wanted above all to "talk" to the king.[15] This of course implied that he and the king would carry on a conversation, that the king would listen and respond to him—would in short recognize his existence.

The psychic damage caused by depersonalization was compounded by the deep sense of cultural inferiority servants often felt in the presence of their masters. Domestic service not only robbed its practitioners of a sense of identity; it also exposed them to a continual bombardment of new ideas, values, manners, and ways of doing things—to a whole new culture, in short, a culture that society labeled infinitely superior to their own. Firmly convinced that their manners and mores were preferable to those of mere peasants, employers exercised a sort of cultural imperialism over their domestics similar to that which European settlers exercised over the indigenous populations they encountered in Africa and America. Masters did their best to reshape the manners and outlook of their servants in their own image—at least insofar as this transformation contributed to their own comfort and convenience and did not challenge their sense of innate superiority. To masters the exposure to superior beings and their superior ways of doing things was one of the great advantages that domestics derived from their employment. Gilbert Cousin, for example, lamented that servants thought of their jobs only in terms of the salaries they earned:

> Most valets . . . always only say: *I have served so many years and I received per year such and such a sum*. Instead this gain should be supplemented thus: *I have been separated for so many years from dissolute company; I have had so many years of board and have been well-treated in this household; I have lived in gentlemanly [honneste] company; I have seen the manners of men; I have learned many things; I have made the acquaintance of gentlemanly people; I have been stripped of my rusticity.*[16]

Domestic service, after all, had long been a school of manners. In the Middle Ages young noblemen—and often women—had lived as servants in the households of great lords in order to acquire the graces of courtly life.

Servants themselves, however, often took a less sanguine view of their exposure to the cultural world of the elite. For them it presented a series of difficult and sometimes impossible challenges which all too often resulted in their complete humiliation. To leave one's village to go to town and enter domestic service was to step into a new and frightening world. First of all, there was the city itself, with its overwhelming size, dirt, and noise, and its complex rituals of life in street and shop which had to be mastered. Next came entrance into a household, which, if rich or noble, was an unfamiliar and disconcerting world of luxury. Mlle. Avrillon, *première femme de chambre* to the Empress Josephine, mentioned in her memoirs how frightening it had been to be led through a seemingly endless succession of exquisitely decorated corridors and *antichambres* for her first interview with her prospective employer, and Mlle. Avrillon should have been as comfortable in rich surroundings as any servant could be, for her parents had been domestics of the Condés, and she had grown up at Chantilly.[17] And once accustomed to their new surroundings, servants had to master the often unspoken rules of a new and infinitely more complex way of life. They had to acquire the skills of their employment: to learn to drive a coach, powder a wig, iron lace, and serve chocolate with éclat. They had to learn to detect the subtle social distinctions among Madame's callers, and to survive cutthroat backstairs intrigues.

Often too they had to learn to function in what was in essence a foreign language: the proper, grammatically correct French of their social superiors. Most domestics of rural origins spoke the local *patois* of their birthplace: the Breton spoken by many Parisian servants, the Occitan of the *gouvernante* in a *parlementaire* household in Toulouse, the German dialect of the Baronne d'Oberkirch's Alsatian maid.[18] If and when they did learn French it was the French of the *menu peuple* of the towns to which they migrated, the French of the streets and markets, crude and ungrammatical, with its dropped syllables, misplaced possessives, added "z" sounds, and its wealth of scatalogical and sexual imagery, which came naturally to people who lived out the most intimate moments of their lives amid the sights and smells of the streets.[19] Such French was almost as "foreign" to masters as their servants' various *patois*. Molière got much comic mileage out of the two different sorts of French spoken in most households. Here, for example, is a scene from his *Les Femmes savantes*, in which Philaminte, the mistress of the house, is shocked by a vulgar word spoken by her maid, Martine:

Philaminte
This creature, who for insolence has no peer,
Has, after thirty lessons, shocked my ear,
By uttering a low, plebeian word
Which Vaugelas deems unworthy to be heard.
. . . .
Martine
I'm sure your preachings is all well and good
But I wouldn't talk your jargon if I could.
Philaminte
She dares describe as jargon a speech that's based
On reason, and good usage, and good taste!
Martine
If people get the point, that's speech to me;
Fine words don't have no use that I can see.
Philaminte
Hark! There's a sample of her style again:
"Don't have no!"

Martine
Good Lord, Ma'am, I ain't studious like you;
I just talk plain, the way my people do.[20]

Many employers insisted, as Philaminte did, on proper French, but the success of servants in ceasing to "talk plain" varied. A few became remarkedly adept at picking up languages, and mastered not only French but foreign tongues as well. The cosmopolitan port of Bordeaux, with its German, Swiss, Dutch, English, Portuguese, and West Indian traders, boasted servants with extraordinary language skills. Bordeaux's newspaper, the *Journal de Guienne*, carried this advertisement in the 1780s: "Man of thirty-six, native of Luxembourg, knowing how to dress hair, shave, and speak French, English, Dutch, German, Russian, and Italian, possessing good references, wants a job as *domestique*; he will attach himself, by preference, to someone who wishes to travel."[21] Even in relatively provincial Toulouse there were *valets de chambre* who could speak English and Italian.[22]

But for most servants just mastering proper French was a difficult struggle. Many, like the Baronne d'Oberkirch's maid, Schneider, never did succeed: "Poor Schneider was never capable of learning a word of French, even in Paris; she constantly made the most comical errors; she said one word when she meant another: for example, 'je vais mal' when she meant 'je vais bien.' "[23] Others tried to cover their ignorance by the use of impressive words and phrases. The Marquise de Villeneuve-Arifat remembered all her life one such domestic in her grandfather's household: "One of his coachmen had pretensions, especially in language, and when he was on duty, 'It is my turn,' he would say, 'to lead the body.' When his master had a carriage made whose interior details were extremely complex, he decided, after an inspection, that the carriage was a veritable *chimique* [chemical]; he meant *chimère* [chimera]. The name stayed with it: 'I will take the chimique,' my grandfather would say."[24]

These anecdotes suggest not only the difficulties servants faced with language but also their employers' amusement at their plight. This amusement was real, and it extended to all the difficulties servants had in adjusting to life among the elite. Eighteenth-century French literature has a wealth of what we might call "ignorant servant stories," anecdotes about domestics newly come to the city who betray their rusticity at every turn. In Nougaret's *Tableau mouvant de Paris, ou variétés amusants*, for example, published in 1787, we find a lackey who, ordered by his mistress always to keep his head covered, answered a nocturnal summons in his nightcap; another lackey who, when sent to read the time from a sundial in the garden, uprooted the thing and carried it back to his master saying, "Well, Monsieur, read the time yourself, because I can't"; a *suisse* who, when asked when his master would return, replied, "Oh, when Monsieur ordered me to say that he was not here, he did not say when he would come back"; and a *domestique* who, when asked how he had enjoyed his first visit to the theater, replied that he found the *salle* and the decorations impressive. "But didn't you like what the actors were saying?" he was asked. "*Ma foi*, no; they spoke of their own affairs, and that didn't interest me."[25] These are not just literary conceits; such humiliating incidents really happened to servants. In *The Horse of Pride*, Pierre-Jakez Hélias's marvelous recollections of Breton village life in the early twentieth century, the author tells of village girls who went to the city to work as domestics and who had never seen oysters until ordered by their masters to serve them. They either thought they were stones and threw them out or carefully disemboweled them and presented the cleaned shells at the table.[26] And in his study of nineteenth- and twentieth-century American servants, David Katzman memorializes a cook who, when asked during a job interview how she made mock turtle soup, replied cheerfully that she first prepared the stock and then, before serving, " 'I gets the little mock turtles and throws them in.' "[27]

Most servants of course adjusted to their new lives sooner or later. How quickly and successfully they did so depended not only on their native wit but also on the type of job they had and the type of household they entered. Grooms who spent all their time in the stables obviously had fewer problems of adjustment than *valets de chambre* who were constantly in their masters' company. Servants in small artisan and middle-class households faced less of a cultural gulf between themselves and their masters than did the domestics in large noble establishments, although in large households there were other servants to ease the shock, while the *servante* of, for example, a *maître libraire* faced her problems alone.

The painful problems and humiliations servants encountered in adjusting to the world of the elite gave servants, I think, a deep-seated sense of inferiority vis-à-vis their masters, those beings who moved so confidently in that culture which their servants found so difficult and alien. This sense of inferiority, combined with the precarious sense of identity produced by the depersonalizing treatment they so often experienced, probably explains much that is puzzling about servants' attitudes toward their masters. It explains, above all, their tendency, so striking to the modern observer, to reject their own backgrounds and personalities and devote themselves totally to their masters, to identify with them and adapt their value system, even when that presupposed their own unimportance and worthlessness.

The Loyal Servant: Self-Abnegation and Identification with the Master

The memoirs of nobles who lived through the French Revolution are full of stories of faithful domestics who hid their employers from revolutionary crowds, interceded for them with revolutionary tribunals, worked to support them when they returned penniless from exile, or, like the Marquis de Barthélemy's Le Tellier, accompanied them to detention and death.[28] Such stories are too abundant to be dismissed as mere royalist wishful thinking. Clearly many servants both before and during the Revolution were genuinely devoted to their masters. Servants like Jean Dorne, *domestique* of the Sr. de Boudriville, were willing to fight to defend their masters' honor. (Boudriville sent Dorne to collect a debt; the debtor started abusing Boudriville, stating that he was not fit to drink from his shoes; Dorne fought back, saying he could not let his master be insulted.)[29] Servants like those of the Rémusat family were so proud of the house they served that it was they, not the master, who taught the heirs of the family its past glories.[30] There were servants who continued to work faithfully for masters who never paid them and beat them regularly: Julien Brunet *dit* Le Brun, servant of Sr. Bonnier, went unpaid for four years and was given a worthless promissory note when he quit his job in 1748, yet the next year he returned to work for Bonnier again; Le Franc, *domestique* of the Marquis de Fimarcon, by his master's own admission regularly endured beatings and punishment in a *cachot* during the ten years he remained in the Marquis's service.[31] Some servants were fond enough of their masters to leave them legacies in their wills: 14.8 percent of the wills of servants in my sample of wills from Bordeaux and Toulouse for the years 1727–29 and 1787–89 included legacies to masters.[32] And there were servants who did not wish to be separated from their masters even by death, and asked to be buried near them or their families.[33]

Much of this devotion is easily explained as a product of the inevitable intimacy of master and servant in patriarchal households. No man may be a hero to his valet, as Hegel noted, but few are total scoundrels either. When one knows another human being as well as most valets knew their masters, when one sees him at his best and worst and shares his triumphs and tragedies, it is hard not to feel at least a little understanding and sympathy for him.

This natural sympathy that could develop between master and servant was often heightened by kind treatment. Employers were capable of extraordinary acts of kindness toward their domestics, and servants naturally responded with gratitude and devotion. One of the few pieces of direct evidence we have about a servant's feelings toward his or her employer is the testimony given by the Toulousan *servante* Jeanne Viguière during the famous trial of her master Jean Calas.[34] Viguière testified that she had worked for the elderly M. and Mme. Calas for many years. She was very fond of them, she said simply, because they had gentle characters and had always treated her well. Even after she stopped working for them, they took her in whenever she needed a place to stay, and once when she fell in the street and broke her arm, they fetched a surgeon and cared for her during the forty-one days it took her arm to knit. Viguière thought it only right to repay the Calas's kindness by testifying for them at their trial, even at the risk of being accused of complicity in their crime.

Often, however, servants showed other and more startling forms of devotion than simple loyalty given in return for kind treatment. One example is the rather amazing tendency of servants to pay their masters the sincerest form of flattery by imitating their dress, speech, and manners. It was almost a maxim during the Old Regime that, as Rousseau put it, "valets imitate their masters," so much so, in fact, that "in Paris I judge the morals of the women of my acquaintance by the air and tone of their *femmes de chambre*, and this rule has never played me false."[35] Servants imitated their masters' mannerisms, gestures, and modes of speech, as Mme. Roland discovered on that famous occasion when she was invited to dinner by a noblewoman and then forced to dine with the servants:

> the *femmes de chambre* played at grandeur. . . . Toilette, carriage . . . nothing was forgotten. Booty fresh from their mistresses gave their appearance a richness forbidden to the honest bourgeoise; the caricature of good taste was joined with a kind of elegance as strange to bourgeois modesty as to the taste of artists. . . . The men were worse: . . . politeness and brilliant clothing of the *valets de chambre* could not hide the gaucheness of manners, the embarrassment of language when they wished it to appear distinguished.[36]

Servants' imitation of their employers frequently went beyond superficialities of dress and manners. Quite often domestics adopted and internalized their masters' ideals and values, displaying, for example, an aristocratic disdain toward the lower classes and especially toward the peasantry from which they themselves had come. A marvelous example of this is found in one of the rare surviving letters of servants, one written by a lackey, Nicolas Brocard, to his employer during a visit Brocard made to his native village to see his father:

> Monsieur, this is to have the honor to let you know that I know that I have arrived at my father's house in good health, *Dieu merci*. I hope that yours is the same, also that of Mme. your wife, without forgetting that of Mlle. your daughter. Monsieur, I tell you that my arrival occupies and worries very much the world of Bassencour: to see me dressed as I am, as they have never seen a man dressed before. You know country people: I have made them believe that the buttons of my vest are gold, that my clothes cost five *louis d'or*, which astonished them very much. Moreover, I have made them believe that I have a suit *chez vous* which cost me 272 livres; that it is braided with gold, but that I have not brought it for fear of having it stolen. That astonished them even more, so much that M. Lear, of Doulencour, has said that he will ask you if that is true. I beg you to say what I have said if someone asks you.[37]

The disdain Brocard shows toward the ignorance and incredulity of countryfolk, the familiarity with which he addresses his employer, and his naive confidence that his employer will back up his boasts all reveal how strongly Brocard identified with his master and how completely he had internalized his master's value system.

Some servants carried their identification with their masters as far as it could go: they fantasized about becoming their masters and occasionally they even acted out their fantasies. Servants notoriously enjoyed dressing up in their masters' clothing, not only wearing the castoffs they were given but also "borrowing" temporarily their masters' best apparel,[38] for literally standing in their masters' shoes helped bring their fantasies closer to reality. Marc Botlan maintains that servants so often stole clothing and pocket watches from their employers not simply because they were obvious items to steal, accessible and easily negotiable, but also because they brought a touch of reality to servants' fantasies of taking on their masters' identities.[39] If Nougaret is to be believed, servants often called each other by the names and titles of their masters: "It is well known that lackeys when together give themselves their masters' names; when they are in the cabaret, Champagne is called by his comrades the Duc de ______; Bourguignon is gratified by the name of Comte de ______; Picard is styled the Marquis de ______, etc., etc."[40] At times they actually tried to pass themselves off as their employers. Damiens, the would-be regicide, often dressed in his master's clothing and wandered about Paris pretending to be a wealthy bourgeois, wasting all his hard-earned wages in generous charity to the poor.[41] Nougaret tells the story of La Fleur, a fictional lackey who probably had many real life counterparts. When his master went away, La Fleur dressed up in his clothes and counterfeited his voice and manner so successfully that the other domestics in the house were fooled. He feasted on *pâté* and drank the best wine in the cellar until his employer returned and unmasked him.[42] The ultimate example of these servant fantasists is probably one François Nyon, valet of Sr. Bouttemont, *curé* of Tourville in Brittany, who murdered his master so that he could take his place. One day in 1699, Nyon hit Sr. Bouttemont over the head and hid his body in the scullery. For the next four days he passed himself off as his late employer, using the time to sell the contents of the house and accumulate a cash reserve so that he could make a getaway.[43]

Clearly such intense identification of servant with master, such pervasive fantasies of replacement and inversion, had deeper psychological roots that the simple gratitude for kind treatment that lay behind the less spectacular forms of servant devotion. It is here that the psychological consequences of servanthood we have postulated may play a role. For if, as suggested, servants tended to suffer from an insecure sense of personal identity and an inferiority complex vis-à-vis their masters, what could be more natural than to compensate by identifying with, emulating, and even trying to take on the identity of those beings who seemed so superior to servants and so secure in their sense of self? After all, servants had always derived ego-boosting power and status from their association with *les grands*. As we have seen, servants were a great family's ambassadors to the outside world, and they were (in theory at least) received in the deferential society of the seventeenth and early eighteenth centuries with all the respect and honor due to the master they served. Such deference was often given spontaneously. Mme. Françoise Verberque employed a maid whose husband, a lackey in the Destrades household, often mistreated her, but Mme. Verberque hesitated to summon the police out of "consideration for the livery that he wore."[44] And if this deference was not freely given it could be easily compelled. The wearing of the livery of a great noble household was a license for servants to bully tradesmen, make scenes in cafes and theaters, and rough up innocent passers-by. Clearly this license to mistreat the *menu peuple* provided domestics with considerable psychic compensation for their own lowly status and sense of inferiority and for the mistreatment they themselves experienced. One servant even explained how this worked. A *garde-chasse* employed by Duc d'Orléans told a visiting English gentleman, Mr. Cradock: "Toward you, Monsieur, or toward people of your rank, I am as polite as possible, but faced with *des petites gens*, oh, then I take on my dignified air, that of my master the duke, and I am not afraid to speak to them *de la bonne façon*."[45]

The opportunity to bully the public was psychologically important to servants. Mme. de Créquy tells in her memoirs of a coachman who refused to work for her because, when he asked to whom he would have to yield the right of way in the street, she replied, to everyone. To financiers? to parlementaires? the coachman asked incredulously. " 'I am used to yielding only to princes of the blood, therefore I will not work for Madame.' "[46] Servants frequently exaggerated the status and honor of their master simply because it brought more status and honor to *them*. One petty Auvergnat noble, the Comte de Montlosier, was often embarrassed by his servant François, who had the habit of addressing him as "Monseigneur" and pretended to all and sundry that his master was a great prince traveling in shabby incognito.[47] Given the psychic compensation servants received from their association with the great and powerful, it seems logical that some of them would carry this association a step further, and try to turn themselves into copies of—or even imagine themselves in the place of—those people who could command such respect and deference.

Whatever its causes, the tendency of servants to imitate their masters is important historically, for it has prompted some historians to picture domestic servants as cultural "mediators," transmitters of manners, values, and assumptions of the elite to the popular masses. In the term of one of the best known historians of popular culture, Peter Burke, domestic servants were "amphibians," participants in both the popular folk culture of their peasant backgrounds and the learned culture of the elite to which their service exposed them.[48] J. Jean Hecht, in his treatment of eighteenth-century English domestics, portrays them as a vital link in the chain of cultural emulation which bound together the upper and lower classes. Servants, he argues, imitated their masters, and they in turn were imitated by their lower-class relatives and friends. Thus elite manners and ways of doing things spread down the social scale.[49] Similarly, Daniel Roche depicts the servants of Paris as a bridge "between the world of the dominant classes and the popular classes. . . . Appropriating the marks of good taste and the ways of living of the privileged, servants participated in a decisive transformation of comportment. Through them, attitudes spread from the sphere of the dominant elites to become the patrimony of the people."[50] Domestic service is thus portrayed as the classic "bridging occupation" of sociologists, providing not only a path by which individual servants could transcend their social origins but a bridge between elite and popular cultures as well.[51]

It is true that servants did fulfill this role, at least on the very superficial level of dress, manners, and consumption patterns. Domestics like Nicolas Brocard who returned to their villages in their silks and satins and told their friends and relatives tall tales of the wonders of the city did expose the lower classes to the life style of the elite. But it is not clear that their roles as transmitters of popular culture to the elite and learned culture to the masses went any deeper than that. Admittedly servants did expose their masters to at least a few elements of folk culture. Children raised by domestics learned to chatter in *patois* (much to their parents' disapproval), and they were entertained by servants' folk tales of ghosts and goblins. Cardinal Bernis remembered all his life the childhood terrors induced by the folk tales of his nursemaids.[52] Even grown-ups occasionally made use of the "folk wisdom" of their servants. When the young would-be philosophe Samuel Dupont de Nemours sought to make a name for himself in the Republic of Letters, he decided that agriculture was a topic that would attract attention, but, having lived most of his life in the city, he knew nothing about farming. Therefore he consulted the only peasant of his acquaintance: the family *cuisinière*.[53] But such cultural interchanges were severely limited by parental vigilance against the "bad influence" of servants and by the general disdain of the cultured for peasant "ignorance."[54] Eighteenth-century France was not nineteenth-century Russia, where the folk tales and wisdom of peasant servants were treasured as part of the genius of the Russian people.[55]

Cultural interchange that flowed in the other direction, was severely limited by formidable barriers of language and literacy which kept servants from any real understanding of or participation in the learned high culture of the elite. As we have seen, many servants did not even speak or understand proper French, the language of the learned culture; some remained ignorant of it throughout their lives. Further, many servants were illiterate even to the extent of being unable to sign their names. The proportion of servants able to sign their names to their marriage contracts in my samples, along with some comparative figures, is summarized in table 18. It shows, first, that servant literacy varied according to the location and the type of town in which the servant was employed. Paris, north of the famous Maggiolo line which di-

TABLE 18

Servants Signing Their Marriage Contracts (in %)

	Men	Women
Servants		
Toulouse		
1727–29	38.6%	1.4%
1787–89	63.0	10.1
Bordeaux		
1727–29	37.7	11.0
1787–89	54.0	17.0
Paris		
1787–89	89.8	61.5
All inhabitants		
Rural areas, Haute-Garonne, 1686–90	12.9	4.7
Rural areas, Haute-Garonne, 1786–90	19.8	8.1
Bordeaux, 1776–86	57.5	36.8
Towns of Bordelais, 1776–86	39.5	21.1

Sources: The figures for servants were derived from the marriage contracts listed in the Bibliography, section I, B. The comparative figures for the rural Haute-Garonne are from François Furet and Jacques Ozouf, *Lire et écrire* (Paris, 1977), 1:33, note. Those for Bordeaux and the towns of the Bordelais are from J. -P. Poussou, "Recherches sur l'alphabétisation de l'Aquitaine au XVIIIe siècle," in ibid., 2:309–10. The following towns were included in the Bordelais: Lombez, Condom, Lectoure, Libourne, Bayle, La Réale, Bazas, Agen.

vided the generally literate north and east from the more uninstructed south and west, shows a striking but typical superiority to southwestern Toulouse and Bordeaux.[56] Typical too is the superiority (with regard to male literacy at least) of Toulouse over Bordeaux. Administrative centers were generally more literate than commercial cities in the ancien régime.[57]

Servant literacy also clearly varied according to sex. Of course, women in general were less likely to be literate than men in Old Regime France, and the gap between the sexes was usually wider in the towns than in the countryside. But the gap between male and female servants was even wider than the 15-20 percentage points that commonly separated the sexes in cities.[58] Except for those in the north of France, female servants were still mired in illiteracy at the end of the Old Regime, despite their advances in the course of the eighteenth century. *Servantes* were much less likely to know how to read and write than the other women of the towns in which they lived (compare, for example, the proportion of the female servants of Bordeaux who signed in 1787–89 with the figures for all the women of Bordeaux from 1776–86). They were even generally less likely to be literate than the peasant women of the country towns of their birth (compare the figures for Toulouse *servantes* with those of the women of the rural Haute-Garonne, where many of them were born, and those for the female domestics of Bordeaux with those of the women of the Bordelais). Male servants, by contrast, were much more likely to be literate than the peasant boys of the villages they had left behind, as table 18 shows. Their literacy was usually on a par with that of the citizens of their adopted towns. On the scale of literacy in most eighteenth-century cities, male servants ranked below artisans (who were often urban born and therefore exposed to educational opportunities and who needed to read and write to keep their accounts) but above their fellow immigrants who ended up as day laborers.[59]

Obviously, then, a large percentage of male servants learned to read and write sometime between their birth and the signing of their marriage contract. The question is when. Did they learn as children in the peasant villages of their birth? Was it in fact the acquisition of these skills and the possibilities for social advancement which they brought that inspired them to set out for town and careers as domestics in the first place? Or did they learn while in service? Did their employers teach them? Or did exposure to the learned culture of the elite inspire them to try to learn on their own?

Unfortunately these questions are difficult to answer. Perhaps the best chance of shedding light on them lies in analyzing servants' literacy patterns by their birthplaces. Urban-born servants had a fairly good chance of acquiring literacy while young, since there were schools in major towns, but rural-born servants did not. Therefore a great gulf between the literacy rates of the urban and rural born would seem to suggest that most servants who could read and write learned as children. If, however, the gap was narrow, or if the rural-born outdistanced the urban-born, then we can assume that literate servants acquired their skills in service. Table 19 summarizes the results of such an analysis. The high proportions of rural-born men and women of the 1727–29 samples who somehow learned to read and write suggests that in the seventeenth and early eighteenth centuries the latter pattern prevailed: those servants who were literate learned not as children but instead while in service. It was, after all, in theory at least, one of the duties of a patriarchal master to provide "instruction" for his domestics. This obligation meant primarily instruction in the basic tenets of religion, but it also meant teaching them how to

TABLE 19

Servants Signing Their Marriage Contracts, Classified by Birthplace (in %)

	Toulouse		Bordeaux		Paris
Birthplace	1727–29	1787–89	1727–29	1787–89	1787–89
Rural-born					
Men	44.8%	55.8%	30.0%	51.7%	89.7%
Women	2.0	6.5	15.3	14.5	55.6
Urban-born					
Men	25.0	85.7	33.0	100.0	100.0
Women	0.0	50.0	25.0	66.7	50.0

Sources: See Bibliography, section I, B.

read and write, skills that would enable them to read moral tracts and other improving literature.[60] At least some masters took this duty seriously. Dlle. Marie Anne Brun, for example, widow of a surgeon in Bordeaux in the 1720s, stated in her will that she had taught her *servante*, Jeanne Fanouil, to read and write and that she intended to provide a dowry for her when she married.[61] Other seventeenth- and early eighteenth-century servants acquired their skills on their own. An example is Gabriel Larrisière, a chef in the noble households of Toulouse before he abandoned service for a life of crime. He was asked during his police interrogation when and how he had learned to read and write. He replied that he learned while in service; his father spent the enormous sum of fifty *écus* in the course of two years for his lessons.[62]

Servants probably looked on the acquisition of such skills as a good investment. Certain types of jobs required literacy: *secrétaires* and *maîtres d'hôtel* obviously needed it, since they had to keep records and accounts.[63] It was also useful for *femmes* and *valets de chambre*, who might be asked to read aloud to their employers, and for nursemaids (*gouvernantes*) who might be required to teach their charges the alphabet. The analysis of servant literacy patterns by the type of jobs they held in table 20 shows that servants in such positions were in fact much more likely to be literate than coachmen, lackeys, and *servantes*.[64] Literacy apparently could also help a servant get a well-paid and prestigious job in a noble household. Analysis of servant literacy patterns by type of household shows that servants employed by nobles generally tended to have rates of literacy above that of servants employed in bourgeois or lower-class establishments.[65]

By the end of the eighteenth century, however, the basic pattern of servant literacy appears to have changed. Table 19 shows, in the samples of the 1780s,

TABLE 20

Types of Servants Signing Their Marriage Contracts (in %)

	Toulouse		Bordeaux		Paris
	1727–29	1787–89	1727–29	1787–89	1787–89
Men					
Secrétaires, maîtres d'hôtel	100.0%	100.0%	—	100.0%	100.0%
Valets	0.0	100.0	50.0	60.0	100.0
Cuisiniers	33.3	100.0	33.3	60.9	83.3
Others	27.2	49.2	39.4	48.2	92.1
Women					
Gouvernantes	—	100.0	—	100.0	—
Femmes de chambre	—	50.0	50.0	60.0	100.0
Cuisinières	—	0.0	0.0	17.4	66.7
Servantes	1.4	2.6	10.4	16.1	50.0

Sources: See Bibliography, section I, B.

a wide gap between the urban-born who were highly likely to be literate, and the rural-born, whose literacy was rising but was now, unlike the 1720s, decidely inferior to that of urban-born servants. This suggests that by the last decades of the Old Regime servants got whatever education they might have had before they entered service. Therefore it was probably the founding of schools in rural areas which fueled the general rise in servant literacy in the last half of the eighteenth century. This is borne out by a study of the spread of schools in Aquitaine which shows that many of the towns that furnished servants, especially men servants, to Bordeaux had primary schools by the eve of the Revolution. This study also helps explain the gap that still remained between male and female servants, for in Aquitaine only the towns near large cities still lacked schools by the end of the eighteenth century, and it was precisely from such towns, like Entre-Deux-Mers, that Bordeaux's *servantes* came.[66]

If these hypotheses are correct, by the end of the eighteenth century employers were faced with an employment pool of literate domestics. This fact does not seem to have pleased them. A distinct change in tone appears in discussions of servant literacy in the domestic manuals of the late eighteenth century. Earlier manuals had emphasized the favorable aspects of servant literacy: servants who could read and write could take messages for their masters and read devotional literature in their free time. But manuals of the immediate pre- and postrevolutionary decades took a dimmer view of the literate domestic. The ability to read, they stated, would allow servants to pry into family secrets[67]—a real concern for employers once they began to value their privacy. The Princess Louise de Condé, for one, endlessly worried that her love letters might fall into the wrong hands, and was careful to entrust them only to the illiterates among her household staff.[68] Domestic manuals also argued that reading exposed servants to morally corrupting novels, and, most importantly, to dangerous ideas which might make them discontented with their place in life.[69]

Such concern was, I think, needless. Literacy seems not to have liberated servants from their dependence on their masters. Instead it deepened it. Being able to read and write seems to have made servants all the more conscious of the cultural gulf between them and their employers. For literacy alone could not make them comfortable in the learned world of the elite. Although probably more servants could read than show up as literate in our statistics,[70] few servants seem to have read well enough to read for pleasure, as suggested by the contents of their libraries. Servants were more likely to own books than were other members of the lower classes. In one sample of Parisian *inventaires après décès* from the prerevolutionary decades, 41 of 196 servant estates contained books.[71] But most of these servant libraries (27 of the 41 cases cited above, for example) were made up exclusively of devotional works, often gifts from their employers. Typical was the library of Parisian *servante* Charlotte

Cousin, who was so proud of her ability to read that she left 100 livres in her will to be used for reading lessons for her rural nieces and nephews. She owned a six-volume edition of *L'Armée chrétienne* and twelve volumes of lives of the saints. All were probably given to her by her master, a *curé*.[72] Male servants were likely to own practical books as well as devotional works. The library of Bernard Arnaud, *officier* in a fashionable Parisian household, for example, came to 143 volumes, most of which were cookbooks, lawbooks, medical and business handbooks, and scientific treatises.[73] In general, servants did not own or read novels or romances. During the Old Regime there was no French equivalent to the English mass audience of literate female servants whose taste for the sentimental romance, so Ian Watt argues, was important in shaping the eighteenth-century English novel.[74] Not until the Restoration, with its growing servant literacy and its cheap lending libraries, the *cabinets de lecture*, which put novels and romances within their reach, did French servants begin to read for pleasure as a leisure-time activity.[75] Instead, Old Regime servants seem to have read as autodidacts engaged in a desperate attempt to close the cultural gap between them and their masters. An example is Le Tellier, the devoted *valet* of the Marquis de Barthélemy, who voluntarily joined his master's revoluntionary exile in French Guiana. When the Marquis, a diplomat, was stationed in England, Le Tellier tried to learn all about the country:

> Instead of abandoning himself to idleness like all the other embassy servants, one always saw him [Le Tellier] in the antechamber occupied in reading solid books on England. He learned the language of the country and came to understand it very well. It was only after his death that I found in his papers an English grammer annotated very carefully in his hand. He also studied the form of government, the administration, the agriculture, the navigation, every thing that concerned industry; all this without affectation, without noise, and with so much modesty that his comrades respected him.[76]

This passage reveals not only Le Tellier's frantic attempts at self-education, but also the condescension of his employer, an attitude that would keep servants from any true and equal membership in the Republic of Letters.

Apart from a certain Mme. Colletet, a seventeenth-century poetess, and Mascarille, an eighteenth-century man of letters, I know of no servants who made any contribution, however minor, to the imaginative literature of Old Regime France.[77] If servants were not yet accustomed to reading for pleasure, they were even less comfortable with expressing their thoughts in writing. Far fewer domestics could write than could read, as we have seen, and the very act of forming their letters was difficult for many. Servants' handwriting was notoriously bad: a poorly educated friend of the Baronne de Montet once said of herself, "I write like a cook," and servants who could write a good hand, like Roch, *valet de chambre* and tutor to the young Duc de Lauzun, were inordinately proud of that accomplishment.[78] It is not surprising therefore that so few letters from servants survive, and that those that do are generally short, stiff, and impersonal. And even those servants who learned to use the pen fluently to communicate their private thoughts and feelings never made the leap into the realm of the more public expression of their personalities through imaginative literature. L'Amireau, the Parisian chef discussed in the last chapter, was extraordinarily spontaneous and eloquent in his descriptions of his feelings about his fellow servants, his masters, and his beloved Rose, but when he attempted something self-consciously literary, like this poem in praise of his fiancée, the results were disastrous:

> Mais Pourquoi ête vous aimable
> Car en verité voilà le mistère
> en Vous aimant on n'est point Blamable
> je l'annoncerois ainsi à toute la terre.[79]

The stiffness of these conceits suggests that even the most "verbal" of domestics was not really at home in the literary culture of the elite.[80] Again not until the Restoration do we find equivalents in France to the eighteenth-century English servant poets Mary or Molly Leapor, Elizabeth Hands, and Robert Dodsley, the last a footman who wrote *A Muse in Livery, or the Footman's Miscellany* (1752) and eventually became a noted bookseller and publisher.[81] In Old Regime France the muses were not yet comfortable in livery, nor were servants at ease in their presence.

All of this suggests that the role of servants as conduits between the learned and popular culture was limited to the superficialities of dress and manners. If servants were, in Burke's term, "amphibians" at home in both cultures, with respect to learned culture they most resembled those sea creatures who first scrambled onto the shore millions of years ago and lay gasping for breath in an unfamiliar and dangerous environment. However much they might desire to participate in it, servants were not really comfortable in the learned culture of the elite. What few elements of learning they managed to pick up were usually barely assimilated and badly misunderstood. The Duc de Croy, who interviewed the would-be assassin Damiens after his attempt on the life of Louis XV, thought that the inspiration for his act had come from the political discussions in his master's house which he had overheard and only half understood: "Here is what comes of talking in front of servants!"[82] And Karamzine, an aristocratic Russian traveling in France, was convinced that a servant he knew committed suicide because he had read—and misunderstood—the "dangerous works of the new philosophes."[83] The conviction that servants did not really comprehend elite culture was not just upper-class prejudice. The minds of servants *were* in fact a strange jumble of traditional folk wisdom and peasant superstition mixed with imperfectly comprehended bits and pieces of learned culture they picked up from their masters. The Parisian chef L'Amireau referred in his letters to the "Supreme Being" with all the aplomb of a philosophe, but he also made a donation to the shrine of Ste. Anne Neuville in the hopes that the saint would make his Rose look favorably on his suit.[84] Servants did not know enough of high culture to act as true cultural transmitters. Instead, they knew just enough to make them aware of the enormous cultural gap between them and their masters. Thus the historical significance of servants' cultural emulation is not that it enabled them to act as ambassadors between elite and popular culture; rather that it increased their already well-developed sense of inferiority vis-à-vis their masters and therefore contributed to that peculiar form of self-abnegation which passed for servant "devotion" during the Old Regime. It is no coincidence that Le Tellier, the anxious autodidact, sacrificed his life for his master during the Revolution.

The Interested Servant: Survival through Role-Playing and Manipulation

Despite the strong psychological pressures in that direction, not all servants developed the persona of the "devoted" servant. In fact many, indeed probably most, domestics withstood the psychological shocks of servanthood and retained a strong sense of their own identity, which was reinforced by their contacts with family, friends, and fellow servants. The whole web of servant sociability discussed in the last chapter doubtless helped servants to preserve their sense of selfhood against the cultural onslaughts of their masters, and probably created in many domestics a sense of solidarity with their fellow servants, of "us" versus "them," which counteracted the strong pressures toward admiration and emulation of their social superiors. Restif tells of a nursemaid in a fashionable household who became extremely proud of the fine clothes and proper French she necessarily acquired during her employment. Her pretensions toward gentility were mercilessly ridiculed by her husband and friends, as she recalled: "*Dame*, c'fallait voir, en c'temps-la [when she worked in the household], comme j'parlais français! Mais, du d'puis, mon mari et mes camarades m'ont dit qu'i'fallait que j'parle tout comme eux, et j'm'y suis s'habituée."[85]

Servants who retained their sense of identity usually viewed their employment only as a means of fulfilling their private ends: survival or marriage or saving for old age. They tended to regard their masters with detached contempt. And they used their skill in role-playing which formed, as we have seen, one of the major psychological legacies of servanthood, not to emulate their masters but to manipulate them toward their own ends. Archetype of the self-interested domestic was Sgnarelle in Molière's *Don Juan*, whose only reaction as he watched his master disappear into the fiery furnace was to shout after him "My wages! My wages!"[86]

The self-interested manipulator was probably the type of servant most frequently found in Old Regime France; he was probably much more common than either his loyal and docile or his more openly rebellious counterparts. But he is the hardest to trace, for the same skill at deception which hid his true feelings from his employer also hides them from us. Yet the correspondence of L'Amireau, the lovelorn Parisian chef, offers some sense of how such servants reacted to their masters. L'Amireau definitely fit the mold of the self-interested servant; his letters show that he had a strong sense of self, took great pride in his skill as a chef, and had great hopes and dreams for the future, hopes that centered on escaping from servitude into bourgeois respectability. His letters suggest that these private hopes and dreams rather than his relationships with his employers dominated his life. In his letters he mentioned his masters only when they interfered in some way with his private concerns. (Admittedly he, as a cook, had little contact with his employers; the letters of a *valet de chambre* might be very different.) The few times that L'Amireau did discuss his employers, his tone was usually a mixture of irritation and contempt. He had a good word to say about them only when they did him some special kindness: a master's sympathetic inquiries about L'Amireau's daughter, ill with smallpox, showed "great sensibility," and another employer's offer to take L'Amireau along on a trip that would include a stop at the latter's native village earned the grudging observation that "this offer by a master could not be more obliging." Otherwise, however, his masters were "those beings who so often torture my poor spirit." Of one mistress he complained that she bored him with her constant lectures, of another that she spoiled her daughter so dreadfully that the child made the whole household suffer from her tantrums. Still another employer had an extraordinarily quick temper, which, as L'Amireau noted, was a luxury only "men of his position" could afford.[87] L'Amireau himself was quick to take offense, but he knew that he had to disguise from his employers the anger and contempt he felt for them. Here is his account, in a letter to his fiancée, of a quarrel with one master:

> My dear love, I am so angry. I was just getting ready to go out last night when M. Amirisson [sp?] asked for me to tell me to clean the pots and pans. I told him that they would do as they were. At that he was overcome with anger against me, telling me that I wished to poison him, with an accompaniment of other similar idiocies. I was entirely beside myself; I had just seen the success of my supper; a thousand compliments awaited me; so life goes, from pain to pleasure and from pleasure to pain. . . . But here is the outcome of the business: as soon as I returned I asked him for my decision [i.e., his decision about my future] and for the honor of his protection, a thing I was far from feeling, but necessary for form's sake. Here is a man who is often overcome with a fury mingled with derision, something that is not appropriate in a man of his station in life. I cannot describe to you all the idiocies I suffered in terms strong enough to make you see them; in another more calm moment I will tell you about that time.

A postscript says, "You can judge my anger by my [bad] handwriting,"[88] and that is certainly true. This extraordinary letter reveals not only the sort of treatment which created resentment among servants but also the extent to which they contrived to hide such feelings from their employer. Here is servant role-playing carried on before our very eyes.

Self-interested and manipulative servants like L'Amireau rarely showed their true faces to their masters; instead they presented their employers with a series of stereotypes that conformed to and reaffirmed their own ideas of servant behavior. The posture of the "devoted servant" often masked anger and resentment, as L'Amireau's example suggests. Servants also often played on their general reputation for idleness, for it allowed them to work at their own pace and shape their tasks to suit themselves.[89] Servant "stupidity" was another convenient mask: it could conceal misdemeanors (the young *aide de cuisine* accused of poisoning Mme. de Genlis's brother maintained steadfastly that "a giant" had done it),[90] and it could cover those intentional "mistakes" and "misunderstandings" which so annoyed and embarrassed masters. No less a personage than Napoleon was once a victim of this sort of masked insolence from a servant. When he was a young officer, desperate to leave behind his Corsican roots and gain acceptance among the French, he was accosted, in the presence of his fellow soldiers, by the servant of an old family friend, who addressed him in Italian. " 'What is all this nonsense?' " Napoleon asked in French.

> He [the servant] replied in Italian, though he could speak French very well, "Signor Napoleon, I do not understand you. You know that in Corsica we poor devils speak only our *patois*. . . ." Bonaparte surveyed the man with a look of surprise: "I left Corsica too young to be able to express myself easily in Italian . . . besides I see no necessity to speak your *patois*. . . . For Signora Catalina tells me in her letter that you have been living for fifteen years on the coast of Provence. . . . Surely, then, you can speak French," said Bonaparte, with impatience. "What do you mean by this insolence, fellow?"[91]

This sort of insolence seems to have been commonplace; in eighteenth-century France veiled insults, too witty or subtle to be openly complained of, yet nonetheless wounding, were known as "mots de laquais."[92] Many servants could judge the border between *mots de laquais* and punishable insolence to a nicety, for they were acute psychologists, who knew their masters through and through and could predict and play upon their reactions. One example is the *femme de charge* in one household where L'Amireau worked, who played up to her mistress's piety by pretending to be devout herself; "she has already been discovered four or five times on her knees, doubtless reciting all the funeral orations of M. Grace, archbishop of Bourges," her fellow servant L'Amireau wrote in disgust.[93] Another is the ten-year-old *jockei*, who, with a pathetic story of being abandoned by his family, managed to cadge free food, lodging, and transportation from Blois to La Rochelle from a soft-hearted traveling Englishwoman, Lady Craven. It is obvious from Lady Craven's remarks in her memoirs that her own servants saw through what he was doing (they kept trying to dissuade her from helping him), but she did not.[94] It was through such expedients that servants survived and prospered, and it was through such veiled insolence and such manipulation that they gained a sense of ascendancy over their masters and found some consolation for the indignities of their lives.

The Rebellious Servant: Occasions for Protest and Rituals of Defiance

There were, however, occasions when replacement fantasies, manipulation, veiled insolence and other such subtle forms of revenge were no longer satisfying; occasions when servants entered into openly rebellious behavior against their masters, and risked dismissal, severe corporal punishment, or even public prosecution for insolence (for this was in theory at least a crime punishable by public shaming, although it does not seem to have been widely prosecuted.)[95] As might be expected from what we have said about the psychological effects of servanthood, most of these occasions arose when servants felt their always precarious sense of identity and autonomy threatened. And as might be expected from their penchant for role-playing, most servant rebellion took the form of public theatrical rituals of protest and defiance.

Rebellious servants were not modern industrial workers. They were not moved to confrontation with their employers over economic issues or over what labor historians term "the conditions of the work place." They do not appear to have resented long hours, low pay, or bad working conditions. What they resented, and what spurred them to active protest, was personal mistreatment. For both domestics and their employers, the master-servant relationship was in essence personal rather than economic. Servants were not hired to perform specific tasks, but instead to present a general posture of obedience and devotion to their employers. And servants did not define themselves primarily in terms of the work they performed. Many factors, including the absence of a guild tradition, the dispersal and isolation of their work place, the uneven rhythms of their work, and the immense variety of their tasks, militated against this. But they *did* define themselves as servants: as men and women who had entered into a certain personal relationship with their employers. Therefore it was the treatment they received within the bounds of this relationship which concerned them most. And because being a servant was so damaging to their sense of self-hood, it was when the actions of their masters threatened their personal autonomy and independence that they were likely to rebel.

The major exception to this generalization is the issue of wages. Police complaints show that this issue was the single most frequent cause of clashes between master and servant.[96] But this was in many ways the exception which proved the rule. For wages had a psychological importance for servants that went beyond purely monetary considerations. They represented for domestics a measure of their worth,[97] a guarantee of their independence (a servant who had some savings could after all always leave a position that had become intolerable), and a hope for the future. Wages represented to a *servante* the dowry that would enable her to marry and leave service, to a *cuisinier* the cabaret that would make him a respectable independent proprietor. Therefore it is not surprising that they were willing to fight for them.

Another reason conflicts over wages were so frequent was the fact that masters and servants held opposite views about what a servant's wages were. As we have seen, the eighteenth century was a period when the long tradition of non- or partial payment of servants' wages was gradually being replaced by a system of true contractual wage labor. But masters naturally tended to cling to the traditional view of servants' wages: to regard their domestics as more than amply compensated by being fed, clothed, housed, and exposed to the company of their betters, and to look upon money wages as a bonus given for extraordinary service purely out of the goodness of an employer's heart. They therefore felt justified in withholding payment if a servant was insolent or otherwise unsatisfactory—or even for no reason at all. One Parisian employer, summoned before the *commissaires de police* in the 1780s for not paying his lackey's wages, stated testily that he had fed and clothed the fellow and supplied all his bodily needs. What more could he possibly desire?[98] Servants, on the other hand, had by the eighteenth century come to take a more modern view of their wages: to them they were compensation for services rendered, something they were unconditionally entitled to. It is not surprising then that many conflicts arose, especially since no written contracts specifying wages existed, and the oral agreements that sealed bargains between employers and domestics were often vague.

After wages, the next most frequent point of conflict seems to have been corporal punishment, and here the threat to servant autonomy and self-esteem was manifest. Until the last decades of the Old Regime masters viewed their right to use corporal punishment on their domestics as unquestionable. It was a basic tenet of patriarchalism, a reflection both of the property rights of a father of a family in the bodies of his wife, children, and servants and of his duty to act as their moral guide and corrector. The right of a master to beat his servants was even sanctified by the Bible: St. Paul had enjoined, "Servants, obey your masters . . . with fear and trembling."[99]

But fundamental as this right was, it was never unlimited. Laws forbade "excès et mauvais traitements" of domestics,[100] and writers of domestic manuals and advice literature constantly enjoined restraint. The late seventeenth-century writer Sylvestre du Four, for example, maintained that employers should "limit . . . their threats and even more their blows," and suggested that they always remember that their servants were their brothers in Christ: "treat them like that, and, however stupid they may be, don't let their conduct arouse your insensibility."[101] And the Abbé Goussault urged masters never to punish servants immediately after the discovery of a mistake, because their justifiable anger and outrage might make them lose control and thus lead to severe injuries to the servant: "All correction made with anger loses its merit and destroys its effect. Punishment is a meat which must be seasoned to be rendered good and useful." He even went so far as to suggest that children and servants were "half justified" in their resentment when their fathers and masters punished them in anger.[102]

"Half justified" but not totally: beatings and blows were part of a servant's lot, something that had to be endured. Despite laws and warnings, masters struck their servants for the slightest misdeed—or none at all. Losing his employer's wallet earned Nicolas, *domestique* of Sr. Duhamel, a German merchant in Paris, a caning; maidservant Sara Cerf's arguments with her fellow domestics were punished by "blows on the head and face" which left her bleeding from the mouth, and Costerine Patou's attempt to collect the wages due her provoked her mistress to pull her hair and try to scratch her eyes out.[103] For the surely minor offense of interrupting his master's dinner to report the results of an errand, François Joseph Pourvin, *suisse* of Sr. Foyer, Parisian banker, was locked in his room, beaten, and hit over the head with the flat of a sword.[104] Violence against servants was almost a reflex action, automatic in a society that had not yet developed modern notions of personal bodily autonomy and the bodily "space" of individuals, a society in which strangers shared beds, street brawls occurred at the drop of a hat, and wives and children as well as servants were regularly beaten, not only for offenses against patriarchal father-figures, but also simply to break their will.[105]

At least until the last half of the eighteenth century, servants seem to have accepted such abuse as their inevitable lot. At any rate they did not complain about it to the police, or use it as an excuse for revenge against their masters. All of the cases mentioned above occurred in Paris in the 1710s and 1720s, and we know about them only because those servants mentioned their beatings to the police during complaints that were primarily concerned with something else.

After 1750, however, attitudes toward corporal punishment seem to have changed. Masters resorted to it less frequently, and servants were more resentful of it when it did occur. Many factors contributed to this transformation. The decline of patriarchal notions of a master's responsibility for the moral conduct of his domestics robbed corporal punishment of its main justification, while the emergence of modern notions of bodily autonomy made it seem insulting, and the humanitarianism of the Enlightenment, which deplored all physical abuse of the helpless, children and animals as well as servants, labeled it as cruel.[106] Household manuals of the late-eighteeenth- and early-nineteenth centuries reflected the change in attitude. As we have seen, earlier domestic advice books merely warned against excessive severity in corporal punishment. But those from the last decades of the Old Regime through the Revolution and Restoration come close to repudiating its use entirely. The Abbé Grégoire's *De la Domesticité* (1814) contained a cautionary tale about a young princess who, caught slapping her maid, was forced by her parents to beg the woman's pardon on bended knee and to serve her her meals for several days. Mme. de Genlis's *Le La Bruyère des domestiques* (1828) noted approvingly that in Switzerland servants who received even the least blow could quit their jobs immediately without losing any pay.[107]

Police records suggest that servants' attitudes changed similarly. Their growing sense of independence and self-worth, fostered by the spread of the market economy and its values, made corporal punishment increasingly intolerable. By the 1750s servants had no hesitation about reporting their beatings to the police. In 1753, for example, Jean Benger, coachman of the Comte de Villefort, tried to quit his job after the comte used "mauvais traitements" against him: when his employer gave him "four blows with his whip, despite the exactitude with which he performed his task," Benger trotted off immediately to the *commissaires de police* to lodge a complaint.[108] And if the servant thought he could get no satisfaction from the police, he took his revenge for beatings in other ways. A Bordelais lackey named, naturally, St. Jean, responded to a caning by sending an anonymous threatening letter to his employer, and, as we have seen, another Bordelais servant, Samuel Coffy, stole his master's purse containing 138 *louis d'or* "in reprisal for the blows he had frequently received."[109] By the late eighteenth century corporal punishment was clearly a major point of conflict between domestics and those employers who continued to use it. Servants regarded it as a personal insult and a blow to the fundamental equality which they believed existed between themselves and their masters. Therefore it was something to be avenged.

Servants also protested verbal insults, and again the majority of their complaints on this issue occurred in the last half of the eighteenth century. Despite—or perhaps because of—the psychological assaults which domestic service entailed, many servants clearly had a strong sense of personal autonomy, and they resented their masters' attempts to regulate their behavior. The *servante* of Marguerite de Beauregard insulted her employer when the latter admonished her about her excessive drinking; Picard, a lackey, quit his job over his master's interference in what he viewed as a private quarrel with a fellow servant.[110]

Servants also resented what they regarded as insults to their honor. Their employers might have scoffed at the idea, but servants did have a sense of personal honor. In their own minds they were, as they stated to the police in their complaints, "honnêtes hommes" and "filles d'honneur et de probité."

Their honor consisted of being good servants: of doing their jobs well, being honest and reliable, and faithfully upholding their masters' interests. Therefore imputations of dishonesty or dereliction of duty offended them. Louis Robert and his wife, employed by the Abbé Boulher, complained to the police when their master's nephew insinuated that they could not be trusted to care for his house in his absence, and Françoise Bezin, *fille domestique,* complained when her mistress accused her first of being pregnant and then of being a thief.[111] Le Franc, *domestique* of M. Emeric de Cassagnac, had endured ten years of severe corporal punishment, according to his master's own account, but it was an unjust accusation—dropping a valuable rifle while drunk—that caused him finally to flare up in anger. "Je suis un honnête homme," he shouted at his employer, and then proceeded to insult him and walk out.[112] Geneviève Berthelemy, employed by the Comtesse Dojelin, walked off *her* job when, during a dispute over the household accounts, the angry Comtesse began to call her a thief and a slut. Berthélemy explained to the police that it was "in her interest to conserve without stain or damage her reputation as a woman of honor and probity, a reputation on which depend her success and her happiness in her calling."[113]

The withholding of wages, corporal punishment, and insults to pride and honor—these were the causes that aroused servants to active protest. Such protest took many forms, running the gamut from the spontaneous and relatively innocuous ritual insult to the premeditated criminal actions of theft and even murder. But most servant protests had two elements in common: they were, first, as we might expect from these chronic role-players, highly public, theatrical, and ritualized, and second, they harked back to traditions, deeply embedded in the popular culture of the peasant villages from which most servants came, of a public appeal to the collective judgment of the community in cases of behavior which violated accepted standards.

The public and ritualized elements of servant protest are clearly visible in its most common form, the ritual insult. I have given it this label because, while insults were spontaneously shouted in the heat of angry moments, they nonetheless followed distinct patterns and rhythms. At their heart were scatological epithets. The same ones recur over and over in police records with monotonous frequency: *gueuse, putain, coquine* if the employer is a woman; *foutre* and *bougre de gueux* if he is a man. These epithets were not confined to master-servant confrontation. They are found in almost all the brawls of street and marketplace recorded in police archives, and they therefore mark, I think, an assertion of the servants' lower-class identity after years of enforced respectability.[114] What was unique to master-servant confrontations was not their vocabulary but their rituals of inversion. Each master-servant shouting match was a carnival in miniature, where roles were reversed and servants could in ritualized gestures express their anger and contempt.[115] Here is a typical master-servant battle, one between the Marquis de Fimarcon and his *domestique* Le Franc. The Marquis had accused Le Franc of being drunk when he apparently was not; Le Franc was so annoyed that he threw down the rifle that he had been cleaning and yelled that he was *not* drunk: "Je suis un honnête homme! Allez faire foutre!" ("I am a respectable man! Go fuck!") The Marquis "felt it his duty to stop this insolence," and slapped him. This set off another round of insults: "Foutin! Jaufort! Va te fair foutre, foutre maître, je me fou de toi et de ton fusil!" ("Fucker! Fatty! Go fuck yourself, fucking master, you and your rifle are driving me crazy!")[116] The elements of inversion here are obvious: Le Franc destroys his master's property (the rifle) he had been hired to care for; such symbolic destruction was common in these cases.[117] And it is the master who is now "tutoyed" and the servant who has become the "honnête homme."

Equally theatrical and ritualized was the departure from one's job. Servants often turned their leave-taking into a grand gesture of protest. There was a right way and a wrong way to go. The wrong way was to disappear quietly after being fired. The right way was to quit, and in doing so, show your employer what you thought of him. Picard, *laquais* of M. François Pichon, Parisian lawyer, was admonished by his master for fighting with the cook. He disliked this interference in his private life, and responded insolently, whereupon Pichon fired him. But Picard said, "I will not leave like that," and departed in high style, throwing the back wages he had just been paid in his master's face and flouncing down the stairs, stripping off his livery as he went.[118]

The satisfactions derived from such theatrical gestures were intense but fleeting. For more lasting revenge servants harked back to the traditions of village popular culture and appealed to the collective judgment of the community against their masters. It was common for a servant who believed himself wronged to complain about his employer to the latter's relatives, friends, and neighbors, in the hope of embarrassing him and ruining his reputation. Marguerite Grolau, for example, avenged herself on a former master who had cheated her out of her wages by the simple expedient of going around to his relatives and telling them what he had done.[119] Another mistreated *servante*, Madelon Nanby, shouted out her accusations against her former master in front of all his friends and neighbors.[120] At times servants' accusations against their masters were farfetched and clearly malicious. A lackey with a grudge against his former employer, Dlle. Marie Elizabeth Parent, spread rumors among her neighbors that that elderly and highly respectable lady was a procuress who lived off the illicit earnings of her two maidservants.[121] And two *servantes* fired by Sr. Antoine Picard, Parisian painter and member of the Academy of St. Luc, made life uncomfortable for him by telling his neighbors that a noxious smell which had been plaguing the district originated in the extremely malodorous sizing for his canvases which Picard brewed in his fifth floor studio. In his complaint to the police Picard angrily denied the charge: he made his sizing, he said, only in a garden he had rented for the purpose in the faubourg St. Antoine, where bad smells were unlikely to be noticed![122] But whether well-founded or simply malicious, such accusations accomplished their purpose of embarrassing masters and damaging their public reputations.

A similar aim, I suspect, rather than any real hope of legal redress, prompted the numerous complaints servants made to the local policc. These at first sight are puzzling, for not only did they go against the strong rural tradition of distrust of the police which most peasant-born servants probably shared, but they also were probably foredoomed to failure, since policemen were more likely to be sympathetic to a respectable property owner than to a poor servant, and indeed many courts—the Châtelet in Paris, for example—automatically took the word of an employer over that of his domestic in cases involving master-servant disputes.[123] But having a policeman come round to your door within sight of the neighbors was certainly embarrassing, and this was probably all that most servants hoped to accomplish. Fetching the police was just one more way to expose a master to the tribunal of public opinion.

In their reliance on public humiliation for revenge against their masters, servants clearly harked back to the village traditions of their rural backgrounds. And the role of village traditions in shaping their protests is even more obvious in those cases in which servants preferred, as La Croix, a *cuisinière* with a grudge against her mistress, put it, "to take justice into their own hands,"[124] and not only appeal to the judgment of the community but also to execute it themselves. To do this they borrowed forms and rituals deeply embedded in popular culture: the *charivari* and "rough music," which collectively and ritually rebuked violators of village notions of correct behavior, and the carnival, with its license for social inversion and public insult of *les grands*.[125] For example, carnivalesque elements are obvious in the public and ritual humiliation suffered by M. Jean Petit, master architect of Bordeaux, who had apparently mistreated his *cuisinière*. In revenge three male domestics, friends of hers, invaded Petit's home while he and his wife were having a dinner party for their neighbors. They stayed for hours, demanding food and drink, spilling wine on the floor, insulting and dancing "a minuet" with the women, and finally roughing up everyone.[126] And the Baron de Jouquières was subjected to a one-woman *charivari* by a disgruntled former *servante*, who for several nights stood beneath the window of the Baron's apartment yelling and otherwise creating *tapages*.[127] So firmly tied to popular culture were servant protests that when popular culture changed, servant protests did too. Historians of popular culture have noted that in the late eighteenth century, with the spread of literacy among the lower classes, new and more "modern" forms like the anonymous threatening letter gradually began to replace the traditional *charivaris* as vehicles for the expression of community judgments and discontents. And from the mid-century on disgruntled servants began to send anonymous threatening letters to their masters.[128]

With the anonymous threatening letter, servant protest reached the borderline of illegality. The types of protest already discussed, the insult and the defiant gesture, the public exposure and humiliation of masters, left the servants who perpetrated them liable, at most, to dismissal and corporal punishment if they were still in their masters' employment (but few were) or to prosecution for "insolence" if they were not. Such prosecutions were rarely undertaken, however, for bringing the police into the case often simply deepened a master's public humiliation. But other forms of servant protest—theft, violence, murder—were clearly illegal and carried severe penalties. Not unexpectedly, then, such protests occurred much less frequently than the more innocuous types: they were usually the last resort of the truly desperate.

As we saw in the last chapter, servant thievery was in reality much less frequent than their master's obsession with *vol domestique* would suggest, and the majority of thefts were committed not by employed servants who robbed their masters but by unemployed domestics who stole from their landlord, fellow lodgers, or chance passers-by.[129] Even many of the cases of apparently genuine *vol domestique* were in reality not thefts at all. Instead they were the result of misunderstandings between employer and employee. Such misunderstandings could easily arise. As we have noted, a certain amount of petty pilfering ("shoeing the mule") was permitted to servants; it is easy to imagine accusations of theft might result when master and servant disagreed on the limits of the permissible. Clothing was another issue that produced misunderstandings. Since employers frequently provided livery and other clothing for their servants, and gave them garments as gifts or in lieu of wages, who actually owned which items of a servant's wardrobe was often unclear. In a typical case *servante* Marianne Faburel was pitted against her mistress, wife of Sr. Jofre, Parisian *marchand quinquaillier*. Faburel's mistress had ordered her to get a new dress, and, contrary to the usual practice, Faburel had paid for it herself. But when she left, her mistress forgot that and refused to let her take the dress.[130] Finally, at least some accusations of *vol domestique* were totally false. Police records suggest that masters often accused their servants of theft to avoid paying them their wages. An example concerns Françoise La Vigne, a *marchande de bière* in Paris, who accused her *servante* Françoise Bezin of taking a six-*écu* piece left on a commode. But Bezin told the police: "This is a maneuver to fire the plaintiff without paying any of her wages except the modest sum of 33 *sous* . . . this mistress often does such things to her domestics. The purpose of these false accusations is to make them afraid to demand anything."[131]

Elimination of such cases leaves only a few genuine *vol domestiques*. Some of these were undoubtedly motivated by nothing more than a simple desire for money, such as the thefts by Guillaume Fournier, a twenty-year-old lackey from Toulouse, who regularly pilfered money and gold watches from the various houses in which he was employed. Another Toulousan thief, Pierre Dubedat, also known as Jean Dangla, aged "about thirty," had worked for over fifty masters in his career and had apparently stolen something from every one of them.[132] On the other hand, many domestic thefts were inspired directly or indirectly by servants' grievances against their masters. As we have seen, the black servant Samuel Coffy stole 138 *louis d'or* "in reprisal for the blows he frequently received." Maidservant Marie Pradel robbed the master who had seduced and impregnated her of enough money to give herself a dowry.[133] And farm servant Guillaume Mazet robbed his employer when he refused to pay his wages:

> interrogated if it is true that he stole . . . a mule, money, clothes and other effects from Sr. Aubanet . . . of whom he was the servant. . . . Responds . . . that it is true that he stole the mule, the money, and the clothes . . . that he had loaned to the aforesaid Aubanet the sum of 72 livres and that the aforesaid Aubanet also owed him 12 *écus* in wages and that the clothes that he took belonged to him except the vest and a pair of culottes valued 30 *sous* which were mixed in with his clothes.[134]

Note Mazet's insistence that he took only what was owed him, except for the vest and culottes which were inadvertently mixed up with his own clothing. Clearly he did not view his act as a theft: he was only reclaiming his own property. Servants who robbed for revenge felt their crimes were justified, and some employers may have agreed with them. The underreporting of servant thievery that historians have postulated may have stemmed as much from guilty consciences as it did from a distaste for rotting corpses hanging in the family doorway.

A servant's ultimate means of revenge against his master was of course murder. But while cases of domestics striking their employers in the course of an argument were relatively commonplace—although by no means as frequent as cases of masters using violence against servants—instances of the *premeditated* murder of a master by his or her servant were quite rare. Most spontaneous servant violence arose out of the rituals of insult discussed above, and its victims were usually women, either female employers (like the Widow Chabert, a *loueuse de carosses*, beaten by one of her employees, François Bulelot),[135] or wives who received blows as surrogates for their husbands, like the wife of M. Jean Jourdan, *écuyer* and *secrétaire du roi*. The Jourdans employed a lackey named Masson, whom they frequently had to reprimand for laziness. One morning Masson slept late, then emerged "half-dressed and spouting a thousand insults against the plaintiff and his wife." M. Jourdan left to go to Mass, telling his wife to fire Masson. When he returned he found her on the floor, suffering from "several infamous injuries."[136]

Premeditated murder was rather different. It was extremely infrequent: in one sample of court cases I looked at, the death sentences handed down by the Parlement of Toulouse between 1633–1728 and 1750–1778, I found only two cases of servants killing their employers.[137] Interestingly enough, neither of these murders seems to have grown out of servant grievances. In one, mistress and servant were rivals in love, and in the other a servant was apparently goaded into killing his master by the man's brother. This suggests that "revenge" murders by servants were quite rare.[138] Yet the upper classes seem to have been possessed by a fear that their servants would rise up and murder them in their beds. This fear is reflected in the extremely brutal punishments allotted to servants who killed their masters. The sentence was inevitably death, as it was in other cases of murder, but not by the normal hanging: servants who killed their masters were usually burned at the stake or broken on the wheel.[139] One young *servante* who murdered her mistress in Cambrai in the 1770s was herself judicially "murdered" in an exact reenactment of her crime, a ritual of inversion staged this time not by a servant but by society. She was driven to the scene of her execution in a garbage cart, then seated in the chair where her mistress had died and (after having her right hand cut off) she was stabbed in the same way that she had killed her mistress with the very knife she had used.[140] Such punishments were a public lesson to any domestic who contemplated challenging the natural order of society by raising his hand against those whom God had set over him.

Masters' fears of harm from their servants appear to have centered on being poisoned. This is not surprising, for fears of poisoning were common in this period. Poison was the standard eighteenth-century explanation for any sudden and unexpected death which the medical profession could not otherwise account for; in this it played the role that witchcraft had in earlier periods.[141] Therefore people often suspected poisoning in quite innocent deaths. But masters were especially fearful of being poisoned by their servants, for poisoning seemed the natural weapon of domestics. They had unparalled opportunities to administer it, and the stealthiness involved in its use seemed to accord with the character of servants, those creatures who listened at keyholes and indulged in petty pilfering. We can see this obsession with poisoning in incidents like the following. Mme. de Genlis was visiting her brother-in-law one day when he became sick after drinking from a glass that had been left standing on a sideboard. He immediately jumped to the conclusion that a servant had put poison in it. "That idea sent a chill into all of us," Mme. de Genlis wrote. After an extensive investigation which upset the household for weeks, suspicion centered on a young *aide de cuisine*, who at first denied the misdeed, but finally admitted putting something in the glass, although he said it was only a mild emetic. He was fired, and his livery was ceremoniously burned.[142] Another case where poisoning by a servant was suspected threatened to end more tragically. A certain M. Huet-Duparc died mysteriously in Caen in the

1780s. Naturally his *servante*, Victoire Salmon, was accused of poisoning him. She was tried and sentenced to be burned alive. But many thought her innocent and raised a public outcry for an appeal to the Paris Parlement, which decided that Huet-Duparc's son was the true culprit and overturned the verdict.[143]

Masters' concern for poisoning, like their obsession with domestic theft, reveals more about their own fears and guilts than it does about servant protest. The psychological pressures on servants were enormous: the depersonalization and challenges to their sense of identity, the feelings of inferiority which grew out of the forced acceptance of a "superior" culture, the constant blows to pride and self-esteem, the irritants of associating with and ministering to people one hated and despised. As Rousseau put it in a famous passage of *La Nouvelle Héloise*, "Servanthood is so little natural to man that it cannot exist without some discontent."[144] But servant discontent was as likely to be sublimated into an awe and admiration for their masters or compensated for by inversion fantasies and manipulation as it was to take the form of open protest. And protests were more likely to be spontaneous, ritualized, and theatrical expressions of discontent than to take the form of theft or murder. All servants probably at heart regarded their masters, in the words of the Old Regime police ordinance quoted at the beginning of this chapter, "as so many enemies." But their means of expressing their hatred were often ambiguous and oblique.

Until now the picture we have presented of the psychological pressures on servants and their consequences suggests few changes over time. But it is tempting to argue that the transformations in servants' private lives in the last decades of the Old Regime—their increasing wealth, ambition, and independence—were paralleled by what might be termed a growth in class-consciousness, as servants became increasingly resentful of their masters and of the insults and degradation that filled their lives. If this were so, we might expect an increase in the active protest by servants as the Revolution neared. But this does not seem to have happened. It is true that servants appear to have been less affectionate toward their masters during the last decades of the Old Regime. This is suggested by a decline in the proportion of servants who left legacies to their masters. In Toulouse in 1727–29, 28.6 percent of all wills of servants contained such legacies; by 1787 only 11.1 percent did so. In Bordeaux the percentage dropped from 17.6 percent in the 1727–29 sample to 5.3 percent in that of 1787–89.[145] It is also true that servants seem to have become increasingly touchy about corporal punishment and other insults to their personal pride in the last decades of the Old Regime. But there does not seem to have been any marked rise in the level of servant protest as a whole. Instead, at least some types of protest, theft as revenge for example, appear to have declined by the eve of the Revolution. An admittedly impressionistic reading of

Parisian police records suggests that in the 1770s and 1780s servants were much more likely to become involved in clashes with ordinary citizens than they were in the conflicts with their employers which dominated the police blotters of earlier periods. Many servants continued to display devotion and loyalty to their masters up to and indeed through the Revolution. The revolutionaries themselves recognized this; one reason they denied the vote to servants was their conviction that most domestics identified with their masters and would vote as they were told. The revolutionaries made active efforts among servants toward what today would be called consciousness-raising. In 1789 a pamphlet appeared in Paris entitled *Avis à la livrée par un homme qui la porte*. This reminded domestics that however much they identified with their masters, the latter did not necessarily accept this identification or appreciate their loyalty: "to most masters we are less precious than their horses or dogs." In the coming struggle servants should remember that they are "of the people," and they should not turn their backs on their friends and relatives.[146] Such consciousness-raising was clearly necessary.

The failure of servants to identify more completely with the other members of the lower classes and to express this identification in increasingly rebellious behavior is, I think, attributable to two factors. First were the very changes in servants' lives that might have been expected to contribute to their increasing discontent—the rise of servant independence and ambition. For it was probably the servant who was canny, literate, and anxious to get ahead who was most likely to be sensitive to the cultural gulf between himself and his master, and consequently to feel the identification and devotion that often grew out of this. And it was the clever and ambitious servant who was more likely to disguise his resentment in role-playing and manipulation rather than express it in overt rebellion.

A second factor behind the relative quiescence of servants on the eve of the Revolution is the fact that their masters probably treated them better than they had in earlier periods and therefore gave them less cause for complaint. There is much to suggest that this was so. By the last decades of the Old Regime patriarchalism was dying, and masters no longer tried to control servants' behavior so strictly or to inflict corporal punishment upon them, thus eliminating basic causes of earlier protest. Also, the increasing physical distancing between master and servant meant that contacts between them were lessened and therefore passions were cooler on both sides. And finally the growing conviction of the equality of all men made at least the more enlightened masters more conscious of their servants' independence and pride and more tactful in their handling of them. Master-servant relationships are two-sided equations, after all.

II

Masters & Servants

5

The Psychology of Mastership: Masters' Attitudes toward Their Servants

"He is my domestic enemy."
—A master, describing his thirteen-year-old valet, in Marana's *L'Espion dans les cours des princes*

The Patriarchal Master in Theory

Masters' relationships with their "domestic enemies" should be easy to define, for in theory they conformed to a model widely disseminated in domestic manuals and religious tracts during the seventeenth century: that of the patriarchal household. While some elements of this model were as old as the ancient world (Xenophon and Quintillian were frequently quoted), the classic texts of French patriarchy were products of the Counter-Reformation, especially of its last phase in the 1670s, 1680s, and 1690s. They came from the pens of churchmen like the Abbé Goussault (*Le Portrait d'un honneste homme*, 1692; *Le Portrait d'une femme honneste, raisonnable, et veritablement chrétienne*, 1694) and their *dévot* followers like Claude Fleury (*Les Devoirs des maîtres et des domestiques*, 1688) who opposed the political and social innovations of the reign of Louis XIV. Patriarchal theory was therefore a product of religious movement devoted to the moralizing of society (hence the emphasis in patriarchal writings on the religious and moral duties of masters) and of a political movement based on a vision of traditional, agrarian, static, and deferential society outmoded even as it was propounded.[1]

The fact that the patriarchal theory of the household grew out of the most important religious and political movements of its time points up the universality of its concepts. In the seventeenth century patriarchy was not simply a theory of the way families and households should function: it was a paradigm for all social organizations, political and religious as well as familial. The family and the household were the basic units of the social order. As Claude Fleury put it, "The family is the image of the state, which is only an assemblage of many families."[2] The authority of the father of the family was the model for all authority: a king was the father of his people, God was the Father of all mankind.

While its precepts held true for all power relationships, the patriarchal vision of authority was especially applicable to master-servant relationships, for the seventeenth-century household by definition *was* a family, and a master by definition *was* the father of his servants. The conviction that the household was a family carried with it important implications about the proper roles and demeanor of master and man. It implied, first of all, that servants were the "adopted children" of the family. They were, therefore, like children, immature, helpless, and dependent. They lacked the essential characteristic of adulthood: the ability to be responsible for their own welfare. In the sixteenth, seventeenth and early eighteenth centuries adulthood implied a certain level of economic self-sufficiency. An adult man was one able to support himself and his family through his own efforts. Those unable to do so, like servants, had to subordinate themselves to someone who could provide for them. In return for financial support, they surrendered their labor, a certain amount of bodily autonomy (see the discussion of corporal punishment in the last chapter), and, most importantly, the freedom of will that was the mark of an adult. Subordination to the will of another was in the seventeenth and early eighteenth centuries considered the essence of servanthood. One patriarchal writer even compared domestic service to the monastic life, for servants like monks gave up their freedom of will: "if a monk never does what he wills, a lackey too must do what he is ordered to do."[3] The duty of servants listed first in every domestic manual was obedience. Only when ordered to do something against the law or the principles of religion could they go against their master's orders.[4]

If the servant was a child, condemned to a child's perpetual submission to adult authority, the master was of course a father, with a father's privileges and responsibilities. A master had certain rights, amounting almost to property rights, over the bodies of his servants, analogous to the rights of a husband over the body of his wife and a father over the bodies of his children. A master had a right to his servants' labor, a right to regulate their behavior and to inflict corporal punishment if necessary, and a right to supervise their sexual conduct and control access to their sexual favors.[5] In return for these rights, however, a master incurred responsibilities similar to those a patriarchal father bore for his wife and children. The conscientious fulfillment of these responsibilities formed in patriarchal theory the essence of mastership.

What were these responsibilities? A master was, first and foremost, responsible for the material welfare of his domestics. He owed them food, shelter, and some sort of financial reward for their services, although not necessarily, as we have seen, a regular wage.[6] Masters, like fathers, were also expected to see that, when their servant-children left the household to fend for themselves, they had an adequate start in life. Employers were expected to provide dowries for their female domestics and apprenticeships for their young men, in sums adequate to place them in their proper station in life, "in the front ranks of the poor."[7] And if his servants fell ill or grew too old to work, the ideal master would not turn them out to starve or die, but instead would care for them as he would for aged or infirm relatives.[8]

Besides providing for the daily bodily needs of his domestics, a master was also required to oversee their moral and spiritual welfare. In patriarchal households the master was in effect a "priest in his house," the intermediary between his wife, his children, his servants, and God, responsible before God for their conduct. Therefore a master owed his domestics spiritual instruction and guidance. This duty was never taken so seriously in Catholic countries as it was in Protestant England. Household prayers, in which the master literally acted as "priest in his house," leading his dependents in worship, were never so widespread in France as they were in England, and unlike English heads of households, French masters were not exhorted to teach their servants to read so that they could read the Bible.[9] But in the France of the Counter-Reformation masters were at least expected to see that their domestics attended Mass and Confession regularly, and to make certain that the ill and dying received the last rites.[10] Masters were also expected to oversee the sexual conduct of their servants, and to discourage drinking, gambling, idle quarreling, and other vices.[11]

Yet another responsibility of masters was to see that their servants did not break the law. According to most French legal codes, an employer could be held legally responsible for his servants' crimes only if they were committed under his direct and explicit orders.[12] But public opinion nevertheless tended to hold employers accountable for their servants' misdeeds, and masters themselves shared this notion, often preferring to punish their erring servants themselves rather than handing them over to the police.[13] For the final duty a master owed to his servant was protection against all other authorities. If a servant submitted himself to a master, that master had the duty to see that he was forced to submit to no one else.

Thus in patriarchal theory masters and servants took the roles of fathers and children, bound together by the same sort of network of mutual rights and duties that bound real fathers and their offspring. Relations between masters and servants should be affectionate, but in the same way that relationships between parents and children were affectionate in the heyday of patriarchy: that is, the affection was measured, distant, decorous, tinged on the child-servant's side with a healthy fear of the all-powerful father-master, and on the father-master's side with a firm conviction that overindulgence was morally harmful for his charges.[14] Bound together by ties of affection and duty, masters and servants would, in theory, take their places in the great chain of similarly obligated superiors and inferiors that constituted the God-ordained social order in the sixteenth, seventeenth, and early eighteenth centuries.

The Patriarchal Master in Reality

How closely did this elaborate theory of patriarchy match the reality of relationships within the household? How seriously did masters take their responsibilities toward their domestics? Did Old Regime France deserve the label that some historians have applied to the antebellum American South: was it "a patriarchy that worked"?

It is hard to know. On the one hand, there definitely were masters who fit the patriarchal model in every respect. One example is Sr. Sentou Dumont, a minor noble who lived near Toulouse from 1690 to 1741. Sentou Dumont took his servants from a small circle of local families; he employed, for example, not only Françoise Dauban but also her niece, Marie Baradate, and he hired the daughter of his valet Louis Gilede when she was old enough to work. He knew his domestics well and treated them generously, caring for them when they were sick, providing dances for them on holidays (his *livre de raison* noted for March 19, 1736, "I have celebrated the feast of St. Joseph, my patron saint, with éclat," at a cost of 24 livres), and opening his purse for their daily needs. He was also concerned to establish them in life. When Françoise Dauban married the son of a fellow servant, Sentou Dumont paid for the banns and the ring, attended the ceremony, provided a house for the couple, and kept them on in his service. When Françoise's niece Marie married yet another of his employees he gave the couple a 100-livre *rente* and 50 livres' worth of household goods, and also spent 15 livres on the wedding feast. But if Sentou Dumont was generous he was also strict, as a good patriarch should be. When his son's tutor seduced the nursemaid, he packed off the guilty couple, although when the woman returned, penniless and repentent, he took her in again.[15] M. Sentou Dumont was not an isolated example. M. François de Mongaillard arranged for his servant to be apprenticed; Dlle. Marie de Boussac left hers a pension for her old age; Marie Ann Brun taught her *servante* to read, cared for her when she was ill, provided her with a dowry, and left her a legacy besides![16]

Thus there were masters who behaved like model patriarchs. But they seem to have been few and far between. The drinking, gambling, and sexual license rampant below stairs in most households suggests that only a minority of employers took their responsibilities for the moral guidance of their domestics seriously. Responsibilities for their material needs were similarly neglected. As we saw earlier, few employers hesitated to fire servants who were too old or too ill to work. And few seem to have felt they owed their servants a dowry or an apprenticeship to give them a good start in life. Only 3 percent of the marriage contracts in my samples from Toulouse, Bordeaux, and Paris stated that employers had contributed to their servants' dowries, and of all the wills I read only three contained provisions by which masters arranged apprenticeships for their domestics.[17]

Probably the best barometer—and certainly the most convenient in terms of making comparisons across periods and classes—of the degree to which masters took their patriarchal obligations seriously are legacies to servants in their wills. In the Old Regime such legacies were not simply generous gestures; they were part and parcel of a master's obligation to provide for the future of his servants. Remembering one's domestics at one's dying moments was essential to a "beautiful death." Priests and notaries present at deathbed scenes constantly exhorted the dying to fulfill their "Christian obligations" toward their faithful domestics.[18] Yet wills show that only a minority of masters took these obligations seriously.

Table 21 summarizes the legacies to servants in testaments from Toulouse and Bordeaux in the late 1720s. Column I shows the percentage of all wills leaving legacies to domestics, classified by social category. But these figures are not a true indication of patriarchal generosity, for the relatively high figures for the nobility and low figures for the lower classes probably simply reflect the fact that many more nobles were more likely to have servants in the first place. Therefore I corrected these figures for patterns of servant employment.[19] The results are shown in Column II.

These figures suggest that only a minority of masters took their patriarchal

TABLE 21

Percentage of Wills Including Legacies to Servants, by Class, 1727–29

	Toulouse		Bordeaux	
	I	II	I	II
Nobility	32.2	35.6	35.6	39.0
Middle class	18.8	35.9	14.5	27.0
Lower class	7.2	28.7	3.4	23.2
Clergy	23.6	39.0	26.7	30.8

Sources: See Bibliography, section I, B.

Note: I = percentage of legacies in total wills, and II = percentage of legacies in wills corrected to reflect patterns of servant employment.

obligations seriously, and that this was true of all social classes. We might have expected bourgeois and lower-class masters to have been more generous with their domestics, since the small size of their households could encourage intimate ties between master and servant. Or, conversely, we might have expected more concern from the nobility because of their sense of noblesse oblige. Yet the figures for all social groups are quite similar—in each only around one-third of the masters remembered their servants in their wills. Not even the clergy, who might have been expected to take the religiously founded precepts of patriarchy more seriously than the laity, were especially generous toward their domestics.

If the social class of masters had little effect on generosity toward servants, neither did their gender. Historians of households have often suggested that relationships between women employers and their female servants were much warmer and closer than those between master and man; that there often developed a mother-daughter relationship between a mistress of the house and her young servant girl or a sisterly affection between mistress and maid who grew old together, sharing the cares of the household.[20] But in Old Regime France it is not clear that this was so. Table 22 suggests that, at least as measured by the barometer of legacies in wills, there was little difference in the relationships of mistress and maid and master and man. It is true that women heads of households, spinsters and widows, were often more generous to their servants than were men.[21] This generosity probably reflected the sisterly relationships that often grew up between such women and their *servantes*. In the ancien régime widows and spinsters usually had little money and little social life. They lived modestly, employing a single *servante* who often remained in their service for decades and became companion, counselor, and friend as well as servant. The warmth of such relationships infuses wills like that of Marguerite Chauvel, widow of a *conseiller* in the Parlement of Bordeaux: "I declare that Marie Philip my *femme de chambre* who has been near me for more than twenty-five

TABLE 22

Percentage of Wills Including Legacies to Servants, by Gender, 1727–29

	Toulouse		Bordeaux	
	I	II	I	II
All men	7.4	32.7	10.1	30.8
All women	12.8		9.9	
Female heads of households	15.1	38.4	14.4	34.5

Sources: See Bibliography, section I, B.
Note: I = percentage of total wills, and II = percentage of legacies in wills corrected to reflect patterns of servant employment. The figures for all women could not be corrected for patterns of servant employment because they include married women who are not listed on tax rolls.

years and who has always served me with the rarest of fidelity and affection . . . merits the greatest kindness from my children."[22]

But married women were rarely so generous with their servants as single women and widows were, in part because they had little control over their money,[23] but also probably because relationships between married women and their domestics were often difficult. For unlike the situation in the nineteenth and twentieth centuries, married women of the Old Regime did not necessarily have undisputed authority over the servants in their households. In the seventeenth century at least the running of a household and the supervision of domestics seem to have been male rather than female responsibilities.[24] Domestic manuals of the period were addressed to men rather than women.[25] In patriarchal theory, and seemingly in practice, the male head of the household bore the ultimate responsibility for its functioning; his wife was at best a lieutenant carrying out his orders. The correspondence of men like the Comte d'Avaux reveals that they were deeply involved in the minutiae of running a household.[26] To be sure, some wives did exercise considerable control over their households, but they often had to fight for this. An example is the Duchesse de Liancourt, who was truly mistress in her house, but only as the result of a bargain with her dissolute husband: he "rendered her mistress of everything, and in return she 'closed her eyes to all which she had to ignore' " in his private life.[27] Other wives were not so fortunate. The Marquise de Courcelles was denied any voice in domestic affairs by her husband: "I did not even have in that household the authority to ask for a glass of water, and I remember that one day [when] I called for a horse . . . my husband's grooms had the insolence to ask me who I was and by what right I gave orders."[28] The seventeenth-century mystic, Mme. de la Mothe Guyon, was not only deprived of control over her servants but also bullied and even physically abused by her maid.[29] Such experiences did not make married women fond of their servants.

Thus while relationships between employer and domestic differed by gender, they did not do so in ways that necessarily made women more generous toward their servants. In fact, for all classes and both sexes levels of legacies to servants in wills hovered around 30 percent in the early years of the eighteenth century. If such legacies are a reflection of an employer's acceptance of his patriarchal responsibilities for his domestics, they suggest that only a minority of masters took these responsibilities seriously.

After all, there was little to make them do so. Admittedly some social opprobrium came with being known as a mean master (such employers were the butt of proverbs: "De maistres gourmans, serviteurs et chiens ont toujours faim"),[30] while to be loved by one's servants reflected well on one's personal reputation. Mme. de Pompadour counted "the attachment of my domestics," along with the kindness of the king, the respect of courtiers, and the fidelity of her friends as one of the blessings of her life, and a conscience-stricken Mme. de Montespan asked the forgiveness of her servants on her deathbed.[31]

But the mild social disapproval accorded the mean master seems to have weighed little against the temptations to tyranny inherent in the very nature of the master-servant relationship. For patriarchal theory, with its network of reciprocal rights and duties binding master and man, was in reality little more than a social myth. It masked a much more unequal relationship in which the master had all the rights while the servant had all the duties. Patriarchal theorists themselves dimly recognized this: their constant exhortations to masters to recognize their servants as their "brothers in Christ," to treat them kindly, "however stupid they may be," to overlook their faults and incapacities, are acknowledgments of the realities of a relationship in which all power lay on the side of the master.[32] In such circumstances there was little to induce masters to behave toward their servants with the benevolent concern of model patriarchs.

Masters' Attitudes toward Their Servants: Indifference and Contempt

If only a minority of masters regarded their servants with paternalistic benevolence, what was the attitude of the rest? In the seventeenth century, in striking contrast to later periods, memoirs and letters offer no clues, only silence. Masters rarely mentioned their servants in their memoirs and letters. A good example is the famed letter-writer Mme. de Sévigné. She wrote literally thousands of letters to her beloved daughter, and few events in her life were too trivial to merit a mention. Yet the thirty-odd servants who shared her household garnered only a handful of comments.[33] And in this she was, I suspect, typical of the men and women of her time. Perhaps this very silence is the key to masters' attitudes toward their servants: they were indifferent to and almost oblivious of their existence. The cliché "domestic enemies," so often used to refer to servants in the sixteenth and seventeenth centuries, was probably an inaccurate representation of the feelings of masters toward their domestics, for it implied an awareness of servants, an active engagement with them, which most masters simply did not have.

The roots of employers' indifference to their domestics lay, I think, in the extraordinary intimacies of households of the patriarchal period. As we have seen, masters rarely had a private moment away from their servants. Employer and employee often shared the same room and sometimes the same bed; and masters lived out the most intimate moments of their lives in full view of hordes of liveried retainers. This intimacy could stimulate close and affectionate relationships between employer and employee, as in the case of single women and their *servantes*, but it did not necessarily do so. For it could also drive masters to indulge in a sort of psychological distancing which served as a substitute for the actual physical distancing separating employer and domestic in the households of later periods. Masters may have preserved their sanity in the face of the immense psychological pressures created by the constant presence in their lives of people who were, in essence, unknown and judgmental strangers by simply refusing to recognize their existence. Thus the intimacy of the households of the patriarchal period was probably at best a pseudo-intimacy; the familiarity of master with servant bred not just contempt but also indifference.

The techniques of psychological distancing were many and varied. We have already discussed some of them: the bestowal of nicknames and sobriquets, which robbed servants of their personal identities, and the enforced wearing of livery, which reduced them from people to things, to *objets d'art* forming part of the decorative background of their masters' lives. Servants were simply *there*, like the furniture; employers took their presence for granted, and refused to recognize or acknowledge their existence as individuals. Masters regarded servants almost as extensions of themselves, not only as instruments to do their will but also as extensions of their very physical being. One early seventeenth-century mistress, the notorious libertine Mme. d'Olonne, saw nothing incongruous in replying, when told by her confessor that she must do penance for her sins, "I'll have my servants fast."[34]

Even when servants did succeed in penetrating their master's consciousness, their employers seem rarely to have recognized them as individual human beings with unique personalities of their own. They saw them instead as representatives of the *genus* servant—a social type characterized by a variety of unfortunate personality traits. Masters seem to have thought of their servants (when they thought of them at all) in terms of stereotypes which were uniformly negative. Servants were widely regarded as licentious, as the *L'Etat de servitude, ou La Misère des domestiques* (an eighteenth-century *bibliothèque bleue* peddled cheaply by wandering booksellers) suggests. In it a lackey laments:

> On le [the servant] croit entaché de
> l'humeur libertine,
> Naturelle et commune à la gente
> Lacquesine.[35]

Servants were also perceived as gluttons and drunkards; in seventeenth-century comedies domestics often bore names like Brodevin (Wine jug), Ferme-à-table (Fixed at the table) and Trinequeboc (Drinking mug).[36] They were also thought notoriously lazy and shiftless. They were cowards, who bullied passers-by whenever they got the chance but trembled before the wrath of their masters: the cringing servant ducking his master's blows was a standard comic turn in seventeenth-century plays.[37] They were fundamentally dishonest ("to lie like a lackey" was a common figure of speech in the Old Regime) and indeed inclined to crimes of every sort (according to Des Essarts' *Dictionnaire universel de police* of 1787 servants were prone to "perfidy, debauchery, corruption, cupidity, and the ignoring of all social virtues; theft, assassination, and poison are the crimes common to them.")[38]

But, above all, servants were stupid and ignorant. This was the most common servant stereotype in the ancien régime, as the abundance of "ignorant servant stories" in the literature of the period attests. Employers regarded stupidity as not only one of the most common traits of servants but also as one of the most desirable. A sixteenth-century nobleman once recommended a *maître d'hôtel* to his son in the following terms: "he writes very well and is very docile—that is, very stupid (*fort sot*)."[39] The stupidity employers attributed to their domestics was of a certain sort, as the use of the word *sot* in the preceding quotation suggests. Servants' stupidity was the loutish stupidity of country bumpkins, who wallowed happily in their ignorance as pigs wallowed in barnyard filth. Servants were "gros réjouis," as the Comte de Montlosier referred to his valet; "sotises gens," as Mme. de Sévigné called her domestics one of the few times she mentioned them.[40]

The connotations of animality in these expressions are noteworthy, for they betray the deeply rooted associations of servants with animals in their masters' minds. Religious tracts and domestic manuals often admonished employers not to think of their servants as "animals of a different species," but they seem to have had little effect.[41] Employers constantly borrowed metaphors and similies from the animal kingdom when referring to their domestics. To Mme. de Sévigné a rough-housing domestic "played like a dog"; to Mme. de Créquy a group of angry lackeys resembled "furious beasts"; and to the Baronne d'Oberkirch a favorite *valet de chambre* was her "chat de maison."[42] The association of servants with domestic animals was a favorite motif in French art of the period (see figure 7). The similarities of pose, treatment, and function of servant and pet in such paintings suggest that artists viewed them as more or less interchangeable. Indeed, a whole *genre* of popular woodcuts in the sixteenth century endowed domestics with the features and attributes of animals: pigs' snouts, asses' ears, and the like.[43] Here is a contemporary verbal exegesis of one such *image du bon valet*:

> He wears on his head a well-made red hat and on his body a proper shirt; he has the snout of a pig, ears of an ass, hoofs of a deer; his right hand is raised and always open, and he has on his left shoulder a yoke, from the two ends of which are hung two sacks of water. . . . In his left hand he carries a pail full of burning coals. The interpretation of this figure is apposite. The good servant must be properly dressed. The pig's snout means that a *valet* must not be choosy about his food, and that he must be content with all sorts of viands. The ass's ears signify that he must hear and support with patience the harsh words that his master says to him. The raised right hand signifies fidelity . . . the deer's hoofs mean that he must be prompt to execute his orders. The water and fire show with what swiftness and industry he must apply himself to his household chores.[44]

FIGURE 7. Antoine Coypel, *Jeune fille caressant un chien*. Reproduced by permission of the Louvre.

The servant as household pet. In seventeenth- and eighteenth-century French art, domestics were often portrayed in close association with animals and occasionally given animalistic characteristics themselves. Note the similar expressions of the pampered lapdog and equally pampered blackamoor.

The prevalence of such images suggest that servants were seen almost as a separate race of men, more animal-like than human in fundamental characteristics. As Fénélon noted in the seventeenth century, "Servants are regarded almost like horses; people believe them to be of a separate race and suppose that they were made for the convenience of masters."[45] Such attitudes were natural to a society like that of sixteenth- and seventeenth-century France, which viewed each estate and occupation as a distinct race and believed that character traits and occupational attitudes—for example, the military prowess and "virtue" of the nobility—were passed down in the blood from generation to generation.[46]

This tendency to see servants as a separate race—surely the ultimate step of psychological distancing—was useful to masters. It relieved the psychological pressures created by the constant presence of servants in their lives, for if domestics were of a separate and inferior race, their judgments on what they saw and heard of their masters' lives simply did not matter. It also justified not conforming to the behavior expected of an ideal patriarch, for if servants were animals, they were simply not worthy of benevolence. Thus it justified the automatic bullying, blows, and scornful insults which seem to have been the normal demeanor of masters toward their servants in the sixteenth, seventeenth, and early eighteenth centuries. It justified the caning Sr. Duhamel meted out to his *domestique* Nicolas when he lost his wallet, the beating François Joseph Fourvin received when he interrupted his master's dinner to report the result of an errand.[47] It justified the indifference with which Mme. de Sévigné watched the physical suffering of her servants: "the abbé's lackey played like a dog [note the automatic animal simile] with the amiable Jacquine [a servant of Mme. de Sévigné]. He threw her on the ground, breaking her arm and dislocating the wrist. The cries that she made were frightful; it was as if a Fury had broken her arm in hell." Madame's reaction to this? "This novelty amused me."[48] This attitude was, I suspect, much more typical of sixteenth-, seventeenth-, and early-eighteenth-century employers than the benevolent concern of Sr. Sentou Dumont.

Masters' attitudes toward their domestics may have a broader historical significance than is obvious at first glance, for they may have helped to shape the general pattern of relationships between the elite and the lower orders in the hierarchal society of the ancien régime. Certainly the way masters viewed their servants, whether as the childlike dependents of the patriarchal model or as the lazy, licentious, and animal-like creatures of the standard stereotypes, were strikingly similar to the way in which they viewed the lower classes as a whole. This was especially true of the poor, who were thought of as lazy, shiftless creatures who wallowed animal-like in their drunkenness, debauchery, and ignorance of the basic tenets of religion, needing the firm moral guidance of their betters.[49] This coincidence of views may reflect nothing more than masters' recognition that their servants were drawn from the poor; masters may have simply applied to their servants the views they held of the lower classes in general. But it is at least possible that the process worked the other way, and that masters' opinions of the lower classes as a whole grew out of their contacts with their servants, who were, after all, the segment of the *menu peuple* they knew best. A major theme of class relationships in seventeenth-century France was a growing gulf between the elite and the lower classes, and a determined assault by the elite on the laziness, licentiousness, and irreligion of the poor.[50] It is possible that this assault had its ultimate psychological roots in the intimacies of master and servant in the patriarchal household. For their experiences with their servants may have taught masters to view the poor in general as in need of reformation. And masters may have tried to achieve in society as a whole the separation from and regulation of their servants, those psychologically threatening presences, which they simply could not achieve within the patriarchal household.

Masters' relationships with and attitudes toward their servants may have further historical significance as well. Their experiences with their servants may have convinced masters not only of the innate inferiority of their domestics—and by extension, of the lower classes as a whole—but also of their own innate superiority and the fact that they fully deserved their position at the apex of the social hierarchy. For surely the major products of the psychological experience of being a master were an affirmation of personal identity and a conviction of superiority, just as the major psychological products of servanthood were a shaky sense of identity and a feeling of inferiority toward one's employers. The superiority of master over servant was implicit in the very relationship itself. It was obvious in both the patriarchal and the indifferent and contemptuous models of mastership. For a patriarchal father was by definition superior to his dependents, while the negative servant stereotypes of the contemptuous model implied that masters had opposite and therefore positive characteristics. This sense of superiority was surely deepened by daily experiences within the household, where masters had their every whim catered to and bullied, beat, and fired their servants with impunity. And it was further confirmed by the behavior of the servants themselves, no matter what they did. Obedient and devoted servants legitimized their masters' right to order them about, while disorderly and rebellious servants confirmed the negative stereotypes of servanthood and thus also, albeit indirectly, confirmed their masters' innate superiority.

A deferential society like that of seventeenth- and early-eighteenth-century France can function only when both those at the top and at the bottom of the social hierarchy are convinced of the innate superiority of the former and the innate inferiority of the latter. What we saw of servants' attitudes in the last chapter suggested that the deference of servants and their acquiescence to a social order that assumed their own inferiority was more complex and problematic than is usually thought. If this was true of servants, whose experiences tended to create a sense of inferiority vis-à-vis their masters, how much more was it likely to be true of artisans or peasants, who had no such experiences? But if the lower classes' acquiescence in their inferior position in seventeenth-century society cannot be taken for granted, the upper classes' conviction of their own superiority was clearly firm and untroubled by doubts. This may have derived in large part from their experiences of mastering servants. The household may have been, in the seventeenth and early eighteenth centuries, a school in which noble, officeholder, and rich bourgeois learned the attitudes and techniques of social dominance.

Changes in Master-Servant Relationships in the Last Half of the Eighteenth Century

In Old Regime France the presentation of servants on the stage closely paralleled the way their masters viewed them in real life, and in the last decades before the French Revolution this theatrical presentation underwent a profound transformation.[51] In earlier centuries, on stage as in reality, servants were everywhere: in the 250 seventeenth-century comedies studied by Michel Lemain, there were no less than 784 domestics, or more than 3 per play.[52] But on the stage as in reality, these swarming servants were scarcely recognized or recognizable as human beings. Their major functions were those traditional to stage servants since the comedies of ancient Greece: through their asides they explained the plot to the audience; through their machinations they kept it moving along. They also provided comic relief with their loutish manners and fractured French, and their stupidity, ignorance, and licentiousness served as dramatic foils for the noble qualities of their masters. On stage the presentation of servants rarely went beyond the level of stereotype. They bore outlandish names: the Pierrots and Columbines of the *commedia dell'arte*; the Merlins and Zélis, Sgnarelles and Dorines of their creators' imaginations.[53] Their behavior conformed to the common image of servants: they were lusty, loutish, cowardly, dishonest, and stupid (except when they had to be conniving to help the plot along).[54] Only in Molière do we find more well-rounded and sympathetic portrayals of servants, and his domestics, with their refreshing common sense and their attractive mixture of sturdy independence and loyalty to their masters, did not influence his immediate successors.[55]

But during the course of the eighteenth century the presentation of servants in French theater underwent a remarkable transformation, one that I think reflected the changed way their masters viewed them in real life. The traditional stereotypes of servants disappeared, drowned in the wave of realism that washed across the stage. With the emergence of the "comédie larmoyante" in the last decades of the Old Regime, true-to-life family conflicts replaced the whirligigs of stratagem and disguise which had earlier passed for plots.[56] Therefore servants were no longer necessary to explain the plot and carry it forward. As a result, they almost disappeared from the stage—a parallel to the contraction of real life households. In, for example, the comedies of Sedaine, who wrote at the end of the Old Regime, there were only four valets in twenty-eight plays.[57]

Those servants who remained were presented much more realistically than servants had been in the seventeenth century. They lost their exotic names in favor of the "Guillaumes" and "Champagnes" they bore in real life.[58] They also shed their stereotypes, displaying instead the characterisitics real servants displayed. They were ambitious, manipulative, self-interested, and often highly critical of their employers, especially in the last half of the century, when they were used as the spokesmen for their creators' increasingly devastating criticisms of the nobility and its way of life.[59] At the same time stage servants took on many of the "good" qualities formerly reserved for their masters: they became increasingly intelligent, dignified, and worthy of respect. They became the *filles de chambre* of Marivaux, as attractive, witty, virtuous, and much more warmhearted and sympathetic than their mistresses.[60] And they became of course Figaro, the servant respectable enough to bear his creator's name,[61] the servant as *honnête homme,* the counter-ideal to all the traditional stereotypes of servant licentiousness, cowardice, and stupidity. With Figaro the servant was not merely the auxiliary who explained the action and provided comic relief; he was the focus of the play, a man of emotions complex enough to make his master look like a wooden stereotype.

This changing image of servants on the stage reflected, I think, changes in the ways masters viewed their domestics in real life. In the last half of the eighteenth century, both the myth and the reality of the patriarchal household disappeared, and with them went the traditional attitudes and patterns of behavior toward servants. In place of the condescending paternalism of patriarchalism came a recognition of the servant's essential equality with his master; in the place of the old automatic assumptions of servant loyalty and devotion came suspicion and uneasiness; in the place of extraordinary intimacies of the traditional household came the physical distancing of master and servant; in the place of the traditional indifference and stereotyping came a fascination with domestics and a recognition of their dignity as human beings. In general master-servant relationships in the last half of the eighteenth century were colder, more distant, and more formal than they had been in earlier periods, but they were also more egalitarian. And at least some masters and servants developed genuine friendships which would have been impossible in an earlier era.

The Demise of Patriarchalism and the Disappearance of the Patriarch

In the last half of the eighteenth century patriarchy as an organizing principle of the social order was in retreat on all fronts. In politics the family and household ceased to be the basic units of society; they were replaced by a society composed of equal and autonomous individuals. And in the family the tyrannical patriarch lost his absolute authority over his wife and children, and became a concerned and loving father and an affectionate and indulgent husband. In these circumstances it was probably inevitable that the patriarch would disappear from master-servant relationships as well.

In the late eighteenth century the patriarch apparently abdicated his traditional authority over household and servants in favor of his wife, the mistress of the house, *la ménagère*. The newly affectionate family life of the last half of the eighteenth century led to a firmer identification of woman as wife, mother, and housekeeper, and this in turn encouraged a new and more strict division of sex roles. Man's role was to go out in the world and work for the sustenance of his family; woman's was to remain at home and organize their daily existence. Or as one domestic manual put it: "All exterior affairs are the domain of the husband; that cannot be doubted. As for the wife, her duty is to oversee all the cares of the interior."[62]

Within the interior the *ménagère* now reigned supreme. It was now she and not the patriarchal head of the household who hired, fired, and supervised domestics. This is reflected in the domestic manuals of the immediate pre- and postrevolutionary eras. Père Collet's *Traité des devoirs des gens du monde, et surtout des chefs de famille,* published in 1763,[63] is the last domestic manual I know of to assume that a male household head would supervise its functioning. Later domestic manuals like Mme. Gaçon-Dufour's *Manuel de la ménagère à la ville et à la compagne* (1805) and Mme. Demarson's *Guide de la ménagère* (1828)[64] reveal in their very titles the assumption that the running of a household is the responsibility of its mistress. Mme. Gaçon-Dufour even gave to the *ménagère* responsibility for hiring and overseeing not only domestic servants but farm servants as well.[65] This change seems to have reflected the way households actually functioned. By the 1780s wives like the Marquise de Courcelles, denied any voice in the running of their households, were clearly things of the past. Instead self-confident and energetic *ménagères* like Mme. d'Albis de Belbèze, wife of a *conseiller* in the Parlement of Toulouse, had *carte blanche* to hire, fire, and supervise the servants. When Mme. d'Albis de Belbèze wrote her husband that she had fired their daughter's governess, his reply indicated that it was unlikely he would ever challenge her authority in household matters. "I am delighted that you fired Thérèze," he wrote. "Anyway, you know that I always approve of everything you do."[66]

The substitution of the *ménagère* for the patriarchal head of the household had an important impact on master-servant relationships. For the mistress of the house was not, in the late eighteenth century at least, burdened with the full weight of responsibilities for the moral and spiritual welfare of her domestics that had been the lot of the patriarchal master. Later this would change, and by the middle of the nineteenth century the *ménagère* would be transformed into an "angel in the house," the moral guide and exemplar of her husband and children as well as her servants.[67] But in the late eighteenth century only a few precursors of this type, like Rousseau's Julie in *La Nouvelle Héloise,* had appeared. This meant that neither the master, who had relinquished his control in the household, nor the mistress, who had not yet become the "angel in the house," was responsible for the morality of their domestics. Instead this responsibility fell on the servants themselves, who were increasingly recognized as adults capable of seeing to their own welfare.

This dismantling of moral responsibilities of the patriarchal master is clearly visible in the domestic manuals of the last decades of the Old Regime. Père Collet's *Traité des devoirs des gens du monde,* dating from 1763, emphasized, as befitted a tract written by a priest, that employers should give their servants a chance to attend Mass and receive religious instruction. But unlike earlier domestic manuals, the *Traité des devoirs* denied that employers had either the right to use corporal punishment on their domestics or the primary moral responsibility for their misdeeds.[68]

Similarly, domestic manuals of the immediate pre- and postrevolutionary decades disavowed a master's traditional patriarchal responsibilities for the material welfare of his servants. No longer did masters have the duty to provide for their servants' futures through dowries or apprenticeships, or to care for them in illness and old age. In fact such duties were explicitly denied. Père Collet stated that firing a servant just because he was too old or too ill to work and sending him away "like a rejected parcel" often "smacks too much of inhumanity," yet on the other hand "a master does not owe a salary to his servant when illness makes it impossible for him to work."[69]

In the domestic manuals of the last years of the Old Regime only a single duty remained to masters, one barely mentioned in earlier handbooks: that they pay their servants' salaries promptly and without complaint. As Père Collet put it: "He [a master] must pay them [his servants] exactly. To treat them badly, even to fire them, because they dare to demand their wages at the end of the year is conduct in which there is neither reason nor justice."[70] Thus the patriarchal father of his servants had become simply an employer. After the middle of the eighteenth century, the language of a market economy invaded domestic manuals, replacing the familial rhetoric of the patriarchal period. The cash-nexus had become the sole tie which bound master and servant.

The Discovery of the Servant: Fear and Fascination within the Household

The master was not the only one to change with the demise of patriarchalism. The intrusion of the language and values of a market economy into the relationships of the household also necessitated a redefinition of the servant. No longer the "adopted child" of a patriarchal family, he became instead an employee, bound to his employer only by the wage he was paid. The new definition of the servant as wage laborer is clearly visible in the domestic manuals of the last years of the Old Regime. To Père Collet a servant was "that man who is paid by you" to perform domestic chores, and this definition was echoed by later writers like the anonymous author of *Des Devoirs des serviteurs, des maîtres, des enfants, des parents, de tous les hommes envers l'église et l'état*, published in Lyons in 1830. He defined servants solely in economic terms: they were "workers obliged to employ their time in return for a daily salary."[71]

The new definition of the servant brought with it a number of implications disturbing to masters. The servant was no longer a docile child; he was instead an adult, the equal to his employer. He was no longer a member of the family circle but instead an unknown stranger. And he was no longer automatically loyal and deferential. He was instead an economic man, motivated by self-interest; he would be loyal to his employer only when it was profitable for him to be so. He was therefore potentially dangerous to his master, and indeed to society at large.

How troubling this new view of servants was to their masters is in the letters and memoirs of the future revolutionary politician Mme. Roland, whose attitudes were probably as typical of those of late eighteenth-century employers as Mme. de Sévigné's had been of those of an earlier era. Mme. Roland expressed much more awareness of her servants than Mme. de Sévigné had been and constantly mentioned them in her memoirs and letters. Indeed, the last letter she wrote before her execution was addressed to her maid.[72] But Mme. Roland was also much more uneasy in her relationships with her domestics than the imperious Mme. de Sévigné had been.

An aspect of the new view of master-servant relationships especially disturbing to Mme. Roland was the fundamental equality of master and servant, a notion implicit in the conception of a cash-nexus relationship binding employer and employee. The two parties to such a contract were equal in a way that the two parties to the "pseudo-contract" binding master and servant (or for that matter, king and subject) in a patriarchal society were not.[73] As Père Collet told masters, "Between you and the man who is paid by you, all is equal in the eyes of humanity."[74]

In the late eighteenth century the recognition of the fundamental equality of domestics inspired a more just and humane treatment of servants. They were paid promptly and in full, and the incidence of corporal punishment declined. But the recognition of the equality of servants also created a certain uneasiness in master-servant relationships, especially among that segment of the population increasingly prominent as servant-employers in the last years of the Old Regime, the bourgeoisie. Bourgeois employers found the equality of servants troubling because their own social status was often insecure. Mme. Roland, that future spokesperson of *Egalité*, is a good example of this attitude. Although she married a robe noble, Manon Philipon's own social origins were modest. Her father was an engraver, a mere artisan. Her parents had always employed a *servante*, but they also had a relative in service: Manon's aunt was *femme de charge* in a noble household. Mme. Roland was ashamed of this fact and disliked the assumption that servants were her equals. It was this feeling that prompted the famous tirade in her memoirs commemorating the time when her aunt's noble employer invited her to lunch and then made her eat in the *office* with the servants.[75] This passage is often interpreted as an attack on noble arrogance in the name of equality for the bourgeoisie. But in reality it is an attack on *servants* and their assumption of equality with outraged Mme. Roland.

A second troubling implication of the new view of the servant, and one that also bothered Mme. Roland, was the notion that he/she was no longer a family member but instead an outsider, a stranger. This troubled those late-eighteenth-century employers who cherished their newly felicitous family life and wished to conduct it in private, hidden from the view of those outside the family circle. It was this desire which prompted the physical distancing of servants within the household which we discussed in chapter 2.

Again Mme. Roland provides a good example of this attitude. She had grown up with servants, but her youthful letters reveal that she felt uneasy with them, simply because they were always around, always watching her, always privy to the secrets of her private life. As a teen-ager she resented the family *servante*'s attempts to help along her flirtations with young men. She wrote, in a passage that epitomizes the new uneasiness many employers felt with their domestics, "I hate the hidden services one receives from that type of person. I boss them, I pity them, but I do not wish to be obliged to them."[76] These sentiments persisted throughout her life. As a young wife and mother Mme. Roland fought running battles to keep her servants out of her private affairs and away from her husband and child.[77]

A final implication of the new definition of servants, and perhaps the most upsetting to their masters, was that as employees servants were self-interested and therefore potentially disloyal. When servants cease to be members of a patriarchal family, employers could no longer expect them to display their traditional devotion to that family and its interests. Instead they were thought to be devoted only to their own advantage. Self-interest was in fact regarded as the salient characteristic of servants in the late eighteenth century. The German traveler J. C. Nemeitz found it a national trait of French domestics; they were, he reported, "*interested* to the last degree."[78] The Marquise de Bombelles also found self-interest the prime characteristic of her employees. Forced to bribe the homesick Swiss nurse of her infant son with the promise of a gold watch if she stayed at her post, the disgusted Marquise wrote to her husband, "So true it is that you cannot count on the attachment of those people except insofar as it is guided by interest."[79] The Princesse Louise de Condé concurred. When a former servant came to visit, the Princesse received her with resignation, asking how large a loan she needed. She was astonished to learn that the servant was prospering and had visited her out of simple devotion.[80]

The recognition that their servants acted primarily out of self-interest, and that their devotion to their masters was therefore often feigned, was a blow to the egos of many employers. The traditional loyalty and affection of servants had flattered masters and had seemed to legitimize their right to rule. Now these props to masters' self-esteem were gone. Many found this hard to bear. The memoirs of the servant-employing classes of the immediate pre- and postrevolutionary decades echo with laments similar to those of the Emperor Napoleon, who discovered that the domestics he had thought devoted refused to go with him into exile on Elba. When even his personal body servant left him, Napoleon wailed: "A servant whom I believed devoted, because I have done everything possible to attach him to me, abandons me on the day of my departure! and I remain at the mercy of people I do not know!"[81]

The revelation of servant self-interest was not only demoralizing for masters, it was also frightening. For what was to prevent these disloyal strangers from making off with the family linen or silver or even murdering them in their beds? In the last years before the Revolution the respectable classes were obsessed with the problem of *vol domestique* and the necessity of policing servants—direct outgrowths, I suspect, of the new view of the servant as self-interested stranger. Lying and dishonesty had always been among the qualities attributed to servants in the traditional negative stereotypes, but they had never before seemed threatening, for they had been counterbalanced by a loyalty taken for granted. Now that this was no longer the case, the servant—self-interested stranger, potential thief, potential murderer—had indeed become the "domestic enemy" of his frightened master.

Therefore it is not surprising that one of the major themes of master-servant relationships in the prerevolutionary decades concerns attempts to guarantee the loyalty and fidelity of domestics. One way to do this was to face up to the fact the servant self-interest and appeal to this very quality to get better and more faithful service. The 1770s and 1780s saw a proliferation of proposals to reward good and faithful servants with prizes, bonuses, and official honors and recognition—proposals that would have been thought absurd and unnecessary in an earlier era. One M. de Montyon founded a prize for a loyal domestic, and the Sociétés d'Agriculture of both Paris and Toulouse awarded faithful farm servants. Even so august a body as the Académie Française gave prizes to servants.[82] There was also a proposal for an honorary royal order, similar to the Chevaliers de St. Louis, for servants who stayed with the same master for at least twenty years. The order was to be called the Chevaliers de la Constance. Members would be nominated by their employers. Each would receive as badges of membership a ribbon for the lapel and a medal "as big as a three-*écu* piece" with a star in the middle and the words "Chevalier de la Constance" around the rim.[83] This proposal, which takes the ambition and self-interest of servants for granted yet assumes that these can be satisfied within a traditional society of orders, is, in its mixture of the notions of corporatism and those of a market society, typical of the social thought of the last years of the Old Regime.

Another solution to the problem of potential servant disloyalty was a stricter policing of the background and references of domestics. This had not been necessary in earlier periods. The trust in servants characteristic of patriarchal society came in part from the fact that masters generally hired only servants they knew something about: children of local families (the Chevalier de la Rénaudie, a seventeenth-century Toulousan noble, took his farm servants almost exclusively from what he described in his *livre de raison* as the "village of Poumies in my parish"),[84] relatives of servants already in the household, domestics recommended by friends. But in the late eighteenth century the rapid turnover among domestics, as ambitious servants moved from job to job in hope of bettering themselves, made the traditional methods of hiring impossible. Employers now had to deal with an impersonal labor market and hire unknown strangers, a practice they found frightening.

To cope with this new situation, in towns like Toulouse local governments passed numerous ordinances to limit the movement and guarantee the bona fides of domestics. In Toulouse an ordinance of 1754 (significantly, the first law concerning domestics service passed in the town in the eighteenth century) cited "the facility with which domestics leave their masters," and required servants to serve out the full term of their contracts. It also required that they provide adequate references of their background and good conduct, and forbade the hiring of servants lacking these.[85] The municipality of Toulouse also tried to regulate the labor market in servants and guarantee their honesty by founding a municipal *bureau d'adresse*, or employment agency. The *bureau* not only matched employers to employees but also vouched for the background and respectability of every servant on its list.[86] *Bureaux d'adresse* were not a new idea; Paris, with its large and impersonal labor market, had one as early as the 1620s.[87] But they did not come to provincial towns like Toulouse and Bordeaux until the 1770s and 1780s, and their foundation was testimony to the new concerns over the potential disloyalty of domestics.

Yet another solution to the problem of servant disloyalty was to hire only those types of servants who could be expected to be docile and devoted to their masters. This helps explain the growing tendency in the late eighteenth century to hire women and boys instead of men servants. It also helps explain employers' preferences for servants fresh from the countryside, uncorrupted by city ways. Newspapers of the 1780s like Bordeaux's *Journal de Guienne* carried many requested from employers seeking: "a *servante*, honest, hardworking, and by preference a peasant" (*Journal de Guienne*, December 27, 1784) and "a robust servant girl, fit to be *aide-de-cuisine* in a good household; preference given to a girl newly arrived from the countryside" (*Journal de Guienne*, January 19, 1786). Servants were not above playing up to the preference for rural naiveté. One young woman seeking a job in Bordeaux advertised herself as "newly arrived from Saintonge"; another described herself as "dressed in the village costume" of the countryside around Clermont in the Auvergne.[88]

Another type of servant popular because of his supposed loyalty in the waning years of the ancien régime was the black domestic. There were only about 5,000 blacks in France in 1789, and most of them worked as servants.[89] They were concentrated in ports that served the Indies and in Paris. Apart from the ports, where even quite modest merchants with connections to the islands might employ a black, they were generally found only in the households of the highest levels of the court nobility. In Paris in the 1780s the fashionable Marquise de La Tour du Pin, Madame de Genlis, and all the ladies of the house of Orléans had their black *femmes de chambre*, *valets*, and pages. There were in fact so many blacks in the households of the Parisian *haut monde* that during the Revolution they provided a whole company of soldiers, commanded by the black servant of Philippe-Egalité.[90] One reason for the popularity of black domestics was therefore sheer snobbery.

But black servants had other attractions besides their social cachet. They were also popular because they could still be viewed and treated in terms of the traditional servant stereotypes, something that was no longer possible with white servants by the end of the eighteenth century. The philosophes may have worked for the abolition of slavery, and they may have found the "noble savage" a useful weapon in their attacks on the abuses of their own society. Nonetheless, like everyone else in eighteenth-century France, they regarded blacks as fundamentally lazy, stupid, and licentious—precisely the same characteristics traditionally attributed to servants.[91] Blacks were frequently compared by their masters to animals, just as servants always had been. The most common comparison was with the *singe*, or monkey, but they were also likened to numerous other household pets. One M. de la Croix, author cf the *Peinture des moeurs du siècle*, maintained that they were the successors to "parrots, greyhounds, spaniels, cats" in the affection of their mistresses.[92] And in paintings black servants were portrayed with animals long after such poses of white servants had fallen out of fashion. (See figure 7.)

Black servants were not only regarded as pets, they were also treated like them. This was especially true of the little boys dressed as blackamoors who became the indulged playthings of their female employers.[93] Even adult black servants were treated with more generosity and indulgence that white domestics. Their masters were less apt to report them for crimes (the courts were even less apt to convict them), and they were much more likely to set them up with dowries and apprenticeships and to leave them substantial legacies.[94] For in their relationships with blacks masters could still assume the patriarchal postures no longer acceptable in their dealings with their fellow Frenchmen. Blacks were, after all, genuinely a race apart. They were seen as childlike and dependent creatures needing care and indulgence. And they were thought to repay these with the traditional servant's virtues of unswerving, doglike devotion and loyalty—qualities so deplorably lacking in the self-interested white domestics of the late eighteenth century. Their loyalty is the characteristic most frequently mentioned in the commentaries on black servants. In the *Le La Bruyère des domestiques* of Mme. de Genlis, for example, a section entitled "true heroic actions by black domestics" contains innumerable stories of black servants who saved their masters' lives. Unlike white servants, who saved their masters by their wits, they did this through sheer physical courage, and they were motivated by the "gentleness, naiveté, and kindheartedness" which Mme. de Genlis saw as fundamental to the character of blacks.[95] This childlike devotion, so similar to the patriarchal stereotype of the ideal servant but so unlike the late eighteenth-century reality, made blacks popular as domestics. Their popularity was a sign of the nostalgia many masters felt for the good old days of the patriarchal household.

There was, however, another and happier side to master-servant relationships in the last years of the Old Regime. If the disappearance of the patriarchal household made servants into threatening strangers it also made them into adults, equal to their masters and deserving of respect. And if the growing distancing between master and servant reflected a new uneasiness in their relationships, it also lessened the psychological pressures that had formerly made masters ignore and stereotype their domestics. When the models and stereotypes of patriarchal society disappeared, employers could for the first time recognize their servants as individual human beings. Therefore while master-servant relationships were in general more distant and uneasy on the eve of the Revolution, at least some masters felt a new affection for their servants, an affection based not on the condescending concern of patriarchalism but instead on respect and even admiration.

The new recognition of servants as individuals is clearly visible in the letters and memoirs from the last years of the Old Regime. Mme. Roland was far from the only employer to fill her letters with references to her domestics. The teen-ager Laurette de Malboissière wrote her closest friend of the doings of her *femme de chambre*; the young wife of the Conseiller d'Albis de Belbèze wrote him about the peculations of the cook; the Comtesse de Sabran relayed to her lover her problems in finding a tutor for her son; the Duc de Bourbon entertained his mistress with an account of the clandestine marriage of two servants in his household.[96] A court beauty writing her memoirs devoted almost as much space to the doings of her domestics as she did to the state visit of Joseph II; a nobleman writing his memoirs devoted almost as much space to the amatory triumphs of his *valet de chambre* as he did to his own.[97] It was as if the elite for the first time woke up to the fact that there were servants all around them.

In these letters and memoirs servants are described not in the traditional stereotypes but instead as individuals, portrayed with accuracy and insight. We get capsule biographies of individual servants. We are told how they looked (the Comte Dufort de Cheverny's *valet* Marnier was "a man of 5′11″, of the handsomest figure that a woman could see, with the strength of an athelete"), how they talked (the Marquise de Villeneuve-Arifat noted the impressive if misused vocabulary of her grandfather's coachman, and the Baronne d'Oberkirch described the fractured French of her Alsatian maid), and how they behaved.[98] Employers like the Baronne de Gerando, who wrote a long account to a friend of her maid's unhappy marriage, displayed at least some knowledge of the private lives of their servants and some empathy with their personal problems.[99]

There was, to be sure, an amused tone to these references which suggests that condescension lurked just below the surface. In the last decades of the Old Regime most masters still undoubtedly felt superior to and contemptuous of their domestics. This contempt showed in their unthinking use of the word *valet* and other servant titles as terms of insult. The Duc de Lauzun, who disliked the American diplomat Arthur Lee, once described him as having "very much the air of a *gros palefrenier*"; the young Laurette de Malboissière found M. de St. Chamas "not worthy of being valet to M. de Choiseul"; and the Restoration essayist J. Joubert called the Devil himself a "*mauvais valet*."[100]

But in the prerevolutionary period the general contempt for the *genus* servant which such passages reveal was often modified by a genuine empathy with and affection for individual domestics. Once servants were seen as individuals, their good qualities could be recognized; once their loyalty and devotion could no longer be taken for granted, servants who displayed such qualities could be appreciated. The memoirs of especially the court nobility show that they sometimes developed genuine friendships with their servants, friendships that cut across class lines and were solidly based on mutual admiration and respect. The relationship of Mme. de La Tour du Pin with the governess who raised her was of this type, as was that of the Comte Dufort de Cheverny and his *valet*-companion Marnier. Even the relationship between the Marquis de Barthélemy and Le Tellier, the *valet de chambre* who died in exile with him during the Revolution, showed something of these qualities.[101]

The possibilities of such affection may explain an otherwise puzzling phenomenon: the fact that legacies to servants in wills rose to what was probably an all-time high in the years right before the Revolution. Table 23 shows the percentages of wills leaving legacies to servants from Toulouse and Bordeaux from 1787 to 1789. Both the corrected and uncorrected figures are substantially higher than those from the 1720s shown in table 21, and this is true of all social classes. This generosity may simply reflect the monetization of servants' work in the period; legacies may have become by the 1780s an expected supplement of servants' wages.[102] Or it may reflect the philanthropic impulse characteristic of the age; John McManners maintains that by the 1780s public opinion judged the generosity of people by the size of their legacies to domestics.[103] But these legacies may also reflect the genuine affection and appreciation many masters felt for their loyal and hard-working servants.

At times the affection of master for servant threatened to turn into idealization. Indeed during the last years of the Old Regime employers showed some danger of falling into a new sort of stereotyping of their servants opposite to that of an earlier era. Their masters' memoirs often pictured servants as Rousseauist children of nature, uneducated but intelligent, with a natural instinct for goodness uncorrupted by civilization. Such was the presentation of the *valet* Marnier by his admiring master, and such was the portrait of the governess Marguerite by Mme. de La Tour du Pin's portrait of her. Marguerite, in fact, resembled no one so much as the totally good and innocent peasant heroine of Flaubert's *Un Coeur simple*. In part such portrayals reflect a sentimentalizing of the "child of nature" common to pre-romanticism, a yearning among the nobility for natural simplicity in their overcivilized lives. Noble memoirs of the late eighteenth century show that many masters harbored fantasies of replacement and inversion similar though opposite to those of their domestics. They fantasized about what it would be like to be a servant, just as their servants dreamed of being masters, and occasionally they made their fantasies come true. Mme. de La Tour du Pin often daydreamed about being

TABLE 23

Percentage of Wills Including Legacies to Servants, by Class, 1787–89

	Toulouse		Bordeaux	
	I	II	I	II
Nobility	56.2	61.2	39.2	49.2
Middle class	25.9	61.7	25.0	54.9
Lower class	3.2	58.1	2.9	54.0
Clergy	26.0	28.6	50.0	52.9

Sources: See Bibliography, section I, B.
Note: I = percentage of legacies in total wills, and II = percentage of legacies in wills corrected to reflect patterns of servant employment.

Marguerite's daughter; when her maid went home for a visit, "I made her tell me all that she did in her village. For several days after, I imagined what I would do if I was a peasant."[104] Mme. de Genlis was so fascinated with her servants' lives that she once disguised herself as a maid and accompanied her *femme de chambre* to a village wedding, dancing with all the local lads.[105] The Duc de Lauzun disguised himself as a royal footman during his pursuit of Marie Antoinette, and the Duc de Richelieu dressed up as a *femme de chambre*, no less, to gain access to his lady-love, Mlle. de Valois.[106] These are just a few of the numerous inversion stories in nobles' memoirs of the period. They suggest a certain amount of play-acting on the part of a social group secure in its privileges, finding titillation in contact with the lower orders. But they also suggest that the fascination servants exercised on their masters was deep and real.

In the twilight of the Old Regime, as in the patriarchal period, masters' attitudes toward their servants may have helped shape their attitudes toward the lower classes as a whole. Certainly the prerevolutionary decades saw a discovery of the "people" similar to the discovery of the servant, and the elite showed the same ambiguities in its attitudes toward the people as it did toward its domestics. On the one hand, the late eighteenth century saw a growing gulf between the elite and the *menu peuple* as the traditional society of orders became a society of classes, and this gulf paralleled that between master and servant with the decline of the patriarchal household. The most marked characteristic of social thought of the period was a rise in social fear. Social theorists and government officials were obsessed with the problems of vagabondage, theft, and social disorder; they were convinced of the need to discipline the people to make them more productive.[107] These concerns had of course a basis in the realities of late-eighteenth-century French society. But they may also have grown out of the new tensions between master and servant within the household. For social theorists of the period showed a striking tendency to blame servants for the ills of French society. It was the unemployed servant who became a vagabond; it was the employed servant who was responsible for the rise in theft. Servants were even blamed for what was perceived, wrongly, as the depopulation of the French countryside and the consequent weakness of French agriculture, for domestic service was thought to draw able-bodied men away from the countryside and into unproductive idleness in towns.[108] Thus the servant was the representative of the people at their most threatening; he became the scapegoat for the social ills of France.

But there was also another side to the discovery of the people, and this too paralleled the changing attitude of the elite toward their servants in the last years of the Old Regime. The private generosity of master to servant was echoed in the public spirit of philanthropy characteristic of the age; needy servants came in for their fair share of the proposals for charities and asylums for the aged, the ill, and the unemployed which were popular at the time.[109]

And the people too were romanticized and idealized just as masters romanticized and idealized their servants, they too were seen as children of nature, sources of folklore, embodiments of the French spirit.[110]

Thus in the last years of the Old Regime the household may still have functioned as a laboratory for social attitudes. Masters may have acquired there the social fear that marked the years of the Revolution and the early nineteenth century, but they may also have discovered there, in the guise of their servants, the "people" in all their glory. The Revolution would, however, lessen the attraction of the "people"; only the social fear would remain.

6

Sexual Relationships between Master and Servant

The ideal serving-woman is faithful, ugly, and unapproachable.
—Bonacossa, *De Servis homnibus proprius et families,* quoted in Abbé Grégoire, *De la Domesticité chez les peuples anciens et modernes*

Most intimate of all the relationships between the "domestic enemies" were sexual affairs between master and servant. Such relationships are worthy of the historian's notice not only because they form an important chapter in the until recently little explored history of sexual behavior and attitudes, but also because they reflect the broader patterns of relationships within the household—and indeed in Old Regime society as a whole. For even this most intimate form of the master-servant relationship was strongly conditioned by the basic assumptions about the social positions and roles of master and servant which governed all associations between employer and domestic within the household. The relationships of the bedroom grew naturally out of those of the *antichambre*, and each affected the other. It was the fundamental premises of patriarchalism that condoned and indeed encouraged the formation of certain types of sexual relationships between master and servant—the seduction of a female servant by her male master, for example—and discouraged others. And it was the atmosphere of what we have termed pseudo-intimacy within the patriarchal household that allowed these acceptable forms of master-servant sexual relationships to flourish. And when, in the last decades of the eighteenth century, the underlying assumptions of patriarchy were challenged and relationships within the household transformed, sexual relationships between master and servant changed too. Revelations of the "secrets of the alcove," as French specialists in *petite-histoire* like to put it, can therefore show us a great deal about master-servant relationships in general.

The Psychology of Sexual Relationships between Male Masters and Female Servants

The most common type of sexual relationship between master and servant was of course that between a male employer and his female domestic. Just how common such relationships were is impossible to say, but all evidence suggests that they were widespread. The major source of information on illicit sexual activity during the ancien régime is the *déclarations de grossesse*, and in every sample of *déclarations* studied by historians a fairly substantial proportion of the women (ranging from a low of 3.6 percent in my sample from Provence for 1750–89 to the high of 36 percent which Depauw found in Nantes in 1737–46)[1] were female servants who stated that they had been made pregnant by their masters. These figures, substantial as they are, probably represent only a small proportion of all master-servant sexual encounters. Many masters who seduced their servants were probably not identified as such in the *déclarations*, and therefore escape our notice. Many doubtless persuaded their servants either to make a false *déclaration* blaming a fellow servant or other lower-class type for their plight, or to conceal or terminate their pregnancy and make no *déclaration* at all. These too would escape our samples. And many servants may have had intercourse with their employers without becoming pregnant, or may have had sexual encounters with their masters that took forms other than completed coitus. Lawrence Stone's well-documented explorations of the sexual habits of English gentlemen show that, in their sexual contacts with female servants, such men often preferred, because of fears of venereal disease or emotional involvement, to stop short of full intercourse and content themselves with fondlings, gropings, and mutual masturbation.[2] There is no reason to believe that the French *gentilhomme* behaved any differently; in fact, the phrase "he wanted to play with me," found frequently in the *déclarations*, probably denotes this kind of behavior. All of these possibilities suggest that master-servant seductions that eventually resulted in a *déclaration* formed only a small proportion of the sexual encounters between masters and servants during the Old Regime. It seems probable that most female servants, unless they spent all of their working lives in exclusively female households, experienced some form of sexual harassment by their masters at one point or another in their careers.

Why were master-servant sexual relationships so widespread? Why did masters pursue their servants so assiduously? And why did servants so often give in to their masters' demands? Of these questions the last is probably the easiest to answer. As we have seen in chapter 3, *servantes* sometimes entered into sexual relationships with their masters from motives of loneliness, sexual frustration, and even genuine affection. But more often they were spurred by self-interest: by promises of care or money if they gave in, by threats of withheld salaries and dismissal if they did not. Living under the same roof as her master, a servant had nowhere to hide if he was bent on her seduction. She was all too easily cornered on her daily rounds or attacked as she slept. Given the immense and inescapable economic, physical, and psychological pressures that masters could bring to bear on their employees, it is not surprising that most *servantes* felt as Thérèse Roux, a farm servant, did. She stated in her *déclaration* that she had at first resisted the propositions of her employer, Louis Seste, but finally gave in to what seemed to her to be inevitable: "since he was my master I was obliged to consent."[3]

Yet if a *servante* was "obliged to consent" to her seduction, her master was not obliged to seduce her. Why so many masters did so is more difficult to answer. In a society like that of Old Regime France, where both arranged marriages and the double standard flourished, it was doubtless inevitable that upper-class men would indulge in pre- and extramarital sexual affairs. And it was only slightly less inevitable that the bulk of these affairs would be with women of inferior social status. A gentleman could not seduce an unmarried girl of his own class without ruining her marriage prospects, and he could not sleep with the wife of a friend without challenging the legitimacy of families and the lawful descent of property. The former prohibition seems to have been effective: in Old Regime France unmarried upper-class girls were rarely seduced by their social equals. Adulterous relationships were more common, especially at the highest levels of the court nobility, where one gathers from the memoirs of noble Don Juans like the Duc de Lauzun and the Comte Dufort de Cheverny that any married woman was fair game.[4] But in the more closely knit and moralistic society of the provincial robe nobility even such adulterous relationships were rare. This left for the sexual adventures of gentlemen only lower-class women: kept mistresses installed in rooms in town; textile workers or street peddlers encountered by chance, who, as the *déclarations de grossesse* show, could be persuaded to have sex by promises of food or money; habitual prostitutes—and the household *servante*.

Among these types of women the servant had certain clear advantages. She was likely to be cheaper than the kept mistress, more certain than the chance pickup, and the less disease-ridden than the prostitute. The servant was *there*, like Mount Everest: under his eye every day, she was bound to catch her master's notice. If she had no other physical attractions (and it is hard to imagine that these ill-nourished country girls did), she usually at least had the bloom of youth, attractive no doubt in a period when the posturing nymphets of Greuze were worshiped. For as we saw in chapter 3, most servant girls seduced by their masters were in their late teens and early twenties. The servant also had the appeal of what has been called "the eroticism of inequality"[5]—the attractions of helplessness and dependency. That many men find such qualities erotically appealing is suggested by the large numbers who have affairs with women dependent upon them: the bosses who sleep with their secretaries, the professors who seduce their female students. Finally, servants had another attraction, probably the most important of all: they were convenient and easy to seduce, eaily cornered as they went about their work, easily pressured by promises or threats.

Perhaps these simple factors are all we need to explain the majority of master-servant seductions. Yet so widespread were such relationships and so automatic was the impulse to seduce one's servant that we cannot help but suspect that these obvious explanations are inadequate, and that sexual attractions of servants stemmed from factors deeply rooted in their masters' psyches. Isolating these factors is not an easy task. Conventional psychological theories offer little help, for few psychologists have explored the question. Historians too have generally ignored it, and those few who have treated it have dealt with nineteenth-century situations which have little relevance for earlier periods. A good example is Leonore Davidoff's ingenious reading of the sexual obsession of English Victorian gentleman Arthur Joseph Munby with his female servants as stemming from his association of them with the forbidden delights of dirt and disorder.[6] But it is hard to imagine that in seventeenth-century households, whose standard of cleanliness fell deplorably short of those espoused by Mrs. Beeton, dirt would have had such an aura of the forbidden as to make it the root of sexual obsessions.

It seems probable that the clues to masters' sexual interest in their servants during the Old Regime can be found in the way the household functioned *in that period*. Here two possible explanations emerge. One grows out of the longstanding tradition that made sexual relationships between master and servant seem "natural" and socially acceptable: the tradition that the enjoyment of the sexual favors of his female domestics was part of the privileges of a patriarch. The belief that a master had the right to exploit his servants sexually was as old as domestic service itself, and like the occupation it had its origins in ancient Greece and Rome. In the ancient world household slaves had no control over their own sexuality. Instead, their sexual favors were controlled by their masters, just as their labor was. Both formed a part of the owner's property rights in his slave. Masters regularly took the female slaves as concubines, and the bastard children of these unions were usually acknowledged by their fathers and raised within his household. Slaves could not bring their masters to court for rape, but owners could sue anyone who raped or seduced their slaves. And slaves of course could not marry without their masters' permission.[7]

The tradition that a master had rights over the sexuality of his servants persisted through the coming of Christianity and the transformation of the slavery of the ancient world into the domestic service of the Middle Ages. Where slavery itself remained, as in fourteenth-century Florence, masters retained their legal rights of access to the sexual favors of female servants, and slaves could not marry without their masters' permission.[8] Where it died out, as in the feudal West, masters gradually lost their legal rights over the sexuality of their domestics, but they continued to behave as though they had not. In medieval France the *droit de seigneur* may have been largely a myth, but the seduction of female servants and other dependent women by their lords was standard practice. In the medieval *domus* master-servant sexual relationships were often self-perpetuating. The bastard offspring of such encounters were raised in the household, and the women among them became what Georges Duby has described as "a kind of pleasure reserve": they in their turn worked as servants and were available for seduction by the young knights of the *domus*.[9]

Even as late as the sixteenth century the legal and popular traditions of a master's right to control the sexuality of his underlings persisted. By a French law of 1567 servants could not marry without their masters' permission, and legally any child of a female servant conceived while she was in her employer's household was automatically considered the offspring of the master unless he could prove otherwise.[10] This law was similar to the legal custom that regarded any child borne by a married woman as the issue of her husband. Both had their roots in the notion of the right of a patriarch to control access to the sexual favors of the women of his household.

Thus there was by the Old Regime a long and quasi-legal tradition of the sexual exploitation of female servants by their masters, a tradition that had its ultimate foundation in the supposed property rights of a master over the bodies of his servants. But this tradition was not without its ambiguities. For by the late seventeenth century there had grown up around the patriarchal household an elaborate ideology whose basic tenets denied a master the right to exploit his servants sexually. In traditional theories of patriarchy, a master's rights over his servants supposedly rested on his performance of certain duties, among the most important of which was the moral supervision of the members of the household. Obviously masters who seduced their servants were not acting as model patriarchs. Indeed, in the light of the familial rhetoric that pervaded the discussions of patriarchy, such masters committed a sin equivalent to incest. It was to this tradition of patriarchal duty that Richardson's Pamela, the most famous seduced servant of the eighteenth century, appealed when she fought off her master's assaults on her virtue. When Mr. B. demanded, "Do you know whom you speak to?" she replied, "Yes I do sir, too well! Well may I forget that I am your servant when you forget what belongs to a master."[11]

Thus on the question of sex between master and servant, patriarchal theory was paradoxical. A patriarch had a clear right to the sexual favors of his servants, but he also had an equally clear duty to refrain from exercising that right. But as we argued in the last chapter, patriarchal theory was generally little more than an ideological veil drawn over the naked reality of a relationship based solely on power. Most masters forgot their inconvenient "duty" and exercised their traditional "right" at will.

The notion that masters had a right to the sexual favors of their servants encouraged sexual relationships between them in two ways. First of all, it provided an excuse for such relationships: they were acceptable because they had always been so. Second, it heightened the awareness of both parties of each other as sexual objects. For if both master and maid have in the back of their minds from the day of her hiring the possibility of an eventual sexual relationship between them, they doubtless act toward each other in ways which help make the possibility a reality.

Similar effects stemmed from another psychological factor that promoted sexual relationships between master and servant: the widespread popular image of the lusty servant. Masters seem to have been convinced that domestics of both sexes were uncontrollably lusty, even more so than other lower-class types, and that their sex lives were a steady series of guiltless gratifications of their base desires.

This is how servants are inevitably portrayed in the literature of the Old Regime. When, for example, the sixteenth-century poet Christophe de Bordeaux wrote his "Le Varlet à louer à tout faire," and "La Chambrière à louer à tout faire," verses that supposedly captured the thoughts and feelings of typical male and female domestics, he had them boast about their amatory accomplishments as proudly as they detailed their skills in the kitchen and *antichambre*. The *servante* announced that she could take her mistress' place in the master's bed and do

> Aussi bien qu'elle ce qu'il fault,
> Soit pour coucher en bas, en haut,
> Au grand lict . . . .

and the valet was even more frank. He bragged of being a:

> Grand despuceleur des nourrices
> Ramonneur de bas et de haut
> Femelles qui ont le cul chaut
> Je les guaris avec froide glace.[12]

Similarly outspoken servants populated the popular comedies of the seventeenth and eighteenth centuries. Plays are full of the love affairs of servants, which are usually deliberately contrasted with those of their masters. Not for servants were the conflicts between love and honor, inclination and interest, which bedeviled their betters. The wooings of servants were straightforward rather than circumlocutory, lewd rather than courtly, and they ended in sexual gratification rather than marriage.[13] On the stage, the world below stairs was, as Michel Lemain, one of the most perceptive commentators on French drama, put it, "a world of liberated sexuality,"[14] and servants were creatures of unbridled lust and untrammeled libido, almost pagan in their instinctual enjoyment of the pleasures of the flesh.

Lemain suggests that the image of the lusty servant arose from the necessity in plays of what he calls "doubles." In real life, people are mixtures of good and bad characteristics, but, Lemain maintains, in a drama the single mixed personality is often split in two, creating *two* characters, one embodying all the good and the other the evil. The stark contrast between the two creates the dramatic tension necessary for the play to succeed on the stage. Lemain argues that in plays servants embodied the "bad" characteristics denied to their noble masters. Masters were all conscience and honor, while servants were pleasures easily and guiltlessly gratified. The lusty servant in plays therefore symbolized the instinctual life which his master had to deny himself in order to remain a gentleman.[15]

There is much to suggest that servants played the same role for their masters in real life. Certainly the image of the sexually promiscuous domestic is found as frequently in memoirs and advice books as it is upon the stage. Domestic manuals take the lustiness of servants for granted. "Finding [sexual] modesty in a lackey," one states, "is like finding the fruits of autumn in the spring. . . . It appears that the name of 'modesty' and that of 'lackey' are so contrary that as soon as a young man puts on livery, he must cease to be modest."[16] Manuals abound with suggestions of how masters might control this lustiness: by keeping male and female servants apart as much as possible, by seeing that they slept in separate beds, and above all, by setting them a good example.[17]

The image of the lusty servant had of course a certain basis in fact. The difficulties servants faced in marrying and the intimacies of life below stairs did tend to encourage illicit sex among them, as shown in chapter 3. But so pervasive was the association of servants with unbridled sexuality that this seems inadequate to account for it. Instead I think that a psychological phenomenon similar to Lemain's notion of "doubles" was at work. The origins of the image of the lusty servant may lie in masters' association of servants with the darker side of their own sexual impulses. This association arose because servants were witnesses to and accomplices in the most private and intimate details of their masters' lives. Servants made their masters' beds, washed their soiled linen, and emptied their slop pails. Servants, even those of the opposite sex, saw their masters and mistresses naked, as the famous example of Mme. du Châtelet bathing in front of her lackey suggests. Domestics performed the most intimate bodily services for their employers. Lackeys laced their mistresses into their stays, and maids combed through their masters' hair for fleas and lice. Servants frequently saw their masters having sex, and not simply because the sharing of a room or even a bed with their masters made this unavoidable. Servants were at times deliberately summoned to watch. The *fille de service* of the newlywed wife of the sixteenth-century apothecary Felix Platter was called in to see her mistress enjoying the privileges of the wedded state, and the seventeenth-century Marquis de Combalet was so proud of his sexual endowments that he frequently summoned his domestics to watch him make love to his wife.[18]

Often servants were not only witnesses but also accomplices in their employers' sexual adventures. Every Old Regime Don Juan knew that the first and most important step in the seduction of a married noblewoman was the bribing of her *suisse* and her *femme de chambre*: the former so that he could have easy access to the lady's *hôtel* at all hours, the latter so that she could be relied on to carry messages, stand guard over the bedroom door, and, if necessary, pretend that she rather than her mistress was the object of his attentions. In his seduction of his first great love, Mme. de Stainville, the Duc de Lauzun followed the classic pattern, bribing the *suisse* to leave open a small gate near the stables, and setting the *femme de chambre* to guard the bedroom door and warn the couple if Madame's husband should approach.[19] Servants also often served as procuresses and pimps for their masters and mistresses. If, for example, the Comte Dufort de Cheverny wanted to spend a quiet evening in female company he had only to give the word—and ten *louis d'or*—to his invaluable servant Marnier, "the most intelligent man possible," to find, when he left the theater that night, a discreet hired house at his disposal, with a supper all laid out and a complaisant young woman waiting. Both the supper and the woman were exactly to the Comte's taste.[20]

Sometimes servants' involvement in their masters' sexual lives went so far as to include the sharing of a sexual partner. Stories of noblemen who surprised their mistresses in the arms of their lackeys are legion, as are those of noblewomen who found their lovers courting their maids.[21] At times these cross-class triangles created painful jealousies. A Toulousan *servante*, Jeanne Bellegarde, poisoned her mistress, the Dame de Lesmitoire, in a quarrel over the favors of their joint lover, the noble François de Timbourne de Montjoie.[22] But more often all parties accepted the situation as inevitable. In the early seventeenth century Mme. de Cornuel had an affair with the Marquis de Sourdis, who amused himself with her maid while he waited in the *antichambre* for Madame to receive him. When the maid eventually gave birth to a son, Mme. de Cornuel had the child raised in her household, "because," as she cheerfully explained, "he was produced in my service."[23]

Thus servants were bound up in the most intimate moments of their masters' lives to a degree that is hard for us to comprehend. This helped to encourage sexual relationships between master and servant in two ways. First of all, the intimate tasks that domestics performed for their employers were often so charged with erotic overtones that they aroused the sexual appetites of both parties. Of course we must be careful here not to project the standards of our own culture back into an earlier one. What would seem sexually charged to us did not necessarily appear so to a society with different standards of privacy, modesty, and shame. Public nakedness, for example, was taken much more lightly in the sixteenth and seventeenth centuries than it is today. It was shameful only to expose the body in the presence of one's superiors; to do so in front of one's inferiors was, on the contrary, a mark of special favor.[24] But it is hard to believe that even in a society with different standards the physical intimacies of the type that occurred between master and servant were completely without erotic overtones. Certainly the act of delousing, to take just one example, had been a standard preliminary to making love ever since the Middle Ages.[25] In the previously quoted boast of the *Varlet à tout faire* that he was a "grand despuceleur des nourrices," the play on the word *despuceleur*, which meant both "delousing" and "deflowering," suggests the close association of the act with sex in the public mind (see figure 8). And Lawrence Stone's researches indicate that at least one English master, Samuel Pepys, took advantage of the intimacy of delousing to make advances to his female servants.[26] It is probable that the other intimate tasks that servants performed were invested with erotic invitation as well. For example, Restif de la Bretonne, surely an expert in eroticism, maintained that the notorious Comtesse du Barry was born of an affair between a noblewoman and her lackey, first consummated when the noble lady summoned her servant to help undo her stays.[27]

Thus the intimate nature of servants' tasks helped promote master-servant sexual relationships by creating erotically arousing situations. But it also contributed to sexual relationships within the household in another way. For it was the intimacy of daily contacts between master and servant which created and reinforced in the minds of employers the image of the lusty servant. Because of servants' close association with the most private and "shameful" aspects of their lives, masters projected onto them their own worst impulses. The resulting image of the promiscuous domestic became something of a self-fulfilling prophecy. It encouraged the master-servant affairs both by heightening employers' awareness of their servants as sexual objects and by providing excuses for masters who wished to seduce their servants, since they could easily convince themselves that their servants welcomed such seduction. In these ways the image of the lusty servant functioned similarly to the tradition of the sexual exploitation of domestics discussed earlier. Both combined to create a situation in which the collective erotic imagination of the master classes was haunted by images of its domestics.[28] It is not surprising then that they so frequently seduced them.

Sexual Relationships between Male Masters and Female Servants

While sexual relationships between master and servant shared a common psychological background, they were not all alike. From the information about them in memoirs and *déclarations de grossesse,* it is possible to distin-

FIGURE 8. Nicolas Lancret, *La Chercheuse de puces, ou La Cuisinière.* Reproduced by permission of the Trustees of the Wallace Collection, London.

The image of the lusty servant. A cook, her legs apart, examines her bodice for fleas. Such tasks of bodily grooming were standard preliminaries to sex in the seventeenth and eighteenth centuries.

guish five different patterns of master-servant sex. Three of these involved a male master and a female servant. The other two were relationships of a female mistress and her male servant and homosexual relationships between employers and domestics of either sex.

The first of the male master–female servant relationships, in the chronological order of the master's life at least, was the sexual initiation of a young man of the elite by a female domestic in his father's household. The memoirs of noblemen that discuss such matters almost always tell of a sexual initiation by a female servant at an early age—thirteen or fourteen, or even, in some cases, as early as nine or ten. So typical were such experiences, in fact, that when an anonymous author decided to concoct the fake memoirs of the "Comte de Bonneval" he included a scene of the young man's introduction to sex by a *fille de lingerie* as a matter of course.[29] And lest it be thought that such seductions were mere literary conventions, we should note that a *servante* was hanged in eighteenth-century Paris for "seducing" and "communicating a venereal disease" to the ten-year-old son of her master.[30]

The extremely early ages of such seductions suggest that these relationships show a reversal of the usual pattern of master-servant sex: in this instance the servant was the aggressor and the master the largely innocent victim. These relationships seem to have been outgrowths of the sexual teasing to which adults regularly subjected children in the seventeenth and early eighteenth centuries. The taunting and abuse endured by the young Louis XIII, whose genitals were caressed by his ladies-in-waiting, and who was encouraged by them to play sexually with himself, his younger sister, and the adult serving women at court, were probably more typical of the experiences of the young men of the French elite than historians have been willing to believe.[31] We know of at least one other victim of such games, Cardinal de Bernis, who wrote a solemn warning about them to parents: "Nothing is so dangerous for morals and perhaps for health than to leave children too long under the care of *femmes de chambre*. . . . I would add that the wisest among them are not always the least dangerous. One dares with a child what one would be ashamed to risk with a young man.[32]

As the boy grew into his teens, these games began to take the form of invitations to sexual intercourse. But the pattern of servant as the aggressor remained, as the Duc de Lauzun's account of his experience as fourteen-year-old with Mlle. Julie, *femme de chambre* of the Duchesse de Gramont, suggests:

> At this time she (the Duchesse) brought me to Menais, to the household of Mme. de Pompadour. Mlle. Julie, *femme de chambre*, who had all her confidence . . . believed that what her mistress kept for herself suited her well also, and destined for me the honor of being initiated into worldly matters by her. She gave me many caresses and provocations [which were] useless, because I was very innocent. One day she put my hand on her throat. My whole body burned for several hours afterward, but I did not advance any further.[33]

The Comte Alexandre de Tilly tells a similar story of an abortive sexual initiation, which occurred at the early age of nine:

> I was nine years old, and my father saw that I was too susceptible to the robust charms of a *femme de charge* named Mme. Roher, whose caresses, pro-

voking my desires, made him suspect my innocence. He wanted to clear everything up, and ordered her to encourage me. I soon came, by pure instinct I believe, to beg her to receive me in the modest alcove where [she slept]. . . . Mounting to the distant room which would become the theater of my precocious felicities, I proposed to receive a lesson which I was scarcely able to render when my father entered quickly by another door armed with a hunting crop. He beat me severely . . . I felt that there had been a plot against me, and this hurt my proud and generous character.[34]

In both these stories we sense uneasiness below the surface bravado. Both young men were exposed to situations and emotions that they simply could not handle, and they knew it. Both got little help from the adults around them. The intervention of Tilly's father, for example (this was one of the few times he paid any attention to his son), obviously did more harm than good. We sense that he staged the scene more for his own amusement than for the edification of his son. Finally, both boys sensed that they were being manipulated, used as playthings, by adults, and both consciously or unconsciously resented this.

For the young men's families the major concern posed by such relationships seems to have been the fear that an unscrupulous servant could manipulate the boy, helpless in the throes of his first love, into an unsuitable marriage. This situation was sketched in the apocryphal memoirs of the "Comte de Bonneval": the seduced thirteen-year-old wanted to marry his mistress, but his mother talked him out of it.[35] It was to guard against such *mésalliances* that the famous Ordinance of Blois of 1579 was promulgated, outlawing the marriage of minors without their parents' consent. This ruling was reinforced by a royal ordinance of 1730 which defined the seduction of a minor child under twenty-five, male or female, by a household servant, for the purpose of luring him or her into an unsuitable marriage, as the crime of *rapt de séduction,* punishable by death.[36]

For the modern historian the greatest danger of such relationships lies in the psychological damage they could do to the young men involved. It is probable that many men who were sexually abused as children had difficulty forming normal heterosexual relationships as adults. Certainly Cardinal de Bernis did, although admittedly his position as a churchman may also have been an inhibiting factor. At any rate, Bernis grew up to be a notorious *voyeur*, best known for watching Casanova service two nuns simultaneously in the courtyard of a Venetian convent.[37] It also seems probable that the teen-agers who suffered through such anxious sexual initiations developed unconscious desires for revenge which poisoned their later relationships with women, especially with women servants. This was apparently true of Lauzun and Tilly at least. Both grew up to be archtypical Don Juans, manipulators of women, whose memoirs are endless catalogs of loveless, heartless seductions. Both were especially nasty in their encounters with female servants. Tilly, for example, once seduced the maid of his former mistress simply to have an excuse to continue to visit the household and see the real object of his pursuit, his mistress's niece. He wrote smugly of this episode: "I put all my effort into corrupting one of her women, and I succeeded."[38]

After their uncomfortable sexual initiations upper-class young men continued to enjoy the sexual favors of female servants, especially while they remained unmarried. In my sample of *déclarations de grossesse* from Provence, 58.8 percent of the master-servant relationships from 1727 to 1749 and 42.0 percent of those from 1750 to 1789 involved young men (sons, nephews, etc.) of the houschold. But as the youths grew into their teens and twenties, the balance of power in these relationships shifted, and the female servant abandoned her unaccustomed role of aggressor to take up her more usual stance as victim. One example is eighteen-year-old Thérèse Cavaillon, *servante* to the *receveur des gabelles* in Berre, who was raped at knifepoint by the son of the house.[39] Such incidents suggest in the households of seventeenth- and early-eighteenth-century France, master-servant sexual exploitation was a self-perpetuating syndrome, which drew generation after generation into a (truly) vicious circle of abuse. Female servants got revenge for the misuse they suffered through the exploitation of the children of the household, and these exploited children grew up to misuse servants in their turn.

For the adult male master, female servants filled two sexual roles. One was that of *servante-maîtresse*, or servant-mistress. She was precisely what her name suggests: a domestic who was the long-term mistress of her employer, and more or less openly acknowledged as such. The servant-mistress was most common among single men. She was the obvious companion of the scion of a robe family waiting to complete his legal studies before marrying, and of the wealthy widower who had suffered through one arranged marriage and could not stomach a second. She was especially likely to be found in the countryside, as the mistress of the cadet of a petty noble family too poor to marry off any son but the eldest.[40] In such households the servant-mistress was a wife in everything but name. She not only shared her master's bed and bore his children (which he often acknowledged), but also ran the household and supervised the other servants, if any.

The servant-mistress seems to have been tolerated by her master's family, as long as she did not attempt to alienate his affection from them, or, worse yet, try to marry into the family herself. It was, for example, the former situation that aroused the ire of the Marquise de Ferrières against Mlle. Guignard, the servant-mistress of her father-in-law. The Marquise noted indignantly in her memoirs that Mlle. Guignard "looked only to blacken us in the mind of her master by bearing a thousand tales, true and false, against us. This woman was a troublemaker (*méchante*) and had similarly aroused my father-in-law against his daughter, whose *femme de chambre* she had been."[41]

Even more likely to cause family tensions was the prospect of a marriage between master and servant-mistress. If the man in question was a minor son of the house, below the age at which he could marry without his parents' consent, the match could of course easily be blocked. In such cases it was apparently the fact that the woman was the young man's *servant*, rather than the fact that she was his *mistress*, which parents found objectionable. At any rate, when the father and mother of Antoine Demortain petitioned the church court to dissolve his engagement to Anne Marie Ghislain, they gave as their reason that she "was a *servante* in the household of the petitioners, at a yearly wage of twelve *écus*, taking care of the cows and going to sell in the market at Quesnoy like other *servantes*. . . . her father is a *journalier* and her sisters and relatives are of the same occupation. . . . Because of this difference of condition the petitioners never dreamed that their son wished to marry a girl of this type."[42]

If, however, the man in question had reached his majority—if he were an elderly widower, for instance—relatives could do little to prevent the match. Widowers did sometimes marry their servants: Sr. Charles Cadithon, Bordelais widower and *cabaretier*, married his servant Marie Surin in 1778, for example.[43] Though not uncommon, such marriages nevertheless met with widespread social disapproval. The memoirs of the Baronne d'Oberkirch record an anecdote that illustrates this. The Duchesse de Bourbon, while doing charity visiting, met an old man, "a sort of King Lear, who complained harshly about his daughters. She gave him money and ended by asking: 'Have you done any wrong to your children? Consult your conscience.' 'No, madame, they have nothing to reproach me for, apart from having married my servant.' 'Isn't that enough?' she answered impatiently. 'You needn't say anything more.' "[44]

Because of such disapproval, few servant-mistresses could hope to regularize their position through marriage. Nonetheless they could expect other, often substantial, rewards. Masters usually felt a duty to "take care of" a servant-mistress "for the rest of her days," as M. François promised his maid Marguerite Donnat when he propositioned her.[45] Such care might take the form of gifts of money, clothing, or jewelry, in the case of widowers often those belonging to their late wives. (One M. Caillol, eager to make his laundress, Marguerite Guierand, his mistress, jumped the gun a bit and gave her his wife's clothing before the sick woman had actually died).[46] Servant-mistresses were also provided for by legacies in their masters' wills. Pierre de Lavaissière, an *écuyer* living in Bordeaux, left land and a house in the country to Françoise Brune "who lives at present in my service," and 6,000 livres to Françoise's (and probably his) bastard daughter Jeanne "to give her an education and favor her establishment" in life.[47] Finally, the future of a servant-mistress might be assured through an arranged marriage with a fellow servant or other lower-class dependent of the master. Such matches usually carried the understanding that the master would support the couple financially and would of course continue to have access to his mistress.[48] The Seigneur de

Haucourt even tried to inveigle his nineteen-year-old nephew into such a match, first getting the youth drunk and then calling in a notary to witness the marriage contract. This marriage was, however, annulled by the church.[49]

While it was fairly common for a bachelor or widower to take a servant-mistress, it was quite unlikely that a married man would do so. This had not always been true. From ancient Greece down through the sixteenth century, married men lived openly with servant concubines and raised their bastard children along with their legitimate families. The sixteenth-century nobleman, Géri de Rabutin, great-grandfather of Mme. de Sévigné, kept an acknowledged servant-mistress, and the Sieur de Gouberville, a sixteenth-century Norman *gentilhomme campagnard*, was raised in a household that included his father's four bastards.[50] But the Reformation and Counter-Reformation, with their emphasis on the conjugal bond and their repression of sexual activity outside its limits, made the flaunting of a servant-mistress by a married man unacceptable.[51] From the seventeenth century on, husbands might still seduce their servants, but they could not live openly with a servant-mistress. What wives apparently found objectionable in these relationships was not the adultery itself, but rather the mistress's public usurpation of honors and attentions that should belong to the lawful spouse. Wives might tolerate a series of casual flirtations with servant-girls who were easily dismissed. But they ran to the church courts to demand separations if their husbands behaved like the Sieur de Henin, who, when his beloved *servante* Marguerite fell ill, had his bed moved into her room and cared for her himself, even emptying the chamber pot; or like Joseph Lecherq, who allowed his *servante* Marguerite to eat at the family table and showed his affection for her by "serving her the best cuts."[52] These two erring husbands at least confined their display of affection within the household. But the Sieur de Biseau, madly in love with his servant, " 'showed her off in front of the whole parish, walking with her, accompanying her to Mass, giving her his arm.' "[53] In this case not just de Biseau's wronged wife but also his neighbors complained to the church court; the open flaunting of a servant-mistress had created a public scandal.

It was this public disapproval which put an end to the acknowledged servant-mistress for married men from the seventeenth century on. Husbands of course continued to seduce the household servants, but now they tried to keep these exploits from public knowledge. If a man wanted a long-time relationship with his servant, he usually removed her from the household and installed her in a room in town which he could discreetly visit. This is what Sr. Louis Cloche did with his servant Suzanne Laugière in a relationship that lasted for nine months.[54] More typically, however, married men contented themselves with short-term affairs, seducing their servants and sleeping with them until either the servant became pregnant, or the wife discovered what was going on, or both happened at once, as was usually the case.[55] When any of the above occurred, the servant was inevitably fired, and the master usually wasted little time in regrets before setting his sights on her replacement.

This sort of casual short-term seduction forms the third and final category of male master-female servant sexual affairs, a category for which I have borrowed the French phrase "ancillary amours."

The ancillary amour was by no means confined to married men; the unmarried who wished to avoid the economic, social, and emotional burdens of a servant-mistress also made use of it. Therefore it was undoubtedly the most common form of sexual relationship between master and servant.

But common as it was, it was by no means inevitable. Evidence from the *déclarations* suggests that it was more likely to occur in some types of households than in others. The major determinants seem to have been household size and location. These are summarized for the "ancillary amours" in my sample of *déclarations* from eighteenth-century Provence in tables 24 and 25.[56]

Table 24 shows that the ancillary amour was more common in rural areas, and that this became increasingly true as the eighteenth century progressed. Most women servants were employed in urban areas, yet even in the first half of the eighteenth century towns contributed only 63 percent of the master-servant seductions. And in the last half of the eighteenth century almost three-fourths of the cases occurred in the countryside.[57] As table 25 shows, certain types of households were more conducive to the ancillary amour than others. Servants employed in the small households of the bourgeoisie and artisanate were more likely to be the victims of their masters' sexual approaches than were servants in the hôtels of the nobility. Noble masters contributed relatively few of our cases—only 8.8 percent of the cases of master-servant sex in our sample of *déclarations* from Provence during 1727–49. This was much lower than we would expect, given the high proportion of female servants employed by the nobility. I have no accurate figures for Aix, but in Toulouse, a city much like Aix in social makeup, in 1750 the nobility employed 18.6 percent of all female servants. Conversely, lower-class households in Tou-

TABLE 24

Master-Servant Sexual Relationships, by Location, Provence, 1727–89 (in %)

	1727–49	1750–89
Rural	37.0%	74.0%
Urban	62.9	26.0
N	35	50

Sources: See Bibliography, section I, C.

TABLE 25

Master-Servant Sexual Relationships, by Type of Household, Provence, 1727–89 (in %)

Household	1727–49	1750–89
Noble	8.8	13.7
Middle class	50.0	49.0
Lower class	41.2	37.3
N	34	51

Sources: See Bibliography, section I, C.

louse employed only 16 percent of all female servants. Yet in Aix lower-class households contributed 41.2 percent of all master-servant seductions.[58]

Two factors seem to lie behind these patterns: the extreme physical vulnerability of servants in small and/or rural households, and the lack of alternative sexual outlets for their masters. The female farm servant on an isolated *bastide* was obviously at her master's mercy. So too was the lone *servante* in a bourgeois or artisan household, forced to sleep on the kitchen hearth or on a *lit de domestique* outside her master's room. In large noble households, by contrast, servants were more likely to have their own quarters and female servants came into contact with their employers relatively rarely. Also, in large households the presence of male domestics provided sexual competition for masters, and the other female servants provided counsel and advice to the object of their attentions. The lone *servante* in a modest household lacked these protections: she was constantly in her master's company, and she had to deal with his advances alone.

Thus the extreme vulnerability of the lone *servante* in small and rural households seems to have been an important factor in the pattern of incidence of the ancillary amour. But probably equally important were the sexual alternatives available to masters. A townsman could take his pick of shopgirl and *comédienne*, textile worker and tavern wench, street peddler and prostitute, but these sexual alternatives to the *servante* were scarce in the countryside. Similarly, noblemen had the money and leisure time to pursue any lower-class woman they wished. And the court nobility also apparently had the option of adulterous relationships with the wives of their friends and acquaintances. But if an artisan or a bourgeois wanted an extramarital fling, his servant was not just his obvious choice but often his only one.

These patterns of the incidence of master-servant sexual relationships are strikingly similar to the patterns of master-slave miscegenation in the antebellum American South. It was on small rural plantations, where slaves lived in the same house as their owner and the owner had few sexual outlets other than his slave women, that master-servant sexual relationships were most likely to take place.[59] But while master-servant sexual relationships may have been more likely in some households than in others, no female servant was really immune from sexual harassment by her master, just as no southern slave woman was immune from the white man's sexual attentions. In both these patriarchal societies, the sexual exploitation of dependent women revealed the hollowness of patriarchal pronouncements about the reciprocity of rights and duties between master and servant, master and slave. In both societies patriarchal relationships were based in reality not on reciprocity but on naked power, and in both societies the female servant, doubly vulnerable because of her status and her sex, was this power's most likely victim.

Sexual Relationships between Mistress and Male Servant

While seduction of a female servant by her master was the most widespread type of sexual relationship between masters and servants, obviously it was not the only possibility. There were also cases of liaisons between a mistress and her male domestic. These relationships were not the simple obverse of the seduction of a maid by her master. In both law and public opinion the two situations were poles apart. A male master had what amounted to a quasi-legal right to the sexual favors of his female servants; socially he suffered few ill-effects if his amorous activities became known. By contrast, sexual relationships between mistress and man were illegal and might carry the death penalty for the servant involved. And any woman rumored to sleep with her male domestics could have her reputation ruined for life. The different way in which the two relationships were regarded is perhaps best epitomized in the royal ordinance of 1730 on *rapt de séduction*. This ordinance made it illegal for a female servant to marry her young master, but it prohibited both marriage *and* sexual relationships between a male servant and the daughter of the house.[60]

More lay behind this distinction than the simple fact that in a society with a double standard respectable women were expected to be chaste while respectable men were not. The most basic notions of the proper functioning of a patriarchal society were involved. Male master–female servant sexual relationships were treated so leniently they offered what was in reality a confirmation of one of the most basic principles of patriarchy: the power of a master over the bodies and souls of his servants. Sexual relationships between mistress and man, by contrast, constituted a flagrant betrayal of patriarchy's most sacred precepts. In patriarchal theory women were regarded as the property of their fathers or husbands, and their chastity was thus a family asset. And in patriarchal theory the first duty of a loyal servant was to guard his masters' property. A servant who seduced his master's wife or daughter therefore was doubly disloyal, robbing his master of the very thing he was to guard. These attitudes were probably summed up best by Saint-Preux, the low-born tutor in Rousseau's *La Nouvelle Héloise*. When he realized that he was falling in love with his employer's daughter Julie, he wrote to her:

> What am I really to your father . . . ? A mercenary, a man paid by him, a kind of *valet*; and he has for my part, to guarantee his confidence, and for the security of that which belongs to him, my tacit word. . . . Now, what is more precious to a father than his only daughter . . . ? [If I seduced her] would I not seem to such a master a scoundrel who tramples on the most sacred rights, a traitor, a domestic seducer whom the law very justly condemns to death?[61]

Death was indeed the penalty faced by a domestic seducer. In the *coutume de Bordeaux* and other law codes of the Old Regime, the rape of his master's daughter by a male servant was classified as *vol domestique*, and it carried the same penalty, death by hanging.[62]

Perhaps because of this, cases of seduction of the daughter of the house by a male servant were relatively rare. I found none in the two samples of *déclarations de grossesse* I analyzed. This of course does not mean much, since families had strong motives to conceal their dishonor by obtaining an abortion, preventing a *déclaration*, or acquiescing in a forced marriage for their daughters. Nonetheless, the scarcity of such cases among *déclarations* suggests that they were in fact infrequent.

The few cases that were recorded suggest that these relationships followed a certain pattern. The flirtation was often initiated by the girl: the Dlle. Elizabeth de Regnoval, daughter of a *lieutenant de robe-courte* in Beauvais, confessed at the trial of her lover, her father's farm servant, " 'that she herself had solicited the *valet* to make love, and that she had had and still had the desire to marry him.' "[63] Apparently flirtations with household domestics were a diversion allowed to young ladies, so long, of course, as they remained platonic. Such relationships gave girls a chance to test their skills with the opposite sex without serious risk to their reputations or their hearts. Typical of these relationships is one of the best documented: that of the future Mme. de Sévigné with her tutor, Gilles Ménage. The sixteen-year-old girl described him as her "dearest Friend," wrote love letters to him and allowed him to embrace her publicly. But apparently she never granted him what her contemporaries called the last favors. The tenor of their relationship is summed up in the following exchange: when Ménage complained of her cruelty and described himself as her "martyr," she tartly replied, "And I, Monsieur, I am your virgin."[64]

But it was not always easy for the girl to control these relationships. She might be betrayed by her own appetites, as Dlle. de Regnoval was, or an unscrupulous servant might take advantage of her interest to try to force a wealthy marriage. This was the motive universally attributed to servants in such cases during the Old Regime. For example, public opinion said of the clerk of the mayor of Cessenon in Languedoc, who seduced his master's daughter, Marie-Louise Milhé: " 'to make his fortune, he had to make the Milhé girl pregnant; he deserves to be shot.' "[65]

But the most frequent target of the male servant on the make was not the daughter of the house but instead the well-off widow. A widow who hired a domestic to help her farm the land or run the shop her husband had left her quite often found herself the object of his advances, and these were not always pleasant. Either because the common reputation of widows for lustiness (Lawrence Stone tells us of an English proverb: "he that wooeth a widow must go stiff before") made their suitors disregard refusals, or simply because their obvious lack of masculine protection made them easy victims, widows were often the targets of sexual violence by their male servants.[66] Typical of the relationships involving a widow and her male domestic is that of forty-year-old Catherine Boule, widow of a Provençal *ménager*, who was raped by Pierre Guivre, the *valet* she hired to help her work her land. According to Boule, Guivre had propositioned her and proposed marriage for months, but she had always turned him down, and she tried to stay out of his way. One night, however, she had to leave her chamber and come into the kitchen where he slept because she had to fix a meal for her young daughter, who was ill. Guivre came up behind her, grabbed her, threw her on the floor, and raped her.[67] In my samples of *déclarations* there were three cases involving widows, and in two of these violence was used.

The most puzzling type of sexual relationship between mistress and man was that between a married woman and her domestic. Were such relationships relatively frequent, or were they not? Certainly rumors of such liaisons abounded in fashionable Parisian and court circles. A German traveler, Baron Pollnitz, wrote of Paris in the 1730s:

> there are Ladies, even of the first Quality, who don't always treat their lackeys like servants. 'Tis true, they most commonly take them out of the Livery, and in order to bring them near their Persons, they make them their Pages or *Valets de Chambre*. Nothing is thought too good for these Favorites of Venus; they are rigg'd out like Princes, and were you to see one of these fortunate Lackeys, you would naturally take him for some Person of Consequence.[68]

Eighty years earlier, Parisian society had rocked with the scandalous behavior of Mme. d'Olonne, who openly pursued her servants. She became so notorious that her tastes were immortalized in song sheets hawked on street corners:

> La d'Olonne
> N'est plus bonne
> Qu'à ragouter les laquais.[69]

And fifty years after Pollnitz wrote, rumors of liaisons between mistress and servant touched even the royal family. The Baronne d'Oberkirch recounted in her memoirs, with a relish not very well concealed by her pious assertions that she, of course, believed not a word of them, the rumors surrounding the Comtesse d'Artois. She was said to display an undue interest in one member of her household, a man, the Baronne wrote, "of a fabulous handsomeness, of a beauty that passes into proverbs and serves as a point of comparison." When he began to boast publicly of his intimacies with the Comtesse, Louis XVI had him arrested and forced him to retract his statements. The Comtesse was applauded at the Opéra the first time she appeared in public after the scandal.[70] Even the most notorious crime of the eighteenth century was said to have its roots in a flirtation between mistress and servant. It was rumored that Damiens, the would-be assassin of Louis XV, was in love with his employer, Mme. de Sainte-Rheuse, who was in turn the mistress of the Marquis de Martiguy, brother of Mme. de Pompadour. The assassination attempt was said to be a blow of revenge against the brother and sister.[71]

How much credence should we give such rumors? It is hard to know. On the one hand, cases of sexual relationships between married mistress and domestic undoubtedly occurred. In 1778 in Toulouse, for example, forty-three-year-old Claire Raynaud, wife of a *ménager* and mother of four children, poisoned her husband in order to marry Pierre Coulet, her young servant.[72] We know of this case only because of its tragic ending. Many others could have occurred leaving no traces for historians to find, since married women who took lovers did not have to make *déclarations*; they could simply pass off the fruit of their illicit adventures as their husband's work. But on the other hand, it is hard to imagine that many women, especially those of high social position, would undertake the risks involved in such relationships. For a married noblewoman who chased her servants appeared not only wanton, but what was even worse, ridiculous. Ridiculous because *déclassé*: a woman, unlike a man, sank to the social level of her sexual partner. And wanton because, given the stereotype of servants as good for bed but little else, it was impossible to imagine that a woman who slept with her domestic could be genuinely in love with him; only overpowering lust could make her do it. Indeed, so deeply embedded was this notion in the common psyche that to accuse a married woman of sleeping with her servants was apparently equivalent to labeling her a common whore. It was for this reason a favorite insult of the scorned lover. An admirer repulsed by the Marquise de Langallery is said to have snapped at her, "Aren't you in the mood to give me what you give your *palefrenier* every day?," and Restif has a story about the would-be lover of a respectable married woman who threatened that if she did not yield to him, "he would dishonor her by writing to her husband, and proclaiming to all the world, that he has surprised her with the lackey."[73]

Given the risks to their personal dignity and reputation, it is hard to imagine that many married noblewomen had affairs with their servants. And the noblewomen of the 1770s and 1780s, newly enchanted with the charms of domesticity and energetically devoting themselves to being model wives and mothers, seem especially unlikely candidates for the role of Lady Booby. Yet in precisely these years rumors and accusations of such behavior were most prevalent. The *libelles* of the gutter press of pre-revolutionary Paris were full of insinuations that "an epidemic [venereal] disease is raging among the girls of the Opéra, it has begun to reach the ladies of the court, and it has even been communicated to their lackeys." Or again, that "The devout wife of a certain *Maréchal de France* (who suffers from an imaginary lung disease), finding a husband of that species too delicate, considered it her religious duty to spare him and so condemns herself to the crude caresses of her butler, who would still be a lackey if he hadn't proved himself so robust."[74]

As the most devoted chronicler of Old Regime smut, Robert Darnton, has pointed out, such insinuations proliferated because they made effective political propaganda. The impotent noble husband whose wife was forced to seek sexual satisfaction with her (inevitably) lusty lackey was a striking metaphor for his whole degenerate class. Sexual relationships between mistress and servant symbolically reversed most basic principles of patriarchy. This explains both their scarcity in real life and their abundance in the mass of rumor, scandal, and innuendo that formed much of the political discourse of prerevolutionary France.

Homosexual Relationships between Master and Servant

A similar dichotomy between facts and rumor is evident in those sexual relationships that reversed not only the principles of the patriarchal social order but also (so it was thought in the eighteenth century at least) those of the order of nature and of nature's God—that is, homosexual relationships between master and servant. Undoubtedly there was a male homosexual subculture in eighteenth-century Paris, as there was in all large European cities, a subculture in which both masters and servants probably participated, separately or as partners. But because of the penalties for homosexual activities—throughout the Old Regime sodomy was punished by burning at the stake—this gay world was necessarily a hidden, underground one.[75] It surfaces for the historian only in police records, especially in the relatively rare legal prosecutions for sodomy (the standard reference, *Les Procès de sodomie au 16e, 17e, et 18e siècles*, discusses only ten cases for a period stretching from 1540 to 1789.)[76] Because these are so rare, one gets the impression that the homosexual world of Paris was rather small. This may not be true, because historians of France have not yet done the sort of digging necessary to uncover a large and socially complex homosexual subculture of clubs and coffee houses similar to that which Randolph Trumbach and Lawrence Stone have found in eighteenth-century London.[77] But on the other hand, it may be that homosexuality was indeed in the eighteenth century "the English vice," and that there were no French equivalents to London's relatively large and visible gay world or of the increasingly open toleration of homosexual behavior which Stone found among the eighteenth-century English elite. The less rigid divisions between male and female spheres in France, the prominence of leisure-time activities in which both sexes took part (the female-dominated salon, so important to both the social and intellectual worlds of eighteenth-century France, had no English counterpart), the absence of the English public school tradition, and the prevalence of early heterosexual experiences among noble youths all may have given the sexual activities of at least the nobility of France a more heterosexual orientation than those of their English contemporaries. This is not to suggest that homosexuality was nonexistent among the French elite. Among those prosecuted for sodomy in the ten published cases were an *écuyer* and two bourgeois.[78] Yet the memoir literature of the period suggests that transvestism, which appealed to the elite's obsession with role-playing in a society of changing social roles (see *Rameau's Nephew*), and voyeurism, increasingly fascinating as conceptions of privacy and prudery altered, were, rather than sodomy, the fashionable eighteenth-century French "vices." The *haut monde* of the salons had goodly numbers of Cardinals de Bernis and Chevaliers d'Eon, but seemingly few Oscar Wildes.

Yet rumors of homosexual activities, especially between master and servant, were plentiful. The ubiquitous Baron Pollnitz has his usual salacious anecdotes about Parisian lackeys:

> There are others of the menial class that enjoy the Favour of their Young Masters, in a Way so uncommon that one knows not what to think of it; and many of those young Gentlemen, forgetting the Respect that is due to their own Persons and their Families, make Parties at Supper with 'em, at which Time I fancy Conversation is the least Part of the Entertainment. But such is the Spirit of Debauchery, that has infected the Generality of the young People at Court.[79]

Restif has tales of noble youths corrupted by their lackeys, for example, the beautiful young woman he followed at a carnival, who turned out to be a beautiful young man: "The youth wanted to run away. Two lackeys stopped him: they put him in a carriage. . . . I draw a veil over the next episodes of this horrible story. Suffice it to say that the boy is today a homosexual; that he occupies a place at———, that this deadly adventure has caused, besides the loss of his morals, the despair of his parents."[80] The *libelles* also have tales of innocent lackeys corrupted by their masters: "The Count de Noail . . . having taken some scandalous liberties with one of his lackeys, this country bumpkin knocked over Monseigneur with a slap that kept his lordship in bed for eight days. . . . The lackey . . . is a Picard of the first order who had not yet been instructed how to serve a Spanish grandee, Knight of the Royal Orders, Lieutenant General, Governor of Versailles. . . ."[81]

But such tales apparently had little basis in fact. None of the published cases involved a master-servant relationship. The prevalence of rumors about such affairs therefore seems to have stemmed less from the facts than from their effectiveness as political propaganda. For whether they pictured the noble as the passive "effeminate" partner, traditionally the object of popular contempt,[82] or as the debauched corrupter of innocent lower-class youth, the stories of the master-servant homosexual relationships conveyed powerful images of a nobility unfit to rule. Doubtless there was a homosexual milieu in Paris and other large French cities, and doubtless both masters and servants were a part of it. But the present, admittedly limited, state of research suggests that tales of male homosexual relationships within the household are simply that: tales with only a slight foundation in fact.

With regard to lesbianism, the situation is reversed. There were probably more lesbian affairs between mistress and maid than there were rumors about them. What lesbianism there was in eighteenth-century France (and in the present state of research we have no idea how much) probably occurred within the household, for lesbians, on the one hand, lacked the public milieu in which male homosexuals could find partners, while, on the other hand, the traditional closeness between mistress and maid may have encouraged physical intimacies to blossom. At any rate, the one lesbian affair for which we have evidence involved an employer and her servant. Parisian police records yield the story of La Maréchale, a petty informer and spy whose specialty was helping prisoners buy their way out of jail. She obtained the release of one Geneviève Pounnier from La Salpêtrière in exchange for her services as maid and sexual partner. When Pounnier complained of mistreatment to the police, La Maréchale replied that "if she knew the pleasure two women could give to one another, she would give up Durot [her lover] and men would cease to mean anything at all to her."[83]

How many other such relationships existed we simply cannot know. Rumors about them are scarce, but this is probably because lesbianism did not provoke the public interest and indignation that male homosexuality did, for it was always considered more "innocent" and less sinful.[84] Also, rumors about lesbian affairs between mistress and servant lacked the social and political overtones that made those about mistress and male servant and master and man so titillating. To modern feminists lesbianism may be the ultimate challenge to the patriarchal organization of society, but it did not appear so in the eighteenth century. In the Old Regime the alliance of two by definition subordinate members of a household was neither an affirmation nor a denial of the patriarchal order. Therefore such an alliance attracted little attention. For, as we have seen, it was the fundamental premises of patriarchy that determined both how master and servant behaved toward each other sexually and how society viewed such behavior.

Master-Servant Sexual Relationships after 1750

Sometime around 1750 a major change occurred in the legal position of domestic servants seduced by their masters. Whereas in the seventeenth and early eighteenth centuries it was assumed that any child born to a servant living under her master's roof was his unless he could prove otherwise, in the last decades of the Old Regime the master was no longer automatically held responsible: it was now up to the woman to prove his paternity.[85] This change is indicative of the revolution in sexual relationships between master and servant which came about with the disappearance of patriarchal conceptions of the household in the last half of the eighteenth century. By the eve of the Revolution masters had lost both their traditional rights over the bodies of their servants and their moral responsibility for their servants' conduct which had characterized the traditional patriarchal household. Servants were now considered free, independent, and adult human beings who were tied to their masters by the terms of their labor contract, but were otherwise totally responsible for their own behavior. The sexuality of a servant was now his or her own property and responsibility, and no longer that of the master. Whereas domestic manuals of the Old Regime had ignored the problem of master-servant sex, those of postrevolutionary France treated it openly, and they stressed that it was the servant's responsibility to see that nothing untoward occurred. For example, *Des Devoirs des serviteurs, des maîtres, des parents, de tous les hommes envers l'église et l'état,* published in Lyons in 1830, stated emphatically that if a master made unseemingly advances a *servante* should immediately "shake the dust of that household off her shoes," although it added reassuringly that such incidents were becoming increasingly rare.[86] This seems to have been true, for the disappearance of the master's traditional and quasi-legal right to the sexual favors of his servants spelled the disappearance of the subtle psychological encouragement this had given to sexual relationships between employer and domestic.

Other factors involved in the decline of the patriarchal household also discouraged sex between master and servant. One was the rise of domesticity, with its emphasis on the joys of family life and of the love and devotion between spouses. The notions of romantic love between husband and wife that appeared among the nobility and upper bourgeoisie in the late eighteenth century may not have made married men less inclined to be unfaithful to their wives, although this is certainly possible. But they definitely made them more anxious to conceal their lapses from their loving spouses. Consequently illicit sexual adventures had to take place outside the home. The household, that nest of conjugal love and domestic felicity, was now a refuge from the dangers and corruptions of the outside world, and it was not to be sullied by sordid sexual encounters. The well-known if rather odd provision of the Code Napoleon that allowed a wife to divorce her husband if he forced her to share a house with his mistress is a testimony to the new inviolability of the conjugal nest.

Another aspect of the decline of the patriarchal household which contributed to the decline of sexual relationships between masters and servants was the emergence of new standards of privacy and decorum. By the late eighteenth century the standards of decorum that we now associate with the nineteenth century were beginning to emerge. The major bodily functions were now considered shameful and performed in isolation; private (let alone public) nakedness was avoided as much as possible. In the sixteenth century Christophe de Bordeaux had his *Chambrière à tout faire* say of her mistress, "I have often seen her nude, but it's all one between her and me."[87] But in the 1780s Marie Antoinette wore a shift when bathing in front of her servants.[88]

As the body was hidden from the gaze of servants, so too was the heart. The newly affectionate nuclear family wanted to enjoy its domestic happiness in private, and did its best to conceal its emotional life from the prying eyes of servants. In the seventeenth century Mme. de Cornuel made her maid her *confidante* in her love affairs, and even shared her lover with her. But in the 1780s Princess Louise de Condé lived in terror that her servants would discover her quite innocent epistolary flirtation.[89] By the eve of the Revolution servants had lost their old rôle as witnesses and accomplices in the most intimate details of their masters' lives. This not only reduced the moments of intimate contact which had earlier provided occasions for sexual relationships between master and servants, but also divested domestics of that aura of sexuality which had made them so attractive to their masters.

The result of all of these changes within the patriarchal household was a massive transformation of the sexual habits of the elite. Upper-class men increasingly refrained from seducing lower-class women, and when they did, they increasingly chose as their sexual partners women outside the home—street peddlers, *couturières*, prostitutes—rather than their servants. The *déclarations,* analyzed in table 26, indicate that the proportion of women seduced by their social superiors decreased over the course of the eighteenth century, as did the proportion of cases involving master-servant relationships, while a growing proportion of women chose a sexual partner from their own social class. Of the female servants who made declarations in the years 1727–49, 32.8 percent claimed their master or some other gentleman as the author of their pregnancies, while in the period from 1750–89 only 26.9 percent did so. (see table 14). And of the upper class men cited in the *déclarations,*

TABLE 26

Patterns of Illicit Relationships, Provence, 1727–89 (in %)

	1727–49		1750–89	
Women seduced by upper-class men	28.7%	(4.5)[a]	19.4%	(3.6)
Women seduced by lower-class men	66.5		71.2	
Short-term encounters	4.7		9.3	
N	796		1,772	

Sources: See Bibliography, section I, C.
[a]Numbers in parentheses indicate servants seduced by masters.

41.9 percent chose servants as their sexual partners in the first part of the eighteenth century, while only 34.5 percent did so in the years from 1750 to 1789.

These patterns are visible in other samples of *déclarations* as well. In Depauw's from Nantes the proportion of illegitimacies resulting from sexual relationships between master and servant shows a dramatic drop, plunging from 36 percent in 1737–46 to 9 percent in 1780–87.[90] Historians have long noticed these trends but they have consistently misinterpreted them. Edward Shorter used Depauw's findings as part of his evidence for a revolution in the sexual mores of lower-class women. He argued that this revolution had its roots in a rejection of traditional values fueled by industrialization and urbanization, was characterized by a search for personal fulfillment through sexual pleasure, and had as its ultimate result the rising rate of illegitimacy in the nineteenth century. Ever since then these statistics have been interpreted as showing a rejection by lower-class women of the sexual advances of upper-class men in favor of relationships with presumably younger and more attractive men of their own social class.[91] But the controversy that grew out of Shorter's hypothesis of a sexual revolution has, I think, proven conclusively that the sexual attitudes of lower-class women did not change during the late eighteenth or indeed during most of the nineteenth century. Levels of illegitimacy seem to have been characterized by immense local variations that grew out of traditional courtship customs and persisted even through industrialization and urbanization.[92] This persistence of traditional modes of behavior in new economic conditions seems to have caused the rise in illegitimacy in the late eighteenth and early nineteenth centuries.[93] And when the lower classes finally did discard their traditional modes of behavior, they apparently did so not in order to assume the individualism and hedonism Shorter postulated, but instead to adopt a middle-class family-centered domesticity.[94] In the face of this evidence, it seems sensible to turn our attention to the other side of the equation, and to interpret the changing patterns of the *déclarations* as the result of a transformation of the sexual behavior of upper-class men rather than lower-class women. The changes that had revolutionized master-servant relationships within the houshold probably made women domestics less attractive sexually to their masters, and men of the upper classes increasingly sought partners for their illicit sexual activities outside the home. This is not to say that sexual relationships between masters and servants disappeared completely. Anne Martin-Fugier's study of late-nineteenth-century Parisian *bonnes* shows that they were still common in that period.[95] Indeed, sexual abuse remains one of the hazards of domestic service to this day, as reports of the sexual exploitation of so-called Tiajuana maids (illegal Mexican immigrants employed as domestic workers in southern California) attests. Nonetheless, the evidence of tables 24 and 25 suggests that in late-eighteenth-century France and probably in the early nineteenth century as well, sexual relationships persisted longest in the sorts of households where they had always been most common: the small households of petty rural landowners and urban artisans. But employers of servants among the urban elite increasingly sought alternative sexual outlets. One of these was the *couturière,* who in the last half of the eighteenth century made her first timid appearance on the sexual stage. The assistant in the shop of a dressmaker or purveyor of other aspects of feminine finery, she copied as well as she could the dress and manners of women of fashion, and this made her attractive to upper-class men—and to male servants who aped their masters' tastes. In my sample of *déclarations* from Bordeaux, 1.5 percent of the seduced women were *couturières,* and of these 24 percent had upper-class lovers and another 47 percent had been made pregnant by male servants.[96]

The ultimate beneficiary of the sexual reorientation of men of the upper classes was, however, the prostitute. Prostitution increased dramatically in the nineteenth century. Most of this increase had its roots in the changes that urbanization and industrialization brought to women's work in the nineteenth century, changes that made more and more women depend on prostitution for survival.[97] But the increased demand of gentlemen of the elite for the services of prostitutes also was a factor. Indeed, Alain Corbin argues in *Les Filles de noce,* his extremely perceptive study of prostitution in nineteenth-century France, that it was the growing demand from gentlemen of the elite that triggered the major change reshaping prostitution in the late nineteenth century: its transformation from the pattern inherited from the Old Regime of casual and part-time "amateur" and uncontrolled prostitution practiced by lower-class women for economic survival to a closed and organized profession that catered to the sexual fantasies of its increasingly middle-class clientele.[98] By the 1880s, when this transformation was complete, the sexual reorientation of the male members of the French bourgeoisie was obvious: the focus of their illicit sexual lives had shifted from the household to the brothel. The monetization of servants' work had therefore an ironic parallel in a monetization of sexual activity: just as masters now had to pay their servants for the labor they had formerly expected as a duty, they now had to pay for the sexual services that had formerly been their "right."

For in the course of the nineteenth century the prostitute took over the sexual functions formerly performed by the female servant. It was the prostitute who now provided the sexual initiation of the young men of the elite, ceremoniously introduced to brothels in their mid-teens by doting uncles or their school fellows. In one nineteenth-century survey 47 percent of the male respondents said they had received their sexual initiation from a prostitute.[99] The prostitute now also provided the sexual outlet of the unmarried student or clerk. The *ménage* of a bourgeois bachelor and his *demimondaine* mistress is a fixture of nineteenth-century literature, as the novels of Huysmans and Alphonse Daudet attest.[100] The prostitute also became in the nineteenth century the ancillary amour of the respectable married man, as visits to the brothel grew to be a standard part of "les dépenses de Monsieur" among the French bourgeoisie.[101] And the prostitute even took over one final sexual role which had fallen to the servant: that of literary symbol of unbridled sexuality. The ultimate hedonist in nineteenth-century literature was not a servant: she was Zola'a Nana. The transformation of relationships within the household in the last half of the eighteenth century had stripped servants of their aura of sexuality, and therefore they ceased to haunt their master's erotic fantasies.[102] By the nineteenth century the traditional patriarchal household was gone, and with it the sexual tensions which had formerly bulked so large in the relationship between master and servant.

7

Relationships between Servants and Their Masters' Children

My mother . . . neglected me a little, and left me too much to the care of the women [servants], who neglected me also.
—*La Vie de Mme. J.M.B. de la Mothe Guion, écrite par elle-même*

The child is not for one hour in the fortnight left to the servants; I never take a step without her.
—Mme. Roland, writing of her daughter Eudora, to M. Birville, April 28, 1785, in *Mémoires de Mme. Roland*

Probably the most intimate and psychologically important of all relationships between master and servant were those which developed between the children of the elite and the domestics who cared for them. Before the last decades of the Old Regime, child-raising in most noble and bourgeois households was left almost totally to servants, as the quote from the autobiography of the seventeenth-century mystic Mme. de la Mothe Guyon suggests. Even in the 1760s, '70s and '80s, when women like Mme. Roland became converts to the cults of domesticity and motherhood, and began to breast-feed their infants and supervise their children's upbringing, household servants still played major roles in child-rearing. The psychological influence of these surrogate parents over their charges was far-reaching. The sort of emotional bond a child developed with the domestics who cared for him—cold and distant, or warm and loving—was crucial for the future development of his personality. The nature of a child's relationship with the household servants also often determined how he would treat his own servants in later life, and indeed it may have helped shape his attitudes and behavior toward all of his social inferiors. Thus relationships between child and domestic did not, like our other "special case," sex between master and servant, simply reflect the broader patterns of relationships within the household: they also helped to form them. The relationships between servants and the children of the household were a vital, though as yet little explored and acknowledged, factor in the social and even political history of the Old Regime.

Child-Raising in the Patriarchal Household: The Nourrice

The role of servants in child-rearing began almost at the moment of birth, when the newborn infant was handed over to a hired wet nurse, or *nourrice*. The predilection of French mothers for employing wet nurses instead of themselves suckling their children is well known. The custom was deep-rooted in France—Paris had a bureau of *recommanderesses*, which arranged for the hiring of nurses, as early as the thirteenth century—and the practice lingered, despite the total disapproval of the medical profession, until after 1900.[1] In the eighteenth century the hiring of *nourrices* was customary not just among the aristocracy but throughout the bourgeoisie and the artisanate as well.

The reasons for the prevalence of wet-nursing were many and various. It was, of course, a necessity if the mother's milk failed, since no adequate substitute nutrient for children was known. To be sure, a few hardy babies thrived on alternative diets. In the sixteenth century the infant Thomas Platter was given cow's milk successfully, and in 1739 the future Mme. de Genlis was fed a mixture of rye bread and watered wine passed through a sieve.[2] But children who could live on such food were definitely the exception rather than the rule. Other motives for wet-nursing were economic: in artisanal families the mother's labor was so vital to the family economy that she could not afford to be incapacitated through nursing. Still others were social: nursing was considered a "vulgar" and "degrading" undertaking which ruined the figures and strained the supposedly delicate constitutions of aristocratic mothers. The hiring of a wet nurse also allowed a father to enjoy a quick resumption of his marital privileges, something that would have been impossible had the mother herself suckled the child, given the folk taboos against sexual intercourse during lactation. And putting children out to nurse spared the parents the sight of their suffering if they died, an all too likely eventuality in the seventeenth century, when one-quarter of all babies born died before their first birthday.[3] Thus the hiring of a wet nurse was both a necessity and a convenience for parents, and it formed the logical beginning of a pattern of child-rearing in which almost all of the care and nurturing was done not by the child's mother and father but instead by hired lower-class parental surrogates, the domestic servants.

Whether or not the *nourrice* herself was a servant was a question of some complexity during the Old Regime. Nurses, like gardeners, were one of those fringe groups which hovered on the edge of domesticity, sometimes defined in law and practice as servants and sometimes not.[4] The difficulty arose because while some *nourrices* moved into their employers' households to perform their duties, more often the child was sent to the nurse's home. Live-in nurses were rare, and they were usually found only in the households of the aristocracy. There were only eleven in Toulouse in 1695, and of these seven were employed by nobles or officeholders.[5] Even noble families often employed a live-in *nourrice* only for the eldest son, putting all the other children out to nurse (this was the custom in the family of the future Cardinal de Bernis, for example).[6] The few live-in nurses were in the eyes of the law true domestic servants, at least according to M. Sallé, an *avocat* who discussed the problem in 1759.[7] Their employers paid a *capitation* for them, as they did for their other servants, and they were subject to the jurisdiction of the *police des domestiques*. But nurses who took infants into their homes had no legal ties to parents, and were mere hired waged laborers in the eyes of the law.

In practice, however, these distinctions blurred, and all nurses were considered the servants of their employers. Indeed, they were the one sort of servant acknowledged to have a special emotional tie with their masters that went beyond that of the reciprocal duties of the patriarchal household. Nursing was thought to create a sort of mystical bond between a child and the woman who fed him. A baby was thought to absorb the personality traits of his nurse when he drank her "whitened blood"; he became in this way as much her child as his parents'. As one seventeenth-century doctor, Jacques Guillemeau, put it: "It is an accepted thing that milk . . . has the power to make children resemble their nurses in mind and body, just as the seed makes them resemble their mother and father."[8] This resemblance supposedly accounted for the affection nurse and child sometimes felt for each other. The baby was in a sense the nurse's child, and this meant that he incurred certain filial obligations toward her. His nurse (and indeed her whole family) therefore became his relatives and dependents. The French nobility apparently took this obligation seriously. Mme. de Chastenay's mother took her nurse's elderly father into her household and cared for him in his old age.[9] An especially strong emotional bond was thought to exist between the child and his *frère* or *soeur de lait*—the nurse's child who shared his or her mother's milk with the stranger. Suckled at the same time by the same woman, these babies supposedly acquired similar personality traits through the milk they imbibed. Their temperments were thought to match perfectly, much more closely than those of blood siblings, making the *frère de lait* the ideal future servant for his young master or mistress. Some indeed eventually played this role. A certain Weber, son of a Viennese magistrate and *frère de lait* of Marie Antoinette, joined her household as a superior sort of servant when she married, accompanied her to

France, and remained with her to the end, heroically defending her against revolutionary crowds—at least according to his memoirs.[10]

The role milk supposedly played in the formation of a child's personality made the selection of a nurse a matter of vital importance. Obviously the ideal nurse would have abundant milk, and would be free of diseases which she might transmit to the nursling. She should also be free of undesirable character traits which might be passed on to the child: nervous, vicious, and melancholic nurses were to be avoided at all costs. Other factors to consider when choosing a nurse were her age (between twenty-five and thirty years was considered best), the sex of her baby (mothers of boys supposedly produced better milk than mothers of girls), the length of time after delivery (right after birth a mother's milk was thought to be thin and watery; it thickened and became more nourishing as time went on), and the nurse's diet (English doctors recommended white bread, veal, mutton, poultry, and fruits; pickles and spices were to be avoided because they heated the milk and made it hard to digest).[11] Nurses seeking employment were always careful to specify such characteristics as their age and the birth date of their child in their newspaper advertisements:

> A woman of thirty, with a healthy complexion, of good morals, and newly delivered, wishes to find a child to nurse . . . (*Journal de Guienne*, September 24, 1784.)
>
> A nurse, aged eighteen, who is ready to wean twins, of whom she was delivered six months ago, desires to find a child to nurse. (*Journal de Guienne*, February 28, 1786)

But in fact the process of finding a nurse was a haphazard undertaking. Nurses were quite scarce, certainly much more so than other servants, and their scarcity was reflected in their higher wages. In the 1650s a nurse received twenty livres per year, more than twice the salary of a *servante*, and during the Revolution *nourrices* charged twenty livres per month, while maidservants got seventy-five livres per year.[12] Because wet nurses were so hard to come by, parents tended to hire the first one they found, accepting any woman produced by a newspaper advertisement or a *bureau des recommanderesses* with no questions asked.[13] As M. de Chamousset noted disapprovingly in 1787, despite the importance of the nurse to the health and well-being of their child, most parents "do more research when it is a question of hiring a *servante* than when they choose a *nourrice*" and hire any "newly arrived woman about whom nothing is known."[14]

Similar insouciance characterized parental attitudes throughout the nursing process. Parents were extraordinarily incurious about the care their children received. Those of Mme. de Genlis, for example, never discovered that the nurse they had hired for their daughter was pregnant and therefore without milk and that she fed the baby exclusively on solid food—even though both infant and nurse were living under their roof![15] Parents whose children were sent away to nurse seemed to have rarely visited them, or even inquired after their progress. And when they did discover something wrong, they were reluctant to do anything about it, for it was thought dangerous to interfere with the bond between nurse and nursling. It was proverbial wisdom in the Old Regime that a child's nurse should not be changed if that could possibly be avoided; Louis Liger, in an agricultural manual written in 1700, advised against changing tenant farmers, "because lands are like infants, who never prosper from a change of nurse."[16]

This parental indifference, stemming both from the superstitions surrounding the nursing bond and from the parents' reluctance to become too attached to their fragile infants, so liable to die, left the *nourrice* free to care for the child as she pleased. We know little about how nurses treated the infants in their care, for neither the evidence of doctors, who had their own professional reasons for attacking the wet-nursing system, nor that of memoirs, written by adults recalling experiences that happened when they were too young to remember, is really trustworthy. Yet these are all we have. They suggest that *nourrices* were extremely careless and neglectful of their charges, although this neglect was occasionally punctuated by loving indulgences that could in their own way be equally dangerous for the future physical and psychological health of the infants.

The system of sending a child out to a wet nurse contained hazards to the infant's health which even the most loving care could not prevent. Babies often died of starvation or exposure before they even reached their nurse. Newborn infants were usually not fed until they arrived at their nurse's home. It was customary to send a child off *chez nourrice* immediately after baptism, which usually took place the day after birth.[17] But sometimes the delay was longer. One Hélie Robert, son of a *lieutenant* of the *élection* of Saintes, was born on May 30, 1642, but not sent out to his nurse, a master mason's wife, until June 3. Probably the only nourishment he received in the interval was a little sugar water.[18] And the journey itself, often made in an open wagon in inclement weather, was frequently dangerous for the child's health.

If the child survived the perils of his first journey, the next challenge he faced was getting enought to eat. It was not easy to achieve a proper "match" between the baby and the nurse's milk and establish a successful nursing bond. Infants often found the milk of their hired wet nurse indigestible. A well-known example is the infant Louis XIII, who went through three different *nourrices* and almost died of starvation before he achieved a satisfactory nursing relationship.[19] Often, too, a nurse's milk failed, either because of ill-health, undernourishment, overwork, or because the nurse, contrary to all medical advice, slept with her husband and became pregnant. Unwilling to give up their lucrative employment, *nourrices* regularly concealed their loss of milk and fed their charges indigestible solid food. The infant Samuel Du Pont de

Nemours almost died at the hands of his wet nurse, who "had no milk at all and gave me only *bouillie*" (the unappetizing mixture of flour or bread soaked in water or wine which was the major alternative to human milk for babies).[20] The future Cardinal de Bernis was also cared for by a milkless *nourrice*; he was fed exclusively on "a soup of cauliflower and lard," to which he attributed his subsequent lifelong good health.[21]

The possibility of starvation was only one of the perils an infant faced *en nourrice*. There was also the danger of serious infection, for nurses frequently took on babies even when they themselves were ill. The sister of Alexandrine des Echerolles was mentally retarded; her family was convinced that this was caused by the mercury her *nourrice* took to cure her syphilis.[22] In addition to illness, infants might fall victim to a variety of accidental injuries. Jacques Guillemeau, a doctor and partisan of maternal breast-feeding, summed these up early in the seventeenth century: "The welfare of infants is left to the discretion of [the nurse], who by accident could suffocate it, or let it fall (the fall killing it instantly), or let it be eaten, bitten or disfigured by some beast, wolf or dog."[23] To which we can add death or injury by burning, drowning, or other household accidents. Nurses seem to have been incredibly careless and callous about the safety and welfare of the children entrusted to them, so much so that Claude Fleury in his handbook for servants felt it necessary to warn *nourrices* that "the life and death of infants lie in their hands, and that if they die by their fault, they are guilty of homicide in the eyes of God."[24] This carelessness is understandable. These peasants' wives were busy women who had to cook, clean, sew, do their share of the endless farm chores, and tend to the needs of their husbands and children. And after all the baby was not theirs; indeed, he was all too often the reason that their own child had to be denied necessary sustenance and care. But understandable as it was, carelessness took a high toll in infant lives. In Lyons on the eve of the Revolution, of the 6,000 babies born each year, between 1,500 and 2,200 died *en nourrice*.[25]

Those children lucky enough to stay alive during their nursing period were apt to emerge from it with grave psychological damage. Modern child psychologists such as Erik Erikson and John Bowlby emphasize that the experiences of the first months of life are vital for the formation of the future adult personality.[26] Especially important is the nursing experience. When infants nurse, they not only take in the nourishment necessary to sustain life—they also make their first explorations of the world outside themselves and their first attempts at human relationships. It is essential that these efforts meet a warm and loving response. But such a response is exactly what was missing in the lives of most infants in the seventeenth and early eighteenth centuries. As we have seen, getting nourishment was itself immensely difficult. The delay in the beginning of feeding, the problems of adjusting to the nurse's milk, and the frequent substitution for milk of indigestible solid food must have inspired in many infants what Erikson called a state of "oral pessimism": a deeply rooted conviction that the world is cold, cruel, and unloving.[27]

This sense of pessimism was probably reinforced by the response these infants received to their first efforts at reaching out to others. *Nourrices* seem to have paid as little attention to the emotional needs of their charges as they did to their physical safety. Babies were swaddled, a practice that produced acute sensory deprivation and therefore retarded both their motor development and the growth of their intelligence.[28] For long periods they were left alone, lying in their excrement, which was thought to be good for them.[29] Nurses seem rarely to have cuddled, caressed, or cooed over their nurslings, but instead just left them to cry. Du Pont de Nemours wrote of his nurse that she was "neither good, nor careful, nor attached to me. . . . She let me make myself sick with crying, and with [my] irritable disposition that was very dangerous."[30] One wonders how he remembered this, but nevertheless it was probably true. The frequent suggestions in servants' handbooks and child-raising manuals that *nourrices* pick up and caress their charges and sing to them and play with them imply that these practices were quite rare.[31] This lack of love, caresses, and responsive care for their bodily needs could only have deepened in children their conviction that the world was cruel and unloving. Even the rare indulgences of nurses could be harmful psychologically. According to contemporary doctors, many nurses fed their charges on demand, whenever they cried, whether they were hungry or not, in keeping with folk beliefs, natural to a society of scarcity, that a fat baby was a healthy baby. But such overfeeding frequently caused digestive upsets and increased the psychological perils of weaning.[32] Occasionally nurslings became the pets of their foster families, but this too could have its dangers. The infant Du Pont de Nemours was the favorite companion of his *nourrice*'s husband, who showed his affection by taking the infant along to the cabaret and giving it *eau-de-vie* to drink![33] And of course, the stronger the attachment that developed between the child and his nurse and her family the more painful was the inevitable parting, when, anywhere from the age of twelve months to three years, the baby was weaned and sent home to its parents.[34] Figure 9, *Les Adieux à la nourrice*, by Etienne Aubry, captures the poignancy of the moment: when the mother takes the child, the baby struggles and looks longingly back at its nurse.

Retarded motor development, "oral pessimism," weaning traumas, and an overwhelming sense of the world as cold, cruel, and unloving: such were the legacies of an infancy spent *en nourrice*. Historians have repeatedly pointed out that such infantile experiences were a perfect apprenticeship for the cold and unloving world of the seventeenth century: they produced adults who were suspicious, prone to violence, and incapable of forming warm and loving relationships with other human beings—in other words, ideal citizens of tradi-

FIGURE 9. Etienne Aubry, *Les Adieux à la nourrice*. Reproduced by permission of the Sterling and Francine Clark Art Institute, Williamstown, Massachusetts.

The pains of parting from a wet-nurse. The peasant couple, with their fine clothes and cottage resembling a Roman ruin, is hopelessly romanticized.

tional patriarchal society.[35] Such infantile experiences also served as a suitable beginning to the typical noble childhood of the seventeenth century, a childhood spent in the hands of servants whose care of their charges was similar to that of the *nourrice*: unsuitable indulgences punctuating long stretches of neglect.

Care for the Toddler: The Gouvernante

Upon return home from the *nourrice* the childhood experiences of the nobility began to diverge from those of other classes. Most children from social classes above the peasantry or the urban poor shared the physical and psychological perils of being put out to nurse. But only the offspring of the nobility and the upper levels of the office-holding bourgeoisie returned home to the hands of hired servants, as table 27 suggests. This shows that in Toulouse at least most specialized children's servants were found in such households, especially in the eighteenth century, when the wage rise and other rising costs of servant-keeping made the employment of domestics by the lower bourgeoisie and artisanate increasingly rare.

Youngsters from households that did not employ special servants for children faced a difficult period of adjustment when they returned from their nurses. They were confronted with a new environment, a new mother figure, and new and usually stricter standards of behavior. Mme. Roland remembered all her life her troubles in adjusting to her parents' home. Her mother and father laughed at her amazement at her first sight of a street light, and she disgraced herself because she had not been taught to use a chamber pot.[36] Similarly, Du Pont de Nemours recalled vividly his parents' shock when he first asked for his customary drink of *eau-de-vie*.[37] But once the initial period of adjustment was over, such children usually settled into a fairly warm and close relationship with their mothers. To be sure, child-raising in the seventeenth and early eighteenth centuries had its elements of harshness—the beatings to break the child's will, for example.[38] But there is little real evidence that mothers were cruel or neglectful. Both Mme. Roland and Du Pont de Nemours became very attached to their mothers and had happy memories of their childhood.

But the children of the nobility and the office-holding bourgeoisie faced a different situation. They returned not to the arms of loving parents but to the hands of hired servants. Therefore their initial adjustment was easier, but ultimately their childhoods were bleaker and psychologically more damaging.

The first servant that the noble child encountered when he or she returned was the *gouvernante*, or nursemaid, who had charge of the child from the end of the nursing period until the age of seven. Before Rousseau described in *Emile* the development of intelligence during infancy, young children were considered incapable of learning, and therefore the *gouvernante*'s responsi-

TABLE 27

Employment of Children's Servants in Toulouse, by Households, 1695, 1750, and 1789

	1695				1750				1789			
	N	G	P	T	N	G	P	T	N	G	P	T
Nobility	7	8	29	44	0	5	0	5	0	16	1	17
Middle class	1	0	33	34	0	1	0	1	0	7	1	8
Lower class	3	1	5	9	0	0	0	0	0	1	0	1
Total	11	9	67	87	0	6	0	6	0	24	2	26

Sources: See Bibliography, section I, A, 1.
Note: N = *nourrice,* G = *gouvernante,* P = *précepteur,* and T =total.

bilities centered primarily on her charge's physical well-being rather than on intellectual or moral training. Chardin, who posed his *La Gouvernante* (figure 10) brushing her young master's hat instead of hearing his lessons, understood this. The duties of a governess, according to Audiger's *La Maison réglée* of 1692, were to feed and clothe the children of the household, keep them, their clothes, and their rooms clean, make certain that they woke up and went to bed at proper hours, and see that they did not suffocate or approach too near the fire. She was also to teach them to pray and take them to Mass, to allow no "naughty" or "bizarre" behavior, and to discipline them "without harshness," but these responsibilities were clearly secondary to those involving the cleanliness and health of her charges.[39] Indeed the *gouvernante* was more akin to a housemaid than to our modern notion of a governess. Often she had other duties in the household besides child care. She might act as *femme de chambre* for her mistress, or care for the household linens, as the following advertisement shows: "One seeks a *femme de chambre*, fit at the same time to be a *gouvernante d'enfans* [sic], having good recommendations [and] knowing how to work in linen and to iron; wages will be proportionate to her talents" (*Journal de Guienne*, January 28, 1789).

If the duties of a *gouvernante* scarcely differed from those of a housemaid, neither did her qualifications. Young girls looking for work seem to have viewed the jobs as interchangeable, advertising for positions as either *fille d'enfants* or *femme de charge*, and citing skill at ironing and working in linen as their only recommendations.[40] *Gouvernantes*, like most *servantes*, were very young; Chardin's earnest adolescent in *The Young Gouvernante* in the National Gallery is a charming example of the species.[41] Again like most *servantes*, they were usually uneducated. The *gouvernante* of Mme. de la Tour du Pin, who as we shall see had immense influence over her charge, was a peasant who could neither read nor write.[42] *Gouvernantes* also enjoyed a reputation for sexual promiscuity even above and beyond that of other servants; so notorious was their conduct that the name *gouvernante* was often used as a synonym for "mistress" in the Old Regime.[43] That an unskilled, uneducated, and perhaps promiscuous teen-ager had complete responsibility for the care of their young child seems not to have worried noble parents. The one quality they might insist upon in a *gouvernante* was a good French accent, so that their children would be exposed to proper pronunciation when they learned to talk. Candidates for the position advertised themselves as "speaking good French," or, shorthand for this, "Parisienne" (a great attraction in provincial towns like Bordeaux and Toulouse).[44] Restif in his *Les Contemporains* had a former governess exclaim, as she recalled her days in the nursery, "Dame! i' fallat voir, en c'temps-la, comme j'parlais françois!"[45] But apart from insistence on proper French, parents seem to have paid little attention to the qualifications or qualities of the young women who cared for their children.

FIGURE 10. Jean-Baptiste-Siméon Chardin, *The Nursemaid / La Gouvernante*. Reproduced by permission of the National Gallery of Canada, Ottawa.

A *gouvernante* and her charge. The boy's solemnity suggests some of the loneliness and unhappiness of noble children raised by neglectful servants.

Education of the Noble Youth: The Précepteur

Only when a child reached the age of seven was he or she considered educable; only then was his or her adult personality thought to take shape. The age of seven was an important watershed for children: they ceased to wear baby clothes, they received their first lessons, and, in the case of noble children, new servants were hired for them, servants who would educate them as well as see to their bodily needs.[46] This change was more radical for boys than girls, since noblewomen were thought to need little in the way of education apart from domestic skills and the social graces. This had not always been true. In the early seventeenth century, when the Renaissance ideal of the educated noblewoman still lingered, girls might be given a male tutor who trained them rigorously in the classics. Mme. de Sévigné, who, as we have seen, flirted with her tutor, Gilles Ménage, is a good example.[47] But the triumph of Counter-Reformation notions of female piety and domesticity put an end to this sort of education for women, and in the eighteenth century most noblewomen were taught only the basics of reading and writing, domestic skills like sewing and embroidery, and social accomplishments like dancing.[48] They might be "educated" in a convent or in a boarding school like the famous St. Cyr. Often, however, they simply remained at home with their *gouvernantes* (who metamorphosed into ladies-maids as their mistresses grew older) and were taught by a series of visiting masters. In the 1780s, for example, the daughter of the Duc de Fitz-James had six different masters to teach her English grammar, history and geography, music, dancing, and the clavichord. Her dancing master was paid twice as much as the man who taught her history and geography.[49] Almost the sole recommendation of this sort of education was that it gave noble girls the reassurance of having around them as they grew up the same servants who had cared for them in early childhood.

For noble boys, however, the age of seven brought a drastic change of personnel. They left their *gouvernantes* behind, often with tears (like poor Elzéar, son of the Comtesse de Sabran, who did not eat or sleep for three days and nights after his governess was sent away),[50] and passed "into the hands of men" to begin their educations. They were given a *précepteur*, or tutor, who either taught them the basic skills until they could be sent to a *collège* (boarding school) at the age of ten or eleven, or, if education at home was preferred, had complete charge of their pupils until they reached manhood. The choice between education at home or at school was a complicated one, and throughout the Old Regime books were published with titles like *L'Honneste garçon* (1642), *De L'Education christienne des enfants* (1666), *De L'Education d'un jeune seigneur* (1728) and *Avantages de l'éducation des colèges sur l'éducasion domestique* (1740),[51] full of advice on the thorny problems of choosing between tutor and *collège* and picking the right *précepteur*. The arguments such books gave in favor of the *collège* were primarily moral, not educational: a *collège* provided greater surveillance and control of behavior, and above all, it kept noble youths out of the hands of servants, who might corrupt them with their bad examples. ("A child is a sort of monkey, who imitates everything he sees," one book cautioned parents; if he is overly exposed to servants he will begin acting like them.)[52] In fact, however, social status more than anything else seems to have influenced these choices. The appeal of *collèges* grew during the eighteenth century, and it was especially strong among the provincial robe nobility and the *anoblis* and bourgeois officeholders who aped their style of life.[53] Consequently in towns like Toulouse where these social groups dominated the private tutor virtually disappeared. As table 27 shows, in 1695, sixty-seven *précepteurs* were employed in Toulouse, but by 1750 there were none.[54] But while certain *collèges* like La Flèche and Louis-le-Grand were fashionable among the highest levels of the nobility, most court nobles preferred to keep their sons protected from the prospect of mingling with *anoblis* and had them educated at home by tutors.[55]

Advice books maintained that the primary qualities to look for in a tutor were moral ones: "probity, gentleness, sincerity, moderation, compassion, candor, [and] justice" made up one formidable list.[56] In the seventeenth century education was thought to consist of two parts, *éducation* (moral training) and *instruction* (reading, writing, etc.), and the former was far more important than the latter. [57] This was especially true for young men of rank, who, unlike future lawyers or officials, had little need of book learning, but who needed to learn how to be good and kindly masters to their families, servants, and underlings.[58] Therefore it was more important that the *précepteur* of a young lord be moral than learned. Intellectuals were "corrupt and undisciplined"—and anyway, specialized masters could always be hired to fill in any gaps in the tutor's knowledge.[59] It was for their moral qualities that elderly clergymen like the one portrayed in Nicolas de Largillière's *A Young Man with His Tutor* (figure 11) were preferred to the younger and probably more intelligent seminarians and law students who were the other obvious candidates. The Comte Dufort de Cheverny remembered his tutor, the elderly Abbé Pupin, as "a very good man, but not very bright."[60]

Many tutors, however, did not have even goodness to recommend them. Despite the reams of advice literature, noble parents seem to have paid no more attention to the choice of a *précepteur* than they did to that of a *gouvernante* or *nourrice*. Memoir after memoir of noblemen of the Old Regime chronicles a woefully neglected education administered by a totally unsuitable *précepteur*. Charles Pinot-Duclos recalled: "My father apparently thought that a son was not an heir, because he was never concerned with my education: he trusted that I would learn from experience. I was given one of those tutors who come directly from a *bureau d'adresse*, who became just one more servant

FIGURE 11. Nicolas de Largillière, *A Young Man and His Tutor*. Reproduced by permission, Samuel H. Kress Collection, National Gallery of Art, Washington.

A seventeenth-century noble youth and his elderly clergyman tutor.

to me."[61] Similarly, Comte Alexandre de Tilly wrote of his father, "He occupied himself very little with my education. . . . I was left to the *valets*, and to a sort of *précepteur* who resembled them in most respects."[62] The *précepteur* of the Duc de Lauzun actually *was* a *valet*:

> The difficulty of finding me a good tutor prompted my father to confide my care to a lackey of my late mother, who knew how to read and write passably, and who was honored with the title of *valet de chambre* to give him more respect. I was also given all kinds of the most fashionable masters, but M. Roch (that was the name of my mentor) was not able to direct their lessons and give me the means to profit from them. He contented himself with passing on to me his talent for penmanship, which was a great source of vanity to him. Here he succeeded very well. At the same time he taught me to read aloud more fluently and more agreeably than is ordinarily done in France.[63]

A lackey's education administered by a lackey may not seem the proper upbringing for a future duke and peer of France, yet Lauzun's experience was probably typical of that of young men of his social status. A court noble's real education came in the ranks of the army, which he entered as an adolescent (Lauzun joined the Guards at age twelve),[64] and in the arms of the beauties of the court, which he entered at about the same time. Before this he could be safely left to servants.

Psychological Consequences of Servant Child-Care

How did domestics treat the children relegated to their charge? This question, like most that deal with the psychological realities of master-servant relationships, is quite difficult to answer. Relationships between servants and the children they care for can take many forms. In Czarist Russia and the antebellum South servants loved, indulged, and spoiled their infant charges.[65] In Edwardian Britain a camaraderie often developed between child and servant, similar in age and in the subordinate positions they occupied within the household.[66] But in seventeenth-and early-eighteenth-century France neither of these patterns is visible. In the memoir material about childhood in this period two themes, one minor and one major, stand out. The minor one is the physical and sexual abuse of children by servants; the major one, overwhelming in its presence in memoirs, is simple neglect.

Servants clearly could treat their charges as they wished, for parents seem to have paid as little attention to how servants did their jobs as they did to their qualifications for them. Some domestics took advantage of this situation to take psychic revenge for the mistreatment they themselves had experienced by abusing the one member of the upper classes too helpless to strike back.[67] The sexual abuse of children by servants, already discussed, probably was not common, but it did happen. Physical abuse was much more widespread. Parents apparently expected servants to use physical discipline on their children, and interfered only in the most extreme cases. One seventeenth-century child-raising manual urged parents not to dismiss domestics when their children complained about mistreatment; seeing that they could cause servants to be fired would make children insolent, and this was much more dangerous for their future welfare than a few blows.[68] We can see what this could lead to in the case of Cardinal de Bernis, who was abused physically as well as sexually as a child. Bernis was given as *précepteur* a young seminarian of devout habits:

> This good man made me fast on bread and water on the eve of religious festivals, ordered me to leave half of my dinner for my good angel, made me pray four times a day kneeling on pointed iron, ordered me to wear armbands of the same material equally pointed, and gave me the *discipline* [scourging] not to correct me, but to nourish in me a spirit of penitence. It was a great crime to complain, and this crime would have been punished very severely.

It speaks volumes for the lack of parental supervision over the child-raising process that although Bernis boasted in his memoirs of his close relationship to his mother, "My parents only learned of my secret austerities from the abscesses that developed on my knees and fingers."[69]

Luckily there were relatively few servants as abusive as Bernis's *précepteur*; much more characteristic of servant child-care was simple neglect. The seventeenth-century Quietist, Mme. de la Mothe Guyon, summed up many childhoods besides her own when she wrote in the passage quoted at the beginning of the chapter that her mother neglected her and left her to the servants, who neglected her also. This neglect is not surprising. As we have seen, parents did not closely supervise their children's upbringing. *Gouvernantes* were young and irresponsible, and they often had other duties in the household besides child-care. *Précepteurs* were frequently intellectually unfit for their tasks, and therefore unlikely to be assiduous about their duties. And the house servants had their own work to do—or, in the overstaffed households of the court and robe nobility, their own lives to lead and love affairs and intrigues to pursue. Little wonder then that children were often left to their own devices. Even their most basic physical needs were often neglected. Hunger was apparently a frequent complaint of noble children. The Duc de Lauzun characterized his boyhood as "like that of all children of my age and class: the most beautiful clothes for going out, but dying of hunger at home," and Mme. de Créquy reported in her memoirs that the children of the Bethune family were reduced by hunger to eating cat food, and that those of the Prince de Montbarrey ate wax.[70] Children were frequently left alone for hours at a time. Mme. de Guyon was so little supervised that she often wandered out into the street, where she played with the neighborhood children "games that were not at all in conformity with my birth." She also had a series of dangerous accidents: "I even fell several times down an airshaft into a very deep cellar filled with wood. A number of other accidents happened to me which I will not speak of because it will take too long. I might have been killed . . . but you protected me, O my God!"[71]

Such neglect caused psychological as well as physical damage to children. The memoirs of seventeenth-and early-eighteenth-century women, especially, have passages about their childhood that display a fear of being abandoned similar to the syndrome of "separation anxiety" which modern psychologists have traced in motherless and/or neglected children.[72] For example, the one childhood incident the Marquise de Ferrières wrote about in detail in her memoirs concerns a time when she, no more than four years old, was abandoned by the servant who was supposed to care for her. The girl had been left in town over the summer while the rest of the family moved to the country; she was cared for by a young *gouvernante* (the Marquise refers to her as "the child") who spent most of her time visiting and gossiping with her friends:

> I remember still a little adventure which earned me a cruel punishment. I ordinarily woke up at eight o'clock; my young girl, counting on that, went out [at night] and left me alone in my bed. One day, waking up earlier than I ordinarily did, I called [to her] to get me up. No one answered. Fear seized me. I left my bed without dressing, wearing only a nightgown; I went down to the entrance to the courtyard; I called but found no one. I went into the courtyard and saw that I was all alone; I went to the gate and saw no one that I knew; I went out into the street, terribly frightened.

She continued her panic-stricken wandering until a passing priest recognized her and took her home.[73] What comes across most clearly in this passage is the child's hysteria on finding herself alone, characteristic of separation anxiety; even the running away to look for the missing mother-figure is symptomatic of the syndrome.[74]

Another account of separation anxiety comes from the pen of Mme. de Genlis, who tells what happened when her five-year-old cousin, the future Mme. d'Arcamballe, was abandoned by her governess. The child wandered disconsolately from room to room, until she stumbled into an antechamber, where she saw someone who sent her into hysterics: a visitor's black servant, the first black man she had ever seen. She screamed and screamed, finally calming down to say, "in a trembling voice, 'Monsieur, if you promise not to eat me, I beg you to lead me to my servant.' "[75] Such overreactions to the strange and unexpected are again characteristic of the syndrome.

Both these accounts of separation anxiety concern young girls, and this is not surprising. Child psychologists have found that little girls are much more prone to this syndrome than boys.[76] The memoirs of noblemen show fewer traces of separation anxiety. They reveal instead a different pattern of servant neglect with different psychological consequences. Characteristic of the childhoods of male nobles is a pattern of conflict between the youth and his *précepteur*, a conflict in which the youth inevitably emerges the victor, gaining ascendancy over his tutor and forbidding him to interfere in any way with his will or pleasure. An example is Charles Pinot-Duclos, who simply made it clear to his *précepteur* (a man who came "direct from a *bureau d'adresse*") at their first meeting that he was not to try to discipline him: "He was simply ordered to follow me, and I forbade him to give me any orders. He played his part well, and he awaited tranquilly the time he would be sent away with the same recompense that he would without doubt have received if he had done anything to deserve it."[77]

For the Comte Dufort de Cheverny establishing independence from his tutor was more difficult. Throughout his childhood he had numerous clashes with his *précepteur*, the "good" but "not very bright" Abbé Pupin. Once he left the poor man marooned in the middle of a lake on an island populated by indignant swans. Their conflict came to a head one evening in Paris when the fifteen-year-old youth wanted to go to the theater:

> My Pupin, as usual, put on his cloak and took his place in the carriage beside me. We were not yet in the rue aux Ours when a sermon and an argument aroused us; I ended by saying that I believed myself the master in my own household and still more in my carriage. I took a tone of authority; that angered him, he wanted to get down; I took him at his word, and right away I gave orders to go to the Comédie Italienne.

Pupin left after this. His replacement was a M. Portier, an ex-music master, with whom the young Cheverny struck a cynical bargain.

> I said to him: "Do you want to attach yourself to me, or to my grandmother [his guardian, who had urged Portier to discipline him]? If the latter, I'll fire you. If the former, on the contrary, I will attach you to me, I will pay all your expenses, I will let you handle my finances, and I will set you up for life." The agreement was soon struck, and from that day we were the best friends in the world. He was complacent, gentle, amiable . . . and I received from my grandmother compliments I did not at all deserve.

After this young Cheverny spent his time as he pleased, mostly attending the theater and patronizing prostitutes.[78]

The most emotionally taxing of these battles for autonomy was that of the Duc de Lauzun. At the age of fourteen he acquired a mistress, the Duchesse de Gramont, much to the disapproval of his tutor: "I was overcome with joy, but M. Roch [his *précepteur*, the ex-lackey who was so proud of his ability to write], who discovered it, and whose high moral standards never weakened, wanted me to go to Mass the next day, which was a Sunday. I refused; we fought; he threatened me with my father, whom I feared very much; I yielded with profound chagrin." At Mass he fainted, for the first and last time in his life. He woke up on the steps of the church, "surrounded by old women who, to help me breathe, had pulled my pants down." When he recovered, he renewed the battle with the aid of his mistress; M. Roch was reprimanded and eventually fired.[79] From that moment on Lauzun led the life of a libertine.

Both the separation anxiety that haunted the childhoods of noblewomen raised by servants and the lack of loving care and discipline that young noblemen who broke free of their tutors experienced seem to have had grave psychological consequences for their adult personalities. Psychologists have found that victims of separation anxiety often suffer "acute or chronic anxiety and depression, and difficulties of every degree in making and maintaining close affectional bonds, whether with parent figures, with members of the opposite sex, or with their own children."[80] This might have been written about the neglected noble children of seventeenth- and early-eighteenth-century France. An extreme example is Mme. de Guyon. Unloved and unloving as a child, and forced into an arranged marriage at fifteen, she was convinced that everyone in her husband's household hated her, and that even the servants spied on her. Her only friend in this sea of hostility was the God who, she thought, had watched over her wretched childhood. Her life became a desperate battle to escape from her family into a convent. In her descriptions of the religious transports she experienced in her later career as a Quietist and her accounts of the emptying of her mind and spirit of selfhood and the filling of her "unworthy vessel" with the presence of the Holy Spirit, we can detect the guilt feelings and dependency needs of the classic deprived child.[81]

The total permissiveness young noblemen enjoyed also left psychological scars. Children need not only the reassurance of the constant presence of a loving and caring parental figure, but also the reassurance of rules and discipline as well. Yet young noblemen like Lauzun and Cheverny were left totally free to do as they pleased, and moreover it was clear to them that they were thus indulged not because their *précepteurs* loved them but because (with perhaps the exception of M. Roch, who seems to have genuinely tried to do his best for young Lauzun) they were totally indifferent to their welfare. Psychologists suggest that childhood experiences of total permissiveness stemming from indifference tends to produce "expedient" children, who constantly "manipulate the people and events around them . . . in an effort to get as much personal gratification as possible . . . and avoid as many social duties as possible which would require them to act in a positively socialized way." They become total hedonists. Their emotional relationships are undertaken for instant gratification, and they never find in them "the human warmth and approval they vaguely but intensely want."[82] Again, this might have been written as a description of Cheverny or Lauzun, whose lives, on the evidence of their memoirs, seem to have been totally devoted to the pursuit of pleasure, especially sexual pleasure. They indulged in endless rounds of seductions, pursuing every woman who crossed their paths, from court beauties to the lowest prostitutes, but they seem never to have achieved any relationships of genuine warmth or affection.

The psychological aftereffects of childhood neglect by servants obviously can explain much about the emotional coldness of the family life of the high nobility in the seventeenth and early eighteenth centuries. But it is possible that they shaped other attitudes and behavior patterns as well. It seems likely, for example, that the childhood experiences of the nobility with servants affected their behavior toward the domestics they employed as adults. Memoirs suggest that emotionally deprived children like Mme. de Guyon had as much difficulty in forming satisfactory relationships with their servants as they did with everyone else. Mme. de Guyon had terrible problems with the servants in her husband's household, and regarded them as her sworn enemies.[83] Is it not possible that the psychological distancing that characterized relationships within the patriarchal household evolved because it allowed masters to coexist with the servants who were so necessary for their existence but who also evoked, from childhood memories of cruelty and neglect, deeply buried but nonetheless powerful feelings of suspicion and hatred?

The relationship of "spoiled" young men like Cheverny and Lauzun with their domestics was rather different. Because they had established clear ascendancy over them, such men were much more comfortable with their servants. Indeed, their memoirs suggest that they were more at home with them than with their social equals. For example, the one person the Comte de Cheverny singled out for praise in his memoirs was his *valet* Marnier, so expert at arranging intimate *soupers* for the Comte and his sweetheart of the moment.[84] Men like Cheverny felt most comfortable in the world below stairs, which was a reminder of that lost paradise of their youth when they could do completely as they pleased. This explains, I think, the *nostalgie de la boue* of their sexual tastes, and also the penchant for disguising themselves as servants, a major theme of their memoirs. (Lauzun, as we have seen, even pretended to be a servant in the king's household during his apparently fruitless pursuit of Marie Antoinette.)[85] But below the surface camaraderie these masters showed to their inferiors lurked a pervasive arrogance and contempt. Such men had learned in their childhood that servants were easily bullied and corrupted, and the lesson had sunk in. The Comte de Cheverny might praise his Marnier, but it was for qualities—physical attractiveness, skill in pursuing women—that confirmed the "lusty servant" stereotype. By his own confession Cheverny knew so little about his *valet* as a person that he was unaware that the man suffered from a grave illness through long stretches of his employment.[86] We can see here the characteristic posture of familiarity masking contempt and indifference which most nobles of the Old Regime displayed toward their servants and toward the lower classes in general. Thus it is at least possible that many of the social attitudes and stances of the elite of the Old Regime toward their inferiors—attitudes and stances that helped bring about the French Revolution—had their roots in the childhood experiences of the nobility at the hands of their servants.

New Attitudes toward Children, 1750–1800

In the last years of the eighteenth century, as we have seen, traditional patterns of patriarchal behavior were under attack in both the family and society at large. On the home front emerged a new concept of the family as a small, close-knit nuclear unit bound together by ties of affection rather than duty. A most important part of this new family was a new attitude toward children and child-rearing. Children came to be recognized as unique and fragile beings who needed infinite love and cherishing, and the care and nurturing of children came to be considered the most important and fulfilling of women's roles. Mothers, even aristocratic ones, now took much more personal interest in child-rearing, and the care children received was much improved. This new interest in mothering did not completely eliminate servants from the child-rearing process. But it did change the way servants treated their young charges, and it altered the relationship between child and servant almost beyond recognition. And since childhood experiences at the hands of servants may have helped shape the general social attitudes of the elite, it is not surprising that these attitudes underwent a profound transformation as well.[87]

The Revolution in Mothering: Maternal Breast-Feeding

The best known and most widely studied aspect of these new attitudes toward children and child-rearing was the craze for maternal breast-feeding in the 1770s and especially the 1780s, a craze that caused countless mothers to renounce hired wet nurses and breast-feed their own offspring.[88] Usually Rousseau's famous passages in *Emile* are cited as its inspiration, but Rousseau's voice was just one of many.[89] From the 1750s through the French Revolution books like Ballexserd's *Dissertation sur l'éducation physique des enfans* (1762), Raulin's *De la Conservation des enfans* (1768), Mme. Le Rebours's *Avis aux mères qui veulent nourrir leurs enfants* (1775), and

Verdier-Heurtin's *Discours sur l'allaitement et l'éducation physique des enfans* (1804) preached the gospel of maternal breast-feeding with equal enthusiasm if less literary skill than the great Jean-Jacques.[90]

The arguments of these books reveal much about the causes and underlying assumptions of the eighteenth-century revolution in child-care. The case for maternal breast-feeding was presented in both positive and negative terms. The positive argument was that maternal nursing was what nature, that god of the eighteenth century, had intended. A mother's milk was the most natural food for an infant; only his or her own mother could produce milk exactly suited to a child's unique nutritional needs. Furthermore, nursing itself was a healthy natural process which not only improved a mother's physical well-being but also satisfied her maternal instinct, which doctors, like almost everyone else in the eighteenth century, were coming to identify as the core of female nature.[91]

The emphasis on the natural was characteristic of the broader revolution in child-rearing of the eighteenth century. For all the thorny problems of parenting the burden of the advice of eighteenth-century doctors and educators was to let nature take its course. Don't swaddle children; that restricts the natural movement of their limbs. Don't force children to learn to walk; they will start walking when they are ready to do so. Don't ignore a crying child; cries are nature's warning signals that something is wrong.[92] The key to raising children successfully was to watch them closely, and anticipate their needs with loving common sense.

This was precisely what a hired wet nurse would not do. Every argument for maternal breast-feeding was also an argument against the mercenary *nourrice*. Not only did she lack a mother's instinctive knowledge of her infant's needs; she was also too much a "slave of custom and prejudice," as Mme. Le Rebours put it, to adopt the new and more natural methods of child-care, clinging instead to outmoded practices like swaddling.[93] Even worse, she was criminally careless and callous toward the infants left in her charge. Books like Chamousset's *Mémoire politique sur les enfans* and the *Mémoire sur la conservation des enfants* by Prost de Royer, the *lieutenant-général de police* of Lyons, documented the high cost of mercenary nursing in infant lives. The horror stories in these books were not new, but the great debate over the French "depopulation" in the late eighteenth century gave them a new significance; wet-nursing, like the employment of male domestics, was seen as one of the chief causes of this national tragedy.[94]

Most of the pro-maternal breast-feeding and anti–wet-nursing propaganda came from doctors, whose position on this question was not entirely disinterested. As Jacques Donzelot has pointed out, the eighteenth century was the period of the professionalization of medicine and the "medicalization" of family life.[95] Doctors were seeking increased respect and social status. One road to this was the colonization of the field of infant care, previously left to the folk wisdom of women. Hence the need to discredit the wet nurse, and hence the effort to replace her with the anxious mother, ever vigilant over the health of her child and willing to call in a doctor when the least little thing went wrong.

The propaganda for maternal breast-feeding attracted so much attention both then and now because it brought together so many themes of late-eighteenth-century thought: the obsession with nature and the natural, the new definition of female nature, the rise of the medical profession, and the depopulation debate with all its ramifications. But the effects of this propaganda were surprisingly muted. Mercenary wet-nursing did not disappear. To be sure, in the 1780s nursing one's own child was *à la mode*. Earnest bourgeoises like Mme. Roland, eager to do the best for their children, perused Rousseau and Mme. Le Rebours and took their infants to their breasts.[96] The craze even reached the court. The Marquise de Bombelles nursed her son, nicknamed Bombon, while she was on duty at Versailles as lady-in-waiting to the Princess Louise, and Marie Antoinette herself expressed an interest in breast-feeding her children.[97] In fact, the fashion for maternal nursing was most prevalent in the upper levels of society. It never spread to shopkeepers and artisans; they still needed their wives' uninterrupted labor in the households, and therefore still put their children out to nurse. In 1787 only one-tenth of the babies in Paris were nursed by their mothers.[98] And the Revolution put an end to the craze even among the nobility, for amid the disruptions of noble family life, the enforced sojourns in the country and the flights to England and Austria, it was often easier and safer to leave newborn infants in the hands of wet nurses.[99]

Thus the craze for maternal breast-feeding had little lasting impact. The great majority of children were still put out to nurse. But their experiences *en nourrice* were quite different from those of infants born earlier in the century. Late-eighteenth-century parents were deeply concerned about their children's welfare, and therefore they went to great trouble and expense to exercise control over the nursing process. One example of such a concerned parent is M. Nicod, a modest Parisian watchmaker. Nicod wrote to the parish priest of his son's nurse asking him to keep an eye on the baby, and he underwrote the cost of postage and of the hiring of a scribe so that the illiterate *nourrice* could send him frequent reports on his son's progress.[100] Other parents made regular visits to the nurse, expeditions immortalized in paintings like Etienne Aubry's *The First Lesson in Brotherly Feeling*, and Fragonard's *A Visit to the Nurse*. The golden glow that bathes the latter picture, with its triangular composition focusing on the sleeping baby, shows that a deep concern for infants was not incompatible with mercenary nursing.[101] It seems likely that this increased parental vigilance made nurses take better care of their charges, which in turn may have saved at least some children's lives. Infant mortality in France shows a slight decline by the 1770s, and it is at least possible that better nursery care contributed to this.[102]

The New Maternal Vigilance

Although the revolution in infant care monopolized attention then as it does now, the care of older children underwent equal and strikingly similar changes in the last decades of the Old Regime. For older children, too, new methods of "natural" child-rearing emerged that greatly expanded the role and responsibilities of the mother. As with infant nursing, some mothers responded to these new theories by taking over full responsibility for their children. Most, however, retained their traditional hired help, but they now made much greater efforts to supervise and control the care their children received.

At the heart of the new methods of child-rearing lay the doctrine of maternal vigilance. All children, it was thought, were born good, and if they were allowed to develop according to nature's plan, all would be well. But such development was possible only in a controlled environment where all corrupting and dangerous influences were carefully excluded. And only a mother could care enough about her children to spend the time and effort necessary to create such an environment. Only she would undertake the ceaseless vigilance necessary to her children's welfare.[103]

Some mothers interpreted this to mean that they themselves should perform all the tasks involved in child care. To them, the hired servants who had earlier cared for children were not only incapable of the ceaseless vigilance necessary to raise a child; they were in fact among the dangerous and corrupting influences which the new protective environment was designed to exclude. Two famous and well-documented cases of mothers who undertook to raise their children without servants have come down to us: Mme. Jacques Necker's care of her ony child, Germaine, the future Mme. de Stael, and Mme. Roland's mothering of her only child, her daughter, Eudora.

Suzanne Curchod, beloved of two of the eighteenth century's most famous men, Edward Gibbon and Jacques Necker (whom she married), was the daughter of a Swiss Protestant minister. Before marrying Necker, she had worked as a *gouvernante*, a most unusual undertaking for a woman of her respectable background in that period. Probably this experience, as much as her reading of *Emile*, prompted her to raise her only child, Germaine, born in 1766, without servants if possible. Mme. Necker herself nursed the baby until she was informed that the four-month-old infant was starving. Then she reluctantly called in a wet nurse. When the child was weaned, Mme. Necker briefly employed a *gouvernante*, but she found her unsatisfactory. "What I should like," she wrote, "is a simple Protestant chambermaid, gentle, pliable, and educated, who can read with perfection and who is well-versed in her religion." Unfortunately what she found was a woman she described as "excellent as far as physical care is concerned, reliable, gentle and virtuous—but stupid, Catholic, uneducated and clumsy."[104] She lasted only until Germaine was two and a half years old; then the *gouvernante* was banished and Mme. Necker took sole charge of her daughter. Until she reached her late teens, Germaine Necker had not only no servants but no playmates as well. She never even left her house. Her sole companions were her parents, especially her mother, who devoted incredible amounts of time and energy to her daughter's education. Germaine knew her catechism before the age of three; at five she could recite long poems in English and Latin, and throughout her girlhood she was a fixture in her mother's salon, trading views on governmental reform and the nature of love with the leading *philosophes* of the day.

In some ways, Mme. Roland's care of *her* only child, Eudora, born in 1781, was even more thoroughgoing. Mme. Roland also nursed her child until the baby starved, but unlike Mme. Necker she refused to hire a wet nurse, and instead fed the baby solid food.[105] Throughout the nursing period Mme. Roland fought a running battle to keep the household servants away from the child. She blamed Eudora's stomach upsets on "the feeling of Marie-Jeanne and the *bonnes femmes* who are always afraid that the little creatures are not eating enough," and who fed the baby after her mother had gone to bed, "thinking they were doing a service for both of us."[106] Mme. Roland's distrust of servants and her determination to keep Eudora out of their clutches increased as the girl grew older, especially after Eudora began to use a swear-word she had picked up from St. Cloud, the family manservant.[107] She never hired a *gouvernante* and took care of the child herself. Throughout Eudora's girlhood her mother's proudest boast was the one quoted at the beginning of this chapter, that "the child is not for one hour in a fortnight left to the servants; I never take a step without her."[108] Mme. Roland, however, lost interest in what she had once described as "the most sacred and at the same time the sweetest of duties"[109] of motherhood earlier than Mme. Necker did. When Eudora was only eight she was packed off to a convent so that her mother could pursue her political career in Paris.

Unsurprisingly, these experiments in good mothering turned out rather differently than their perpetrators had hoped. Germaine Necker grew up to hate her mother, while her love for her father (more or less excluded from the child-rearing process) was such as to raise eyebrows in this post-Freudian age. "I adore my father," she wrote. "It is a cult." And: "Of all the men in the world it is he whom I would have wished for a lover."[110] Germaine de Stael's spectacular romantic career was not only an avid pursuit of the perfect lover which fate had denied her when it made him her father, but also a complete and total repudiation of her pious and straight-laced mother's childhood precepts. Eudora Roland was of course a much less flamboyant personality (perhaps because her mother lost interest in her so much earlier). But in the course of a long and retiring life she attracted public notice at one point: when she protested that Lamartine's *History of the Girondins* had glorified her mother at the expense of her father.[111] Obviously being a good mother in the context of the modern affectionate nuclear family was more complex than these heroic pioneers had realized.

Mme. Necker and Mme. Roland had in common a basic distrust of servants (typical of many employers in the last half of the eighteenth century), a restless intelligence which had few outlets other than mothering, and an iron determination to succeed. Probably all these qualities were necessary for the sort of heroic mothering they undertook. Most women interpreted the new mothering in a less strenuous fashion. To them being a good mother did not mean doing without servants—something that at least the noblewomen among them would have found utterly strange and unnatural.[112] Instead it meant exercising constant vigilance over the care servants gave to their offspring. Such mothers were extremely particular about the servants they hired to care for their children and they supervised them closely.

Evidence of the new and strong maternal involvement in the child-raising process appears in the correspondence of noblewomen in the decades before and during the Revolution. A good example is the Marquise de Bombelles, the domestically minded noblewoman who had nursed her infant son Bombon while a lady-in-waiting at Versailles. Her letters suggest that to the Marquise the finding and keeping of competent personnel to care for Bombon was a source of endless worry. Probably influenced by Rousseau's panegyrics on the domestic habits of the Swiss, the Marquise imported a Swiss nurse, Mme. Giles, to help her care for the baby. Unfortunately Mme. Giles became homesick and wanted to leave just as Bombon was being weaned. This upset the Marquise: "I was not expecting to see her leave at the moment when the baby's teeth are going to appear and when it needs her most."[113] Mme. Giles's defection was especially troublesome because the only other servant available was too young and inexperienced to help at such a crucial time. But the nurse was persuaded to stay by the promise of a gold watch, and the crisis of weaning passed peacefully. When Mme. Giles finally did depart, the Marquise faced the problem of finding a successor. A long search yielded only one likely candidate, a certain Agatha, who did not seem entirely satisfactory. She was hired on a trial basis, and the Marquise ordered her *femme de charge*, "who understands children perfectly," to watch her and report back on how she treated Bombon.[114] Meanwhile she made contingency plans to find another *gouvernante*. Fortunately, Agatha worked out well and Bombon was spared the ordeal of another "new face"—and his mother the problems of another hiring.

The Marquise de Bombelles was not the only noblewoman who anguished over finding the right servant to care for her child. Another concerned mother was the Comtesse de Sabran, who was perhaps even more upset than her son Elzéar when the time came to replace the boy's *gouvernante* with a *précepteur*:

> I am very disturbed right now because of Elzéar; the grief that he feels at being parted from his nurse has upset him so much that he is sick. For the last

> three days he has neither eaten nor slept and he has a slight fever. . . . I can't tell you how unhappy this makes me, how worried I am. . . . Luckily the *abbé* who is near him [the new *précepteur*] is an extremely gentle and understanding man, and he gives him all his patience and gentleness.[115]

But unfortunately for the Comtesse's peace of mind, Elzéar did not like his new tutor. He was fired, and a number of others were tried before one was found whom the boy accepted. In her letter recounting this the Comtesse noted: "He [the new tutor] will not come to live here until next Monday. I want to have some time to accustom myself to him. It is hard for me to give up suddenly the notion of all the dangers that my poor child is facing, and not to shudder to think that I am putting him in the hands of a man whom I do not know at all."[116]

Such letters clearly indicate that aristocratic mothers of the 1770s and 1780s expended a great deal of time and thought in finding and keeping the right servants to care for their children. It is also clear that their primary criterion in hiring was that the person be gentle and kind with the child, and that the child accept him or her. But finding a servant whom the child liked could create its own problems, as Mme. Necker once noted. "*Gouvernantes*," she wrote, "always have one great disadvantage; if they are qualified for their calling, they intercept the child's affection for its mother."[117] It was a commonplace in the late eighteenth century that infants could develop strong emotional attachments to those who cared for them, so strong in fact that they might die of grief if parted from the loved one. So common were such notions that even as unlikely a person as Napoleon once had a long conversation about the strength of children's emotional attachments with his friend Laura Junot.[118] Mothers knew that if they found competent and caring servants for their children, they ran the risk of having to share with them their children's love. We can detect maternal jealousy in the Comtesse de Sabran's description of Elzéar's attachment to his departing *gouvernante*: "his love is not at all that of a child. His affection for this woman is more love than friendship," and we can see it too in the Baronne d'Oberkirch's reaction when leaving on a journey that would take her away from her daughter: "I cried a great deal on parting from my daughter; it was true grief for me. . . . Schneider [her servant] cried also, which made me angry. *She* was not leaving behind a cherished child."[119]

Probably many mothers shared the feelings of the Comtesse de Sabran, who once confessed that she sometimes wished she could raise her children by herself as lower-class mothers did: "These unfortunate types don't need *précepteurs*; they raise their children themselves, and that is compensation for their burdens."[120] But however much they might envy lower-class mothers, few noblewomen emulated them. To most noblewomen of the late eighteenth century, good mothering meant picking competent and kind servants to care for their children, and jealousy of these servants was the price they had to pay for their children's welfare.

The Revolution in Education

One final aspect of the new attitudes toward children of the late eighteenth century which had important consequences for the relationship between children and servants was the revolution in education. A major theme of the intellectual history of the decades immediately preceding the Revolution was an obsession with the importance of education, both for individuals and for society at large. These years saw the publication of innumerable tracts on such subjects as how school curricula should be reformed, whether universal state-supported schooling was possible and desirable, and what sort of education was suitable for each social class.[121]

Noble parents apparently shared this concern, at least to the extent of resolving that their own offspring be well educated. Fewer and fewer followed the old tradition of entrusting the task of teaching their children to whatever servants happened to be around. One parent who kept this tradition alive was Jules Constant, father of the future novelist Benjamin Constant, born in 1767. Young Benjamin was "educated" by, successively, a sadist who alternately beat him and smothered him with kisses, a convicted rapist who took him to live in a bordello, a music master who left him to his own devices (the boy ruined his eyesight reading pornography at the local lending library), an author whose lessons consisted of setting the boy to copy his own works (since he disapproved of Benjamin's penmanship, the youth never advanced beyond the preface), and a defrocked monk who eventually committed suicide.[122] But as nobles took a greater interest in their children's welfare, horror stories like this became increasingly rare.

Many noble parents solved the problem of how to educate their sons by sending them off to *collèges*. The proportion of *collège* students of noble background shows a steady increase throughout the eighteenth century.[123] But some noble fathers disliked the seemingly moribund curriculum and harsh discipline of these institutions. They sent their sons instead to *pensions*, where a private master took a few boys for lessons in his own lodging, or hired *précepteurs* to educate them at home, where they themselves could supervise the process.[124]

The tutors of the prerevolutionary decades were however a far cry from the doddering *abbés* and illiterate lackeys of the past. We can trace the evolution of the *précepteur* over the course of the century in the education of the generations of the de Croy family. The first Duc, born in 1713, had as a tutor a lackey whose only educational qualification was that he was born in the Rhineland and therefore spoke German. The second Duc was educated by his father, not very well, one suspects. But the third Duc, born in 1765, had as *précepteur* the Abbé Clouet, "a man of great talent and well known," the author of an *Atlas de géographie moderne* published in 1767.[125] To find a man of the Abbé Clouet's attainments in the post of *précepteur* was not at all unusual in the late eighteenth century. The tutor finally hired for the Comtesse de Sabran's son Elzéar also had a fine academic background, as the Comtesse boasted to her friends: "He is an *abbé*; he studied at the Petit-Séminaire de St. Sulpice, and from there he went to the *collège* of Montaiger, where he has been for ten years. He is twenty-eight, intelligent and learned, and with a good, open and fresh face. He knows Latin very well, because he took diplomas in theology and mathematics."[126]

It seems clear that by the 1780s parents were making every effort to see that the tutors they hired for their sons were well qualified. The newspaper advertisements placed by *précepteurs* in those years stress both their own educational attainments ("sustained at age sixteen general theses of philosophy and mathematics," "knows Italian and English well") and their skill at teaching ("can teach Latin very well in a third of the time schools take, so that in eighteen months he can put into Rhetoric classes young students who had no previous knowledge of the tongue").[127] Many of these *précepteurs* seem to have had a genuine talent for teaching. At least the Abbé Pouard, tutor of Charles and Edouard, scions of the great ducal house of Fitz-James, not only gave his charges the poems of Alexander Pope as well as the more standard Caesar's *Commentaries* and Colot's *Explication des premiers vérités de la religion*, but also had the imagination to take them to the opening of the Estates-General at Versailles in 1789.[128] Even one of Benjamin Constant's disastrous tutors taught him Greek grammar by encouraging him to "invent" the rules of a new language.[129]

The emergence of talented and dedicated *précepteurs* led to a "professionalization" of the role of the tutor, similar to that of musicians, *hommes d'affaires*, and chefs at the end of the eighteenth century (see chapter 1). Tutors ceased to think of themselves as mere servants; instead they began to identify with their fellow teachers outside the household and to regard themselves as educators, trained men performing tasks important to society. This led them to claim "professional" middle-class status and respect. Tutors might still be domestics, but they commanded salaries (as much as 600 livres per year) and special marks of status which set them off from the lowly lackey or *valet de chambre*. (One advertisement seeking a *précepteur* promised that he would be "lodged, shod, dressed, lighted and fed like the masters of the house," and another promised a yearly pension of "1000 to 1200 livres," a solidly bourgeois income.)[130] The post could be held by a respectable bourgeois with no loss of status. Indeed, certain elements of the bourgeoisie eagerly sought jobs as *précepteurs*. Penniless young men from the provinces found positions as tutors in the households of the high nobility the perfect *entrée* into the intellectual world of Paris. Such young men were treated with respect by their employers, who introduced them to salons where they could make contacts important for their future. Alan Kors, in his study of the philosophes in D'Hôlbach's *coterie*, found that almost every one of them who was not wealthy or of noble birth used this pathway to a career as an intellectual. Morellet, Suard, Augustin Roux, and the scientist Darcet all began as tutors.[131] This of course ended when the Revolution irrevocably separated the intellectual world from the *haut monde*. But the Revolution compensated for this by its establishment of a nationwide state-supported public school system that gave educators new career opportunities and new social pretensions and pushed them further along on the road to professional status which they would tread in the nineteenth century.

The growing professionalization of education even had an impact on the activities and status of the lowly *gouvernante*. To be sure, in the decades before the Revolution most *gouvernantes* were still young, ill-paid, and ignorant, and most were still, as M. Formey, a *précepteur* very conscious of his educational mission, noted indignantly, "charged with other functions very discordant with those of education; they are made into a sort of housekeeper who watches over the household economy, into ladies' maids obliged to dress the mistress and children, into dressmakers and embroiderers and I don't know what all!"[132] And the education of young noblewomen still consisted mostly of sewing lessons and music lessons and listening to the *femmes de chambre* discuss their love affairs. But in the 1770s and 1780s at least some parents wanted a better education for their daughters, and some *gouvernantes* were capable of providing it.

Archetype of the new-style *gouvernante*, as well educated and as earnest about her task as any *précepteur*, was the famous Mme. de Genlis. Appointed, in defiance of the tradition that only men should educate growing boys, to teach the sons and daughters of the Duc d'Orléans (one of whom became King Louis-Philippe), Mme. de Genlis shocked public opinion not only by her sex but also by her unconventional teaching methods. She educated boys and girls together, she hung ropes from the schoolroom ceiling for her pupils to climb, and she took her charges to factories and workshops so that they would understand how things were made.[133] Her writings on teaching, especially the *Lessons of a Governess* and *A New Method of Instruction for Children from Five to Ten Years Old*, give her a place in the front ranks of eighteenth-century educational reformers, right behind Rousseau and Pestalozzi, although admittedly her unorthodox methods seem to have left little mark on her highly conventional pupil Louis-Philippe.[134]

If Mme. de Genlis was the most notorious of the newly efficient *gouvernantes*, she was not the only one. Mme. de Chastenay remembered with gratitude her governess, a Mlle. de Sully: "Her teaching had nothing routine or rote about it. There were sometimes repetitions of the catechism and recitations of verses, but with these exceptions, all was done by reasoning. I pointed out on the map the geography I studied, I debated the meaning of the chapters of grammar I had to learn."[135]

The Baronne de Gerando wrote admiringly of a similarly dedicated teacher, Mlle. Seitz, *gouvernante* of a friend's daughter: "When I see a person of great merit . . . consecrate herself again to the fundamentals of education . . . when I see her take up a task so painful, without the least personal interest, through the simple triumph of the duties that she prescribed for herself and the good that she wishes to do; oh! I find myself very inferior to her, very guilty of not having made the best use of the years of my youth."[136] Nothing could better express both the new level of professional competence and dedication of the educators of the young or the new respect this earned them in the eyes of their employers. The new parental concern over children encouraged the hiring of competent personnel as child-raisers, and this competence gave the role of educator increased status and respect.

Servants' Child-Care in the Late Eighteenth Century

With the new competence of servants hired to care for children and the new parental supervision over the child-raising process, children received better care from servants in the late eighteenth century than they had in the past. Self-interest, if nothing else, prompted servants to treat their charges well. On the one hand, they could lose their jobs if their charges complained of mistreatment to their doting parents. When four-year-old Poulou, daughter of a *conseiller* in the Parlement of Toulouse in the 1780s, was beaten by her *gouvernante*, she ran to her mother and poured out the story "in her baby talk"; the *gouvernante* was promptly fired.[137] (What a contrast to poor Cardinal de Bernis, whose parents did not discover his beatings until the welts had festered!) On the other hand, servants who gained the affection of the capricious beings around whom the household now revolved had a powerful weapon for self-advancement. Children fought to protect the servants they were fond of: both Mme. de Genlis and Mme. de La Tour du Pin, for example, threw tantrums when their beloved *gouvernantes* were threatened with dismissal.[138] Children could also be used to wheedle favors from their parents. When Mme. de Campan, teacher of young Hortense de Beauharnais, daughter of the Empress Josephine, wanted to place a protégé as *femme de chambre* in the empress's household, she wrote to her pupil singing the woman's praises. "Read my letter to your mother," she urged, and added—three times—be sure to tell her what I have said.[139]

The end result was that children in late-eighteenth-century households were treated gently and kindly by servants, not just by those especially hired for them but also by all the domestics of the household. Memoirs written by nobles born in the last decades of the Old Regime dwell for the first time on *happy* memories of childhood, and household servants figure largely in these accounts. Madame de Chastenay, for example, eulogized in her memoirs the father of her mother's *nourrice*, taken into the household in his old age. He had been a mason, possessed a "gentle character," and "his patience was inexhaustible." He was the constant companion of her childhood, taking her and her brothers and sisters on walks, telling them endless stories, and teaching them to appreciate the beauties of nature. "We called him grandfather, [and] our real grandfather could not have been more respected or loved."[140] Similarly, the Marquise de Villeneuve-Arifat seems to have spent most of her childhood in the kitchen, listening with a fascination tinged with disbelief to the tales Naret, the family cook, told about the years he had spent in the army.[141] Mme. de La Tour du Pin was another toddler who apparently spent most of her childhood in the kitchen. The servants taught her to cook and sew, skills that she put to good use on a farm in upstate New York when she was exiled during the Revolution.[142]

The new intimacy with the children of the household doubtless tried many a servant's patience. Domestics now had to endure constant interruptions in their work, constant teasing, temper tantrums, and even blows (when Poulou d'Albis got a new *gouvernante* to replace the cruel Thérèze, her mother noted, "Poulou knows very well the right she has over her; she hits her every time the fancy takes her").[143] We get a rare servant's eye view of the permissive child-rearing of the prerevolutionary era in a letter written in 1786 by L'Amireau, our Parisian chef, to his fiancée Rose Farcy, describing the daughter of his employers: "It is la Diderot [a maid] who cares for the child, who has reached during the trip a summit of naughtiness. If you had had responsibility for her you would have ended sooner or later by abandoning your job, which would have driven you crazy. I cannot begin to tell you how spoiled she is by her mother."[144] But while the new child-raising was difficult for servants, it was marvelous for children. By the eve of the Revolution households had become in a sense extended families for noble children, and servants played the role of surrogate aunts and uncles, grandmothers and grandfathers, not only caring for their bodily needs but also spending time with them, playing with them, telling them stories, answering their questions—in fact, acting as considerate relatives would.

Effects of the New Methods of Child-Rearing

It seems likely that these changes in child-raising among the nobility had a substantial impact on the adult attitudes and behavior of that class, but this was probably less far-reaching than it might have been because infantile experiences, which psychologists tell us are the most important for personality formation, were the least affected by the new child-rearing methods. Most elite children—indeed, most children of all but the poorest classes—still had wet nurses who still followed traditional, careless, and psychologically damaging modes of infant care. Some change did occur, to be sure. The new parental vigilance over the nursing process probably inspired at least some nurses to take better care of their charges, and the slow diffusion of the new "natural" methods of infant care eliminated many of the psychologically harmful aspects of traditional child-rearing. The gradual disappearance of swaddling, for example, allowed the child to explore and learn from his environment, and the elimination of demand feeding eased the psychological pains of weaning.[145] But in general infant care changed only gradually—*nourrices* and swaddling were still very much in evidence in at least some parts of France throughout the nineteenth century—and it continued to leave scars on the psyche.

Only after the child's return home did the really revolutionary changes in child-raising have their impact. The new maternal vigilance guaranteed that children were raised in a warm and caring environment, indulged by their parents and well treated by the servants of the household. With the mother's new assertion of her authority over the child-rearing process, youngsters had a single loving mother figure to identify with, even though they still spent most of their time in the hands of servants.[146] And these servants clearly treated their charges with more care and attention than had been the rule previously. It seems probable therefore that the separation anxieties and the "expedient" and manipulative character traits that had formerly marked children raised by servants were much less in evidence in the noble children of the 1760s, 70s, and 80s. It seems probable, too, that these children, raised with careful attention, were much less violent and aggressive in their attitude toward the world and much more open and comfortable in their personal relationships than their seventeenth-century ancestors had been.[147] It seems likely that they grew up into warm, loving, and domestic-minded adults, that they became the affectionate spouses and doting parents portrayed in the noble memoirs of the revolutionary period. The turn toward domesticity of the nobility in the late eighteenth century may have originated in changes in child-rearing as well as caused them.

More important for our purposes, however, than the impact of the new methods of child-care on noble family life were the changes they may have brought to the master-servant relationship and consequently to the attitude of the nobility toward the lower classes in general. As we have seen, in the late eighteenth century master-servant relationships seem to have been more distant than they had been in the era of patriarchalism, but they were also more egalitarian. These relationships were characterized by a basic recognition of the servant as a fellow human being with his or her own cares and desires. This sea-change in relationships within the household had many causes—the penetration of the market economy in domestic service and the rise of egalitarian social philosophies, to name only two. But it is probable that the altered relationship between servants and the children of the elite also played a role. The relatively happy childhood experiences of the nobility in the prerevolutionary decades probably helped eradicate the contempt that had marked master-servant relationships in earlier generations. Mme. de Chastenay wrote of the prerevolutionary court nobility, "We of the Old Regime were all raised in the ideal of the equality of men, of scorn for worthless distinctions . . . the teachers of young people were almost all imbued with these ideas."[148] Given the fact that many young nobles were tutored by would-be philosophes, this is probably true. But it is also probable that theoretical lessons in equality were reinforced in the minds of young nobles by their practical experiences with domestic servants. Clearly their teachers were worthy of respect, although they lacked the distinctions of birth, and even the lesser servants appeared, to these children at least, as decent and kindly human beings. Contacts with such servants probably gave noble children at least some sense of the dignity and worth of the lower classes. And through the endless stories these domestics told of their families and their childhoods (stories that to their listeners must have seemed as exotic and fascinating as any fairy tale), noble children probably gained at least a slight insight into the realities of life among the people.

This process is visible in the memoirs of two noblewomen who developed very close attachment to the servants who cared for them as children: Lucy Dillon, later Marquise de La Tour du Pin, and Stéphanie de Saint-Aubin, later the notorious Comtesse de Genlis. Both of these women came from the highest levels of the court nobility, and both had mothers who, despite the revolution in mothering, did not take much interest in their daughters, but who did at least care enough to choose exceptional servants to raise them.[149] Mme. de Genlis's *gouvernante* Mlle. Mars and Mme. de La Tour du Pin's *gouvernante* Marguerite, like most governesses in the ancien régime, were young and uneducated. Mlle. Mars, equipped with "no wordly learning," although well schooled in both music and religion as the daughter of a cathedral choirmaster, was only sixteen when she took on the care of the seven-year-old Mme. de Genlis; Marguerite, an illiterate peasant woman, was twenty-five when she came to serve the twelve-year-old Lucy Dillon.[150] But both were exceptionally talented women who cared for their charges with intelligence, insight, and imagination, as well as love. Both Mme. de Genlis and Mme. de La Tour du Pin soon became passionately attached to their *gouvernantes*. Indeed, their memoirs suggest that these relationships became the emotional centers of these women's lives. Certainly they wrote about them in their memoirs with more genuine feeling than they did of their parents, their husbands, or even their children. The emotional highpoint of Mme. de Genlis's autobiography is a chance meeting with Mlle. Mars in the Palais-Royal more than twenty years after they were parted in her childhood, a meeting so disturbing that it provoked hysterical fits of weeping.[151] Mme. de La Tour du Pin did not record such a scene, for, with the exception of a few years of exile during the Revolution, she was never parted from her Marguerite. But even when she wrote her memoirs at age fifty-five she remembered the terror that the threat of such a parting had provoked in her when she was young.[152]

Both Mme. de La Tour du Pin and Mme. de Genlis grew up not only to love but also to respect their *gouvernantes*. Mme. de Genlis wrote of the "natural intelligence, gentle and serious character, noble and sensitive soul and most sincere piety" of Mlle. Mars, and Mme. de La Tour du Pin praised the "sensible judgment, accurate mind, and strong soul" of her Marguerite.[153] Both women consciously modeled their behavior on that of their *gouvernantes*, and both tried to adhere to the high moral standards they set.[154] Both contrasted the moral world of their *gouvernantes* with that of their parents—and both found the latter wanting. As Mme. de La Tour du Pin put it: "The princes, the dukes, the grands of the earth were judged by a girl of twelve and a peasant of twenty-five, who knew only the hamlet in which she was born and the house of her parents."[155] Both women grew up to be rebels against the social values of their own milieu: Mme. de La Tour du Pin mildly, Mme. De Genlis strongly.[156] Both found the world of servants (as represented by their *gouvernantes*) preferable to their own, and both fantasized as children about being servants themselves. Mme. de Genlis's favorite childhood game was to play at being a *gouvernante*, while Mme. de La Tour du Pin spent most of her time with the household servants and persuaded them to let her "help" them cook and sew. When her Marguerite went home to visit her mother, "I made her tell me all that she did in her village. For several days after, I imagined what I would do if I were a peasant, and I envied the lot of those that I visited in the village who were not, like, me, obliged to hide their tastes and their ideas."[157]

Remarkably enough, both women as adults turned their childhood fantasies into reality. The happiest period of Mme. de La Tour du Pin's life was her year of exile in America during the Revolution, which she spent on a farm in upstate New York. While her army officer husband sat around in his uniform and brooded on past glories, she cooked and sewed, mothered her children, milked the cows, and churned butter and sold it at the local market—a true peasant daughter of her Marguerite at last.[158] And Mme. de Genlis of course, grew up to be the most famous *gouvernante* of the Old Regime.

These are extreme cases, to be sure, made possible by the unusually strong characters of the two *gouvernantes*. But probably this sort of thing occurred in a milder form in many noble families. The liberalism and egalitarianism of the high nobility in the 1780s may have owed as much to the attachment of nobles to the servants of their childhood and to the taste for peasant life—admittedly idealized and sentimentalized—which they acquired from them as it did to the writings of the philosophes.

In 1688 in *Les Devoirs des maîtres et des domestiques* Claude Fleury had warned *gouvernantes* that if the children in their charge died through their carelessness and neglect they were guility of murder in the sight of God.[159] In 1828 the anonymous author of *Les Domestiques chrétiens* urged servants to give the children they cared for at least some measure of the rules and discipline their doting parents refused to provide.[160] Between the publication of these two works lay a revolution not only in the attitude of parents toward their children but also in the relationship between the children of the household and the domestic servants who cared for them. This revolution probably had immense repercussions on the way the French elite viewed both its domestic servants and its social inferiors in general. The Revolution of 1789 might be therefore in some small part traceable back to the nursery.

8

Epilogue: The Revolution and After

The law does not recognize the state of servanthood [domesticité]; *only a bond of solicitude and acknowledgment may exist between the employee and his employer.*
—The Declaration of the Rights of Man and Citizen, June 14, 1793

With this ringing statement the Jacobins, who tried to reshape so many other aspects of French society during their brief period in power, sought to reform the institution of domestic service. Throughout the French Revolution the legislators of the successive representative bodies, the National Assembly, the Constituent Assembly, the Legislative Assembly, the Convention, worried periodically about the problems posed by domestic service. These were of course only a minor concern in comparison with the legislators' major tasks of reordering France's government and legal system, reshaping church-state relations, creating a society that functioned according to the principles of Liberty, Equality, and Fraternity, and protecting these accomplishments against the foes of the Revolution both foreign and domestic. But the relative lack of urgency of the problem of domestic service did not make it any less intractable.

The issue of domestic service put the revolutionaries in a quandary. On the one hand, they had many reasons to dislike both the occupation itself and those who practiced it. Most of them probably shared the concern of prerevolutionary philosophes and economists that domestic service was an unproductive use of male labor and drained the countryside and the agricultural sector, backbones of *la patrie*, of much needed workers. Many probably also shared the traditional negative stereotypes about servants: that they were lazy, lusty, dishonest, and possessed of a low, animal-like cunning—in short, hardly suitable citizens for the new society of reason and justice. Further, they objected to the dependence and servility that, they believed, the occupation inevitably produced in those who practiced it. Again these were qualities that rendered servants unfit to be part of the new society of free and equal men.[1]

But undoubtedly the greatest drawback of the occupation from the point of view of the men of 1789 was its traditional association with the nobility. Servants had for so long functioned as the public representatives of *les grands*, protecting them against insult and making certain that they received the deference that was their due, that the men of the Revolution found it difficult to conceive of them in any other role. This function, of course, did not endear them to the revolutionaries, committed as they were to a society based on natural equality rather than the distinctions of birth. Even worse, the association of servants with the nobility seemed to pose a threat to the very survival of the Revolution. For if servants remained loyal to their noble masters, would they not constitute a sort of fifth column which could rise up in support of the aristocratic opposition to the revolutionary government?

It was this threat that prompted the men of the Constituent Assembly to deny servants the right to vote and to hold public office. Their debates over the issue show that they were convinced, as indeed the Puritans and Levellers had been during the English Revolution a century before, that no man in a position of dependency on another could make an independent, free, and rational choice when he voted.[2] One member, D'André, even proposed denying the vote and the right to hold office to all wage earners on the grounds that they too were, in effect, servants dependent on their employers: "I believe that everyone who is not only in a state of servanthood [*domesticité*] but also who is in a state of immediate dependence on another person, be it the king or private citizen, must be excluded from the legislature. Any man who is absolutely dependent on another is not free to express his will."[3]

In part the legislators' concern over dependency stemmed from a general fear of the possible corruption of the body politic by monied interests, a major theme in eighteenth-century writings about representative government in England and America as well as in France.[4] This fear was expressed in a later portion of D'André's speech: "I ask if it is not possible for such men to make a coalition among themselves to fill the legislative body with their people. If they have the means to put men of talent on their payroll . . . could they not then employ seduction, intrigue, even corruption [murmurs] to get them elected?"[5] But their concern also stemmed from the special nature of servant dependency: from the fact that servants were likely to be the tools of *noble* masters. As a certain M. Thouret pointed out in the course of the debate, "It is not the influence of a simple private citizen that we must fear."[6] It was rather the influence of *les grands*, an influence inevitably counterrevolutionary.

In light of such fears, it is not surprising that the revolutionaries directed a steady stream of propaganda at servants in hopes of cutting their ties of dependency to their masters and winning them over to the principles of 1789. Typical of this propaganda was the pamphlet *Avis à la livrée par un homme qui la porte*, which was published, probably in Paris, in 1789. Ostensibly written by a domestic for the edification of his fellows, the *Avis* painted a grim picture of the personal humiliations that servitude entailed: "How many brutalities, how many fits of ill-humor to endure, like the epithets of *drôle, coquin, gredin,* which rain down on us for the least little trifle!" Why be loyal to masters who refused to recognize that you were their equal, and indeed respected you less and treated you worse than they did their dogs and horses? Instead, the pamphlet exhorted, remember that you were "born citizens, *enfants de la patrie*"; remember that your family and friends are of the people. Throw in your lot with them and with their revolution: "Therefore, it is necessary, comrades, when our masters sound us out, to declare frankly that we are of the people, and that we will never abandon the people for them."[7]

The *Avis* is interesting because it illustrates the ambivalence of the revolutionaries' feelings toward servants. It shows both why they disliked and feared servants and why, at the same time, they hoped servants might turn out to be good revolutionaries after all. For servants were, as pamphlets like the *Avis* so frequently pointed out, born good sans-culottes and therefore potential allies of the Revolution. They certainly had good reason to dislike their noble masters. As for their unfortunate choice of occupation, they were after all wage earners who had to support themselves; they could not really pick and choose the work they did. Furthermore, much of their work served a social purpose. The men of the Revolution were, at heart, good bourgeois; most of them employed at least a *servante*. Therefore they realized how important domestic help was in the smooth running of a home. Indeed, given the revolutionaries' emphasis on the family as the cradle of virtuous and patriotic *citoyens*, the contributions servants made to the creation of tranquil domesticity took on some of the lineaments of a patriotic duty.

Thus the men of the Revolution had reasons to both like and dislike the occupation of domestic service and those who practiced it. Given this ambivalence, it is not surprising that revolutionary policy toward servants was contradictory. In essence the revolutionaries wanted, as they proclaimed in the passage of the Declaration of the Rights of Man quoted at the beginning of this chapter, to do away with "the state of *domesticité*," by which they meant the outmoded dependency and inequality which were so deeply embedded in the master-servant relationship. But at the same time they wished to preserve the socially useful aspects of the occupation and to help the good sans-culottes who practiced it. As the founders of a Parisian mutual aid society for servants proclaimed in 1789, they wanted to give "domesticity, which under an arbitrary government is by turn tyrannized and tyrannizing," its "rightful role, that of a useful part of the family."[8]

This contradictory attitude led the revolutionaries to deny servants the right to vote and to hold public office and to tax them as a luxury, while at the same time they founded numerous public welfare institutions to aid domestics who were aged, ill, or unemployed.[9] But the heart of the revolutionaries' policy was their attempt to change the way people thought about domestic service. To accomplish this they relied on the introduction of a new vocabulary. During the Terror the terms *laquais* and *domestique*, with their traditional degrading connotations, were forbidden; servants were instead to be called *familiers* or *hommes de peine*.[10] When the Comtesse Dufort de Cheverny wanted to send a servant to care for her ailing husband during his imprisonment, she was informed by her jailer that there was no such thing as a servant: "a French citizen is not a *domestique*." However her husband could have the help of an "*aide*" if he wished.[11] This attempt to transform the vocabulary of domestic service was less silly than it may appear at first glance. One of the major achievements of the Revolution, after all, was the creation of a new vocabulary for political and social discourse. The revolutionaries recognized that the traditional vocabulary of domestic service had acquired connotations of dependency and inferiority over the centuries. They wanted a fresh vocabulary suitable for a new sort of *domesticité*, in which masters and servants would be, at last, genuine equals, employer and employee bound only by the cash-nexus. Their vision of master-servant relationships is epitomized by this passage in *Le Catéchisme français*, published in 1797 as a primer for use in primary schools:

> *What are the duties of masters toward their servants?*
> My fellow creature, forced to sell me his labor,
> Expects from me kindness, regard, reason, justice;
> With money I don't need I buy long service
> In this unequal exchange, it is I who gives less.
>
> *What are those of a servant toward his master?*
> That he be reliable, vigilant, sober, active, circumspect.
> No duty is too vile; only vice can be that.
> A *valet* steeped in vice is nothing but an abject slave;
> An honest servant is the equal of a good master.[12]

This new vision of *domesticité* was shared by both the liberal bourgeoisie dominant in the early years of the Revolution and by the more radical Jacobins. They differed only in their optimism about the timing of the transformation. The liberal revolutionaries of the Constituent and Legislative assemblies did not think that they could transform the traditional postures of master and servant overnight; hence their denying domestics the right to vote. The Jacobins were more optimistic. They truly thought that it would be easy to do away with the dependency that had been the hallmark of master-servant relationships in the past. They wanted to do what two enterprising playing-card manufacturers did in 1793 when they produced a deck of cards suitable for the revolutionary era: to replace all *valets* (jacks) with good revolutionary sans-culottes.[13]

Servants' Attitudes toward the Revolution

How well did the revolutionaries succeed in their attempt to change *valets* into sans-culottes? Did they succeed in winning servants over to the Revolution? These questions are difficult to answer, for the attitude of servants toward the Revolution was every bit as complex and ambivalent as was the revolutionaries' attitude toward them. Both as individuals and as a group, servants had much to lose from the Revolution—but also much to gain.

Clearly many domestics came to despise the Revolution and all its works. They were, after all, viewed with suspicion by the revolutionaries and denied any political role in the new order. This treatment was a cause of much resentment and sparked most of the relatively infrequent servant demonstrations during the Revolution. In August 1789, for example, servants took to the streets of Paris to demand the right to vote, to attend district assemblies, and to enroll in the National Guard. They were only with difficulty dissuaded by the National Guard from staging a march of 40,000 servants down the Champs Elysées.[14]

Servants also resented the Revolution because of the hostility directed at them by patriotic sans-culottes. As we have seen, the relationship between servants and the rest of the *menu peuple* had been tense throughout the Old Regime. As symbols for the surrogates of the hated nobility, servants had always been targets for popular attack and abuse. With the coming of the Revolution, such attacks naturally increased in number and ferocity. By the spring of 1791 any manservant who appeared on the streets of Paris in his livery was simply asking to be assaulted. Crowds shouted "A bas des valets" as well as "A bas des aristocrates" whenever they caught a glimpse of a nobleman and his liveried retainers.[15] By 1793 even lowly *servantes* who appeared on the streets in the clean white aprons that were the traditional badges of their calling were liable to insult and injury. One day in the summer of 1793 Mme. de la Tour du Pin's beloved *gouvernante* Marguerite was walking in Paris, wearing her customary "spotless" apron, when she was stopped by a cook, who warned her, "An apron like that will get you arrested and guillotined."[16]

Subject to discrimination by revolutionary legislation and to attack by militant sans-culottes, many domestics naturally turned against the Revolution. The revolutionaries' suspicion of the loyalty of servants, like their doubts of the loyalty of priests, had elements of a self-fulfilling prophecy. These groups gradually became antirevolutionary because the Revolution had already turned against them.

Another factor that made at least some servants antirevolutionary was simple loyalty to their noble masters. We have seen that such loyalty was quite common among domestics, and that its roots lay deep within the psychological experience of being a servant. Therefore it was often strong enough to survive even the outbreak of a revolution whose main enemy was the nobility. A servant like Le Tellier, *valet de chambre* to the Marquis de Barthélemy (see above, chapter 4), who had wholeheartedly adopted his master's value system, was unlikely to be shaken in his loyalties by revolutionary attacks on the nobility. Nor, on a simpler psychological level, was a servant like Mme. de la Tour du Pin's Marguerite, who almost looked upon her mistress as her own child, and knew her to be a kindly and decent woman who bore little resemblance to the frivolous and decadent noble of revolutionary propaganda. To such servants the persecution their masters suffered during the Revolution seemed unwarranted. Many expressed their loyalty by saving their masters from the guillotine. The Comte de Périgord was saved by the devotion of his servant Beaulieu, who carefully threw away all the petitions and pleas for mercy entrusted to him by the Comte and his family. Completely forgotten by the Committee of Public Safety, the Comte survived the Terror and was released at Thermidor. A *valet* named Bontemps rescued the daughter of his mistress from a prorevolutionary lynch mob in the Vendée. The elderly Duchesse de Villeroi survived the emigration through the devotion of her *femme de chambre*, who supported her penniless mistress with her own meager savings.[17] Such examples could be multiplied indefinitely, and they clearly show that one of the major causes of antirevolutionary sentiment among servants was loyalty to their persecuted noble masters.

But probably the most important single factor in turning servants against the Revolution was simple self-interest. For with its persecution of the nobility—and, during the Terror, the rich in general—the Revolution caused widespread unemployment among servants. What happened in many noble households is illustrated in the following letter, written in March 1790, by one M. Venez to his uncle, M. de Boissey, one of those Swiss Calvinist bankers so prominent in Parisian financial circles before 1789:

> The bankers will not make loans at any price; you know as well as I do that no one has received a *sou* from *rentes* bought in 1789; therefore I had for my living expenses last year only my revenues from my land, from which I had to deduct all the *lods* and *cens* [feudal dues] which my peasants did not want to pay me, since I did not wish to be burned out or put *à la lanterne*. . . .I have therefore been reduced to firing three servants and selling my horses.

He added, with some prescience, "God preserve us from the evils that threaten us, but I believe that the revolution is a tragedy in five acts, of which we have as yet seen only the prologue."[18]

Countless other wealthy families experienced economic setbacks similar to those outlined by M. Venez, and countless families took similar measures of retrenchment: they fired their servants.[19] Unemployment among servants grew even greater in 1792, 1793, and 1794, as more and more noble families fled France and the growing radicalism of the Revolution. Few aristocrats took along their full household when they emigrated; considerations of both cost and safety prohibited that. Some nobles took with them their personal attendants, their *valets* and *femmes de chambre*, but most fled unaccompanied by servants, planning to hire new ones when they reached Germany, Italy, or England. Of every ten aristocrats who emigrated, only one seems to have been accompanied by a domestic.[20] To be sure, at least a few of the servants left behind when their masters fled remained on the family payroll, charged with caring for the houses and furniture so precipitously abandoned. One example was Venier, *domestique* to the Comtesse de Balbi. Throughout the year 1791 he was bombarded with letters from his former colleague, Pierre Farcy, the Comtesse's *valet de chambre*, who had fled to Coblentz with his mistress and who relayed Madame's instructions about the furniture and porcelain left behind.[21] But such employment occupied only a handful of domestics. When their noble masters fled the country or withdrew to their rural estates to ride out the storm, most servants were thrown unceremoniously onto a drastically shrunken job market. Unfortunately it is impossible to find any accurate statistics on the extent of unemployment among servants during the years of the Revolution, but clearly it was substantial. One indication is the estimate that the population of Versailles dropped by as many as 20,000 between 1789 and the Year II, as domestics and other "hangers-on of the *ci-devants*," unemployed when their masters emigrated, went off to Paris to look for work.[22]

Unemployment was always an economic disaster for servants, and never more so than during the Revolution, when added to the lack of employment opportunities were the hardships of wartime shortages and runaway inflation. The results show up on the rolls of the governmental agencies of public assistance which replaced the private charities of the ancien régime. During the Revolution domestic servants began for the first time to appear as clients of institutions of public assistance in proportions comparable to their representation among the *menu peuple*. Of the inmates of the new *dépôt de mendicité* established at St. Denis in December 1789, for example, 16 percent of the men and 14 percent of the women were servants.[23]

One formerly proud and prosperous domestic driven to seek public welfare during the Revolution was Nicolas Petit, once *officier* in the household of the Duc de Villeroy. His papers, preserved when his widow was arrested, apparently for royalist sympathies, show that during the ancien régime Petit, son of a *manouvrier* from Menecy, had had a successful career as a servant in Paris. When he married in 1761 both he and his bride had substantial savings, and he received a share of the family land, worth 875 livres, as a wedding settlement. During the 1770s and 1780s both husband and wife regularly received appeals for financial help from poor relations. But after 1789 the now elderly couple themselves had to seek help to survive. Petit, once the proud *officier* of a ducal household, was reduced to working as a humble *portier*—when he could find a job. He paid only three livres in taxes in 1791 and 1792, and during the Terror he was excused from military service on the grounds of indigence as well as old age. He died in a Parisian *hospice d'humanité* on 11 *brumaire an* 4. After his death his widow struggled on alone. She was constantly dunned by her landlady for not paying the rent, and she survived only through the help of the *Comité de Bienfaisance* of her local section, which in the Year 5 described her as being "without any resource whatsoever."[24]

It is not surprising that servants like the widow Petit eventually fell foul of the revolutionary authorities, for while part of her troubles were simply the natural concomitants of servant old age (see above, chapter 3), her situation was clearly aggravated by the hardships resulting from the Revolution. Police records of the revolutionary years are full of the seditious utterings of servants like Marie Petit who felt themselves victimized by revolutionary politics. For example, *domestique* Louis Blanchet was arrested in July 1790 while drinking in a tavern in Aix-en-Provence for uttering threats against the National Assembly, which he blamed for the widespread unemployment among servants. He is reported to have said "that the time will come when action must be taken because servants and workers are increasingly unhappy . . . that if that continues, unemployed servants and workers must take to the streets."[25] And Eugene Gervais, an unemployed Parisian cook, was arrested at the Palais Royal for inciting his fellow *domestiques sans conditions* against the bourgeois National Guard in the explosive summer of 1789. Gervais reportedly stated "that all the bourgeois guard and all the people who wear the uniform are all j____f____s and that 10,000 servants are capable of f____ing all the j____f____s who wear blue coats with white trim . . . and that there are 60,000 servants in Paris who could unite with the workers of different crafts and that one would then see all the j____f____s hide themselves at home in their f____ing uniforms."[26]

Gervais is interesting because he was obviously against the Revolution not simply because it had put him out of work but also because to him it seemed the work of the rich and well-born, whom he hated with an instinctive visceral hatred. Such sentiments were of course common among servants, and they prompted servants to support the Revolution as well as to oppose it. For there was another side to the coin. Many domestics were prorevolutionary simply because they hated their masters and therefore identified with a movment which took the aristocracy, and, later, the rich in general, as its targets. Many servants seem to have viewed the Revolution as a perfect opportunity to get revenge for the insults that were so much a part of their lives. Apparently one such servant was the *domestique* of M. Suard, a *ci-devant* minor philosophe; at any rate he took advantage of the chaotic conditions in Paris during the September Massacres to rob his employer of 8,000 francs. The theft greatly surprised M. and Mme. Suard, because the servant had been with them for several years and had never before shown any signs of dishonesty or discontent.[27] While there is no real proof of this, it seems probable that servant protest, in its traditional forms of robbery for revenge, ritualized insult and insolence, and the public blackening of a master's reputation, increased during the years of the Revolution. At least it is clear that many servants denounced their masters to revolutionary tribunals.[28]

Apart from a desire for revenge, servants had other reasons to support the Revolution. Some favored it simply because they approved of its basic principles. Even deep-seated loyalty to a master did not necessarily preclude such sentiments, as Mlle. des Echerolles discovered when she talked to her former *gouvernante*, who had devoted her life to caring for her mistress's mentally retarded sister. Mlle. des Echerolles assumed that, since the woman had remained loyal to her employers throughout the upheavals of the period, she naturally shared their counterrevolutionary sentiments. She was astonished to discover that in fact the nurse thought the Revolution had been a good thing and hoped it would triumph.[29]

Still other domestics supported the Revolution because they saw it as an opportunity for a better life. Some viewed the Revolution as a chance to improve the conditions of their occupation. Apparently this hope inspired a group of Parisian domestics who gathered at a theater in the Belleville district of the city to petition the Estates General in August 1789. They demanded that salaries for domestic servants be doubled, that they no longer be required to wear livery, and that the employment of blacks as servants be prohibited.[30]

Other servants saw the Revolution as a chance to leave their occupation behind and find other more satisfying and more lucrative employment. The widespread unemployment among domestics, especially the male servants of noble households, was therefore not necessarily a tragedy. As we have seen, many men servants had abandoned the occupation even before the Revolution, and many more dreamed of doing so and embarking on careers in commerce. For such people the unemployment of the revolutionary period often provided the final spur to make them leave domestic employment behind once and for all and try to make their dreams come true. Although it is impossible to find much evidence about this, it seems probable that the years of the Revolution saw a substantial movement of male servants into petty commerce and the crafts. The one aspect of this flight of the male servant which can be traced concerns the chefs of great noble houses. Many of them were able to turn their inevitable unemployment to their advantage, either emigrating to England, where they were lionized by high society, or staying in France and opening public restaurants.[31] Either way they found not only well-paying employment but also the social recognition as respectable bourgeois which they had desired for so long.

The spectacular career of Bertrand Arnaud is an example of a servant canny enough to take advantage of the opportunities the Revolution offered. His papers, like those of Nicolas Petit, were confiscated and preserved by the revolutionary tribunals. Before 1789 Arnaud had been a humble lackey in the household of one M. Sevelinge, *écuyer* and *secrétaire du roi* residing in Versailles. But even then he was ambitious to make his fortune. Like many other servants he was a moneylender, and once in the 1770s he went to court to collect a debt of only 27 livres. An opportune legacy (of 350 livres cash and all his household goods) from his master, who died in 1792, gave him more substantial funds to invest, and he soon put them to work in the profitable speculations opened up by the Revolution. In 1793, for example, he invested thousands with bankers in La Rochelle, probably in privateering. He became quite rich and made munificent donations to the various forced loans of the revolutionary period. Not surprisingly, Arnaud was strongly prorevolutionary, and he even served for a time in the municipal government of Paris, thus becoming one of the very few servants or former servants to hold public office during the Revolution.[32]

Doubtless Arnaud was more adept than most in seizing the economic opportunities of the revolutionary years. But even less canny male domestics could turn the Revolution to their advantage by riding out the worst of the unemployment (1792–94) through service in the revolutionary armies,[33] and then either setting themselves up as petty *commerçants* or returning to an occupation now hungry for their labor. For from Thermidor on, employing a servant, even a male domestic, was once again politically acceptable. Therefore unemployment among servants disappeared, and there was in fact an acute shortage of servants, especially men servants. This situation lasted as long as the wars of the revolutionary and Napoleonic eras did, for it was the army's need for men that kept civilian labor in short supply. The Comtesse de Bézémont complained about the shortage in 1809. "In Paris," she wrote, "everyone mounts guard on their employees; for *domestiques, portiers,* everyone most necessary to a person there are absolutely no replacements."[34] Naturally this shortage pushed servants' wages up to very high levels. As table 28 shows, salaries for all types of servants surpassed their prerevolutionary highs during the years from 1789 to 1815, although the general inflation of the period made the gains less striking than they appear at first sight. Clearly once

TABLE 28

Average Wages for All Types of Servant, Pre- and Post-Revolution (in Livres)

	1770s, 1780s	1789–1815
Male lower servants	46.4	152.8
Male upper servants	190.5	262.7
Female lower servants	36.4	67.5
Female upper servants	78.6	123.0

Sources: See Bibliography, section I, D.

the dangers and dislocations of the early years of the Revolution had passed, domestic service again became one of the more economically advantageous occupations for the lower classes.

For domestic servants the effects of the French Revolution were mixed. To some it brought unprecedented economic and personal disasters. Because of the Revolution they lost the jobs that had brought them not only income but also the vicarious social prestige that came from their association with *les grands*. They saw their respected masters persecuted, and they themselves were vilified for practicing an occupation unsuited to the new egalitarian society. For other servants, however, the years of the Revolution were years of opportunity. They found in the Revolution a chance to assert the dignity of their calling and their own sense of equality with their employers; to take revenge for a lifetime of insults; and even to leave the occupation behind altogether and try to make their fortunes.

Thus it is not surprising that some servants favored the Revolution while others did not. A domestic's attitude toward the events of 1789 was probably shaped by both his economic and social circumstances and by his perception of them—by his temperament, in short. Among servants, as among the barristers of Toulouse studied by Lenard Berlanstein—and probably among most other social groups as well—it was the adventurous, the ambitious, the far-sighted who most welcomed the Revolution, while those who were more temperamentally inflexible and set in their ways disliked it for the changes it brought to their lives.[35]

Their essentially private and personal reaction to the events of 1789 explains the relative quiescence of servants during the revolutionary years. Servants on the whole were not conspicuously politically active either for or against the Revolution. Domestics did not take the lead in the great *journées* of the Revolution; they were not prominent among the *vainqueurs de la Bastille*. George Rudé found only 32 servants among his 1,536 identifiable participants in crowd actions and riots between 1787 and 1795.[36] During the Revolution servants did not hold public office (obviously, since this was prohibited in the early years of the Revolution), join the Jacobin clubs, or volunteer for the army or National Guard in any large numbers.[37] Yet servants also did not figure prominently among the *émigrés* or the victims of Terror. Servants formed a mere 1.7 percent of all those who left France during the Revolution; they contributed only 3 percent of the victims of the Terror.[38] The conflicting loyalties servants felt to both their masters and to their own family and class, plus the fact that the Revolution could both help and hurt them, prevented any widespread politicization of domestic servants. Most of them saw the Revolution solely in terms of its effect on their own private lives, and most, when asked afterward what they had done during the Revolution, would have replied with the Abbé Siéyès, "I survived."

Even in retrospect servants' reactions to the French Revolution retained a private and personal character. During the Restoration many domestics who were old enough to have been in service before 1789 regretted the passing of the Old Regime. This was especially true of those who had been members of great noble households. In her memoirs the Marquise de Villeneuve-Arifat noted that her mother's cook Naret, who returned to their household after the Terror, constantly complained about the economy that his now relatively penurious mistress enjoined upon him and constantly recalled with regret the good old days before 1789 when he had cooked for twenty, thirty, and forty people a day.[39] Similarly, the Restoration politician Charles de Rémusat recalled that as a chid he first learned of the Revolution from the tales of his family's servants, who "spoke of the ancien régime with a certain regret, with a sort of esteem." But, as Rémusat shrewdly noted, this regret and esteem were rarely translated into political support for ultra-royalism. They were purely private regrets for a "time when they had been part of a great household" and had "nothing of the retroactive enthusiasm for the Old Regime so common later among the enemies of the Revolution."[40] Among most servants nostalgia for the Old Regime was simply nostalgia for the great noble household with its "public" domestic service which had disappeared with the Revolution.

The Effects of the Revolution on Domestic Service

The impact of the Revolution on the lives and fortunes of individual servants may have been limited and ambiguous, but its impact on the occupation as a whole was clear-cut, obvious, and undeniable. Domestic service in the France of the 1850s was very different from domestic service in the France of the 1750s: private instead of public, bourgeois rather than aristocratic, feminine rather than masculine, egalitarian rather than patriarchal. The Revolution did not initiate these transformations; as we have seen, they had their beginnings in the last decades of the Old Regime. Instead the Revolution acted as a catalyst, speeding up these changes to a point where, with the economic and social changes of the nineteenth century, they became irreversible.

The Revolution had perhaps its most obvious impact on patterns of servant employment. It doomed the great noble household and its public style of servant-keeping. The Revolution created a society egalitarian in theory if not in practice, and such a society had no use for the liveried lackey who demanded public deference for his master. The Revolution also accelerated the replacement of the nobility by the bourgeoisie as the leading employers of servants. During the Revolution nobles had to dismantle their households, and their establishments would never again be so large as they had been before 1789. The *noblesse* of the Restoration was not only poorer than its prerevolutionary counterpart, it was also, understandably, more discreet about displaying its wealth.[41] With the retreat of the nobility, the bourgeoisie, its ranks greatly expanded by the economic growth of the nineteenth century, came into its own and took the leading place as servant-employers. In the nineteenth century the bourgeoisie employed the majority of servants, and indeed the keeping of a domestic was an almost infallible sign of middle-class status.[42]

The bourgeoisification of domestic service of course brought with it a feminization of the occupation. The bourgeoisie had always preferred female domestics; this pattern continued in the nineteenth century. During the Revolution the bourgeoisie adopted the values of domesticity as a badge of class identity. They believed religiously in the home as women's sphere and housework as women's work. Middle-class homes were the domain of the *ménagère*, and cared for by her in partnership with an inevitably female servant.[43]

The feminization that marked domestic service in the nineteenth century was a product not only of the emergence of the bourgeoisie as leading servant-holders but also of the flight of male servants from the occupation. Here again the Revolution was a crucial turning point. The unemployment of the revolutionary years was worse for male servants than for women, and men suffered more from the revolutionaries' attacks on the occupation as one unworthy of a free man and citizen. Yet, as if in compensation, the Revolution also opened up more alternative employment opportunities for them than it did for their female colleagues. The result was a massive flight of men from domestic service. This trend accelerated in the nineteenth century, when the quickening pace of economic change created attractive alternative employment opportunities for men at first in petty crafts and in the growing commercial sector, both traditional havens of male domestics, and later in factory labor. During the nineteenth century domestic service became progressively less attractive for men as the wages of male servants failed to keep pace with those of other occupations. For women, however, the economic growth and industrialization of the nineteenth century had the opposite effect, narrowing rather than increasing the choice of occupation. In the nineteenth century the wages of a *bonne* were better than the pittance that a female factory worker could earn, and domestic service continued to provide a chance to save for a dowry and make a respectable marriage. Thus domestic service remained one of the most worthwhile of the dwindling employment opportunities for women.[44] This provided the final impetus for the feminization of the occupation. In Aix-en-Provence in the eighteenth century about 60 percent of the servants were women; by 1835 the figure was 80 percent. And in France as a whole the percentage of women servants rose from 68 percent in 1851 to 83 percent by 1911.[45]

Thus with regard to patterns of servant employment and the sexual make-up of the occupation, the Revolution speeded up transformations already under way, transformations that would be brought to completion by the economic and social changes of the nineteenth century. In the realm of master-servant relationships, however, the impact of the Revolution was more complex. The revolutionaries took an egalitarian, cash-nexus view of master-servant relationships. They defined servants as wage laborers hired to do housework, thus completing the transition of the occupation from *état* to *métier* and ridding it once and for all of those ambiguous types like family members, apprentices, and gentlemanly upper servants.[46] They also made a concerted attack on the remnants of patriarchy and the dependency it entailed. But the postrevolutionary period, and indeed the nineteenth century in general, saw a reversal of the latter trend.

The most striking feature of master-servant relationships in the nineteenth century was the attempt by masters to restore patriarchal values and patterns of behavior to relationships within the household. This effort was clearly visible in the domestic manuals of the postrevolutionary period. Books like François Perennes's *De la Domesticité avant et depuis 1789* (1844) displayed a strong nostalgia for the golden age of patriarchy, "before the Revolution . . . when religion reigned in every heart. . . . The servant was born in the shadow and under the very roof of the château of his master. . . . Between master and servant there was a true union and community of sympathies, affection, and interest. . . . The one obeyed as the other commanded, by a sort of original instinct, without debasement on the one side or arrogance on the other."[47] Nineteenth-century domestic manuals and religious and moral tracts intended for servants showed a clear attempt to restore this mythical golden age. While they revealed traces of the changes in the occupation in the last half of the eighteenth century (servants were deemed responsible for their own sexual conduct, and a major duty of masters was paying their servants promptly), most of what they said about master-servant relationships could have been written in the seventeenth century. Mme. Le Prince de Beaumont, the French equivalent of Hannah More, wrote innumerable novels and tracts for the newly literate servants of the 1820s; her lists of the duties of masters (they should oversee their servants' behavior, provide them with religious instruction, and care for them in illness and old age) and her exhortations to servants to accept the lowly place to which God had called them could have come from the pages of Claude Fleury.[48]

This nostalgia for the golden age of patriarchy was, ironically, a product of the Revolution itself. It was the class war of the revolutionary era that made masters uncomfortable with an egalitarian conception of master-servant relationships. In the last decades of the Old Regime the disintegration of patriarchy had brought a new uneasiness and distancing to the relationships between the "domestic enemies" but it had also brought equality, camaraderie, and even affection. The Revolution killed the latter tendencies; only the uneasiness remained. This uneasiness was manifested in further physical and psychological distancing between master and servant. In the nineteenth century, all domestics, even for the first time women, were put into uniforms. And they were banished from the household itself into attic *chambres de bonne*. Some masters even hoped to do without servants entirely. The rise of the *faiseuse de ménage*, who "lived out," is a testimony to this. Another sign of the uneasiness of master-servant relationships in the nineteenth century was the attempt to restore patriarchy to relationships within the household. Nineteenth-century employers tried to exercise a strict control over their servants' private lives. They restricted their free time, supervised their social contacts ("no followers"), and gave them edifying reading and religious instruction. They took, or at least pretended to take, a personal interest in their welfare. And they demanded discipline, docility, and unquestioning obedience in return.

In general employers got what they wanted, for the work force was young, female, and fresh from the country. In the nineteenth century a new literary image of the servant appeared on the scene, an image different from both the lusty and animal-like creature of the patriarchal period and the proud and ambitious Figaro of the prerevolutionary decades. The new image was that of the peasant heroine of Flaubert's *Un Coeur simple* and the family cook in Proust's *Remembrance of Things Past*. She was inevitably female, a simple country girl, docile and pious, who devoted herself to her employers and had no other life outside the household.[49] This image represented what the worried employers of the nineteenth century desperately hoped their servants would be.

Yet however much they wanted to believe that their servants were like this, nineteenth-century employers did not delude themselves with the notion that this image fit the lower classes as a whole. For yet another heritage of the Revolution to domestic service was the fact that the household ceased to be a laboratory of class attitudes, and employers ceased to project their images of their domestics onto the lower classes. The class war of the Revolution taught employers that their loyal and obedient servants were not representative of the people at large. In the nineteenth century "the people" wore the guise not of pious servant girls but of peasants to be dragged from rural sloth and ignorance and turned into Frenchmen, of factory workers to be made hard-working and industrious, and, above all, of the criminally-inclined "dangerous classes" of the bourgeoning urban slums.[50] The very different image of the servant exemplified the effort of nineteenth-century employers to make their households into places apart, havens in the heartless world of industrialization, where the social peace and harmony of an earlier era would prevail. But they could not delude themselves that these havens of peace and harmony were representative of the world outside their walls.

Thus a divorce between the popular image of the servant and that of "the people" was the Revolution's final legacy to the occupation of domestic service. In the nineteenth century domestic service remained an important occupation for the lower classes, especially for lower-class women. It also remained an important factor in the domestic and family life of the new ruling classes. But it lost its former role as the prime shaper of the social attitudes of both the lower classes and the elite. Domestic service was no longer so central to the social history of the period as it had been in the Old Regime, when the relationships between the "domestic enemies" had both mirrored and shaped those of society as a whole.

Notes

Preface

1. For the history of the phrase see Iris Origo, "The 'Domestic Enemy': The Eastern Slaves in Tuscany in the Fourteenth and Fifteenth Centuries," *Speculum* 30 no. 3 (July 1955), 322. (I wish to thank my colleague at Syracuse University, Edward Muir, for this reference.) For the use of the phrase in ancien régime France see John Andrews Van Eerde, "The Role of the Valet in French Comedy between 1630 and 1789 as a Reflection of Social History," (Ph.D. diss., The Johns Hopkins University, 1953), 104–5.

2. Albert Babeau, *Les Artisans et les domestiques d'autrefois* (Paris, 1886); Alfred Franklin, *La Vie privée d'autrefois* (Paris, 1887–1902); J. Jean Hecht, *The Domestic Servant Class in Eighteenth-Century England* (London, 1956).

3. Examples are Franklin L. Ford, *Robe and Sword* (Cambridge, Mass., 1953), and Robert Forster, *The Nobility of Toulouse* (Baltimore, 1960).

4. The rise of these new fields incidentally turned the former liabilities of servants as topics (the fact that so many servants were women, and they lived and worked within the private and domestic rather than the public and productive spheres) into assets. Consequently the late 1970s saw an outpouring of excellent studies on domestic servants in various times and places, including Theresa McBride's pioneering work on domestics in nineteenth-century France and England (*The Domestic Revolution* [New York, 1976], and David Katzman's study of servants in the United States in the nineteenth and twentieth centuries (*Seven Days a Week: Women and Domestic Service in Industrializing America* [New York, 1978]). Even servants in Old Regime France received some attention: they were the subject of two excellent dissertations, one French and one American (Marc Botlan, "Domesticité et domestiques à Paris dans la crise [1770–1790]" [*thèse*, École des Chartes, Paris, 1976]; Sarah Crawford Maza, "Domestic Service in Eighteenth Century France" [Ph.D. diss. Princeton University, 1978]), and one fine book, Jean-Pierre Gutton's *Domestiques et serviteurs dans la France de l'ancien régime* (Paris, 1981). My work draws heavily on these studies, and I thank M. Botlan and Professor Maza for generously making copies of their work available to me. But my approach differs from these largely prosopographical studies in its attention to the psychology of master-servant relationships.

5. A model for such a study is a recent work on English farm servants, Ann Kussmaul's *Servants in Husbandry in Early Modern England* (Cambridge, 1981).

6. In this my major inspiration was Lawrence Stone's magisterial *The Family, Sex, and Marriage in England, 1500–1800* (New York, 1977), which makes superb use of memoirs to explore family relationships. Alert readers will notice that I borrowed not only the use of memoirs but also much of my interpretation of the timing and causes of changes in family life from Stone.

Chapter 1

1. For the estimate of 100,000 see J. C. Nemeitz, *Séjour de Paris, c'est-à-dire, instructions fidèles pour les voiagers de condition* (Leyden, 1717), 92. This is undoubtedly exaggerated. But

there were probably 75,000 to 80,000 servants in Paris by the eve of the Revolution. See Botlan, "Domesticité et domestiques," 190.

2. Fanny Cradock, *Journal de Mme. Cradock: Voyage en France (1783–1786),* trans. Mme. O. Delphine-Balleyquier (Paris, 1896), 16.

3. For guidebooks, see Nemeitz, *Séjour de Paris,* 85–92; L. Liger, *Le Voyageur fidèle ou le guide des étrangers dans la ville de Paris* (Paris, 1715), 403; and Luc-Vincent Thierry, *Almanach du voyageur à Paris . . .* (Paris, 1783), 115. For visitors' comments, see B. L. de Muralt, *Lettres sur les anglois et les françois et sur les voiages,* ed. Charles Gould and Charles Oldham (Paris, 1933), 27; Elizabeth Craven, *A Journey through the Crimea to Constantinople* (Dublin, 1786; facsimile ed., New York, 1980), 31–32; and Prince Karamzine, *Voyage en France, 1789–90* (Paris, 1885), 286–90.

4. For the exportation of French servants to foreign countries see Barbara Wheaton, *Savoring the Past* (Philadelphia, 1983), 160–72.

5. A higher figure, 17 percent for the city as a whole, is often cited (eg., in Maza, "Domestic Service," 6, and "Porphyre Petrovitch," "Recherches sur la criminalité a Paris dans la seconde moitié du 18e siècle," in A. Abbiateci et al., *Crimes et criminalité en France sous l'ancien régime: 17e–18e siècles* [Paris, 1971], 246). This figure is Daumard and Furet's calculation (Adeline Daumard and François Furet, *Structures et relations sociales à Paris au milieu du XVIIIe siècle* [Paris, 1961], 18–19) of the percentages of servants among the male Parisians who made marriages contracts in 1749. But marriage contracts are a source weighted to favor servants over less prosperous and sophisticated members of the lower classes like *gagne-deniers,* who were much more likely to marry without a contract. Therefore the figure is probably slightly inflated, and 15 percent is a more realistic estimate. The latter is the calculation of Daniel Roche, *Le Peuple de Paris* (Paris, 1981), 27.

6. For Aix in 1695 see Jean Paul Coste, *La Ville d'Aix en 1695: Structure urbaine et société* (Aix, 1970), 2:712; for the mid-eighteenth-century figure, see Maza, "Domestic Service," 6. The figures for Toulouse are my calculations based on the number of servants listed in the *capitation* rolls for these years; they will be explained at length later.

7. For Bordeaux see Paul Butel and Jean-Pierre Poussou, *La Vie quotidienne à Bordeaux au dix-huitième siècle* (Paris, 1980), 40; and Poussou, "*Les Structures démographiques et sociales,*" in F.-G. Pariset, ed., *Bordeaux au dix-huitième siècle* (Bordeaux, 1968), 367. For Marseilles see Maza "Domestic Service," 8. In minor commercial centers the proportion of servants was even smaller. In Elbeuf, a Norman textile town, there were only 150 servants in a population of 4,000 to 5,000 (Jeffry Kaplow, *Elbeuf during the Revolutionary Period: History and Social Structure* [Baltimore, 1964], 74).

8. An example is the Provençal town of Digne, where around 3 percent of the population were servants (Maza, "Domestic Service," 6).

9. These figures are based on the statistics in Gutton, *Domestiques et serviteurs,* 102, and Peter Laslett, *Family Life and Illicit Love in Earlier Generations* (Cambridge, 1977), 32. In the present state of our knowledge it is impossible to say what factors determined the employment of farm servants, rather than sharecroppers or hired day laborers, as agricultural laborers. The two areas where farm servants were most frequently found, Gascony and the Rouergue, were otherwise very different in social and family structure, patterns of landholding, and type of agriculture practiced (see Gutton, *Domestiques et serviteurs,* 102–3; 108–9). Much more research is needed on this subject.

10. There are no reliable statistics on the socioeconomic makeup of both country and town in the ancien régime. But given what we know about it, these seem good guesses.

11. This was the estimate of the eighteenth-century statistician Moheau, and it is generally accepted today. See Gutton, *Domestiques et serviteurs,* 7–8, and Maza, "Domestic Service," 5.

12. There are no reliable statistics for the proportion of servants in the population in the Middle Ages. In the seventeenth century Marcel Cusenier estimates that about one-sixth of the population were domestics (*Les Domestiques en France* [Paris, 1912], 13), but this seems doubt-

ful. A more likely figure is 6–7 percent (Maza, "Domestic Service," 4). In the nineteenth century only around 2.5 percent of the population were servants (McBride, *Domestic Revolution,* 35).

13. For de la Touche see Robert Forster, *Merchants, Landlords, Magistrates* (Baltimore, 1980), 112–14; for Jeanne Leconte, see Archives Départementales, Gironde (hereafter ADG) 12B 287, Procédures et informations de la jurat de Bordeaux, 1746. (See Bibliography for archival abbreviations.)

14. *Webster's Third International Dictionary* (New York, 1976), 2075.

15. Quoted in Gutton, *Domestiques et serviteurs,* 11.

16. The best description of the medieval household is Mark Girouard, *Life in the English Country House* (New Haven, 1978), 13–29. He deals primarily with England, but there is no reason to suppose that French households were significantly different.

17. For the changing conception of "service" over the centuries see Philippe Ariès, "Le Service domestique: Permanence et variations," *XVIIe Siècle* 32, no. 4 (October–December 1980), 415–20.

18. For a sixteenth-century household which included such types see Nancy L. Roelker, *Queen of Navarre: Jeanne d'Albret, 1528*–1572 (Cambridge, Mass., 1968), 26.

19. For this usage see Charlotte Arbaleste de Mornay, *Mémoires de Mme. de Mornay* (Paris, 1868), 175.

20. Ariès, "Le Service domestique," 418; Girouard, *English Country House,* 143.

21. For the provisions of the *capitation* see Marcel Marion, *Les Impôts directs sous l'ancien régime* (Facsimile ed, Geneva, 1974), 48–61. For laws on the *police des domestiques* see Des Essarts, *Dictionnaire universel de police* (Paris, 1787), 3:467; andBN Manuscrits FF 21800, Collection Delamare, Ordonnance de Roi, April 8, 1717.

22. Compare what follows with Gutton, *Domestiques et serviteurs,* 12–15.

23. Quoted in Jean-Louis Flandrin, *Familles: Parenté, maison, sexualité dans l'ancienne société* (Paris, 1976), 11.

24. Comte d'Avaux, *Correspondance inédite du Comte d'Avaux (Claude des Mesmes) avec son père, Jean-Jacques de Mesmes, Sieur de Roissy*, ed. A. Boppe (Paris, 1887), 38; [Audiger], *La Maison réglée d'un grand seigneur et autres, tant à la ville qu'à la campagne, et le devoir de tous les officiers et autres domestiques en général* (Paris, 1692), preface, pages unnumbered.

25. The changing nature of family life and family ties over the centuries has recently received much attention from historians. The two best works on the patriarchal phase of the family unfortunately deal with England; they are Stone, *The Family, Sex and Marriage*, 123–221; and Randolph Trumbach, *The Rise of the Egalitarian Family* (New York, 1978), 119–65. The nearest French equivalent to these studies is Flandrin, *Familles*, but it is rather idiosyncratic. David Hunt, *Parents and Children in History: The Psychology of Family Life in Early Modern France* (New York, 1970), and Philippe Ariès, *Centuries of Childhood: A Social History of Family Life*, trans. Robert Baldick (New York, 1962), are suggestive but not definitive.

26. Claude Fleury, *Les Devoirs des maîtres et des domestiques*, reprinted in Alfred Franklin, *La Vie privée d'autrefois*, (Paris, 1898) 23:210.

27. For more on the patriarchal vision of the servant, see below, chapter 5.

28. See Gordon J. Schochet, *Patriarchalism in Political Thought* (New York, 1975).

29. Fleury, *Les Devoirs des maîtres et des domestiques*, 212.

30. For the economy and society of Toulouse see Robert Forster, *The Nobility of Toulouse* (Baltimore, 1960); Lenard Berlanstein, *The Barristers of Toulouse* (Baltimore, 1975); Georges Frêche, *Toulouse et la region Midi-Pyrénnés au siècle des lumières (vers 1670–1789)* (Paris, 1974); Jean Sentou, *Fortunes et groupes sociaux à Toulouse sous la Révolution, 1789–1799* (Toulouse, 1969).

31. This table (and also tables 2, 3, and 4) are drawn from the tax rolls of seven of the eight districts, or *capitoulats*, in the city of Toulouse: those of Daurade, La Pierre, St. Pierre, Pont-Vieux, St. Sernin, St. Barthélemy, and Dalbade. The tax roll for the eighth, St. Etienne, also exists for 1695, but I omitted it because its tax rolls do not exist for the years 1750 and 1789, and

therefore a table that included it would not be valid for later comparisons. This omission is unfortunate, because St. Etienne was a large and fashionable district with a high concentration of domestics.

32. For more on the payment—or nonpayment—of servants, see below, chapter 2.

33. These estimates are based on the costs of feeding hospital inmates in this period from Cissie C. Fairchilds, *Poverty and Charity in Aix-en-Provence, 1640–1789* (Baltimore, 1976), 63, 75, and are deflated to the level of seventeenth-century prices.

34. This income estimate is based on the chart of page 518 of Pierre Deyon, *Amiens: Capitale provinciale* (Paris, 1967), with salaries of wife and children added.

35. ADHG C 1082, Rolle de la capitation de la ville de Toulouse, 1695, Dalbade.

36. Girouard, *English Country House*, 27.

37. It should be noted that merchants, *procureurs*, surgeons, and the like often employed large numbers of male clerks (or in the case of surgeons, apprentices) in their businesses, but this was not the same as employing a liveried lackey.

38. In Bordeaux the *capitation* was recorded by occupation, not district, and few of its records have survived. I was unable to find the *capitation* rolls of Bordeaux's prosperous overseas merchants, the *négociants*, for the late seventeenth century. But one indication that even these dynamic merchants were reluctant to employ male domestics is the fact that only 16 percent of the male servants who made marriage contracts in Bordeaux in 1727–29 were employed in middle-class households, while 72 percent were employed by the nobility. (For sources for these figures see Bibliography, section I, B, 3.)

39. McBride, *The Domestic Revolution*, 18–19.

40. Pierre-Jean-Baptiste Nougaret, *Tableau mouvant de Paris, ou variétés amusants* (Paris, 1787), 3: 74.

41. Nemeitz, *Séjour de Paris*, 135.

42. [Jean Meusnier], *Nouveau traité de la civilité qui se pratique en France parmi les honnestes gens* (La Haye?, 1731), 39–40.

43. In Bordeaux in 1716 the judges of the Cour des Aides averaged 2.93 servants each, while those of the Parlement averaged 5.80. And in the Parlement the households of *conseillers* averaged 4.44 domestics each, and those of *présidents* 8.69, while the *premier président* of the Grande Chambre had a household of 20 (ADG C 1082, Rolle des domestiques de la cour de Parlement, 1716).

44. ADHG C 1082, Rolle de la capitation de la ville de Toulouse, 1695.

45. Charles de Ribbe, *Une Grande Dame dans son ménage au temps de Louis XIV, d'après le journal de la Comtesse de Rochefort (1689)* (Paris, 1889), 137.

46. Audiger, *La Maison réglée*, 1–2.

47. Gutton, *Domestiques et serviteurs*, 42–43, 28, 32; de Ribbe, *Une Grande Dame*, 137.

48. The family and domestic life of the nobility is thoroughly described below, especially in chapters 2 and 7. See also the works cited in note 25.

49. Richard Sennett, *The Fall of Public Man* (New York, 1976), 47–122, esp. 64–88.

50. E. P. Thompson, "Patrician Society, Plebeian Culture," *Journal of Social History* 7, no. 4 (Summer 1974), 382–405. This brilliant article inspired much of my thinking about master-servant relationships and social relationships in general during the seventeenth and eighteenth centuries.

51. The most persuasive statement of this view is Michel Vovelle, "Le tourant des mentalités en France, 1750–89: la 'sensibilité pré-révolutionaire,' " *Social History* 5 (1977), 605–30.

52. This table is less trustworthy than the earlier ones, for after 1695 *capitation* rolls became both less abundant and less accurate. For the 1750 figures I was able to find tax rolls from approximately that date for the same seven of Toulouse's eight *capitoulats* that were used for the 1695 figures. The rolls for Daurade, La Pierre, and St. Pierre dated from 1750 itself; those of Pont-Vieux and St. Sernin are from 1757; that of St. Barthélemy is from 1748, and that of Dalbade is from 1741. But for the 1789 figures I could find rolls for only five *capitoulats*: La Pierre,

Pont-Vieux, and St. Pierre for 1789; Dalbade for 1788, and Daurade for 1764. Therefore the figures for 1789 are not truly comparable with those of 1695 and 1750. Also, the *capitation* rolls became progressively less accurate in the course of the eighteenth century, with more people listed only by name with no occupation given (as the large category of "other" in my table show) or even omitted entirely. This makes these later figures even more dubious. But in the absence of better data I think their use is justified.

53. The figure probably was even larger, for many of the unknowns in the category "other" were middle-class types who employed servants.

54. Marquise de Villeneuve-Arifat, *Souvenirs d'enfance et de jeunesse, 1780–1792* (Paris, 1902), 3031.

55. AN T 208[1], Comptes du maréchal et maréchale de Mirepoix, 1749–77, Etat des nourriture, gages, mémoires de depense . . . des gens de Mme. la Maréchale, janvier 1788; T 491[2], Papiers du Prince de Lambesc, Etat de la maison de S. A. Mgsr. le Prince de Lambesc; Comte Dufort de Cheverny, *Mémoires*, ed. Robert de Crévècoeur (2nd ed.: Paris, 1909), 1:164.

56. For an explanation of why these figures rather than the *capitation* rolls were used, see above, note 38.

57. Craven, *A Journey through the Crimea*, 31.

58. This change will be traced in detail below, especially in chapters 2, 6, and 7. For further information see Flandrin, *Familles*; James F. Traer, *Marriage and the Family in Eighteenth Century France* (Ithaca, 1980); Margaret Darrow, "French Noblewomen and the New Domesticity, 1750–1850," *Feminist Studies* 5, no. 1 (Spring 1979), 41–65; Cissie Fairchilds, "Women and Family," in *French Women and the Age of Enlightenment*, ed. Samia Spencer (to be published by Indiana University Press), and Elisabeth Badinter, *Mother Love: Myth and Reality* (New York, 1981).

59. Flandrin, *Familles*, 13.

60. See below, chapter 2.

61. See for example Abbé Grégoire, *De la Domesticité chez les peuples anciens et modernes* (Paris, 1814), 1.

62. This is how freedom is defined in the *Social Contract*, for example. See Maurice Cranston's introduction to the Penguin edition (New York, 1968), 42.

63. Ordinance of police, of November 6, 1778, quoted in Des Essarts, *Dictionnaire universel de police*, 3:478.

64. Quoted in Gutton, *Domestiques et serviteurs*, 11.

65. Quoted in ibid., 12.

66. The professionalization of tutors is discussed below, chapter 7. For the emancipation of musicians from the ranks of servants see Judith Tick, "Musician and Mécène: Some Observations on Patronage in Late 18th-Century France," *International Review of the Aesthetics and Sociology of Music* 4 (1973), 245–56; and for the changes in musical taste that made this possible see William Weber, "Musical Taste in Eighteenth-Century France," *Past and Present* 89 (November 1980), 58–85.

67. Sieur de La Varenne, *Le Cuisinier françois* (Paris, 1654), Preface; Menon, *Les Soupers de la Cour, ou L'Art de travailler toutes sortes d'alimens* . . . (Paris, 1755), vi; M. A. Carême, *Le Maître d'Hôtel français* (Paris, 1822), iv.

Chapter 2

1. Christophe de Bordeaux, "Chambrière à louer à tout faire" and "Varlet à louer à tout faire" in Anatole de Montaiglon, ed., *Recueil de poésies françoises des 15e et 16e siècles* (Paris, 1855).

2. Robert Darnton, "Work and Culture in an Eighteenth Century Printing Shop" (paper

presented at the Library of Congress, 1981), has an excellent discussion of the uneven rhythm that characterized not only the eighteenth-century printing trade but preindustrial work in general. I thank Professor Darnton for sending me his paper, which has since been printed in Robert Darnton, *The Literary Underground of the Old Regime* (Cambridge, 1982), 148–66. My citations are to the original paper.

3. Audiger, *La Maison réglée*, 136–42.

4. *Affiches, Annonces . . . de Toulouse*, April 2, 1788.

5. See below, chapter 3.

6. [Anon.], *Mémoires du Comte de Bonneval, ci-devant général d'infanterie au service de sa Majesté Impériale et Catholique* (London [?], 1737), 1:86.

7. Goujon, *Journal du maître d'hôtel de Msgr. de Belsunce durant la peste de Marseille, 1720–1722* (Paris, 1878), 22.

8. Audiger, *La Maison réglée*, 34–36.

9. AN T 208^{1}, Comptes du maréchal et maréchale de Mirepoix, 1749–77.

10. AN T 186^{45}, 186^{50}, 186^{56}, Papiers du duc et duchesse de Fitz-James.

11. Comtesse de Genlis, *Le La Bruyère des domestiques, précédé de considerations sur l'état de domesticité en général et suivi d'une nouvelle* (Paris, 1828), 30; *Mémoires de Mlle. Avrillon, première femme de chambre de l'Impératrice, sur la vie privée de Josephine* (Paris, 1833), 369; Audiger, *La Maison réglée*, 53; G. Vanel, *Une Grande Ville au 17e et 18e siècles: La Vie privée à Caen, les usages, la société, les salons* (Caen, 1912), 165.

12. [Anon.], *La Maltôte des cuisinières, ou la manière de bien ferrer la mule: Dialogue entre une vieille cuisinière et une jeune servante*, reprinted in Franklin, *La Vie privée d'autrefois* (Paris, 1898), 344–56.

13. Grégoire, *De la Domesticité*, 140; AN T 254, Papiers de Pierre Farcy, valet de chambre.

14. *Mémoires du Comte Dufort de Cheverny*, 19.

15. [Anon.], *Avis à la livrée par un homme qui la porte* (N. p., 1789), 4–5.

16. *Journal de Guienne*, September 12, 1784.

17. For an amusing description of these hair styles see the *Mémoires de la Baronne d'Oberkirch sur la cour de Louis XVI et la société française avant 1789*, ed. Suzanne Burkard (Paris, 1970), 56.

18. Laurette de Malboissière, *Lettres d'une jeune fille du temps de Louis XV (1761–66)*, ed. Marquise de la Grange (Paris, 1866), 194.

19. *Journal de Guienne*, January 20, 1785.

20. Laurette de Malboissière, *Lettres d'une jeune fille*, passim.

21. Louis Nicolardot, *Ménage et finances de Voltaire, avec une introduction sur les moeurs des cours et des salons au 18e siècle* (Paris, 1854), 106; Comtesse de Genlis, *Mémoires inédites de Mme. La Comtesse de Genlis, sur le dix-huitième siècle et la Révolution française, depuis 1756 jusqu'à nos jours* (Paris, 1825), 6:272; Laure Junot, Duchesse d'Abrantes, *The Home and the Court Life of the Emperor Napoleon and His Family* (London, 1893), 1:271.

22. For an example of servants joining in entertaining guests, see Mme. de Genlis, *Mémoires inédites*, 1:183; for a discussion of their involvement in their employers' love-lives, see below, chapter 6.

23. Fanny Cradock, *Journal de Mme. Cradock*, 325.

24. *Mémoires de Madame du Hausset, femme de chambre de Madame de Pompadour*, ed. M. F. Barrière (Paris, 1847), esp. 129.

25. Evidence about the hours of meals comes from Le Grand d'Aussy, *Histoire de la vie privée des françois* (Paris, 1815), 3:309–10; and Laurette de Malboissière, *Lettres d'une jeune fille*, 6, 7. These are the hours for meals during the last decades of the ancien régime. Meals had been getting progressively later since the seventeenth century, when the *diner* took place at twelve or one and the *souper* in the early evening. These earlier hours would return during the Revolution.

26. Marquise de La Tour du Pin, *Journal d'une femme de cinquante ans, 1778–1815* (Paris, 1907), 1:7.

27. [Menon], *La Cuisinière bourgeoise, suivi de l'office à l'usage de tous ceux qui se mêlent de dépenses de maisons* (Paris, 1746), 12–14.

28. See the description of a dinner in a great noble household in [Nicolas de Bonnefons], *Les Délices de la campagne, suitte de jardinier françois* (Amsterdam, 1655), 373–78.

29. Maurice Caillet, "Le Livre des dépenses de la maison de l'Archevêque Lomenie de Brienne," *L'Auta* 273 (April 1958), 54.

30. See the sample table settings in *Le Cannameliste français, ou nouvelle instruction pour ceux qui diserent d'apprendre l'office . . .* (Nancy, 1768), and the description in Wheaton, *Savoring the Past*, 138–42.

31. Wheaton's is the best history of the evolution of French cuisine during the Old Regime.

32. See the instructions for molding and coloring ices and jellies in M. Emy, *L'Art de bien faire les glaces d'office . . .* (Paris, 1768).

33. Wheaton, *Savoring the Past*, 102, 106.

34. Marquise de Villeneuve-Arifat, *Souvenirs d'enfance*, 4.

35. Wheaton, *Savoring the Past*, 108–9.

36. Cusenier, "Les Domestiques en France," 200.

37. Marquise de Sévigné, *Lettres* (Pléiade ed, Paris, 1953), 1:272–75.

38. The Marquise de Villeneuve-Arifat tells of chambermaids in her grandfather's household who refused to eat at the same table with the lackeys; her grandfather pointed out that they did not refuse to sleep with them, so they could surely share a table (*Souvenirs d'enfance*, 4).

39. Ordonnance du roy, contre les domestiques compris sous la nom de gens de livrée . . . , 8 avril 1717, in BN FF 21800, Collection Delamare: Serviteurs et manouvriers.

40. Phillis Cunnington, *Costume of Household Servants: From the Middle Ages to 1900* (London, 1974), 15–17.

41. For the ordinances see Dubois de St. Gelais, *Histoire journalière de Paris* (Paris, 1716), 2: 139–40; for warning see Nemeitz, *Séjour de Paris*, 82.

42. Comte Dufort de Cheverny, *Mémoires*, 20.

43. For an example, see Isambert, Jourdan and Decrusy, *Recueil général des anciennes lois françaises depuis l'an 420 jusqu'à la révolution de 1789* (Paris, 1822–23), 20:584, Ordinance of February 8, 1713.

44. Quoted in Vanel, *Une Grande Ville*, 167.

45. *Journal de Guienne*, October 9, 1784.

46. *Affiches, Annonces . . . de Toulouse*, April 30, 1788.

47. The functions of the *gens de livrée* are well analyzed in Maza, "Domestic Service," *passim*. Much of my description is derived from hers.

48. For complaints about the lack of skill of French coachmen, see John Moore, *A View of Society and Manners in France, Switzerland, and Germany* (Boston, 1792), 232; for an example of an accident, see Anne Robert Jacques Turgot, *Lettres de Turgot à la duchesse d'Enville (1764–74 et 1777–80)*, ed. Joseph Ruivet et al. (Louvain and Leiden, 1976), 52.

49. Mme. de La Tour du Pin, *Journal*, 1:38.

50. *Journal inédit du Duc de Croy, 1718–84*, ed. Vicomte de Grouchy and Paul Cottin (Paris, 1906), 4:292.

51. *Avis à la livrée*, 5–6.

52. Laurette de Malboissière, *Lettres d'une jeune fille*, 182.

53. This phrase, and much of the description which follows, comes from Girouard, *English Country House*, 126–28, 144.

54. The function of the *cabinet* is perhaps best conveyed in the memoirs of the seventeenth-century Quietist, Mme. de la Mothe Guyon. Trapped in an arranged marriage and forced to live in a household in which her husband, his relatives and friends, and even the servants despised and mistreated her, she treasured the time spent in the room she referred to as "my dear *cabinet*." It was the only place where she could be truly alone. (*La Vie de Mme. J.M.B. de la Mothe Guion, écrite par elle-même* [Cologne, 1720], 1:108.)

55. Jean-François de Bastide, *Dictionnaire des moeurs* (LaHaye [?], 1773), 8.

56. For English vails, see Hecht, *The Domestic Servant Class*, 158–68. For contemporary opinion that vails were much less prevalent in France, see Abbé Le Blanc, *Lettres de M. L'Abbé Le Blanc* (Amsterdam, 1751), 153–59; and Vicomte de Grondy, "Un Voyageur français en Angleterre en 1764: Elie de Beaumont," *Revue Britannique* 71, no. 11 (November 1895), 98.

57. Charles-Louis, Baron de Pollnitz, *Memoirs: Being the Observations He Made in His Late Travels, from Prussia through Germany, Italy, France . . .* (London, 1737), 2:244–45.

58. For an example of such laws see BN Manuscrits FF 21800, Collection Delamare: Serviteurs et manouvriers, ordinance of the Paris Parlement, August 28, 1737; for an example of domestic manuals, see [Anon.], *Devoirs généraux des domestiques de l'un et de l'autre sexe, envers Dieu, et leurs maîtres et maîtresses . . .* (Paris, 1713), 132–33. Account books of noble households indicate that the bribing of the *gens de livrée* was widespread. Those of the Prince de Lambesc, for example, show that he distributed money to the *suisses* of the Apartements du Roi and the Ministre de Guerre whenever he went to Versailles. (AN T 491², Papiers du Prince de Lambesc.)

59. R. P. Toussaint de St. Luc, *Le Bon Laquais ou la vie de Jacques Cochois dit Jasmin . . .* (Paris, 1739), 21; Fleury, *Les Devoirs*, 292.

60. AN Y 14518, Commissaires de police, St. Germain (Paris), 1722; AN Y 14543, Commissaires de police, St. Germain, 1753.

61. AN Y 14518, Commissaires de police, St. Germain, 1721.

62. *Lettres de M. de Marville, lieutenant-général de police, au ministre Maurépas, 1741–47*, ed. A. de Boislisle (Paris, 1896), 2:5, 45, 182.

63. Vanel, *Une Grande Ville*, 164.

64. The Collection Delamare (BN Manuscrits FF 26468) contains royal edicts forbidding servants to carry arms promulgated in 1609, 1629, 1665, 1670, 1671, 1676, 1678, 1679, 1680, 1682, 1685, 1687, 1689, and 1695.

65. There was also a specialized group of servants who cared for the children of the household; they are discussed separately in chapter 7.

66. For example, in Toulouse in 1695 the household of a *président* of the Parlement contained eleven domestics, but only one of them was a *servante*. (ADHG C 1082, Rolle de la capitation de Toulouse, capitoulat de St. Pierre.)

67. Audiger, *La Maison réglée*, 85.

68. Quoted in Allan Braham, *The Architecture of the French Enlightenment* (Berkeley, 1980), 14.

69. See *Lettres de Madame du Boccage, contenant ses voyages en France, en Angleterre, en Hollande et en Italie pendant les années 1750, 1757, et 1758* (Dresden, 1771), 78.

70. These are printed as endpapers in Girouard, *English Country House*.

71. For examples see Dufort de Cheverny, *Mémoires*, 1:204; Laurette de Malboissière, *Lettres d'une fille*, 348; *Mémoires de M. de Gourville, concernant les affaires auxquelles il a été employé par la cour, depuis 1642, jusqu'en 1698* (Paris, 1724), 2:295–300.

72. This conclusion is based on the almost total silence in domestic manuals about the subordination of lower to upper servants.

73. For the prevalence of corporal punishment in Old Regime households see below, chapter 4.

74. The best evidence of the proportion of Parisian servants who "lived out" comes from Daniel Roche's analysis of *inventaires après décès*. Fifty-one percent of the servants who died intestate in Paris from 1695 to 1715 and 47 percent of those who died intestate from 1775 to 1790 lived apart from their masters. (Roche, *Le Peuple de Paris*, 107). This source exaggerates the number of servants living on their own, for it is drawn mostly from the elderly, many of whom had left service and therefore their masters' households. Nevertheless the proportion of servants who "lived out" in Paris was probably quite high. For married couples with their own apartments, see

below, chapter 3. An example of a household where lackeys were given money for room and board rather than being housed by their master is that of the Prince de Lambesc; see AN T 491², Papiers du Prince de Lambesc; Etat de la maison de S. A. Monseigneur Le Prince de Lambesc, janvier 1777. For the servants who hired themselves out to foreign visitors see Karamzine, *Voyage en France*, 286; and Nemeitz, *Séjour de Paris*, 85–87.

75. M. de St. Amans noted in his *livre de raison* that his male servants all slept in a room "next to the stables facing the tower." (BN Manuscrits, N A 6580, Livre de raison de famille St. Amans.)

76. ADHG 3E 10802, Fonds Roc, 1788; 3E 1182, Fonds Saurine, 1787.

77. ADG 3E 20393, Fonds Gatellet, 1789; ADHG 3E 10936, Fonds Rieux, 1729; ADHG 1285, Fonds Brios, 1788–89.

78. The living conditions of nineteenth-century *bonnes* are described in McBride, *Domestic Revolution*, 51–55; and Anne Martin-Fugier, *La Place des bonnes: La Domesticité feminine à Paris en 1900* (Paris, 1979), 115–36.

79. For the organization and functioning of the hôtel in the seventeenth and early eighteenth centuries see Orest Ranum, *Paris in the Age of Absolutism* (New York, 1968), 151–55.

80. AN T 208¹, Comptes du maréchal et maréchale de Mirepoix, 1749–77.

81. Daniel Roche's analysis of the estate inventories of Parisians who died intestate shows that servants were much more likely to own fine furniture than the rest of the lower classes. (*Le Peuple de Paris*, 131–57.)

82. For such arguments see Fleury, *Les Devoirs*, 235.

83. AN T 208¹, Comptes, du maréchal et maréchale de Mirepoix, 1749–77.

84. Hester Lynch Piozzi, *Observations and Reflections Made in the Course of a Journey through France, Italy and Germany*, ed. Herbert Barrows (Ann Arbor, 1967), 37.

85. [Meusnier], *Nouveau traité de la civilité*, 1:47, 209.

86. *Les Mémoires de Messire Roger de Rabutin, Comte de Bussy* (Paris, 1696), 30; Laurette de Malboissière, *Lettres d'une jeune fille*, 157.

87. *Mémoires de Mlle. Avrillon*, 1:243.

88. For the farm servants' holiday see Pierre-Jakez Hélias, *The Horse of Pride: Life in a Breton Village*, trans. June Guicharnaud (New Haven, 1978), 245–46.

89. AD BdR XXH I E 45, Déclarations de grossesse, 1774–75; XH I E 44, Déclarations de grossesse, 1772–73; XH I E 43, Déclarations de grossesse, 1770–71.

90. ADG 12B 287, Procédures et informations de Jurat, 1746.

91. *Journal de Mme. Cradock*, 8.

92. Duchesse d'Abrantes, *Home and Court Life of the Emperor Napoleon*, 1:376; *Souvenirs de Mme. Louise-Elizabeth Vigée-Lebrun* (Paris, 1835), 2:357.

93. Jacques Viollet de Wagnon, *L'Auteur laquais, ou Réponse aux objections . . . faites au corps de ce nom, sur la vie de Jacques Cochois, dit Jasmin . . .* (Avignon, 1750), 62.

94. AN T 254, Papiers de Pierre Farcy, valet-de-chambre de Mme. la Comtesse de Balbi.

95. Mlle. Avrillon, *Mémoires*, 74, 78.

96. For the banning of liveried lackeys from public gardens see John Andrews, *Letters to a Young Gentlemen, on His Setting Out for France . . .* (London, 1784), 529, and Nemeitz, *Séjour de Paris*, 157–58. La Mésangère, *Le Voyageur à Paris: Tableau pittoresque et morale de cette capitale* (Paris, an V, 1797), 2:39, and Pollnitz, *Memoirs*, 2:285 have stories of lackeys accosting noble ladies.

97. AN T 254, Papiers de Pierre Farcy.

98. Viollet de Wagnon, *L'Auteur laquais*, 1.

99. Nicolas Edmé Restif de la Bretonne, *Les Nuits de Paris* (Paris, 1930), 111–14.

100. The best description of the recreations of farm servants is Hélias, *The Horse of Pride*, 287–88. This deals with the nineteenth century, but there is no reason to suspect that servants' recreations differed greatly in that period from those of earlier centuries.

101. For fairs and their attraction for servants, see Robert M. Isherwood, "Entertainment in

the Parisian Fairs in the Eighteenth Century," *Journal of Modern History* 53 (March 1981), 30–31.

102. Fanny Cradock gave her servants time off to see Blanchard make his flight from the Champs de Mars in March 1784. (*Journal de Mme. Cradock,* 10)

103. For such imitation and the psychology behind it see below, chapter 4.

104. Picard was, of course, fired for his insolence. (Mme. de Sévigné, *Lettres*, 1:340–41).

105. AD G 12B 276, Procédures et informations de la Jurade, 1741.

106. For an extensive discussion of servants' family origins see the next chapter.

107. Jacques-Louis Ménétra, *Journal de ma vie*, ed. Daniel Roche (Paris, 1982), 163, 145, 107, 73.

108. AN 14515B, Commissaires de police, St. Germain, 1718; 14542B, Commissaires de police, St. Germain, 1750.

109. Of course not all people who signed as witnesses were necessarily close acquaintances of the affianced couple; occasionally notaries used chance passers-by. But it is safe to assume that most witnesses to marriages were in fact acquaintances of the bride and groom.

110. ADHG 3E 1184, Fonds Saurin, 1789; 3E 14132, Fonds Savy, 1727.

111. Quoted in George Sussman, "Three Histories of Infant Nursing in Eighteenth-Century France" (paper, Berkshire Conference on Women's History, Northampton, Mass., August 1979), 25. This has since been published in George O. Sussman, *Selling Mothers' Milk* (Urbana, 1982). My citations are to the original paper.

112. The following remarks are based on the first Duc's memoirs, *Journal inédit du Duc de Croy*.

113. Laurette de Malboissière, *Lettres d'une jeune fille*, 31–32.

114. Charles Antoine Jombert, *Architecture moderne ou L'Art de bien bâtir pour toutes sortes de personnes* (Paris, 1764), plate 45; Johann Karl Krafft and Pierre Nicolas Ransonette, *Plans, coupes, élévations de plus belles maisons et des hôtels construits à Paris et dans les environs, 1771–1802* (Facsimile ed., Paris, 1902), plate 10.

115. Both the new rooms for entertainment and the new traffic patterns are visible in plans like that of the Maison Epinnes, in the faubourg St. Honoré, published in Krafft and Ransonette, *Plans, coupes, élévations*, plate 28.

116. Mme. Vigée-Lebrun, *Souvenirs*, 93.

117. Gallet, *Stately Mansions*, 118, discusses the many changes which contributed to the increasing comfort of the private areas of the household.

118. Nowhere was the English influence more striking—and the French nobility's new-found passion for informal but luxurious comfort more visible—than in clothing. For both men and women a drastic change in styles occurred in the 1780s as *habits à la français* gave way to those *à l'anglais*. For women the simple straight-lined *robe à l'anglaise* in cotton or muslin replaced the elaborately panniered *robe à la française* of taffeta or brocade, and men abandoned the emroidered waistcoats and satin breeches of their formal court dress (known as the *habit habillé* or *habit français*) for the sober English broadcloth frockcoat. (See Paul M. Ettesvold, *The Eighteenth-Century Woman: Catalogue of an Exhibition at the Costume Institute, Metropolitan Museum of Art* [New York, 1982]; and Philip Mansel, "Monarchy, Uniform and the Rise of the *Frac*, 1760–1830," *Past and Present* 96 [August, 1982], 103–32.)

119. Mme. Vigée-Lebrun, *Souvenirs,* 112. Mme. Lebrun probably was Calonne's mistress despite these disclaimers.

120. See below, chapter 8.

121. Wheaton, *Savoring the Past,* 195–212.

122. [Menon], *La Cuisinière bourgeoise.* For the significance of this work see A. Girard, "Le Triomphe de 'La Cuisinière Bourgeoise': Livres culinaires, cuisine et société en France au 17e et 18e siècles," *Revue d'histoire moderne et contemporaine* 24 (October–December 1977), 499–523.

123. [Jean-Charles Bailleul], *Moyens de former un bon domestique, ouvrage ou l'on traite de la manière de faire le service de l'intérieur d'une maison; avec des règles de conduite à observer pour bien remplir ses devoirs envers ses maîtres* (Paris, 1812).

124. Ibid., 59, 66–67.

125. Compare Fleury, *Les devoirs des maîtres et des domestiques,* 258, and Bailleul, *Moyens de former un bon domestique,* 151–52.

126. This was the case in the house of D'Argenson, figure 4.

127. Most of the plans in Krafft and Ransonette show no servants' quarters on the main floors of the buildings, suggesting that they were housed in the attic or cellar. There was, however, one exception to the banishment of servants: personal body servants still occasionally slept within call of their master or mistress. As we have seen, the Empress Josephine preferred that her *femme-de-chambre* sleep near her.

128. Compare the arrangement of servants' beds in the plan in figure 3, dating from the early eighteenth century, to the Maison Hosten in Krafft and Ransonette, *Plans, coupes, élévations,* plate 10.

129. Ibid., plate 10. See also Botlan, *Domesticité et domestiques,* 113.

130. Gallet, *Stately Mansions,* 114–15.

131. Ibid.

132. Bailleul, *Moyens de former un bon domestique,* 117, 93, 56, 66–67, 9, 11, 131–37.

133. L. F. Fouin, *De l'Etat des domestiques en France et des moyens propres à les moraliser* (Paris, 1837), 50.

134. For sources see Bibliography, section I, B.

135. ADHG 3E 1122, Fonds Pratrieul, 1728; 3E 10935, Fonds Rieux, 1728. Hiring *à récompense* was not confined to the provinces; Roland Mousnier found similar patterns of payment for servants in the wills of seventeenth-century Parisians. (*Paris au XVIIe siècle* [Paris, n.d.], 233).

136. ADHG E605, Livre de raison du Chevalier de la Rénaudie.

137. Ibid.

138. ADHG J 550, Livre de raison de Guillaume Escaffié, curé de St. Pierre de Calvaignac, 1701–21; E 701, Cahier de famille de Sentou Dumont, 1690–1743.

139. This graph was derived from the salaries in the *livres de raison* listed in section I, D, of the Bibliography. Since they were drawn from three different areas of the country, these figures tend to blur regional differences, but they have the advantage of approaching some sort of national average.

140. ADHG E 635, Marquis de Barneval, Registre pour mes domestiques.

141. Nougaret, *Tableau mouvant,* 3:315.

142. ADHG E 635, Marquis de Barneval, Registre pour mes domestiques; ADG I Mi 684, Livre de raison de Jean Bernard Daleau, 1761–76; AN T 208[1], Comptes du maréchal et maréchale de Mirepoix; AN T 491[2], Etat de la maison du Prince de Lambesc.

143. The figures for servants' salaries in this graph were derived from figure 5. For the seventeenth century, the journeyman's salary was taken from table 26 bis in Pierre Deyon, *Amiens: Capitale provinciale* (Paris, 1967), 519. The value of the food and shelter received by servants was derived from the prices of bread in Deyon's table 26 bis, calculated on an average consumption of 1½ pounds per day, with twenty livres added to cover shelter and other essentials. For the eighteenth century, the journeyman's salary is from C. E. Labrousse, *Equisse du mouvement des prix et des revenus en France au XVIII siècle* (Paris, 1933), 2:476, and the cost-of-living figures from Fairchilds, *Poverty and Charity,* 63. N.B. The journeyman's salary was calculated on the basis of Deyon's average working year for a mason of 200 days. Journeymen in other crafts worked more frequently and therefore earned more.

144. C. E. Labrousse, as cited in A. Soboul, *La France à la veille de la Révolution,* 1:56–57.

145. For examples see ADHG E 642, Livre de raison de M. de Cambon, 1767–90; 12 J 41,

Château de Castelnau, Comptes de maison, 1753–61; E 639, Livre de raison de M. Bernardet, curé. In nineteenth century France farm servants were sometimes still hired *à récompense*, and left unpaid for long periods, but this was unusual.

Chapter 3

1. Maria Ribaric Demers, *Le Valet et la soubrette de Molière à la Révolution* (Paris, n.d.), 211–12.

2. For Mazarin's career as a "creature" see Orest Ranum, *Richelieu and the Councillors of Louis XIII*; for Gourville see *Mémoires de M. de Gourville.*

3. This is at least what masters thought their servants' attitudes were (see Fleury, *Les Devoirs de maîtres et des domestiques,* 253). We do not know how servants really felt.

4. C. B. MacPherson, *The Political Theory of Possessive Individualism* (Oxford, 1962), 56–61.

5. In the Minutier Central of the Archives Nationales, which houses the records of Parisian notaries, these records are classified by the street in which the notary had his office. For my sample I chose to analyze all the marriage contracts of servants registered during 1787–89 with the notaries of the rue St. Martin, a major north-south thoroughfare which ran through some fashionable districts of the city, but was for the most part a street of relatively poor shopkeepers and artisans. I thought that this sample would be more representative of Parisian servants than one drawn from a street in a wealthier district.

6. For Toulouse, these were the dioceses of Montauban, Lombez, Rieux, Mirepoix, St. Papoul, and Lavaur; for Bordeaux, the dioceses of Saintes, Périgueux, Agen, Bazas, and Dax. Dioceses were chosen as the unit of analysis because they were given much more frequently in marriage contracts than the names of provinces or regions. In classifying birthplaces I relied on the following reference works: *The Times (of London) World Atlas* (New York, 1980); *The New York Times World Atlas* (New York, 1978); the *Dictionnarie des Communes* (Paris, 1964); and Dom Dubois, "Cartes des diocèses de France des origines à la Révolution," *Annales E. S. C.* (1965) 680–91. (I thank Professor Timothy Tackett for telling me about the last reference.)

7. This includes the dioceses of Auch, Lectoure, Condom, Agen, Tarbes, Comminges, Couserans, Pomiers, and Alet. For a description of the economy of this region see Frêche, *Toulouse et la région Midi-Pyrénnés.*

8. Included in it are the dioceses of Limoges, Tulle, Cahors, Rodez, Lectoure, Agen, and Condom. Alain Corbin's *Archaisme et modernité en Limousin au XIXe siècle* (Paris, 1975) gives the best picture of the economic conditions in this area.

9. For migration patterns see Olwen Hufton, *The Poor of Eighteenth-Century France, 1750–1789* (Oxford, 1974), 69–106 and Abel Châtelain, *Les Migrants temporaires en France de 1800 à 1914* (Villeneuve d'Arcq, 1976).

10. Our sample of Parisian servants is small, and therefore its results are doubtful. But they accord with the statistics on geographical origins Marc Botlan derived from a sample of 255 Parisian servants whose deaths are recorded in the Châtelet from 1771 to 1790. (Botlan, "Domesticité et domestiques," 156). Therefore I believe they are representative of Parisian servants as a whole.

11. Richard Cobb, *Paris and Its Provinces, 1792–1802* (Oxford, 1975), 57–86.

12. See the references in note 9, and also, for Toulouse, Jean Rives, "L'Evolution démographique de Toulouse au dix-huitième siècle," *Bulletin d'histoire économique et sociale de la Révolution française* (1968), 132 ff; for Bordeaux, Jean-Pierre Poussou, "Les Structures démographiques et sociales," in F.-G. Pariset, ed., *Bordeaux au dix-huitième siècle* (Bordeaux, 1968) 333–48; and for Paris, Cobb, *Paris and Its Provinces,* passim.

13. See the Poussou citation in the note above.

14. Posts as *gardes-chasse* continued to be popular with army veterans even in the nineteenth century. See Isser Woloch, *The French Veteran from the Revolution to the Restoration* (Chapel Hill, 1979), 256.

15. *Journal de Guienne,* June 4, 1789.

16. ADHG E 705, Livre du raison du Chevalier de la Rénaudie, 1689 ff.

17. Nicolas Edmé Restif de la Bretonne, *Les contemporains* (Paris, 1930), 98.

18. Arlette Farge, *Vivre dans la rue à Paris au dix-huitième siècle* (Paris, 1979), 67.

19. Restif, *Les Contemporains,* 99.

20. AD BdR XXH E 40, Déclarations de grossesse, 1764–65.

21. Restif, *Les Contemporains,* 183.

22. Liger, *Le Voyageur fidèle,* 403, advises travelers who wish to hire servants in Paris to seek them at the *petite porte* of the Palais Royal.

23. AN Y 14543, Commissaires de police, St. Germain, 1752.

24. For servant-girls newly arrived in cities and reduced to prostitution, see Hufton, *The Poor of Eighteenth-Century France,* 311, and for juvenile delinquency see Yvonne Bougert, "Délinquance juvenile et responsabilité pénale du mineur au XVIIIe siècle," in Abbiateci, *Crimes et criminalité,* 49–91.

25. See above, chapter 2.

26. ADG 3E 15432, Fonds Dugarry, 1788.

27. ADHG 3E 2121, Fonds Campmas, 1787.

28. ADHG E 635, Papiers du Marquis de Barneval, Registre pour mes domestiques. For more on the necessity of quitting a job to get a raise see Botlan; "Domesticité et domestiques," 77, and Maza, "Domestic Service," 74.

29. These statistics were based on the following *livres de raison*: ADHG J 550; J 262; 12J 33; E 701; E 705; 12J 41; E 635; ADG IIE 412; IIE 1568; IIE 1696; I Mi 683; BN Nouvelles acquisitions françaises: 6541; 6580.

30. ADHG E 635, Marquis de Barneval, Registre pour mes domestiques.

31. Botlan, "Domesticité et domestiques," 213.

32. Ibid., 295.

33. There is evidence that servants made wide use of both these techniques, A Mlle. Bellefort was the *femme de chambre* of an abbess in the convent where Mme. de Genlis regularly took a rest cure. She tactfully made her talents known to the visitor, got herself fired, and left the convent as Mme. de Genlis's personal maid. (Comtesse de Genlis, *Mémoires inédites,* 1:181–84). And one Lefevre, a servant, once wrote to his friend Pierre Farcy, *valet de chambre* of the Comtesse de Balby, urging him to do what he could to get Lefevre's wife hired as lady's maid to the Comtesse. (AN T 254, Papiers de Pierre Farcy, valet de chambre.)

34. Alan Williams, *The Police of Paris, 1718–1789* (Baton Rouge, 1979), 283.

35. The best evidence we have that unemployment among servants was tied to the price of bread comes from Marc Botlan, who found that the percentage of the unemployed among servants tried for crimes at the Châtelet in Paris during the last half of the eighteenth century peaked when the price of bread did. (Botlan, "Domesticité et domestiques," 228–29).

36. Ibid., 203.

37. Quoted in ibid., 234.

38. This figure of 150 livres is based on the cost of living calculations in Fairchilds, *Poverty and Charity,* 75.

39. Botlan, "Domesticité et domestiques," 234–35.

40. AN Y 14542, Commissaires de police, St. Germain, 1750.

41. For examples of police ordinances to curb servant criminality, see Des Essarts, *Dictionnaire universel de police,* 3:468 and AM Toulouse BB 161, Ordonnances des Capitouls, ordinance of February 15, 1769; for a modern historian who accepts the traditional view of servant theft, see Williams, *The Police of Paris,* 283 (but cf. 192).

42. For the proportion of servants in the Parisian population see above, chapter 1; for the proportion of criminal servants see "Pophyre Petrovitch," "Recherches sur la criminalité à Paris, dans la seconde moitié du dix-huitième siècle," in Abbiateci, 212.

43. For the population figures see above, chapter 1. The percentage of accused criminals who were domestics was derived from Jean Cavignac, "Répertoire numérique de la Cours des Jurats de Bordeaux, sous-série 12 B" (undated typescript in ADG).

44. ADHG 51 B 21–27, Parlement de Toulouse, Procès-verbaux d'exécution à mort et de torture.

45. "Petrovitch," "La Criminalité à Paris," 245–46.

46. Botlan, "Domesticité et domestiques," 293.

47. The dichotomy between the violent crimes prevalent in rural areas and the crimes against property that characterized cities and towns is, so far as I know, found in every country in Western Europe from the thirteenth through the nineteenth centuries.

48. See "Petrovitch," "La Criminalité à Paris," 212–13.

49. Ibid.

50. Mme. Vigée-Lebrun, *Souvenirs,* 286–88.

51. That most servant theft was not *vol domestique* was also true in late nineteenth-century Paris; there the typical servant's theft was shoplifting in the newly invented department stores. (Martin-Fugier, *La Place des bonnes,* 233–34.)

52. Women servants, like women in general, were much less likely to commit (or at least to be accused of and prosecuted for) crimes than men. In Marc Botlan's sample of servant criminals prosecuted at the Châtelet, only around 30 percent were women. (Botlan, "Domesticité et domestiques," 238.)

53. For the *revendeuse* see Hufton, *The Poor of Eighteenth-Century France,* 259.

54. ADHG 51B 22 and 51B 23, Parlement de Toulouse, Procès-verbaux d'exécution à mort et de torture, 1687–1700 and 1702–28.

55. For an example of such servant accomplices, see ADHG 51B 23, Procès-verbaux d'exécution à mort et de torture, 1702–28.

56. Ibid.

57. Alexandre Parent-Duchâtelet, *De la Prostitution dans la ville de Paris,* (Paris, 1857), 74.

58. Hufton, *The Poor of Eighteenth-Century France,* 306–17 and esp. 312.

59. AM Toulouse FF 614, Police, 1733–89, Condemnations à La Grave.

60. Butel and Pousseau, *La Vie quotidienne à Bordeaux*, 314.

61. AM Bordeaux FF 75, Filles publiques.

62. This is based on my recollection of a paper given by Mme. Erica-Marie Benabou at the Conference on Women and Power, University of Maryland, 1977. Mme. Benabou has found voluminous records about the backgrounds and clients of prostitutes in eighteenth-century France. Those of us interested in the study of sexual practices in eighteenth-century France hope that her important work will soon be completed and published.

63. See Alain Corbin, *Les Filles de noce: Misère sexuelle et prostitution aux 19e et 20e siècles* (Paris, 1978), esp. 79–80; and Frances Finnegan, *Poverty and Prostitution: A Study of Victorian Prostitutes in York* (Cambridge, 1979) 73.

64. M. Fournel, *Traité de la séduction, considerée dans l'ordre judiciaire* (Paris, 1781), 49–50.

65. ADG 12B 287, Procédures et informations de la Jurat, 1746.

66. AD BdR XXH I E 44, Déclarations de grossesse, 1772–73.

67. AD BdR XXH I E 43, Déclarations de grossesse, 1770–71; XXH I E 44, Déclarations de grossesse, 1772–73.

68. The distinction between casual and professional prostitution and the tolerance for the former among the poor is well demonstrated in Judith Walkowitz, "The Making of an Outcast Group," in *A Widening Sphere,* ed. Martha Vicinus, (Bloomington, 1977), 72–94.

69. McBride, *The Domestic Revolution,* 98.

70. See above, chapter 2.

71. ADHG 3E 10935, Fonds Rieux, 1728; ADHG 3E 2124, Fonds Compmas, 1789.

72. AN LXXXV 715, Fonds Gilles Lecointre, 1789.

73. Poussou, "Les structures démographiques et sociales," 367; Jean Sentou, *Fortunes et groupes sociaux à Toulouse*, 437.

74. Daumard and Furet, "Structures et relations sociales," 18.

75. Briquet's will, which details his complicated financial dealings, can be found in ADHG 3E 6964, Fonds Pratrieul, 1728.

76. Maza, "Domestic Service," 304, has numerous examples of servant traders.

77. Roche, *Le peuple de Paris*, 80.

78. In the eighteenth century over 7 percent of the *rentes* sold by the Hôpital-général in Aix-en-Provence were purchased by servants. This was the highest proportion of any group among the lower classes. (Fairchilds, *Poverty and Charity*, 65.)

79. AN Y 14543, Commissaires de police, St. Germain, 1753. For further examples see Maza, "Domestic Service," 305.

80. ADHG 3E 6092, Fonds Boyer, 1727, will of Louis Vintrou; AN Y 14517, Commissaires de police, St. Germain, 1720.

81. AN Y 14516, Commissaires de police, St. Germain, 1719; ADHG 3E 14019, Fonds Sans, 1781; ADHG 3E 10935, Fonds Rieux, 1728; ADG 3E 17871, Fonds Hazera, 1787. Often employers neglected to repay these loans.

82. AN Y 14517, Commissaires de police, St. Germain, 1720.

83. AN Y 14533, Commissaires de police, St. Germain, 1752.

84. Babeau, *Les Artisans et les domestiques*, 262–63.

85. *Journal de Guienne*, November 6, 1786; April 10, 1789.

86. Ibid., August 6, 1787; AN Y 10442, cited in Botlan, "Domesticité et domestiques," 178.

87. D. Dessert, "Le Laquais financier au Grand Siècle: Mythe ou réalité?" *XVIIe Siècle* 122 (January–March 1979), 21–36.

88. AN T 254, Papiers de Pierre Farcy, valet de chambre.

89. Ibid.

90. These arguments are from Duchesse de Liancourt, *Règlement donné par une dame de haute qualité à sa petite-fille* . . . (Paris, 1698), 124; Bailleul, *Moyens de former un bon domestique*, 187–88; and Francesco Barbaro, *Les deux Livres de l'estat du mariage* . . . (Paris, 1667), 138. Other more generalized warnings against the employment of married servants can be found in domestic manuals as widely separated in time as Père de Cambry, *Maison du Prince réglée, tout en économie, que discipline domestique* (Brussels, 1652), 82; and Mme. Aglaé Adamson, *La Maison de campagne* (Paris, 1822), 150.

91. H. Richard, *Du Louage des services domestiques en droit française* (Angers, 1906), 27.

92. Flandrin, *Familles*, 140.

93. ADG IIE 1696, Livre de raison, famille de Lamourous, 1674–1739.

94. *Journal de Guienne*, October 14, 1784.

95. Duc de Bourbon, *Correspondance inédite de Duc de Bourbon avec Mme. la Comtesse de Vaudreuil, 1798–99* (Paris, 1886), 211.

96. It is almost impossible to calculate the proportion of servants who never married, because the obvious source for such figures, burial records, usually do not give either the marital or social status of the deceased. Other sources indicate a high percentage of celibates. For example, of those servants who made wills in Toulouse and Bordeaux in my sample years of 1727–29 and 1787–89, 64 percent had never married. But this source is weighted in favor of celibates, because married couples automatically inherited from each other and therefore did not need to make wills. A less prejudiced source is the inventories of those who died intestate. Daniel Roche's investigation of such inventories in Paris from the beginning and the end of the eighteenth century found that 21 percent of the servants who died intestate from 1695–1715 and 25 percent of those from

1775 to 1790 were celibate. Comparable figures for salaried workers were 3 percent and 13 percent. (Roche, *Le Peuple de Paris,* 90).

97. Again, because of gaps in the sources, it is almost impossible to determine the average age of marriage of domestics. Marriage registers give the ages but not the occupation of the spouses, while marriage contracts usually give occupations but not ages. Marriage contracts, however, often do state whether the prospective spouse had reached the age of majority, which was twenty-five for women. In the marriage contracts from Toulouse and Bordeaux for which we have such information, 93.8 percent of the women servants were twenty-five or older when they married. And in the few contracts in which the actual age of marriage was shown, it averaged 29.8 years. This suggests that most female servants were in their late twenties or early thirties when they married—that is to say, considerably older than the average age of marriage for women in the period, which was twenty-five–twenty-six years. (François Lebrun, *La Vie conjugale sous l'ancien régime* [Paris, 1975], 31.)

98. Marcoul, "Les Domestiques à Toulouse," 83.

99. In the remaining 25.7 percent of the cases the servant provided part of her dowry herself, but her family or master also made contributions.

100. These and the following figures are based on the marriage contracts among the sources listed in the Bibliography, section I, B, Toulouse.

101. The following table shows the average size, in livres, of dowries of female servants working in the various types of households in Toulouse and Bordeaux:

	Toulouse		Bordeaux	
	1727–29	1787–89	1727–29	1787–89
Nobility	139.3	475.8	303.6	667.7
Middle class	152.7	207.2	334.5	569.9
Lower class	141.3	117.3	185.0	187.0
Agricultural	30.0	53.3	35.0	—

Sources: See Bibliography, section I, B.

102. Lebrun, *La Vie conjugale,* 26.

103. In Toulouse, for example, 23 percent of the female servants who made marriage contracts in 1727–29 returned to the country to marry, but by 1787–89 the figure was only 12 percent.

104. For the legal background of the *déclarations* see Marie-Claude Phan, "Les Déclarations de grossesse en France (XVI-XVIIIe siècles): Essai institutionel," *Revue d'histoire moderne et contemporaine* 17 (1975), 61–88.

105. The Bordelais registers are A M Bordeaux FF 77, Déclarations des filles enceintes, registre des déclarations, 1772–77; FF 78, Filles enceintes, registre de declarations, 1779–82; FF 79, Registre de déclarations des filles enceintes, 1782–84. For Toulouse, no *déclarations* from the *ancien régime* seem to have survived, although François Galabert analyzed three registers for the year 1792 in "La Recherche de la paternité à Toulouse 1792 et les volontaires nationaux," *Revue des Pyrénnés* (1911), 353–92. But I was unable to find these registers in the municipal archives, and since Galabert's article is not very informative, I have decided to ignore this small Toulousan sample in favor of the much broader one from Aix-en-Provence.

106. This sample formed the basis of my article "Female Sexual Attitudes and the Rise of Illegitimacy: A Case Study," *Journal of Interdisciplinary History* 8, no. 4 (Spring 1978), 627–67, reprinted in Robert I. Rotberg and Theodore K. Rabb, eds. *Marriage and Fertility: Studies in Interdisciplinary History* (Princeton, 1980), 163–203. The pitfalls of my sample and my methods of analysis are explained more fully there.

107. See Beatrice Gottlieb, "The Meaning of Clandestine Marriage," in *Family and Sexuality in French History,* ed. Robert Wheaton and Tamara Hareven (Philadelphia, 1980), 49–84.

108. It should be noted that we have only the woman's word about the identity of her lover, and since fathers could be sued for the support of a bastard, it was in the woman's interest to accuse a wealthy man. On the other hand, gentlemen often forced their paramours to conceal their identity, suggesting that they accuse instead a lower-class type or a "man unknown." I assume for the sake of simplicity that these two types of lies cancel each other out and accept the women's identification of their seducers.

109. AD BdR XXH E 43, Déclarations de grossesse, 1779–81.

110. Ibid.

111. For a discussion of this tradition and its psychological effects on master-servant relationships, see below, chapter 6.

112. AD BdR XXH E 34, Déclarations de grossesse, 1747–57.

113. AD BdR XXH E 35, Déclarations de grossesse, 1752–57.

114. Maza, "Domestic Service," 112.

115. Of the forty-eight servant-servant cases in my sample from Provence for which the location is recorded, twenty-one took place in châteaux during the summer.

116. Admittedly these two tables are not really comparable, because they involve different cities. But I am sure that the trend they indicate is real.

117. AN Y 14519, Commissaires de police, St. Germain, 1722.

118. The wills are those of Marie Jacquette Arthaud, wealthy enough to leave a *rente* of 650 livres to her bastard daughter (ADHG 3E 2124, Fonds Compmas, 1789), and Marie Rivière, *servante* to a *négociant* for twenty-nine years, who left 50 livres to her bastard son (ADHG 3E 14021, Fonds Sans, 1789).

119. These cases are from ADHG 51B 23, Parlement de Toulouse, Procès-verbaux d'exécution à mort et de torture, 1702–28; and 51B 22, Procès-verbaux, 1687–1700.

120. Quoted in Farge, *Vivre dans la rue,* 109.

121. *L'Etat de servitude ou La Misère des domestiques,* printed in Geneviève Bollême, *La Bibliothèque bleue: Litterature populaire en France du XVIIe au XIXe siècles* (Paris, 1971), 104–6.

122. ADG 3E13, 497, Fonds Marin, 1787.

123. See the statistics on petitioners for divorce in Roderick Phillips, *Family Breakdown in Late Eighteenth-Century France: Divorces in Rouen, 1792–1803,* (Oxford, 1980), 89. These are drawn from Rouen, a textile center, and therefore, not surprisingly, the largest occupation category of divorce-seekers is textile workers. But Phillips states that servants were well represented among divorce petitioners.

124. Gutton, *Domestiques et serviteurs,* 88–89.

125. AN Y 14543, Commissaires de police, St. Germain, 1753.

126. Her decision provoked an angry letter from L'Amireau: "I want first of all to tell you briefly the pain that you gave me by telling me impassively that you have become the *gouvernante* of the two children of Mme. de Fresne; you have without doubt very assuredly caused me a great deal of pain." (AN Y 254, Papiers de Pierre Farcy.)

127. AN Y 14542^{B}, Commissaires de police, St. Germain, 1751. Roche, *Le Peuple de Paris,* 108, has other examples of married servants living apart from their spouses.

128. AN T 254, Papiers de Pierre Farcy.

129. AN Y 14543, Commissaires de police, St. Germain, 1753; Y 14542^{B}, Commissaires de police, St. Germain, 1750; Y 14517, 1720.

130. AN Y 14542^{B}, Commissaires de police, St. Germain, 1750.

131. For the poem, see following chapter.

132. AN T 254, Papiers de Pierre Farcy.

133. Sentou, *Fortunes et groupes sociaux,* 437.

134. Gutton, *Domestiques et serviteurs,* 196. See also Roche, *Le Peuple de Paris,* 76–79.

135. Roche argues that servants were the first among the *menu peuple* to acquire the spending habits of a modern consumer economy. See his discussion in *Le Peuple de Paris,* 131–97.

136. Peter N. Stearns, *Old Age in European Society: The Case of France* (New York, 1976), 43–45.

137. AN T 462[2], Papiers de Nicolas Petit, domestique de Duc de Villeroy et sa femme Marie Madelaine Jolly, condamnés à réclamé (à fer).

138. For an example of such an attitude in a servant, see below, chapter 4.

139. AN T 254, Papiers de Pierre Farcy; AN T 462[2], Papiers de Nicolas Petit.

140. See below, chapter 5.

141. ADHG 3E 5802, Fonds Milhet, 1728.

142. For examples see the wills of Dlle. Françoise de Carrière and Dlle. Jacquette de Pezan in ADHG 3E 1122, Fonds Pratrieul, 1728.

143. ADHG 3E 13898, Fonds Miss, 1789.

144. ADHG 3E 1182, Fonds Saurine, 1787.

145. AN XXII 58, Fonds Julien Lesacher, 1789.

146. Louis Vintrou, a former cook in Toulouse, left ten livres, almost his total estate, to the woman hired to care for him during his illness; and Anne Galioreau, *ci-devante servante* in Bordeaux, made her landlady, a *patissière,* her heir because of her kindness when she was sick. (ADHG 3E 6092, Fonds Boyer, 1727–28; ADG 3E 21.602, Fonds Naceville, 1787.)

147. ADG, Fonds Barbaret, 1787.

148. For the fear of dying in a charitable institution see Fairchilds, *Poverty and Charity,* 99.

149. Ibid., 78.

150. ADHG 3E 4028, Fonds Forêt, 1729; 3E 2856, Fonds Couderc, 1727; 3E 5803, Fonds Milhet, 1729; 3E 14133, Fonds Savy, 1728; 3E 11106, Fonds Maignac, 1727; 3E 3074, Fonds Damans, 1727; 3E 4026, Fonds Forêt, 1728; 3E 10762, Fonds Cabissol, 1789; ADG 3E 20.445, Fonds Duprat, 1787; 3E 25.004, Fonds Brun, 1787; 3E 23.130, Fonds Dufaut, 1787; 3E 21.602, Fonds Nauville, 1787; 3E 23.442, Fonds Rideau, 1787; AN XXII 54, Fonds Julien Lesacher, 1788; LXXXV 713, Fonds Gilles Lecointre, 1789; XXXIII 707, Fonds Toussaint Girard, 1787.

151. Mme. de Guerchois, *Avis d'une mère à son fils* (Paris, 1743), 119–20.

152. AN T 254, Papiers de Pierre Farcy.

Chapter 4

1. N. Evreinov, quoted in James H. Billington, *Fire in the Minds of Men: Origins of the Revolutionary Faith* (New York, 1980), 47.

2. Sennett, *The Fall of Public Man,* 45–122; Michael Fried, *Absorption and Theatricality: Painting and Beholder in the Age of Diderot* (Berkeley, 1980).

3. I owe this observation to Evreinov quoted in Billington, *Fire in the Minds of Men,* 47.

4. For an example of this attitude see Lawrence Towner, "A Fondness for Freedom: Servant Protest in Puritan Society," *William and Mary Quarterly,* 3d Ser. 19, no. 2 (April 1962), 201–19.

5. For Coffy see ADG 12B 287, Procédures et informations de la Jurade, 1746; for Le Tellier see Marquis de Barthélemy, *Mémoires,* ed., Jacques de Dampierre (Paris, 1914).

6. Christian Miller, "A Scottish Childhood: The Castle," *The New Yorker* (November 12, 1979), 114.

7. Alexandrine des Echerolles, *Side Lights on the Reign of Terror, Being the Memoirs of Mademoiselle des Echerolles translated from the French by Marie Clothide Balfour* (London and New York, 1900), 19.

8. ADHG E 635, Marquis de Barneval, Registre pour mes domestiques.

9. These servant nicknames were gleaned from AN Y 145 42^{B}, Commissaires de police, St. Germain, 1748; AN X 2, Parlement de Paris, Chambre criminelle, Table des accusés, 1750–80; AD BdR XXH G 32, Livre des expositions des femmes enceintes commencé le 27 mars 1752. Nicknames were not confined to servants; many among the lower classes had them. But the nicknames of artisans and wage laborers were usually chosen by the person himself or his friends. They were proclamations of his personality, whereas servants' nicknames, so often chosen by masters, were denials of it.

10. Mme. de Maintenon, *Entretiens sur l'éducation des filles*, ed. Théophile La Vallée (Paris, 1854), 107. Another warning against this practice is M. Baudouin, *De l'Education d'un jeune seigneur* (Paris, 1728), 308.

11. *Mémoires de Mme. La Vicomtesse Fars Fausselandry, ou Souvenirs d'une octogénaire* (Paris, 1830), 3:259.

12. Richard Cobb, *Death in Paris* (Oxford, 1978), 23.

13. Alison Lurie, "From Rags to Rags" (a review of Anne Hollander, *Seeing through Clothes*), *New York Review of Books* (December 7, 1978), 25.

14. Mlle. Avrillon, *Mémoires*, 1:21–22.

15. Pierre Rétat, ed., *L'Attentat de Damiens: Discours sur l'événement au XVIIIe siècle* (Lyons, 1979), 222.

16. *Traité de Gilbert Cognatus ou Cousin, entitlé de l'office des serviteurs*, published with Barbaro, *Les Deux Livres de l'estat du marriage*, 347.

17. Mlle, Avrillon, *Mémoires*, 1:44, 6–11.

18. For the Breton of Parisian servants, see Hélias, *The Horse of Pride*, 149; for the Occitan-speaking *gouvernante*, Auguste Puis, ed., *Une Famille de parlementaires toulousains à la fin de l'ancien régime: Correspondance du Conseiller et de la Conseillère D'Albis de Belbèze* (Paris and Toulouse, 1913), 165; for the Baronne d'Oberkirch's maid, Burkard, *Mémoires de la Baronne d'Oberkirch*, 194.

19. Jeffry Kaplow, *The Names of Kings: The Parisian Laboring Poor in the Eighteenth Century* (New York, 1972), 106–7; and Farge, *Vivre dans la rue*, 114. These discuss only the French of the poor in Paris, but it is unlikely that apart from regional accents and local slang, the French spoken by the *menu peuple* in other towns and cities was very different.

20. Molière, *The Learned Ladies*, trans. Richard Wilbur (New York, 1978), act two, scene six.

21. *Journal de Guienne*, December 20, 1784.

22. See the advertisement in the *Affiches, Announces . . . de Toulouse*, March 12, 1788.

23. Baronne d'Oberkirch, *Mémoires*, 194.

24. Marquise de Villeneuve-Arifat, *Souvenirs d'enfance*, 21. The language barrier between master and servant continued even with the rise of public education in the nineteenth century, but by then servants clung to their bad French as a badge of identity, and masters were reluctant to correct them for fear of giving offense. (Martin-Fugier, *La Place des bonnes*, 225).

25. Nougaret, *Tableau mouvant*, 2:298–99.

26. Hélias, *Horse of Pride*, 256.

27. Katzman, *Seven Days a Week*, 165.

28. For examples of such stories see *Mémoires de Mme. La Marquise de la Rochejaquelein, écrites par elle-même* (Paris, 1817), 343–44; Comte Dufort de Cheverney, *Mémoires*, 2:80, 108; Duchesse d'Abrantes, *The Home and Court Life of the Emperor Napoleon*, 1:165; *Souvenirs de Mme. Louise-Elizabeth Vigée-Lebrun*, 2:187. These are just a few highlights of a mammoth literature.

29. AN Y 14543, Commissaires de poice, St. Germain, 1752.

30. Charles de Rémusat, *Mémoires de ma vie*, ed. Charles H. Pouthas (Paris, 1958), 1:21.

31. AN Y 14542^{B}, Commissaires de police, St. Germain, 1748; AN Y 14543, Commissaires de police, St. Germain, 1753.

32. It is possible that some of these legacies were coerced by employers, yet the figures are striking.

33. Philippe Ariès, *The Hour of Our Death,* trans. Helen Weaver (New York, 1980), 77.

34. ADHG J 598, Déclaration de Jeanne Viguière, ancienne domestique des Sr. et Dame Calas de Toulouse, touchant des bruits calomnieux qui se sont répandus.

35. Jean-Jacques Rousseau, *La Nouvelle Héloise,* in *Oeuvres complètes de Jean-Jacques Rousseau* (Paris, 1909), 4:320.

36. *Mémoires de Mme. Roland* (Paris, 1820), 1:140.

37. Marc Botlan discovered this wonderful letter in AN Y 10335, and quoted it in his "Domesticité et domestiques," 296.

38. For complaints about this see Bailleul, *Moyens de former un bon domestique,* 29.

39. Botlan, "Domesticité et domestiques," 298, 301.

40. Nougaret, *Tableau mouvant,* 2:35–36. Other evidence for this practice can be found in [Turmeau de la Moranderie], *Police sur les mendians, les vagabonds, . . . les domestiques . . .* (Paris, 1764), 101.

41. Botlan, "Domesticité et domestiques," 295.

42. Nougaret, *Tableau mouvant,* 2:36–37.

43. Vanal, *Journal d'un bourgeois de Caen,* 57.

44. AN Y 14542B, Commissaires de police, St. Germain, 1751.

45. *Journal de Mme. Cradock,* 41.

46. Mme. de Créquy, *Souvenirs,* 2:178–81.

47. Comte de Montlosier, *Souvenirs d'un émigré, 1791–98,* ed. Comte de Larouzière-Montlosier (Paris, 1951), 133–34.

48. Peter Burke, *Popular Culture in Early Modern Europe* (New York, 1978), 28, 63. It should be noted that Burke does not specifically discuss servants as cultural mediators, yet they fit his model well.

49. Hecht, *The Domestic Servant Class,* 200–28, esp. 205–19.

50. Roche, *Le Peuple de Paris,* 283.

51. See L. Broom and J. H. Smith, "Bridging Occupations," *British Journal of Sociology* 14, no. 4 (December 1963), 321–34. This article, like most of the work of sociologists on this topic, emphasizes the role of bridging occupations for social mobility but largely ignores their role as cultural transmitters.

52. *Mémoires et lettres de François Joachim de Pierre, Cardinal de Bernis, 1715–58,* ed. Frederic Masson (Paris, 1878), 9. For an example of a child speaking patois, see Puis, *Une famille de parlementaires toulousains,* 165.

53. Samuel Du Pont de Nemours, *L'Enfance et la jeunesse de Du Pont de Nemours* (Paris, 1906), 201–2.

54. For a further discussion of parental vigilance see below, chapter 7. On elite disdain of popular culture, see Burke, *Popular Culture,* 207–43; for an opposing view see Isherwood, "Entertainment in Parisian Fairs," 30–31.

55. See the suggestive remarks in Marc Raeff, *Origins of the Russian Intelligentsia* (New York, 1966), 123–24; 141–42.

56. For nationwide patterns of literacy in eighteenth-century France see François Furet and Jacques Ozouf, *Lire et écrire: L'Alphabétisation des français de Calvin à Jules Ferry* (Paris, 1977), esp. 1: graph c.

57. Ibid., 1:241.

58. Ibid.

59. This was the pattern in Lyons (Maurice Garden, *Lyon et les Lyonnaise au 18e siècle,* [Paris, 1970], 242–43, 246–47, 254–55, 265–66, 309–13, 350–53, 449–51) and in the towns of the Eure and Seine-Inférieure (M. Jéorger, "L'Alphabétisation dans l'ancien diocèse de Rouen au XVIIe et au XVIIIe siècles," in Furet and Ozouf, *Lire et écrire,* 2:144.

60. For such arguments see Fleury, *Les Devoirs,* 210; and Prince de Conti, *Mémoires de*

Monseigneur le Prince de Conty [sic] touchant les obligations d'un gouverneur de Province et la conduite de sa maison (Paris, 1669), 80–81. On the meaning of "instruction," see Botlan, "Domesticité et domestiques," 284.

61. ADG 3E 11941, Fonds Treyssac, 1729.

62. ADHG 51B 23, Procès-verbaux d'exécution à mort et de torture, 1702–28.

63. Domestic manuals stressed literacy as a requirement for such jobs. See Audiger, *La Maison réglée*, 34.

64. Daniel Roche found a similar pattern in his much larger sample of Parisian servants. (Roche, *Le Peuple de Paris*, 209).

65. This may simply be due to the fact that nobles were more likely to employ those sorts of servants—*secrétaires, femmes de chambre,* etc.—who needed literacy for their jobs. Nonetheless the pattern is clear, as the following table shows:

Servants Signing Their Marriage Contracts, Classified by Household (in %)

	Toulouse		Bordeaux		Paris
	1727–29	1787–89	1727–29	1787–89	1787–89
Male Servants					
Nobility	45.0%	64.9%	15.8%	69.0%	88.2%
Middle class	33.3	44.4	0.0	45.0	100.0
Lower class	0.0	50.0	0.0	66.7	—
Clergy	33.3	66.7	50.0	100.0	100.0
Female Servants					
Nobility	10.0	20.0	27.8	50.0	100.0
Middle class	0.0	11.5	11.1	14.3	75.0
Lower class	0.0	0.0	0.0	0.0	—
Clergy	0.0	0.0	0.0	0.0	100.0

Sources: See Bibliography, section I, B.

Note. This table includes only those servants in households for which information exists. Therefore, the sample is quite small and the figures are not statistically significant.

66. P. Butel and G. Mandon, "Alphabétisation et scolarisation en Aquitaine au XVIIIe et au debut du XIXe siècles," in Furet and Ozouf, *Lire et écrire*, 2:11; J. P. Poussou, "Recherches sur l'alphabétisation de l'Aquitaine au XVIIIe siècle," in ibid., 2:344.

67. Bailleul, *Moyens de former un bon domestique*, 25–27.

68. Louise de Condé, *Lettres intimes de Mlle. de Condé à M. de la Gervaisais, 1786–87*, Intro. Paul Viollet (3d ed., Paris, 1878), 161–62.

69. Comtesse de Genlis, *Le La Bruyère des domestiques*, 2, 3; M. Formez, *Traité d'éducation morale . . . ou Comment on doit gouverner l'esprit et le coeur d'un enfant, pour le rendre heureux et utile* (Liège, 1773), 22–23. The warnings about the possibly dangerous effects of education on servants were similar to elite worries about educating the lower classes in general. See Harvey Chisick, *The Limits of Reform in the Enlightenment: Attitudes toward the Education of the Lower Classes in Eighteenth Century France* (Princeton, 1981).

70. This was common in the ancien régime, because reading was usually taught first and cost less to learn than writing. Therefore more people could read than sign their marriage contracts. See Furet and Ozouf, *Lire et écrire*, 1: 89–91, 131.

71. Botlan, "Domesticité et domestiques," 278. Daniel Roche found a similar pattern in his much larger sample of Parisian inventories. (Roche, *Le Peuple de Paris*, 217.)

72. AN CI 700, Fonds Legrand (Jean Maupas), 1787.

73. AN T 273, Papiers de Bernard Arnaud, laquais: Etat de livres de Sr. Arnaud.

74. Ian Watt, *The Rise of the Novel* (Berkeley, 1957), 47.

75. For servant patronage of the *cabinets de lecture* see F. Parent, "Les Cabinets de lecture dans Paris: Pratiques culturelles et espace social sous la Restauration," *Annales E. S. C.* 34, no. 5 (September–October 1979), 1030, and James Smith Allen, "The *Cabinets de Lecture* in Paris, 1800–1850" (paper presented at the American Historical Association, Washington, 1980), 5.

76. Barthélemy, *Mémoires*, 69–70.

77. For Mme. Colletet, see Dorothy Anne Liot Backer, *Precious Women* (New York, 1974), 251–52; for Mascarille see Marcoul, "Les domestiques à Toulouse," bibliography.

78. *Souvenirs de la Baronne de Montet, 1785–1866* (Paris, 1904), 47; *Mémoires du Duc de Lauzun, 1747–83*, ed. Louis Lacour (Paris, 1858), 3.

79. AN T 254, Papiers de Pierre Farcy.

> But why are you lovable?
> That in truth is the mystery.
> One can't help loving you;
> I announce this to all the world.

80. Here I differ with Daniel Roche, who argues that at least Parisian upper servants were accustomed to expressing themselves in writing. (Roche, *Le Peuple de Paris*, 213–16.)

81. For the English servant poets see Hecht, *Domestic Servant Class*, 191–92; and for at least one French servant poet of the Restoration see Edgar Newman, "*L'Ouvrière: elle souffre et se plaint rarement*: The Politics and Spirit of the French Women Worker Poets of the July Monarch, 1830–48" (unpub. paper), 1–3.

82. Duc de Croy, *Journal inédit*, 1:385.

83. Karamzine, *Voyage en France, 1789–90* (Paris, 1885), 289.

84. AN T 254, Papiers de Pierre Farcy.

85. Restif de la Bretonne, *Les Contemporains*, 220; "Lord, you should have seen how I spoke French then! But since then, my husband and my friends have said that I must speak like them, and I am used to it by now."

86. Cited in Maza, "Domestic Service," 359.

87. AN T 254, Papiers de Pierre Farcy.

88. Ibid.

89. David Katzman shows that many American black "cleaning ladies" of the nineteenth and early twentieth centuries also used this ploy, playing on the reputation of blacks for laziness to do their work at a bearable pace. Katzman, *Seven Days a Week*, 195.

90. Mme. de Genlis, *Mémoires inédites*, 2:100.

91. Duchesse d'Abrantes, *The Home and Court Life of Napoleon*, 1:120–21.

92. Van Eerde, "The Role of the Valet," 106.

93. AN T 254, Papiers de Pierre Farcy, letter of Amireau, May 2, 1786.

94. Craven, *A Journey through the Crimea*, 7–10.

95. I found only one reference to such a prosecution, a statement in the Parisian *Annonces, affiches et avis divers* of September 28, 1751, that the Paris Parlement had affirmed the sentence of one Charles Bonnin for insolence toward his mistress. It does not say what this sentence was.

96. This statement is based on an impressionistic rather than quantitative analysis of the records of the Parisian *commissaires de police* listed in section I, F of the Bibliography.

97. See the remarks in MacPherson, *Possessive Individualism*, 56–91.

98. Cited in Botlan, "Domesticité et domestiques," 39.

99. See Flandrin, *Familles*, 117–18.

100. Des Essarts, *Dictionnaire universel de police*, 3:479, quoting an *ordinance de police* of November 6, 1778.

101. Sylvestre du Four, *Instruction morale d'un père à son fils, qui part pour un long voyage, ou Manière aisée de former un jeune homme à toutes sortes de virtus* (Paris, 1679), 197.

102. Abbé Goussault, *Le Portrait d'un honnête homme* (Paris, 1692), 69. For other conduct books that counseled leniency toward servants, see M. Baudouin, *De l'Education d'un jeune seigneur* (Paris, 1728), 308; and Jacques Bouyer de St. Gervais, *Conseils d'un gouverneur à un jeune seigneur* (Paris, 1727), 67.

103. AN Y 14517, Commissaires de police, St. Germain, 1720; AN Y 14518, Commissaires de police, St. Germain, 1721; AN Y 14516, Commissaires de police, St. Germain, 1719.

104. AN Y 14515, Commissaires de police, St. Germain, 1718.

105. For the concept of bodily autonomy see Norbert Elias, *The Civilizing Process: The History of Manners*, trans. Edmund Jephcott (Oxford, 1978), 69ff., and Maza, "Domestic Service," 342–43. For beatings to break the will, see Hunt, *Parents and Children*, 133–58.

106. See the discussion of this point in Stone, *The Family, Sex and Marriage*, 237–38.

107. Grégoire, *De la Domesticité*, 205; Mme. de Genlis, *Le La Bruyère des domestiques*, XXIII.

108. AN Y 14543, Commissaires de police, St. Germain, 1753.

109. Both cases are in ADG 12B 287, Procédures et informations de la Jurade, 1746.

110. AN Y 14542B, Commissaires de police, St. Germain, 1750; AN Y 14516, Commissaires de police, St. Germain, 1719.

111. AN Y 14517, Commissaires de police, St. Germain, 1720; AN Y 14543, Commissaires de police, St. Germain, 1753.

112. AN Y 14543, Commissaires de police, St. Germain, 1753.

113. AN Y 14542B, Commissaires de police, St. Germain, 1750.

114. See Kaplow, *Names of Kings*, 106–7.

115. For the inversion of carnival see Natalie Zemon Davis, "The Reasons of Misrule," in *Society and Culture in Early Modern France* (Stanford, 1975), 97–123; and Burke, *Popular Culture*, 178–204.

116. AN Y 14516, Commissaires de police, St. Germain, 1719.

117. Robert Darnton found a marvelous case in which the workers in an eighteenth-century Parisian print shop ceremoniously executed their master's cat. Darnton, "Work and Culture," 18–21.

118. AN Y 14516, Commissaires de police, St. Germain, 1719.

119. AN Y 14542B, Commissaires de police, St. Germain, 1750.

120. Ibid., 1751.

121. Ibid., 1748.

122. Ibid.

123. For the traditional distrust of the police in French villages see Hufton, *Poor of Eighteenth Century France*, 222, 247, 289. For the legal preference for the word of masters over servants (its justification was that the master was a gentleman and therefore would not lie) see J. B. Denisart, *Collection de décisions nouvelles et de notions relatives à la jurisprudence* (Paris, 1754), 2:8–9. It would be interesting to know how master-servant cases were finally decided, to ascertain if the police did indeed display a bias in favor of masters. But unfortunately this is hard to trace, for the great majority of complaints recorded in police archives give no hint about the action taken on them or about how they were finally settled. Perhaps Philippe Usinky's forthcoming University of Michigan Ph.D. dissertation on the functioning of the police in eighteenth-century Rouen will shed some light on this matter.

124. AN Y 14543, Commissaires de police, St. Germain, 1753.

125. Davis, "The Reasons of Misrule," in *Society and Culture*, 97–124; Burke, *Popular Culture*, 178–204.

126. ADG 12B 276, Procédures et informations de la Jurade, 1746.

127. AN Y 14542B, Commissaires de police, St. Germain, 1748. Servants were not the only lower-class group to adopt the forms and traditions of popular culture as modes of expressing their grievances toward their employers. This practice was also common among artisans. For

example, Robert Darnton has found ritualized and carnivalesque forms of protest among eighteenth-century printers. See his "Work and Culture," 18–21.

128. On the replacement of the charivari by the threatening letter see E. P. Thompson, "The Crime of Anonymity," in Douglas Hay et al., *Albion's Fatal Tree: Crime and Society in Eighteenth Century England* (New York, 1975), 255–308. Cases in which French servants sent anonymous letters to their employers can be found in ADG 12B 276, Procédures et informations de la Jurade, 1746, and AN Y 14542B, Commissaires de police, St. Germain, 1748.

129. See above, table 10, chapter 3.

130. AN Y 14517, Commissaires de police, St. Germain, 1720.

131. AN Y 14543, Commissaires de police, St. Germain, 1753.

132. ADHG 51B 25, Parlement de Toulouse, Procès-verbaux d'exécution à mort et de torture, 1761–67.

133. ADHG 51B 23, Parlement de Toulouse, Procès-verbaux et d'exécution à mort et de torture, 1702–28.

134. ADHG 51B 25, Parlement de Toulouse, Procès-verbaux d'exécution à mort et de torture, 1761–67.

135. AN Y 14543, Commissaires de police, St. Germain, 1753.

136. AN Y 14515B, Commissaires de police, St. Germain, 1718.

137. ADHG 51B 21–27, Parlement de Toulouse, Procès-verbaux d'exécution à mort et de torture, 1633–1728 and 1750–78.

138. This was also apparently true in nineteenth-century France. None of the nineteenth-century murders of masters by servants discussed by Anne Martin-Fugier was, on the surface at least, motivated by revenge. Instead they occurred in the course of robberies or grew out of sexual jealousy. (Martin-Fugier, *La Place des bonnes*, 236–39.)

139. Maza, "Domestic Service," 227; E. Lamouzèle, ed., *Toulouse du dix-huitième siècle d'après les "Heures Perdues" de Pierre Barthes* (Toulouse, 1914), 164.

140. Maza, "Domestic Service," 227.

141. For the traditional propensity to blame unexplained illnesses on witchcraft, see A. D. J. MacFarlane, *Witchcraft in Tudor and Stuart England* (London, 1970), 178.

142. Mme. de Genlis, *Mémoires inédites*, 2:99–103.

143. Vanel, *Une Grande Ville*, 173–74.

144. Jean-Jacques Rousseau, *La Nouvelle Héloise*, part 5, letter 10.

145. For sources see Bibliography, section I, B.

146. *Avis à la livrée par un homme qui la porte*, 9, 13.

Chapter 5

1. For the moralizing thrust of the Counter-Reformation see Michel Foucault, *Histoire de la folie à l'âge classique* (Paris, 1961); Jean-Pierre Gutton, *La Société et les pauvres: L'Exemple de la géneralité de Lyon* (Paris, 1970); and Fairchilds, *Poverty and Charity*, 22–35. For the political vision of the *dévots* see Lionel Rothkrug, *Opposition to Louis XIV* (Princeton, 1965) and Carolyn Lougee, *Le Paradis des Femmes* (Princeton, 1976). Both these discuss Fleury extensively.

2. Fleury, *Les Devoirs des maîtres et des domestiques*, 207.

3. Toussaint de St. Luc, *Le Bon Laquais*, 2–3.

4. [Benigné Lordelot], *Les Devoirs de la vie domestique, par un père de famille* (Paris, 1704), 123.

5. For a more detailed discussion of a master's rights over the sexuality of his domestics see below, chapter 6.

6. Fleury, *Les Devoirs des maîtres et des domestiques*, 214.

7. Mme. de Guerchois, *Avis d'une mère*, 119–20.

8. This care was one of the duties of mastership most stressed in domestic manuals. For examples see Audiger, *La Maison réglée*, preface; Fleury, *Les Devoirs des maîtres et des domestiques*, 237; Mme. de Guerchois, *Avis d'une mère*, 118.

9. For the importance of household prayers in Protestant England, see Trumbach, *Rise of the Egalitarian Family*, 141–45; and Stone, *The Family, Sex, and Marriage*, 245–46. For the duty of Protestant masters to teach their servants to read, see Elizabeth L. Eisenstein, *The Printing Press as an Agent of Change* (Cambridge, 1980), 425. In French domestic manuals references to household prayers are sparse. The only two I found were in the *Mémoires de Msgr. le Prince de Conty*, 80; and Fleury, *Les Devoirs de maîtres et des domestiques*, 282. Both concern great noble households which employed chaplains to celebrate daily Mass and instruct servants in their catechisms. References to teaching servants to read so that they could read the Bible and other religious works are even more scarce. Only Fleury, 218, 222, argues that this is an essential part of a master's duties.

10. Conti, *Mémoires de Msgr. le Prince de Conty*, 80, 97; Fleury, *Les Devoirs des maîtres et des domestiques*, 223.

11. Fleury, *Les Devoirs des maîtres et des domestiques*, 235; Conti, *Mémoires de Msgr. le Prince de Conty*, 82, 97.

12. Richard, *Du Louage de services domestiques*, 37.

13. The correspondence of the Parisian *lieutenant-général de police* de Marville shows that masters often intervened with him to protect their servants from prosecution. (M. de Marville, *Lettres*, passim.) One seventeenth-century master even hid from the police a servant accused of murder. (BN, MS, Nouvelles acquisitions françaises, 6580, Livre de raison de famille St. Amans.)

14. See the discussions of relationships within patriarchal families in Stone, *The Family, Sex, and Marriage*, 159–206; Trumbach, *The Rise of the Egalitarian Family*, 119–65; Flandrin, *Familles*, passim; and Hunt, *Parents and Children*, passim.

15. ADHG E 701, Cahier de famille de Sentou Dumont, 1690–1743.

16. ADHG 3E 10934, Fonds Rieux, 1727; ADHG 3E 50802, Fonds Milhet, 1728; ADG 3E 11941, Fonds Treyssac, 1729.

17. These figures of course reflect only formal arrangements actually recorded in wills and marriage contracts. It is possible that many employers made informal provisions for the future welfare of their servants which would not appear in such records.

18. John McManners, *Death and the Enlightenment: Changing Attitudes to Death among Christians and Unbelievers in Eighteenth-Century France* (Oxford, 1981), 237.

19. This was done by multiplying the total number of wills in each category by the percentage of households of that social class which employed servants, as shown in the *capitation* roll of Toulouse, 1695.

20. See Katzman's remarks in *Seven Days a Week*, 154–58.

21. The pattern of women being more likely to leave legacies to their servants than men is typical of early modern Europe and can be found in England as well as France. (See Richard T. Vann, "Wills and the Family in an English Market Town," *Journal of Family History* 4, no. 4 [Winter 1979], 364–65.) This pattern may reflect only the fact that women's money was generally more "discretionary"; it was not usually considered part of the family fortune, and therefore more apt to be put to personal use. But women's legacies to their servants may also reflect the closer ties of their shared domestic concerns.

22. ADG 3E 20446, Fonds Duprat, 1788.

23. The legal provisions concerning married women's property in Old Regime France are immensely complex and deserve a book to themselves. For a clear brief treatment, see Traer, *Marriage and the Family*, 40–45.

24. The question of which sex had the primary responsibility for the direction of the household in the seventeenth century is an immensely difficult one. As Carolyn Lougee has shown us, the period was one of intense debate over the proper social role of women, especially noble

women: should they play public roles as court ladies and *salonnières*, or should they remain within the private sphere as wives, mothers, and *ménagères*? Ironically, the most vehement advocates of the latter role were the religiously inspired social conservatives, such as François de Grenaille, who were also among the most eloquent proponents of patriarchy. (See Lougee, *Le Paradis des Femmes*, 59–69, 85–110.) Yet the notion of women's supremacy within the home contradicted the basic premises of patriarchy, for patriarchy gave supreme control to a masculine head of the household. Obviously sex roles were in flux in the seventeenth century, and much more work is needed to sort them out.

25. Of all the seventeenth-century domestic manuals I read, only three were addressed to women.

26. The Comte appears to have regarded the supervision of the household as women's work (he once prefaced a bit of gossip about a servant in a letter to his father with the remark that it concerned a "minor domestic matter more suitable for my mother than for you"), but his correspondence shows that he played an active role in the hiring, firing, and disciplining of servants. (Comte d'Avaux, *Correspondance inédite*, 232 and passim.)

27. Duchesse de Liancourt, *Règlement*, 9–10.

28. *Mémoires de la Marquise de Courcelles, née Marie-Sidonia Lenoncourt, et sa correspondance* (Paris, 1869), 200–201.

29. *La Vie de Mme. J.M.B. de la Mothe Guion*, 54–55, 106–9.

30. Quoted in Gutton, *Domestiques et serviteurs*, 155.

31. *Lettres de Mme. La Marquise de Pompadour, depuis MDCCLII jusqu'à MDCCLXII inclusivement* (Londres [sic], 1771), 160; Ariès, *The Hour of Our Death*, 18–19.

32. du Four, *Instruction morale d'un père à son fils*, 197–98. For other examples see Mme. de Guerchois, *Avis d'une mère*, 116–17; and Goussault, *Portrait d'une femme honneste*, 85, 94.

33. Mme. de Sévigné, *Lettres*, passim.

34. Backer, *Precious Women*, 211.

35. The servant is believed to be tarnished with the libertinism / Natural and common to this type. The *L'Etat des domestiques* is reprinted in Bollême, *La Bibliothèque bleue*, 105.

36. Gutton, *Domestiques et serviteurs*, 150.

37. Jean Emelina [Michel Lemain], *Les Valets et les servantes dans le théâtre comique en France de 1610 à 1700* (Cannes and Grenoble, 1975).

38. Gutton, *Domestiques et serviteurs*, 155; Des Essarts, *Dictionnaire universel de police*, 3: 468.

39. Comte d'Avaux, *Correspondance inédite*, 18.

40. Comte de Montlosier, *Souvenirs*, 136; Mme. de Sévigné, Lettres, 1:320.

41. Fleury, *Les Devoirs de maîtres et des domestiques*, 210.

42. Mme. de Sévigné, *Lettres* 1:365–66; Mme. de Créquy, *Souvenirs*, 4:174; Baronne d'Oberkirch, *Mémoires*, 179.

43. Eisenstein, *Printing Press*, 259.

44. *Traité de Gilbert Cognatus ou Cousin, entitlé de l'office des serviteurs*, published with François Barbaro, *Deux Livres de mariage*, 349–50.

45. Fénélon, *L'Education des filles*, ch. 13, quoted in Cusenier, *Les Domestiques en France*, 188.

46. The best brief explication of this racialism so prevalent in the ancien régime is Davis Bitton, *The French Nobility in Crisis, 1560–1640* (Stanford, 1969), 77–91.

47. AN Y 14517, Commissaires de police, St. Germain, 1720; AN Y 14516, Commissaires de police, St. Germain, 1719.

48. Mme. de Sévigné, *Lettres*, 1:365–66. Such indifference to suffering of course was widespread in the seventeenth century; people watched children and animals suffer with similar *sang-froid*.

49. For elite views of the lower classes in the seventeenth century, see Gutton, *Domestiques et*

serviteurs, 154–55, which stimulated my thinking along these lines. See also the works cited in note 1.

50. See the works cited in note 1 and also Burke, *Popular Culture*, 207–43.

51. My remarks on the treatment of servants in the French theater are based on Emelina, *Les Valets et les servantes*; Demers, *Le Valet et le soubrette*; and Van Eerde, "The Role of the Valet."

52. Emelina, *Les Valets et les servantes*, 73–93, 131.

53. Demers, *Le Valet et la soubrette*, 211; Emelina, *Les Valets et les servantes*, 333–50.

54. Emelina, *Les Valets et les servantes*, 221–45.

55. Demers, *Le Valet et la soubrette*, 23–60. Regnard, one of the founders of the Comédie-Française, wrote almost a quarter century after Molière, yet the servants in his plays conformed to the traditional stereotypes and displayed none of the individuality and humanity of Molière's domestics.

56. Ibid.

57. Ibid.

58. Ibid., 212.

59. Van Eerde, "Role of the Valet," 19–24.

60. Demers, *Le Valet et la soubrette*, 152.

61. At least some authorities maintain that Figaro was an anagram of *fils de Caron*, Beaumarchais's family name. (Ibid., 212).

62. Mme. Henriette Demolière, *Conseils aux jeunes femmes, ou Lettres sur le bonheur domestique* (Paris, 1836), 206.

63. Père Collet, *Traité des devoirs des gens du monde, et surtout des chefs de famille* (Paris, 1763).

64. Mme. Gaçon-Dufour, *Manuel de la ménagère à la ville et à la campagne* (Paris, 1805); Mme. Demarson, *Guide de la ménagère* (Paris, 1828).

65. Mme. Gaçon-Dufour, *Manuel de la ménagère*, 23–28.

66. Puis, ed., *Une famille de parlementaires toulousains*, 56.

67. The "angel in the house" was primarily an Anglo-Saxon phenomenon; she was given her classic formulation in Coventry Patmore's poem of that title. But she had her counterparts in nineteenth-century France, where women became the guardians of religion and traditional moral values in the face of the secularism and aggressive ethics of the marketplace espoused by their menfolk. See Bonnie L. Smith, *Ladies of the Leisure Class* (Princeton, 1981.)

68. Collet, *Traité des devoirs*, 230; 233.

69. Collet, *Traité des devoirs*, 241.

70. Ibid., 240.

71. [Anon.], *Des Devoirs des serviteurs, des maîtres, des enfants, des parents, de tous les hommes envers l'église et l'état* (Lyons, 1830), 11; Collet, *Traité des devoirs*, 225.

72. *Mémoires de Mme. Roland* (Paris, 1820), 2:259–60.

73. See MacPherson, *Possessive Individualism*, passim, for the equality of contracting parties in a market society; and see Schochet, *Patriarchalism*, 82, for the inequality of the parties to a patriarchal "pseudo-contract."

74. Collet, *Traité des devoirs*, 225.

75. Mme. Roland, *Mémoires*, 1:137–42.

76. *Lettres inédites de Mlle. Philipon—Mme. Roland—adressées aux Dlles. Cannet de 1772 à 1780*, ed. Auguste Breuil (Paris, 1841), 1:175.

77. See below, chapter 7.

78. Nemeitz, *Séjour de Paris*, 89–90.

79. AD Seine-et-Oise E 434, Correspondance de la Marquise de Bombelles, quoted in Sussman, "Three Histories of Infant Nursing," 31.

80. Avrillon, *Mémoires*, 1:13.

81. Ibid., 2:391–92.

82. Cusenier, *Les Domestiques*, 294; Mme. de Genlis, *Le La Bruyère des domestiques*, XXXI.

83. Viollet de Wagnon, *L'Auteur laquais*, 111–66.

84. ADHG E 705, Livre de raison du Chevalier de la Rénaudie, 1688ff.

85. AM Toulouse BB 161, Ordonnances des capitouls, 1764–80. As early as the sixteenth century servants had been required by law to have written *congés*, or references, from former employers. But these laws seem not to have been enforced, so they were repassed in the last decades of the Old Regime.

86. Ibid.

87. For the foundation and functioning of the *Bureau d'adresse* in Paris see Howard M. Solomon, *Public Welfare, Science, and Propaganda in Seventeenth Century France* (Princeton, 1972), 40–44, 227.

88. *Journal de Guienne*, September 9, 1784; November 8, 1784.

89. William B. Cohen, *The French Encounter with Africans: White Response to Blacks, 1530–1880* (Bloomington, 1980), 111.

90. Mme. de La Tour du Pin, *Journal*, 1:247; Mme. de Genlis, *Le La Bruyère des domestiques*, 61–68.

91. Cohen, *French Encounter*, 60–99, describes the many contradictions and paradoxes in eighteenth-century French attitudes toward blacks.

92. M. de la Croix, *Peinture des moeurs du siècle, ou Lettres et discours sur differens sujets* (Amsterdam [?], 1777), 147.

93. Ibid., 148–50; Mme. de Genlis, *Le La Bruyère des domestiques*, 65-67.

94. For the leniency of the courts see "Petrovitch," "Recherches sur la criminalité," 240. The tendency of masters to be more generous toward their black servants is well illustrated in Bordeaux, where there were many such domestics. In my two sample periods, 1727–29 and 1787–89, employers left average legacies of 683 livres to their black servants; the average legacy to whites was only 389. White servants seem to have resented the favored treatment of blacks. In August 1789 a group of Parisian servants met to petition the Estates-General. They demanded a doubling of their salaries, an end to the wearing of livery—and the dismissal of all black domestics, "who annoyed white servants." (Cohen, *French Encounter*, 113.) It is not clear whether such anti-black actions arose from racism or simple jealousy. We do not know how deeply engrained racism was among the *menu peuple*. On the one hand, a serious race riot took place in Bordeaux in the 1770s. (Cohen, *French Encounter*, 113). On the other hand, blacks and whites intermarried, despite laws forbidding this, and there were whites like the wife of a modest *marchand de poterie* in Bordeaux, who, when the black servant Samuel Coffy sought refuge in her house, stated that "it didn't matter that he was black provided that he was a *brave garçon*." (ADG 3E 20.449, Fonds Duprat, has an example of a black servant who married a white servant; the Coffy case is in ADG 12B 287, Procédures et informations de Jurat, 1746).

95. Mme. de Genlis, *Le La Bruyère des domestiques*, 61–115.

96. Laurette de Malboissière, *Lettres d'une jeune fille*, passim; Puis, *Une famille parlementaire*, 65; Comtesse de Sabran, *Correspondance inédite de la Comtesse de Sabran et du Chevalier de Boufflers, 1778–1788* (Paris, 1875), 45–46, 205–6; Duc de Bourbon, *Correspondance inédite*, 21.

97. Baronne d'Oberkirch, *Mémoires*; Comte Dufort de Cheverny, *Mémoires*.

98. Comte Dufort de Cheverny, *Mémoires*, 167–68; Marquise de Villeneuve-Arifat, *Mémoires*, 21; Baronne d'Oberkirch, *Mémoires*, 194.

99. *Lettres de la Baronne de Gerando*, 240.

100. Duc de Lauzun, *Mémoires du Duc de Lauzun, 1747–1783*, ed. Louis Lacour (Paris, 1858), 58; Laurette de Malboissière, *Lettres d'une jeune fille*, 100; J. Joubert, *Pensées de J. Joubert, précédés de sa correspondance*, intro. Paul de Raynal (Paris, 1864), 1:53.

101. The last of these relationships is discussed in chapter 4; the first two are analyzed in great detail in chapter 7.

102. I argued this in my article "Masters and Servants in Eighteenth Century Toulouse," *Jour-*

nal of Social History 12, no. 3 (Spring 1979), 380–81. But evidence from memoirs about affection between master and servant in the period has caused me to change my mind, and to see such legacies as springing from genuine feeling on the part of masters.

103. McManners, *Death and the Enlightenment*, 242.

104. Mme. de La Tour du Pin, *Journal*, 1:20.

105. Mme. de Genlis, *Mémoires inédites*, 1:182.

106. Baronne d'Oberkirch, *Mémoires*, 182; Baron de Besenval, *Mémoires de M. le Baron de Besenval, Lieutenant-Général des armées du roi sous Louis XV et Louis XVI* (Paris, 1805), 162.

107. The best introduction to the perception of social problems in the last years of the Old Regime is Hufton, *The Poor of Eighteenth-Century France*.

108. The literature connecting servants to vagabondage, theft, and especially the depopulation of the countryside is voluminous. Among the most typical and important works are Moranderie, *Police sur les mendians*; Des Essarts, *Dictionnaire de police*, esp. 3:467–85 and M. de Chamousset, "Mémoire concernant les ouvriers et les domestiques," in *Oeuvres complètes* (Paris, 1787), 2:46. It should be noted that only the *male* domestic was blamed for these social ills. The female servant was not thought nearly so threatening. In the depopulation debates, for example, it was argued that domestic service was an unproductive use of male labor, but a productive and, indeed, given the growing identification of the household as woman's sphere and housework as women's work, a "natural" use of female labor. These debates therefore both reflected and contributed to the growing feminization of domestic service in the late eighteenth century.

109. Two examples of plans for charitable asylums for domestics: Viollet de Wagnon, *L'Auteur laquais*, 111ff.; and M. de Chamousset, "Mémoire sur un établissement en faveur de servantes . . . ," in *Oeuvres complètes*, 2:53ff. Such plans were, incidentally, an acknowledgment that the day of the master's patriarchal responsibilities for his servants' illness and old age had indeed passed.

110. For the idealization of the people in the last years of the Old Regime see Burke, *Popular Culture*, 281–86.

Chapter 6

1. For my sample see above, chapter 3, and Cissie Fairchilds, "Female Sexual Attitudes and the Rise of Illegitimacy." For Depauw see Jacques Depauw, "Illicit Sexual Activity and Society in Eighteenth Century Nantes," in *Family and Society*, ed. Robert Forster and Orest Ranum (Baltimore, 1976), esp. 167.

2. Stone, *The Family, Sex, and Marriage*, 546–603; see especially the cases of Samuel Pepys and William Bryd.

3. AD BdR XXH E 34, Déclarations de grossesse, 1747–57.

4. The amorous proclivities of these two gentlemen will be discussed below in some detail.

5. The phrase is from Sandra M. Gilbert and Susan Gubar, *The Madwoman in the Attic: The Woman Writer and the Nineteenth-Century Literary Imagination* (New Haven, 1979), 506.

6. Leonore Davidoff, "Class and Gender in Victorian England: The Diaries of Arthur J. Munby and Hannah Cullwick," in *Feminist Studies* 5, no. 1 (Spring 1979), 87–141.

7. Sarah B. Pomeroy, *Goddesses, Whores, Wives and Slaves: Women in Classical Antiquity* (New York, 1975), 90–91.

8. Origo, "The Domestic Enemy," 343–45.

9. Georges Duby, *Medieval Marriage: Two Models from Twelfth-Century France*, trans. Elborg Forster (Baltimore, 1978), 94.

10. Richard, *Du Louage des services domestiques*, 27; Fournel, *Traité de la séduction*, 132.

11. Samuel Richardson, *Pamela, or Virtue Rewarded* (New York: Norton edition, 1958), 16. I owe this interpretation of this quotation, and indeed the arguments of this whole paragraph, to

Randolph Trumbach's excellent discussion of master-servant sexual relationships in English patriarchal theory in *The Rise of the Egalitarian Family*, 145–50.

12. Christophe de Bordeaux, "Chambrière à louer à tout faire," and "Varlet à louer à tout faire," in Montaiglon, *Recueil de poésies françaises*, 95; 85.

As well as she what is necessary
To sleep below or above
In the big bed. . . .

Great deflowerer (delouser) of nurses
Sweeping them out below and above.
Women who have hot asses
I cure (plow) with cold ice.

13. These remarks are based on Emelina [Lemain], *Les Valets et les servantes*, esp. 245–58 and 287–96.

14. [Lemain], *Les Valets et les servantes*, 258.

15. Ibid., 290–303.

16. Toussaint de St. Luc, *Le Bon Laquais*, 78.

17. For two of the many possible examples of such suggestions, see Liancourt, *Règlement donné par une dame de haute qualité*, 126; and Fleury, *Les Devoirs des maîtres et des domestiques*, 235.

18. *Mémoires de Felix Platter, médecin bâlois* (Geneva, 1866), 86; Backer, *Precious Women*, 96.

19. *Mémoires du Duc de Lauzun*, 33–34. Another example can be found in the Comte Alexandre de Tilly's pursuit of the lovely Sophie. "I soon found means of seeing her in secret," he wrote. "It was by bribing the *suisse*." Sophie's maid was persuaded to pretend to be the object of the Comte's interest to deflect the suspicions of the girls' guardian aunt. (Comte Alexandre de Tilly, *Mémoires . . . pour servir à l'histoire des moeurs de la fin du dix-huitième siècle* [Paris, 1830], 101–2.

20. *Mémoires*, 168. An example of a female servant serving as sexual intermediary for her mistress can be found in Lauzun, *Mémoires*, 92. Rosalie, one of Lauzun's former loves, eventually became the mistress of a rich *Américain*. He negotiated for her favors (which cost him 10,000 livres of *rentes viagères*) with her *femme de chambre*.

21. An example of the former situation can be found in *Lettres de Mme. Du Montier à la Marquise de______, sa fille, avec les responses: ou l'on trouve les leçons les plus épurées et les conseils les plus délicats d'une mère, pour servir de règle à sa fille, dans l'état de mariage . . .* (Lyons, 1756), 248–50. For the latter situation see Comte Bussy de Rabutin, *Mémoires*, 78.

22. ADHG 51B 21, Parlement de Toulouse, Procès-verbaux d'exécution à mort et de torture, 1633–1686.

23. Backer, *Precious Women*, 243.

24. Elias, *The Civilizing Process*, 139.

25. Emmanuel Le Roy Ladurie, *Montaillou: The Promised Land of Error*, trans. Barbara Bray (New York, 1978), 141–42.

26. Stone, *The Family, Sex, and Marriage*, 558.

27. Restif de la Bretonne, *Les Contemporains*, 456.

28. I owe this phrase to Maza, "Domestic Service," 359.

29. *Mémoires du Comte de Bonneval*, 1:6–7.

30. "Petrovitch," "La Criminalité à Paris," 215–16.

31. For Louis XIII see Hunt, *Parents and Children in History*, 162–63. Many critics of Hunt have suggested that Louis's case was atypical, that his position as heir to the throne and future king, who had to sire an heir for the good of the kingdom, caused the adults around Louis to focus

on and encourage his sexuality to an unusual degree. (For an example, see the review by Etienne van de Walle in the *Journal of Interdisciplinary History* 2, no. 2 [Autumn 1971], 361–62.) But the evidence of memoirs suggests that Louis's experiences were fairly commonplace.

32. Cardinal de Bernis, *Mémoires et lettres,* 7–8.

33. Lauzun, *Mémoires,* 7–8.

34. Tilly, *Mémoires,* 14–15.

35. *Mémoires du Comte de Bonneval,* 1:7–8.

36. Fournel, *Traité de la séduction,* 306–7; 321–23.

37. Casanova, *Mémoires* (Pleiade ed., Paris, 1958), 1:837–45.

38. Tilly, *Mémoires,* 86.

39. AD BdR XXH E 43, Déclarations de grossesse, 1770–71.

40. Alain Lottin, J. R. Machirelle et al., *La Désunion du couple sous l'ancien régime: L'Exemple du Nord* (Paris, 1975), 169.

41. *Souvenirs en forme de mémoire d'Henriette de Monbielle d'Hus, Marquise de Ferrières-Marsay, 1744–1837* (St. Brienne, 1910), 32.

42. Quoted in Lottin et al., *La Désunion du couple,* 68.

43. ADG 3E 31.338, Fonds Maillères, 1788.

44. Baronne d'Oberkirch, *Mémoires,* 324.

45. AD BdR XXH E 34, Déclarations de grossesse, 1747–51.

46. AD BdR XXH IE 44, Déclarations de grossesse, 1772–73.

47. ADG 3E 25.006, Fonds Brun, 1789.

48. For English examples of servant-mistresses who continued to receive their former masters even after they were wed, see G. R. Quaife, *Wanton Wenches and Wayward Wives: Peasants and Illicit Sex in Early Seventeenth Century England* (New Brunswick, 1979), 134.

49. Lottin, et al., *La Désunion du couple,* 142.

50. Mme. de Sévigné, *Lettres,* 1:11–12; E. Le Roy Ladurie, ed., *Un Sire de Gouberville: Gentilhomme campagnard au Contentin de 1553 à 1562* (Paris, 1972), XX.

51. Flandrin, *Familles,* 179. For the sixteenty-century redefinition of the family, restricting it to the conjugal bond, see Natalie Zemon Davis, "Ghosts, Kin, and Progeny: Some Features of Family Life in Early Modern France," *Daedalus* 106, no. 2 (Spring 1977), 87–114.

52. Lottin, et al., *La Désunion du couple,* 174, 120.

53. Quoted in ibid., 155.

54. AD BdR XXH G 28, Expositions des femmes enceintes, 1722–29.

55. One example among many: Elizabeth Deniser was the *servante* of the M. Thomassin, actor in the Comédie-Française. From the moment she entered his household, he "showed criminal desires toward" her. She fended him off, until "finally, worn out by the attempts which were daily more frequent and more brutal, and seduced by his caresses and his promises, which became more extravagant every instant," she gave in. But when she became pregnant, "he did not blush to fire her in concert with his wife." AN Y 14542B, Commissaires de police, St. Germain, 1749.

56. In these tables I eliminated what seemed to be the cases of sexual initiation and servant-mistresses from the master-servant relationships in my sample of *déclarations* and classified all the remaining cases as "ancillary amours." Doubtless there are mistakes in this classification, given the paucity of information about many of the cases.

57. It is possible that the proportion of urban servants shrank because they were more adept than their rural sisters at using birth control or avoiding making a *déclaration*. But this seems unlikely.

58. Admittedly these percentages are not really comparable, since they come from different towns and periods. But the towns were similar in social makeup, and the figures do give some idea of the disproportionate number of seductions that occurred in artisan households.

59. This pattern was first suggested on the basis of impressionistic evidence, in Genovese, *Roll, Jordan, Roll,* 414, and it has recently been confirmed through quantitative analyses by Richard H. Steckel, "Miscegenation and the American Slave Schedules," *Journal of Interdisci-*

plinary History 40, no. 2 (Autumn 1980), 251–63. Further similarities in the patterns of master-servant sexual relationships in the two societies are suggested by Kenneth M. Stampp's discussion of the slave as the sexual initiator of white adolescents and of the prevalence of "servant-mistresses" among unmarried southern planters. (*The Peculiar Institution: Slavery in the Ante-Bellum South* [New York, 1968], 355.)

60. Fournel, *Traité de la séduction,* 358.

61. Jean-Jacques Rousseau, *La Nouvelle Héloise,* in *Oeuvres complètes de Jean-Jacques Rousseau* (Paris, 1909), 4:56, letter 24.

62. Fournel, *Traité de la seduction,* 359.

63. Quoted in ibid., 360.

64. Mme. de Sévigné, *Lettres,* 1: 21.

65. Quoted in Nicole Castan, *Justice et répression en Languedoc à l'époque des lumières* (Paris, 1980), 59.

66. For the proverb, see Stone, *The Family, Sex, and Marriage,* 281. The high level of sexual violence against widows has been noted in seventeenth-century England as well as in France. See Quaife, *Wanton Wenches and Wayward Wives,* 145.

67. AD BdR XXH G 33, Livre des expositions des femmes encientes commencé le 27 mars 1752.

68. Baron de Pollnitz, *Memoirs,* 2:275.

69. Quoted in Backer, *Precious Women,* 210. "La d'Olonne is no longer good for anything but arousing lackeys."

70. Baronne d'Oberkirch, *Mémoires,* 325–26.

71. Rétat, *L'Attentat de Damiens,* 191.

72. ADHG 51B 27, Procès-verbaux à mort et de tortures, 1772–78.

73. *Mémoires du Marquis de Langallery* (La Haye, 1743), 9; Restif de la Bretonne, *Les Nuits de Paris*, 7.

74. From *Le Gazetier cuirasse,* quoted in Robert Darnton, "The High Enlightenment and the Low-Life of Literature in Pre-Revolutionary France," *Past and Present* 51 (May 1971), 107, 106.

75. Kaplow, *The Names of Kings,* 142.

76. Lodovico Hernandez, *Les procès de sodomie au 16, 17 et 18e siècles* (Paris, 1920). It is not clear whether these constitute all the cases "Hernandez" (the name is a pseudonym for Fernand Furet and Louis Perceau) could find for the period, or whether they are just selected examples. And if the latter, the authors' principles of selection are not explained.

77. Randolph Trumbach, "London's Sodomites: Homosexual Behavior and Western Culture in the Eighteenth Century," *Journal of Social History* 7, no. 1 (Fall 1977), 1–33; Stone, *The Family, Sex, and Marriage,* 541–42.

78. Hernandez, *Les Procès de sodomie.* Other defendants include a *gagne-denier,* a shoemaker, a *garçon perruquier,* and a *commis* of the *fermes du Roi.*

79. Pollnitz, *Memoirs,* 2:275.

80. Restif, *Les Nuits de Paris,* 26.

81. *Le Gazetier cuirasse,* quoted in Darnton, "The High Enlightenment and the Low-Life of Literature," 106.

82. See the remarks by Trumbach, "London's Sodomites," 2.

83. This case is described in Williams, *The Police of Paris,* 106–7. Williams does not make it clear whether Pounnier worked as a servant for La Maréchale, but the circumstances of the story imply it.

84. Lillian Faderman, *Surpassing the Love of Men: Romantic Friendship and Love between Women from the Renaissance to the Present* (New York, 1981), 23–30, 74–75.

85. Fournel, *Traité de la séduction,* 131–35.

86. *Des Devoirs des serviteurs,* 40. Randolph Trumbach shows a similar shift of responsibil-

ity for the sexual conduct of domestics from master to servant in English domestic manuals in the eighteenth century. (*The Rise of the Egalitarian Family,* 145–50).

87. Christophe de Bordeaux, "La Chambrière à tout faire," 94–95.

88. Flandrin, *Familles,* 93.

89. Louise de Condé, *Lettres intimes,* 161–62. Mlle. de Condé wrote to her lover: "My love, I am worried about my letters. . . . I believe that several of my people can't read . . . and entrusting my letters openly, without concealment, to any one of them who comes along should prevent their suspicions. But I am careful not to give them to the *valet de chambre* who knows you."

90. Depauw, "Illicit Sexual Activity," 167.

91. For Shorter's arguments see his "Illegitimacy, Sexual Revolution, and Social Change in Modern Europe," *Journal of Interdisciplinary History* 2 (1971), 237–72; "Sexual Change and Illegitimacy: The European Experience," in *Modern European Social History,* ed. Robert J. Bezucha (Lexington, Mass., 1972), 231–69; "Female Emancipation, Birth Control, and Fertility in European History," *American Historical Review* 78 (1975), 605–40; *The Making of the Modern Family* (New York, 1975).

92. This is the argument of the articles in *Bastardy and Its Comparative History,* ed. Peter Laslett, Karla Oosterveen, and Richard M. Smith (London, 1980).

93. Louise A. Tilly, Joan W. Scott, and Miriam Cohen, "Women's Work and European Fertility Patterns," *Journal of Interdisciplinary History* 6 (1976), 447–76; Fairchilds, "Female Sexual Attitudes," passim.

94. The argument that the rise in illegitimacy in nineteenth-century France was due to the adoption by the poor of the ideals of domesticity has been made persuasively in Lenard Berlanstein, "Illegitimacy, Concubinage, and Proletarianization in a French Town, 1760–1914," *Journal of Family History* 5, no. 4 (Winter 1980), 360–75.

95. Martin-Fugier, *La Place des bonnes,* 294–303.

96. AM Bordeaux FF 77, Déclarations des filles encientes, 1772–77; FF 78, Filles encientes, registre de déclarations, 1779–82.

97. The connection between the growth in prostitution and female employment opportunities is clearly demonstrated in Walkowitz, "The Making of an Outcast Group." See also Finnegan, *Poverty and Prostitution,* 68–114, 136–64.

98. Corbin, *Les Filles de noce,* esp. 190–315.

99. Theodore Zeldin, *France, 1848–1945.* Vol. 1: *Ambition, Love, and Politics* (Oxford, 1973), 306.

100. See the analysis of this phenomenon in Corbin, *Les Filles de noce,* 287–300.

101. Ibid., 286.

102. This statement is not strictly true. Anne Martin-Fugier's study of late-nineteenth-century Parisian servants shows that both master-servant sexual relationships and the literary and popular image of the lusty servant persisted in that period. The scheming servant slept her way to fame and fortune in countless nineteenth-century novels, and *fin-de-siècle* Parisian newspapers rarely lost an opportunity to titillate their readers with the immoralities of the *sixième* (the top floor of Parisian apartment houses which contained the *chambres de bonne*). (*La Place des bonnes,* 171–98, 125–29.) But I am convinced, first of all, that the nineteenth-century image of the lusty servant had psychological roots different from the earlier one. It grew not from the traditions of the patriarchal household and the close association of servants with their masters' sex lives but instead from first, the new sexlessness of respectable women in the nineteenth century, which cried out for an antithesis, and second, as Davidoff has suggested (see above, note 6), from masters' association of servants with dirt and disorder, so abhorred by the nineteenth-century bourgeoisie. I am also convinced that in the nineteenth century the image of the lusty servant was much less prevalent than in earlier periods. Martin-Fugier herself shows that in the nineteenth century the literary image of the lusty servant had to contend with a very different image of the female

domestic as a saintly innocent (see below, chapter 8), something inconceivable in earlier periods. In sum, I think that there was, despite a certain persistence of the image of the lusty servant, a massive desexualization of master-servant relationships in the nineteeth century.

Chapter 7

1. There is an extensive bibliography on wet-nursing in France, especially during the early modern period. The best general surveys are Hunt, *Parents and Children,* 100–124; Elizabeth Wirth Marvick, "Nature versus Nurture: Patterns and Trends in Seventeenth Century French Child-Rearing," in *The History of Childhood,* ed. Lloyd de Mause (New York, 1974), 259–73; Jacques Gélis, Mirielle Laget, and Marie-France Morel, *Entrer dans la vie: Naissances et enfances dans la France traditionelle* (Paris, 1978), 109–15; 151–71; and Lebrun, *La Vie conjugale,* 124–33. The thirteenth-century *recommanderesses* are cited in Des Essarts, *Dictionnaire universel de police,* 7: 250. For the final disappearance of wet-nursing see George D. Sussman, "The End of the Wet-Nursing Business in France, 1874–1924," in *Family and Sexuality in French History,* ed. Robert Wheaton and Tamara K. Hareven (Philadelphia, 1980), 224–52.

2. Thomas Platter, *Autobiographie,* ed. Marie Helmer (Paris, 1964), 21, cited Gélis, et al. *Entrer dans la vie,* 133; Mme. de Genlis, *Mémoires inédites,* 1:6.

3. Hunt, *Parents and Children,* 102–9; Gélis, et al., *Entrer dans la vie,* 158–60; Lebrun, *La vie conjugale,* 139.

4. See above, chapter 1.

5. ADHG C 1082, Rolle de la capitation de la ville de Toulouse, 1695.

6. Cardinal de Bernis, *Mémoires et lettres,* 7.

7. M. Sallé, avocat au Parlement, *Traité des fonctions, droits et privilèges des Commissaires au Châtelet de Paris* (Paris, 1759), 2:447.

8. Jacques Guillemeau, *De la Nourriture et gouvernement des enfans . . .* (Paris, 1609), X.

9. *Mémoires de Mme. de Chastenay,* ed. Alphonse Roserot (Paris, 1896), 29–30.

10. Weber, *Mémoires,* see esp. 9–10.

11. Guillemeau, *De la Nourriture des enfans,* ix; Sieur Guerin, *Méthode d'éléver les enfans selon les règles de la medicine . . .* (Paris, 1675), 24; Marvick, "Nature versus Nurture," 266; Trumbach, *Rise of the Egalitarian Family,* 199.

12. BN, Nouvelles acquisitions françaises, F 6541; BM Toulouse, LmC 6326; ADHG J 246; Marcoul, "Les Domestiques à Toulouse au XVIIIe siècle," 85.

13. The best known bureau that arranged for the hiring of nurses was in Paris. It was regulated by royal ordinances, and in 1769 was given the exclusive right to represent nurses seeking employment in the capital. (Des Essarts, *Dictionnaire universel de police,* 7:250.)

14. M. de Chamousset, "Mémoire politique sur les enfans," in *Oeuvres complètes,* 1:224.

15. Mme. de Genlis, *Mémoires inédites,* 1:6–7.

16. Louis Liger, *Oeconomie générale de la campagne, ou Nouvelle Maison rustique* (Paris, 1700), 22.

17. Lebrun, *La Vie conjugale,* 119; Gélis, et al., *Entrer dans la vie,* 150.

18. For Hélie Robert see Gélis, et al., *Entrer dans la vie,* 156–7. The information that babies were fed sugar-water until they reached their nurses comes from a personal communication from Elizabeth Wirth Marvick, March 14, 1981. Delays in baptizing babies and sending them out to nurse seem to have been more characteristic of the seventeenth century than the eighteenth. See the table of ages at baptism in Mireille Laget, "Childhood in Seventeenth and Eighteenth Century France: Obstetrical Practices and Collective Attitudes," in *Medicine and Society in France,* ed. Robert Forster and Orest Ranum (Baltimore, 1980), 145.

19. Hunt, *Parents and Children,* 113–14.

20. Du Pont de Nemours, *L'Enfance,* 60.
21. Bernis, *Mémoires et lettres,* 7.
22. des Echerolles, *Side Lights on the Reign of Terror,* 250.
23. Guillemeau, *De la Nourriture et gouvernement des enfans,* 5.
24. Fleury, *Les Devoirs des maîtres et des domestiques,* 318.
25. Garden, *Lyon et les lyonnais,* 140.
26. Eric Erikson, *Childhood and Society* (New York, 1963), esp. 72–76; *Identity and the Life Cycle: Selected Papers* (New York, 1959), 55–65; John Bowlby, *Attachment and Loss,* 2 vols. (New York, 1969–73). It will be obvious to any informed reader that in my use of these writings, I have drawn on Hunt's imaginative use of Erikson in *Parents and Children,* esp. 113–32, and Trumbach's equally insightful use of Bowlby in *Rise of the Egalitarian Family,* esp. 187–235.
27. Erikson, *Identity,* 61; Hunt, *Parents and Children,* 119.
28. For swaddling see Gélis, et al., *Entrer dans la vie,* 115–18. For its harmful psychological effects see Stone, *Family, Sex, and Marriage,* 101.
29. Gélis, et al., *Entrer dans la vie,* 119–20.
30. Du Pont de Nemours, *L'Enfance,* 60.
31. For examples see Audiger, *La Maison réglée,* 91; and M. Formey, *Traité d'éducation morale . . . Comment on doit gouverner l'esprit et le coeur d'un enfant, pour le rendre heureux et utile* (Liège, 1773), 46.
32. Gélis et al., *Entrer dans la vie,* 111–12.
33. Du Pont de Nemours, *L'Enfance,* 61.
34. Gélis et al., *Entrer dans la vie,* 124–25.
35. Hunt, *Parents and Children,* 146–58; Stone, *Family, Sex, and Marriage,* 93–102.
36. Mme. Roland, *Mémoires,* 1:7–8.
37. Du Pont de Nemours, *L'Enfance,* 62.
38. Hunt, *Parents and Children,* 133–58.
39. Audiger, *La Maison réglée,* 88–90.
40. One example of such an advertisement comes from the *Journal de Guienne* for November 8, 1784: "A young girl of eighteen, having good references, costumed as a peasant from the countryside of Clermont in Auvergne, knowing how to iron and work in linen, wants to be placed in a household as a *fille d'enfans* [*sic*] or *femme de charge.*"
41. There is some debate over whether this picture really portrays a *gouvernante.* Today it is officially titled *The Schoolmistress,* and some critics suggest that it portrays the elder sister of a bourgeois family teaching the alphabet to her young brother. But in the eighteenth century the painting was called *The Young Schoolmistress* or *The Gouvernante,* the latter being the title of a popular engraving of the painting by Lépicié, which had a caption remarking on the girl's youth. (Pierre Rosenberg, *Chardin: 1699–1779* [Bloomington, 1979], 228–30.)
42. Mme. de La Tour du Pin, *Journal,* 1:5.
43. For an example of such usage see Du Pont de Nemours, *L'Enfance,* 126. This usage may have its origin in decrees of the Council of Trent which prohibited priests from employing *servantes* but allowed them to have *gouvernantes* (presumably their old nurses) in their households. It is impossible to judge how far *gouvernantes* deserved their reputation for promiscuity. But at least some definitely carried on flirtations with the gentlemen of the household. One example is Marianne, *gouvernante* of the young Benjamin Constant, who was his father's mistress and bore him two illegitimate children. (J. Christopher Herold, *Mistress to an Age: A Life of Madame de Stael* [New York, 1958], 137.) The usage of *gouvernante* as a synonym for mistress continued even in the nineteenth century. See Martin-Fugier, *La Place des bonnes,* 58.
44. For examples of such advertisements see *Affiches, annonces . . . de Toulouse,* February 22, 1787.
45. Restif, *Les Contemporains,* 220. "God, you should have seen how I spoke French then!"
46. For an excellent description of this important watershed, see Hunt, *Parents and Children,* 180–86.

47. See above, chapter 6.

48. Lougee, *Le Paradis des Femmes,* 173–209, gives a fine account of the impact of the rise of domesticity on women's education in the late seventeenth century.

49. AN T 186[45], Papiers du Duc et Duchesse de Fitz-James.

50. Comtesse de Sabran, *Correspondence inédite,* 45.

51. Sieur de Grenaille, *L'Honneste garçon* (Paris, 1642); [Alexandre Varet] *De L'Education chrétienne des enfants, selon les maximes de l'Ecriture Sainte et les instructions des saintes pères de l'Église* (Paris, 1666); M. Baudouin, *De L'Education d'un jeune seigneur* (Paris, 1728); L'Abbé Castel de St. Pierre, *Avantages de l'éducasion du colèges sur l'éducasion domestique* (Amsterdam, 1740).

52. Baudouin, *L'Education d'un jeune seigneur,* 307.

53. For the social composition of the student bodies of eighteenth-century *collèges,* see R. Chartier, M. M. Compère, and D. Julia, *L'Education en France du XVIe au XVIIIe siècles* (Paris, 1976), 179–96.

54. Other factors may also have contributed to the disappearance of the *précepteur.* For one thing, the rising cost of servant-keeping may have discouraged his employment, as it did that of other skilled upper servants. Then, too, the disappearance may be purely illusory. The *capitation* roll of 1695 was far more accurate than that of 1750. Masters in 1750 may simply have not reported the *précepteurs* they employed.

55. Here I differ with Guy Chaussinand-Nogaret, *La Noblesse au XVIIIe siècle: De la Féodalité aux lumières* (Paris, 1976), 98–103, which argues that the high nobility was more likely to patronize *collèges* than provincial nobles were, and that they were therefore better educated than the robe nobility. The evidence of memoirs suggests that most court nobles were "educated," if that is the word, at home by tutors. But a comprehensive study of the education of the eighteenth-century nobility is badly needed.

56. Baudouin, *L'Education d'un jeune seigneur,* 7.

57. Hunt, *Parents and Children,* 182.

58. [Jacques Bouyer de St. Gervais], *Conseils d'un gouverneur à un jeune seigneur* (Paris, 1727), passim.

59. Baudouin, *L'Education d'un jeune seigneur,* 5.

60. Dufort de Cheverny, *Mémoires,* 5.

61. Charles Pinot, Sieur Duclos, *Mémoires pour servir à l'histoire des moeurs du dix-huitième siècle* (Paris, 1751), 5–6.

62. Tilly, *Mémoires,* 14.

63. Lauzun, *Mémoires,* 3.

64. Ibid., 4.

65. For the childhood experiences of the Russian nobility see Marc Raeff, *Origins of the Russian Intelligensia: The Eighteenth Century Nobility* (New York, 1966), 123; for the southern mammy see Genovese, *Roll, Jordan, Roll,* 352–61.

66. Miller, "A Scottish Childhood," 116.

67. Lawrence Stone suggests that servants were cruel to children simply because that was the way they themselves had been raised. (*The Family, Sex, and Marriage,* 470.) But I think desires to compensate for their own ill-treatment at the hands of their masters must have played at least some role in their persecution of their charges.

68. *De L'Education chrétienne des enfants,* 144–45.

69. Bernis, *Mémoires et lettres,* 11.

70. Duc de Lauzun, *Mémoires,* 4; Mme. de Créquy, *Souvenirs,* 6: 232–34.

71. *La Vie de Mme. de Guyon,* 18, 12.

72. For "separation anxiety" see Bowlby, *Attachment and Loss,* vol. 2: *Separation,* XII; 52–65.

73. Marquise de Ferrières, *Souvenirs,* 12.

74. Bowlby, *Attachment and Loss,* vol. 2: *Separation,* 257–58.

75. Mme. de Genlis, *Mémoires inédites,* 5:116.

76. Bowlby, *Attachment and Loss,* vol. 2: *Separation,* 187–88.

77. Pinot-Duclos, *Mémoires,* 5–6.

78. Dufort de Cheverny, *Mémoires,* 5–6, 11, 19.

79. Lauzun, *Mémoires,* 9–10.

80. Bowlby, *Attachment and Loss,* vol. 2: *Separation,*xiii.

81. *La Vie de Mme. de Guion,* passim. Lawrence Stone finds similar links between the childhood emotional deprivation and the religious transports of English enthusiasts. See *The Family, Sex, and Marriage,* 101.

82. Bowlby, *Attachment and Loss,* vol. 2: *Separation,* 332, 335. For similar modern examples of the psychological problems of children raised by servants, see M. H. Stone and C. J. Kastenbaum, "Maternal Deprivation in Children of the Wealthy," *History of Childhood Quarterly* 2 (1974), 76–96.

83. *La Vie de Mme. de Guion.* 55, 106–7.

84. Dufort de Cheverny, *Mémoires,* 168.

85. Baronne d'Oberkirch, *Mémoires,* 182.

86. Dufort de Cheverny, *Mémoires,* 167–69.

87. I differ here with Lawrence Stone, who in *The Family, Sex, and Marriage,* 478–80, denies that any real change in child-rearing attitudes and practices took place in France until the Revolution. My reasons should be obvious from the argument to follow.

88. The best works on this aspect of the eighteenth-century revolution in child-care are Marie-France Morel, "Théories et pratiques de l'allaitement en France au dix-huitième siècle," *Annales de démographie historique* (1976), 393–427; "City and Country in Eighteenth Century Medical Discussions and Early Childhood," in *Medicine and Society in France,* 48–65; and Sussman, "Three Histories of Infant Nursing in Eighteenth Century France."

89. Jean-Jacques Rousseau, *Emile* (Everyman ed., London and New York, 1963), 11–13. For the arguments about maternal breast-feeding see Badinter, *Mother Love,* 169–70.

90. M. Ballexserd, *Dissertation sur l'éducation physique des enfans, depuis leur naissance jusqu'à l'âge de puberté* (Paris, 1762); Raulin, *De la Conservation des enfans* (Paris, 1768); Mme. le Rebours, *Avis aux mères qui veulent nourrir leurs enfants* (3d ed., Paris, 1775), Verdier-Heurtin, *Discours et essai aphoristique sur l'allaitement et l'éducation physique des enfans* (Paris, 1804).

91. Raulin, *De la Conservation des enfans,* 3:172; Dessessartz, *Traité de l'éducation corporelle des enfants en bas âge, ou Réflexions pratiques des moyens de procureur une meilleure constitution aux citoyens* (Paris, 1760), 183, 189, 195; William Buchan, *Médecine domestique, ou Traité complet des moyens de se conserver en santé* (Edinburgh, 1775), 1:4, 9–10; Mme. Le Rebours, *Avis aux mères,* 203.

92. Mme. Le Rebours, *Avis aux mères,* 185; Alphonse Leroy, *Recherches sur les habillemens, ou Examen de la manière dont il faut vêtir l'un et l'autre sexe* (Paris, 1772), passim; Buchan, *Médecine domestique,* 64; Dessessartz, *L'Education corporelle,* 230–37.

93. Mme. Le Rebours, *Avis aux mères,* 185.

94. For the depopulation debate, see Prost de Royer, *Mémoire sur la conservation des enfants,* (Lyons, 1778), 19ff., and read Chamousset's *Mémoire politique* in connection with the rest of his *Oeuvres complètes.*

95. Jacques Donzelot, *The Policing of Families,* trans. Robert Hurley (New York, 1979), 9–22. But see also Jean-Pierre Goubert, "The Art of Healing: Learned Medicine and Popular Medicine in the France of 1790"; Daniel Roche, "Talent, Reason, and Sacrifice: The Physician during the Enlightenment," and Mireille Laget, "Child-birth in Seventeenth and Eighteenth Century France: Obstetrical Practices and Collective Attitudes," all in *Medicine and Society in France*; and J. -N. Biraben, "Le médecin et l'enfant au 18e siècle: Apercu surla pédiatrie au 18e siècle," *Annales de démographie historique* (1973), 215–23.

96. For Mme. Roland's misadventure with maternal breast-feeding see Sussman, "Three Histories of Infant Nursing," 12–23.

97. See ibid., 23–35, for the Marquise de Bombelles. For Marie Antoinette, see Morel, "L' Allaitement au 18e siècle," 406.

98. Gélis et al., *Entrer dans la vie,* 158.

99. One noblewoman who discovered this was the Comtesse de la Bouère. She wanted to nurse her baby, but decided it was safer to leave the child with a *nourrice* when the Vendean civil war broke out and she was forced to flee. (Comtesse de la Bouère, *Souvenirs: La Guerre de la Vendée, 1793–96* [Paris, 1890], 114–15.

100. The remarkable letters of Nicod and the nurse he hired were discovered and analyzed by George Sussman in "Three Histories of Infant Nursing," 5–10.

101. This painting is labeled by its current owner, the National Gallery in Washington, as *A Visit to the Nursery.* But the simplicity of the surroundings and the tattered rags of the nurse and her offspring, who stare wide-eyed at the fashionable strangers, suggest that it portrays a visit to the nurse in her own home.

102. For the decline in infant mortality, see Gélis et al., *Entrer dans la vie,* 185, and Lebrun, *La Vie conjugale,* 139. The decline is only slight; infant death rates rose again with the disruptions of the Revolution in the 1780s and 1790s. Also, other factors, especially the availability of food and the price of bread, were important in determining the infant death rate. Nonetheless, that increased parental vigilance saved at least some infant lives remains an intriguing possibility. For a similar argument with regard to England see Trumbach, *The Rise of the Egalitarian Family,* 187–88.

103. Donzelot, *Policing of Families*, 20–21; Leroy, *Recherches sur les habillemens*, 90–91; Raulin, *De la Conservation des enfans*, 238.

104. Quoted in Herold, *Mistress to an Age*, 23–24. This work is my major source for Mme. de Stael's childhood.

105. Sussman, "Three Histories of Infant Nursing," 21.

106. Quoted in ibid., 20.

107. Mme. Roland, *Mémoires*, 1:292; letter of Mme. Roland to M. Birville, April 28, 1785.

108. Ibid.

109. Quoted in Sussman, "Three Histories of Infant Nursing," 16.

110. Quoted in Herold, *Mistress to an Age*, 37, 46.

111. Sussman, "Three Histories of Infant Nursing," 22–23.

112. In this they apparently differed from English noblewomen of the same period, who quite often did exclude servants from the child-raising process. (Stone, *The Family, Sex, and Marriage*, 456–57). This difference is just one more indication of how much further advanced domesticity was in England than in France at the end of the eighteenth century.

113. Quoted in Sussman, "Three Histories of Infant Nursing," 31.

114. Ibid.

115. Comtesse de Sabran, *Correspondance inédite*, 45–46.

116. Ibid., 205–6.

117. Quoted in Herold, *Mistress to an Age*, 23.

118. Duchesse d'Abrantes, *Home and Court Life of the Emperor Napoleon*, 1:339–42.

119. Comtesse de Sabran, *Correspondance inédite*, 45; Baronne d'Oberkirch, *Mémoires*, 138.

120. Comtesse de Sabran, *Correspondance inédite*, 205–6.

121. The best treatments of the outpouring of interest in education are Chartier et al., *L'Education en France*, 207–8; and Chisick, *The Limits of Reform in the Enlightenment*.

122. Herold, *Mistress to an Age*, 138. Benjamin Constant should not really be included in this study, since he grew up in Switzerland, not France, but the example is irresistible.

123. Chartier, et al., *L'Education en France*, 193.

124. For an example of a father who decided to send his son to a *pension*, see Comte Dufort de

Cheverny, *Mémoires*, 1:353. There was a similar movement away from the harsh discipline of the public school toward the more sympathetic pensions and home instruction among the English aristocracy in this period. See Stone, *The Family, Sex, and Marriage*, 432–37; and Trumbach, *The Rise of the Egalitarian Family*, 265–81.

125. Duc de Croy, *Journal inédit*, 1:2; 4:100–101.

126. Comtesse de Sabran, *Correspondance inédite*, 205.

127. *Affiches, annonces . . . de Toulouse*, March 26, 1788; ibid., supplement no. 47, 1781.

128. AN T 186^{56} and T 186^{50}, Papiers du Duc et Duchesse de Fitz-James.

129. Herold, *Mistress to an Age*, 138.

130. *Affiches, annonces . . . de Toulouse,* April 2, 1788; March 5, 1788.

131. Alan Charles Kors, *D'Hôlbach's Coterie: An Enlightenment in Paris* (Princeton, 1976), 166, 169, 176, 284.

132. Formey, *Traité d'éducation morale*, 171. Most *gouvernantes* were young and uneducated even in the nineteenth century. See Theresa McBride, " 'As the Twig Is Bent': The Victorian Nanny," in *The Victorian Family: Structure and Stresses*, ed. Anthony S. Wohl (New York, 1978), 49.

133. Mme. de Genlis, *Lessons of a Governess to Her Pupils, or Journal of the Methods Adapted by Mme. de Sillery-Brulart (Formerly Countess de Genlis) in the Education of the Children of M. D'Orléans, First Prince of the Blood-Royal* (Dublin, 1793), 73, 91.

134. See Louis Philippe, *Memoires, 1773–1793,* trans. John Hardman (New York and London, 1977), 12–18, for his memories of Mme. de Genlis.

135. Mme. de Chastenay, *Mémoires*, 1:20.

136. Baronne de Gerando, *Lettres*, 57.

137. Puis, ed., *Une famille de parlementaires toulousains*, 55.

138. Mme. de La Tour du Pin's tantrum worked: she was to keep her beloved Marguerite at her side throughout her life. Mme. de Genlis was not so lucky; her Mlle. Mars was fired. (Mme. de Genlis, *Memoires inédites*, 1:79; Mme. de La Tour du Pin, *Journal*, 1:21.)

139. *Correspondance inédite de Mme. Campan avec la Reine Hortense*, ed. J.A.C. Buchon (Paris, 1835), 38–39.

140. Mme. de Chastenay, *Mémoires*, 29–30.

141. Marquise de Villeneuve-Arifat, *Souvenirs d'enfance*, 5–6. The children even wrote a poem about Naret's stories, a parody of the *Mort de César:*

> Avec quelque raison Naret peut l'entreprendre
> Après ce qu'on a vu dans les guerres de Flandre
> Ou, par mille aloyaux, volailles et gigots
> Il arrêta souvent les plus fameux héros.

> With some justification Naret could undertake it
> After what he had seen in the wars of Flanders
> Where, by a thousand sirloins, chicken breasts and legs of lamb
> He often stopped the most famous heroes.

142. Mme. de La Tour du Pin, *Journal*, 1:36: 338ff.

143. Puis, *Une famille de parlementaires toulousains*, 55.

144. AN T 254, Papiers de Pierre Farcy.

145. See note 32 above.

146. For a discussion of the ways in which an aristocratic mother could assert her control over the child-raising process and thus attach the child to her rather than to the servants see Trumbach, *Rise of the Egalitarian Family*, 229.

147. See the judicious discussion in ibid., 230–35.

148. Mme. de Chastenay, *Mémoires*, 1:29.

149. For the lack of interest of their mothers in child-rearing, see Mme. de La Tour du Pin, *Journal* 1:4–5 and Mme. de Genlis, *Mémoires inédites*, 1:23. But we must take these statements with a grain of salt, for they may be attempts to excuse the authors' seemingly unnatural and thus guilt-inducing preference for their *gouvernantes* over their own mothers.

150. Mme. de Genlis, *Mémoires inédites*, 1:22–23; Mme. de La Tour du Pin, *Journal*, 1:5.

151. Mme. de Genlis, *Mémoires inédites*, 2:354.

152. Mme. de La Tour du Pin, *Journal*, 1:21.

153. Mme. de Genlis, *Mémoires inédites*, 1:23; Mme. de La Tour du Pin, *Journal*, 1:5.

154. Ibid.

155. Mme. de La Tour du Pin, *Journal*, 1:5.

156. Mme. de Genlis shocked her society by flamboyantly pursuing careers as novelist, teacher, and educational reformer, as well as openly living in sin with the Duc d'Orléans. On the eve of the Revolution her political opinions were extremely liberal. Mme. de La Tour du Pin was also a liberal at the beginning of the Revolution. Her defiance of social norms took the milder form of a genuine preference for the simple life as a farmer's wife in New York she experienced when in exile during the revolution over that of a court lady.

157. Mme. de Genlis, *Mémoires inédites*, 1:11–12; Mme. de La Tour du Pin, *Journal*, 1:20.

158. Mme. de La Tour du Pin, *Journal*, 1:338ff.

159. See above, note 24.

160. [Anon.], *Les Domestiques chrétiens, ou La Morale en action des domestiques* (Paris, 1818), 103–7. For another example of a postrevolutionary domestic handbook that urged servants to discipline children spoiled by their parents, see Mme. Demolière, *Conseils aux jeunes femmes*, 278–79.

Chapter 8

1. Such sentiments occasionally surface in debates over giving the vote to servants. They seem to lie behind the careful distinctions the revolutionaries inevitably made between secretaries, tutors, and other respectable types of domestics who were allowed to vote and hold office and servants proper, who were constantly defined by the fact that they were "of a servile condition" and engaged in "servile work." See *Réimpression de l'Ancien Moniteur* (Paris, 1840), 2:4, debate of October 27, 1789. I owe this reference to Maza, "Domestic Service," 420.

2. For the Puritan and Leveller objections to servants voting, see MacPherson, *Possessive Individualism*, 104.

3. *L'Ancien Moniteur*, 8:622.

4. See Bernard Bailyn, *The Ideological Origins of the American Revolution* (Cambridge, 1967).

5. *L'Ancien Moniteur*, 8:623.

6. Ibid., 8:622.

7. *Avis à la livrée*, 7, 9, 12–13.

8. *L'Ancien Moniteur*, 3:63.

9. For the public welfare institutions to aid servants in the revolutionary era see Alan Forrest, *The French Revolution and the Poor* (New York, 1981), 105.

10. Abbé Grégoire, *De la Domesticité*, 187.

11. Count Dufort de Cheverny, *Mémoires*, 2:141.

12. Reprinted in Bollême, *La Bibliothèque bleue*, 145.

13. In this deck the kings were replaced by philosophes like Voltaire and Rousseau, and queens by female figures embodying republican virtues. See Abbé Grégoire, *De la Domesticité*, 187, note 1. These cards have recently been reproduced and are on sale at the Metropolitan Museum of Art in New York and the Bibliothèque Nationale in Paris.

14. George Rudé, *The Crowd in the French Revolution* (Oxford, 1959), 65. I owe this reference to Maza, "Domestic Service," 417.

15. Weber, *Mémoires*, 310; *Journal d'émigration du Comte d'Espinchal* (Paris, 1912), 9.

16. Mme. de La Tour du Pin, *Journal*, 2:132.

17. Laure Junot, Duchesse d'Abrantes, *The Home and Court Life of the Emperor Napoleon*, 1:165–66; Marquise de la Rochejaquelin, *Mémoires*, 343–44; Mme. Vigée-Lebrun, *Souvenirs*, 187.

18. AN T $161^{21\text{-}22}$, Lettres de famille de M. de Boissey, letter from M. Vinez, March 1, 1790.

19. For the effects of the Revolution on the financial position of the nobility see Robert Forster, "The Survival of the Nobility," *Past and Present* 37 (July 1967), 71–86.

20. These figures are based on table VIII, "The Vocational Incidence of the Emigration," in Donald Greer, *The Incidence of the Emigration during the French Revolution*, (Cambridge, 1951), 132–38. It shows a total of 16,431 nobles who emigrated, and a total of 1,699 servants. Of course not all servant *émigrés* necessarily accompanied a master; some may have fled on their own.

21. AN T 254, Papiers de Pierre Farcy.

22. Cited in Cobb, *Paris and Its Provinces*, 95. The estimate is clearly exaggerated, but I think it gives an accurate sense of the dimensions of the problem. Servant unemployment during the Revolution was not confined to domestics of the former nobility; the tumults of the Revolution also adversely affected many more modest bourgeois types, and their servants too probably lost their jobs.

23. The figures are 35 of 215 men and 22 of 154 women. See *L'Ancien Moniteur*, 3:48. For other examples see Forrest, *The French Revolution and the Poor*, 91, 105.

24. AN T 462^2, Papiers de Nicolas Petit, domestique du Duc de Villeroy, et sa femme Marie Madelaine Jolly, condamnés à réclame (à fer).

25. Quoted in Maza, "Domestic Service," 418.

26. Quoted in Rudé, *The Crowd in the French Revolution* 65, note 5. I owe this reference to Maza, "Domestic Service," 418.

27. Mme. Suard, *Essais de mémoires sur M. Suard*, in M. de Lescure, ed., *Mémoires biographiques et littéraires*, vol. 37 (Paris, 1881), 198.

28. Abbé Grégoire, *De la Domesticité*, 151.

29. Mlle. des Echerolles, *Side Lights on the Reign of Terror*, 195.

30. Cohen, *French Encounter*, 113.

31. For the migration of French chefs to England during the Revolution see Comte de Montlosier, *Souvenirs*, 189–90. An example of a chef who remained in France and opened a public restaurant is A. Beauvilliers, who described himself on the title page of the cookbook he wrote as "former *officier* of Monsieur Comte de Provence . . . actually restauranteur at no. 26, rue de Richelieu." (A. Beauvilliers, *L'Art du Cuisinier* [Paris, 1814].)

32. AN T 273, Papiers de Bernard Arnaud, laquais. It is not clear at what period during the Revolution he held office, or what his politics were. The only evidence that he served in the municipal government is a document among his papers which describes him as an "ex-officier municipale de la commune de Paris."

33. It is not clear how many male domestics served in the various armies of the revolutionary and Napoleonic eras. Men servants do not seem to have volunteered for the defense of their country in great numbers (see Maza, "Domestic Service," 418), but they do appear with some frequency on lists of draftees once compulsory military service was introduced in 1793, as Alan Forrest shows in *The French Revolution and the Poor*, 145. Forrest argues that the lower classes disliked military service, but I suspect that at least some of them, especially domestic servants, found it a welcome alternative to the unemployment of the revolutionary period.

34. Comtesse de Bézémont, *Lettres écrites de 1809 à 1828 par la Comtesse de Bézémont au Comte de Bruc de Livernière*, ed. Baron Gaitan de Wismes, (Vannes, 1895), 8.

35. Berlanstein, *Barristers of Toulouse*, 181.

36. Rudé, *The Crowd in the French Revolution*, Appendix IV, 246–48.

37. In Marseilles, for example, not one servant enrolled in the National Guard or the Jacobin club, and only 21 of the 433 volunteers who marched to Paris on the eve of the August 10 crisis were domestics. (Maza, "Domestic Service," 418).

38. Greer, *Incidence of the Emigration*, 132–38; Donald Greer, *The Incidence of the Terror during the French Revolution* (Cambridge, 1935), 154–60.

39. Marquise de Villeneuve-Arifat, *Souvenirs d'enfance*, 5.

40. de Rémusat, *Mémoires de ma vie*, 21.

41. Forster, "Survival of the Nobility," passim; Theodore Zeldin, *France: 1848-1945*, 1, 393–427.

42. McBride, *Domestic Revolution*, 15, 18.

43. The literature on nineteenth-century middle-class domesticity is voluminous. Among the works most influential on my views of the topic was Smith, *Ladies of the Leisure Class*.

44. For the comparative wages of male and female servants and factory workers see McBride, *Domestic Revolution*, 60–64.

45. Maza, *Domestic Service*, 12; R. Forster, "Review of Marcel Bernos, *Histoire d'Aix-en-Provence, American Historical Review* 83, no. 4 (October 1978), 1022; McBride, *Domestic Revolution*, 45.

46. The types remained, of course—Balzac's murderess Thérèse Raquin was a poor relation taken into a relative's household to do domestic labor—but they were no longer classified as servants.

47. François Perennes, *De la Domesticité avant et depuis 1789, ou Discours sur cette question: comparer les rapports actuels des domestiques et des maîtres, avec ce qu'ils étaient avant la Révolution et indiquer les moyens d'améliorer ces rapports* (Paris, 1844), 28.

48. Marie Le Prince de Beaumont, *Farmers', Mechanics', and Servants' Magazine, translated from the French* (New York, 1812), 2:124; 1:162–63, 169.

49. Martin-Fugier, *La Place des bonnes*, 139–71, perceptively delineates this nineteenth-century image of the servant.

50. For nineteenth-century attitudes toward the people see Eugen Weber, *Peasants into Frenchmen* (Stanford, 1976) and Louis Chevalier, *Laboring Classes and Dangerous Classes*, trans. Frank Jellink (London, 1973).

Bibliography

Archives: The repository of many respectable chimeras and useful lies.
—Jean-François de Bastide, *Dictionnaire des moeurs*

I. Archival Sources

A. Tax Rolls

1. Toulouse

Archives Départementales, Haute-Garonne, (ADHG) Series C 1082, Rolle de la capitation de la ville de Toulouse, 1695.
Includes the following capitoulats: St. Sernin, St. Pierre, Dalbade, La Pierre, Pont-Vieux, Daurade, and St. Barthélemy.

Archives Municipales (AM), Toulouse, Series CC.
CC 1004, Rolle de Capitation de la ville de Toulouse, au capitoulat de Dalbade pour l'année 1741
CC 1041, Daurade, 1750
CC 1046, La Pierre, 1750
CC 1062, Pont-Vieux, 1751
CC 1072, St. Barthélemy, 1748
CC 1086, St. Pierre, 1750
CC 1120, St. Sernin, 1751
CC 1008, Dalbade, 1788
CC 1041, Daurade, 1784
CC 1056, La Pierre, 1789
CC 1069, Pont-Vieux, 1789
CC 1116, St. Pierre, 1789

2. Bordeaux

Archives Départementales, Gironde (ADG), Series C.
C 2693, Rolle du capitation, 1716: Domestiques du Parlement et de la Cour des Aydes de Bordeaux et du Bureau des finances de Guienne.
C 2713, Rolle des domestiques du Parlement de Bordeaux, 1737.
C 2781, Rolles de capitation, 1767: Les domestiques des officiers du Bureau des finances; chambre des enquêtes; noblesse d'élection de Bordeaux.
C 2792, Capitation des bourgeois de Bordeaux et ses faubourgs, 1777.
C 2793, Role du bourgeois de la ville de Bordeaux, 1784.

B. Marriage Contracts and Wills

1. Toulouse, 1727–29

Archives Départementales, Haute-Garonne, Series 3E: 3E 4028; 4472; 2855–58; 7337; 6092–93; 7420; 6456; 4627–28; 6426–64; 5801–3; 3404; 1829–31; 5958–59; 14132–33; 10934–36; 3961–62; 1106–8; 3982; 7235; 3074; 5265–66; 722; 6317–18; 6913–14; 7410; 4023–27; 3674–76. These include every marriage contract and will registered in Toulouse from 1727 to 1729, except for those in E 7777, which was too mildewed to be legible.

2. Toulouse, 1787–89

3E 1867; 14183–85; 2121–221; 2124–51; 13939; 13941; 13896–98; 13908–9; 5662–63; 1064–69; 6486–87; 10802–3; 1182–84; 14016–21; 10913–15; 10873–75; 1284; 10994–96; 10761–62; 7365–66; 11096–97. These include all marriage contracts and wills registered in Toulouse from 1787 to 1789.

3. Bordeaux, 1727–29

Archives Départementales, Gironde, Series 3E 428–29; 20.542; 1237–45; 24.951–53; 23.027–29; 2047; 2874–77; 2878–79; 11948; 3419–20; 24.850–52; 7127–28; 5255; 7353–61; 8788–89; 11.712–13; 13025–26; 10831–32; 30.919; 13.120–22; 2236–42; 15.328–30; 6813–15; 8011–19; 8827–28; 9288–93; 21.528–30; 14977–79; 11.929–44; 440–63. All marriage contracts and wills registered in Bordeaux, 1727–29.

4. Bordeaux, 1787–89

3E 23.088–90; 20444–49; 23.258–59; 15.037; 23.260; 15.038–39; 20.607–11; 13.177–79; 25.004–6; 24.288–93; 19.186–91; 24.893–95; 23.130–36; 15.429–34; 20.385–95; 17.880; 20.672–74; 31.335–41; 13.272; 15.497–500; 21.601–6; 23.442–45; 13.077–79; 24.085–88; 19.334–41; 13.373; 24.451–56; 23.456–57; 23.087. All marriage contracts and wills registered in Bordeaux, 1787–89.

5. Paris, 1787–89

Archives Nationales (AN), Minutier Centrale, XXII 51–60; XXXIII 707–29; LXXXV 706–17; CI 699–720; CX 514–530. All marriage contracts and wills registered with notaries of the rue St. Martin, 1787–89.

C. *Déclarations de grossesse*

1. Bordeaux

Archives Municipales, Bordeaux, Series FF 77–79.

2. Aix-en-Provence

Archives Départementales, Bouches-du-Rhône (AD BdR; Annex in Aix-en-Provence), Series XXH.

XXH E 33–34, 40, 43–52; G 28–33.

D. *Livres de raison* and Household Accounts

1. Toulouse

Archives Départementales, Haute-Garonne. E 635, Marquis de Barneval, Registre pour mes domestiques, 1769ff.

E 639, Livre de raison de Bernadet, curé.

E 642, Livre de raison de M. de Cambon, 1767–80.

E 701, Cahier de famille de Santou-Dumont, 1690–1743.

E 705, Livre de raison du Chevalier de la Rénaudie.

IMi 55, Livre de raison de moi, Fortune François Xavier de Bec, officier royal du corps d'artillerie.
J 246, Livre de raison de Charles Louis Tournier, Comte de Vaillac, 1796–1822.
J 262, Livre de raison de la famille Lacaze-Manbel, 1720–40.
J 550, Livre de raison de Guillaume Escaffié, curé de St. Pierre de Calvairac, 1701–21.
4J 22 No. 26, Dépense annuelle de la maison de M. Le Procurer-général Riquet de Bonrepos, 1756.
9J 4, Livre de raison de la famille de Montlezun, 1702–24.
10J 20, Fonds de Montaigut de St. Paul.
12J 33, Famille de Palarin, Livre de comptes de maison et de recolte, 1659–1749.
12J 41, Château de Castelnau, Comptes de maison, 1753–61.

2. Bordeaux
Archives Départementales, Gironde.
2E 412, Famille de Bourran, Livre de raison, 1664–73 and 1693–1707.
2E 1562, Livre de raison de famille Labarthe, 1702–53 and 1723–63.
2E 1696, Livre de raison de Lapourous, 1674–1739.
2E 1718, Dépenses annuelles de Curé Lapaure, 1766–85.
2E 1749, Famille de Laroque, Baron de Budos, Livre de raison, 1709–84.
I Mi 683–84, Livres de raison de Jean-Bernard Daleau, 1761–76 and 1728–70.

3. Paris
Archives Nationales, Series T.
T 186^{45}, 186^{50}, 186^{56}, Papiers du Duc et Duchesse Fitz-James.
T 208^{1}, Comptes de Maréchal et Maréchale de Mirepoix, 1749–77.
T 399, Papiers de La Moine de Crécy, premier valet de chambre du roi.
$T446^{B}$, Papiers de Jacques-Edouard Renard, valet de garde robe de Monsieur, frère du roi.
T 491^{2}, Papiers du Prince de Lambesc.
Bibliothèque Nationale (BN), MS, Nouvelles acquisitions françaises.
6187, Fragments d'un livre de raison d'un bourgeois de Rodez, 1635–88.
6541, Livre de raison de famille St. Amans, 1604–66.
6542, Livre de raison de St. Amans d'Agen, 1666–1749.
6580, Livre de raison de famille St. Amans, 1774ff.
Bibliothèque Nationale, MS, Collections Joly de Fleury.
2489, Comptes de maison du Président Omer Joly de Fleury, 1769–72.
2490, Comptes de maison du Président Omer Joly de Fleury, 1772.

E. Family Correspondence
Archives Nationales, Series T.
T $161^{21\text{-}22}$, Papiers de M. de Bossey.
T 169^{19}, Papiers de M. de Bossey.
T 254, Papiers de Pierre Farcy, valet de chambre de la Comtesse de Balbi.
T 273, Papiers de Bernard Arnaud, laquais.

T 462[2], Papiers de Nicolas Petit, domestique du Duc de Villeroy et sa femme Marie Madelaine Jolly, condamnés à réclame (á fer).

F. Police and Court Records

1. Toulouse

Archives Départementales, Haute-Garonne, Series B.

51B 21 Parlement de Toulouse, Procès-verbaux d'exécution à mort et de torture, 1633–86

51B 22, 1687–1700

51B 23, 1702–28

51B 24, 1750–60

51B 25, 1761–67

51B 26, 1768–71

51B 27, 1772–78

Archives Municipales, Series FF.

FF 613, Police, justice, et répression, 1661–1783. Condemnations à La Grave.

FF 614, Police, justice, et répression, 1733–89. Condemnations à La Grave.

2. Bordeaux

Archives Départementales, Gironde, Series B.

12B 276, Procédures et informations de la Jurade, 1741.

12B 287, 1746.

12B 358, 1778.

Archives Municipales, Series FF.

FF 75, Filles publiques.

3. Paris

Archives Nationales, Series X and Y.

X[2], Parlement de Paris, Chambre criminel, Table des accusés.

Y 14515[B], Commissaires de police, St. Germain, 1717–18.

Y 14516, 1719

Y 14517, 1720

Y 14518, 1721

Y 14519, 1722

Y 14542[B], 1749–52

Y 14543, 1752–53

G. Police Ordinances Concerning Servants

1. Toulouse

Archives Municipales, Series BB.

BB 159, Livre des arrêts, judgements et ordonnances rendues en fait de police, 1725–33

BB 160, Registre pour servir à y transcrire les ordres de police rendues par M. des capitouls, 1739–64.

BB 161, Ordonnances des Capitouls, 1764–80.

BB 163, Ordonnances des Capitouls, 1780–85.

BB 164, Ordonnances des Capitouls, 1785–90.

BB 165, Ordonnances capitulaires, 1655–1738.

2. Paris
Bibliothèque Nationale, Manuscrits.
FF 21800, Collection Delamare, Serviteurs et manouvriers.

II. Printed Original Sources

A. Memoirs and Correspondence

Abrantes, Laure Junot, Duchesse d'. *The Home and Court Life of the Emperor Napoleon and His Family*. London, 1893.

Anthonie, garçon de la chambre du Roy. *Fragment du journal de le maladie et de la mort de Louis XIII*. Fontainbleau, 1888.

______, Les frères. *La Mort de Louis XIV*. Paris, 1880.

Arnauld D'Audilly, Robert. *Mémoires de Messire Robert Arnauld d'Audilly*. Paris, 1824.

Avaux, Claude de Mesmes, Count d'. *Correspondance inédite du Comte d'Avaux, Jean-Jacques de Mesmes, Sieur de Roissy*. Ed. A. Boppe. Paris, 1887.

Avrillon, Mlle. *Mémoires de Mlle. Avrillon, première femme de chambre de l'Impératrice, sur la vie privée de Josephine*. Paris, 1833.

Barthélemy, François, Marquis de. *Mémoires*. Ed. Jacques de Dampierre. Paris, 1914.

Bassompierre, Maréchal François de. *Journal de ma vie*. Paris, 1870–77.

Béarn, Pauline, Comtesse de Galard de. *Souvenirs de quarante ans, 1789–1830, récits d'une dame de Mme. la Dauphine*. Paris, 1861.

Beauvais-Nangis, Nicolas de Brishanteau, Marquis de. *Mémoires de M. de Beauvais-Nanges*. Paris, 1665.

Bernis, François Joachim, Cardinal de. *Mémoires et lettres de François Joachim de Pierre, Cardinal de Bernis, 1715–58*. Ed. Frederic Masson. Paris, 1878.

Berthoud, S. Henry. *Mémoires de ma cuisinière*. Paris, 1846.

Besenval, Pierre-Victor, Baron de. *Mémoires de M. Le Baron de Besenval, Lieutenant-Général des armées du roi sous Louis XV et Louis XVI* . . .Paris, 1805.

Bézémont, Comtesse de. *Lettres écrites de 1809 à 1828 par la Comtesse de Bézémont au Comte de Bruc de Livernière*. Ed. Baron Gaetan de Wismes. Vannes, 1895.

Bonneval, Claude-Alexandre, Comte de. *Mémoires du Comte de Bonneval, ci-devant général d'infanterie au service de Sa Majesté Impérial et Catholique*. Londres(?), 1737.

Boudeville, Marquise de. *Lettres de Madame la Marquise de Boudeville à la Dame de Briux, sa fille*. N.p., n.d. (c.1730).

Bouère, Comtesse de la. *Souvenirs: La Guerre de la Vendée, 1793–96*. Paris, 1890.

Boufflers, Stanislas-Jean, Marquis de. *Lettres du Chevalier de Boufflers à la Comtesse de Sabran*. Paris, 1891.

Bouille, Louis-Joseph-Amour, Marquis de. *Mémoires du Marquis de Bouille*. Paris, 1821.

Bouillon, Elisabeth de Nassau, Duchesse de. *Les Deux Duchesses: Lettres de Mme. de Bouillon à Mme. de La Trémoille, 1621–22*. Paris, 1858–66.

Bourcier, Jean-Leonard, *Journal du président Bourcier, 1649–1726*. Nancy, 1891.

Broglie, Albertine-Ida-Gustavine, Duchesse de. *Lettres de la duchesse de Broglie, 1814–38*. Paris, 1896.

Bussy, Roger de Rabutin, Comte de. *Les mémoires de Messire Roger de Rabutin, Comte de Bussy*. Paris, 1696.

Buvat, Jean. *Journal de la Régence, 1715–23*. Paris, 1865.

Campan, Jeanne-Louise-Henriette. *Correspondance inédite de Mme. Campan avec la Reine Hortense*. Ed. J.A.C. Buchon. Paris, 1958.

Casanova, Jacques. *Mémoires*. Pléiade ed. Paris, 1958.

Chastenay, Victorine, Comtesse de. *Mémoires de Mme. de Chastenay, 1771–1815*. Paris, 1896.

Cheverny, Jean-Nicholas Dufort, Comte de. *Mémoires du Comte Dufort de Cheverny*. Intro. Robert de Crévècoeur. 2d. ed. Paris, 1909.

Chorllon, J.-B.-Alexis. *Mémoires du président Chorllon, 1635–1685*. Gueret, 1886.

Clairon, Legris de Latude. *Mémoires de Mlle. Clairon*. Ed. M.-F. Barrière. Paris, 1846.

Condé, Prince de. *Correspondance inédite de Duc de Bourbon avec Mme. la Comtesse de Vaudreuil, 1798–99*. Paris, 1886.

Condé, Princesse Louise de. *Correspondance de la Princesse Louise de Condé: . . . Lettres écrites pendant l'émigration*. Ed. R.-P. Dom Rabocy. Paris, 1889.

———. *Lettres intimes de Mlle. de Condé à M. de la Gervaisais, 1786–87*. 3d ed. Paris, 1878.

Courcelles, Marie-Sidonia Lenoncourt, Marquise de. *Mémoires de la Marquise de Courcelles, née Marie-Sidonia Lenoncourt, et sa correspondance*. Paris, 1869.

Créquy, Rénée, Marquise de. *Souvenirs de la Marquise de Créquy de 1710 à 1803*. Paris, n.d.

Croy, Emmanuel, Duc de. *Journal inédite du Duc de Croy, 1718–84*. Ed. Vicomte de Grouchy and Paul Cottin. Paris, 1906.

Dangeau, Philippe de Courcillon, Marquis de. *Mémoires et journal*. Paris, 1830.

D'Anger, Comtesse. *Souvenirs d'émigration*. Caen, 1858.

D'Angleterre, Bruno. *Mémoires du Chevalier Bruno D'Angleterre*. Paris, 1851.

Dubuisson, Simon-Henri. *Lettres du Commissaire Dubuisson au Marquis de Caumont, 1735–41*. Paris, 1882.

Dubus-Préville, Pierre-Louis. *Mémoires de P.-L. (Pierre-Louis) Dubus-Préville*. Ed. M.-F. Barrière. Paris, 1846.

Du Pont de Nemours, Samuel. *L'Enfance et la jeunesse de Du Pont de Nemours*. Paris, 1906.

Echerolles, Alexandrine des. *Side Lights on the Reign of Terror*. Trans. Marie Clothilde Balfour. London and New York, 1900.

Espinchal, Comte Thomas d'. *Journal d'émigration*. Paris, 1912.

Fausselandry, Vicomtesse de Fars. *Mémoires de Mme. La Vicomtesse de Fars Fausselandry, ou Souvenirs d'une octogénaire*. Paris, 1830.

Faydit de Terssac, Comte Pierre-Paul. *Mémoires du Comte Pierre-Paul Faydit de Terssac, 1726–1820*. Foix, 1901.

Ferrières-Marsay, Henriette de Monbielle d'Hus, Marquise de. *Souvenirs en forme de mémoires d'Henriette de Monbielle d'Hus, Marquise de Ferrières-Marsay, 1744–1837*. St. Brienne, 1910.

Ferrquières, Antoine de Pas, Marquis de. *Mémoires*. Londres(?), 1736.

Gaillardet, Frédéric, ed. *Mémoires du Chevalier d'Eon, publiées pour la première fois sur les papiers fournis par sa famille . . .* Paris, 1836.

Genlis, Stéphanie de St.-Aubin, Comtesse de. *Mémoires inédites de Mme. La Comtesse de Genlis, sur le dix-huitième siècle et la Révolution française, depuis 1756 jusqu'à nos jours*. Paris, 1825.

Gerando, Marie-Anne, Baronne de. *Lettres de la Baronne de Gerando, née de Rathsamhausen, suivées de fragments d'un journal écrit par elle de 1800 à 1804*. Paris, 1880.

Goujon. *Journal du Maître d'Hôtel de Mgr. de Belsunce durant la peste de Marseille, 1720–22*. Paris, 1878.

Gourville, Jean-Hérault. *Mémoires de M. de Gourville, concernant les affaires auxquelles il a été employé par la Cour, depuis 1642, jusqu'en 1698*. Paris, 1724.

Gramont, Antoine III, Maréchal de. *Mémoires du Maréschal de Gramont . . .* Paris, 1716.

Guyon, Jeanne-Marie Bouvières de La Motte. *La Vie de Mme. J.M.B. de la Mothe-Guion, écrite par elle-même*. Cologne, 1720.

Hausset, Mme. du. *Mémoires du Mme. du Hausset, femme de chambre de Mme. Du Pompadour*. Ed. M.-F. Barrière. Paris, 1847.

Joubert, J. *Pensées de J. Joubert, précédées de sa correspondance*. Intro. Paul de Raynal. Paris, 1864.

Langallery, Philippe de Genlis, Marquis de. *Mémoires*. La Haye (?), 1743.

La Tour du Pin, Henriette-Lucie Dillon, Marquise de. *Journal d'une femme de cinquante ans, 1778–1815*. Paris, 1907.

Lauzun, Armand-Louis, Duc de. *Mémoires du Duc de Lauzun, 1747–1783*. Ed. Louis Lacour. Paris, 1858.

Louis-Philippe, *Memoirs, 1773–1793*. Trans. John Hardman. New York, 1973.

Malboissière, Laurette de. *Lettres d'une jeune fille du temps de Louis XV (1761–66)*. Ed. Marquise de la Grange. Paris, 1866.

Ménétra, Jacques-Louis, *Journal de ma vie*. Ed. Daniel Roche. Paris, 1982.

Montet, Baronne du. *Souvenirs de la Baronne du Montet, 1785–1866*. Paris, 1904.

Montlosier, François-Dominique, Comte de. *Souvenirs d'un emigré (1791–98)*. Ed. Comte de Larouzière-Montlosier. Paris, 1951.

Montresor, Claude de Bourdeille, Comte de. *Mémoires de M. de Montresor*. Cologne, 1723.

Mornay, Charlotte Arbaleste, *Mémoires de Mme. de Mornay*. Paris, 1868.

Nemours, Marie, Duchesse de. *Mémoires de la Duchesse de Nemours*. Paris, 1824.

Oberkirch, Henriette-Louise, Baronne de. *Mémoires de la Baronne d'Oberkirch sur la cour de Louis XVI et la société française avant 1789*. Ed. Suzanne Burkard. Paris, 1970.

Pinot-Duclos, Charles. [Ch. Pinot, Sieur Duclos]. *Mémoires pour servir à l'histoire des moeurs du dix-huitième siècle*. Paris, 1751.

Platter, Felix. *Mémoires de Felix Platter, médecin bâlois*. Geneva, 1866.

Pompadour, Jeanne-Antoinette Poisson, Marquise de. *Lettres de Mme. de Pompadour, 1753–62*. Ed. François, Marquis de Barbe. Londres(?), 1771.

Puis, Auguste, ed. *Une Famille de parlementaires toulousains à la fin de l'ancien régime: Correspondance du Conseiller et de la Conseillère D'Albis de Belbèze*. Paris and Toulouse, 1913.

Rémusat, Charles de. *Mémoires de ma vie*. Ed. Charles H. Pouthas. Paris, 1958.

Rémusat, Claire-Elisabeth, Comtesse de. *Lettres de Mme. de Rémusat, 1804–14*. Paris, 1881.

Rochejaquelein, Marquise de la. *Mémoires de Mme. la Marquise de la Rochejaquelein, écrites par elle-même*. Paris, 1837.

Roland, Marie-Jeanne Phlipon, *Lettres autographes de Mme. Roland, adressées à Mancal-des-Issarts, membre de la Convention*. Paris, 1835.

———. *Lettres inédites de Mlle. Philipon–Mme. Roland—adressées aux Dlles Carnet de 1772 à 1780*. Ed. Auguste Breuil. Paris, 1841.

———. *Le Mariage de Mme. Roland: Trois Années de correspondance amoureuse, 1777–1780*. Ed. A. Join-Lambert. Paris, 1896.

———. *Mémoires de Mme. Roland*, Paris, 1820.

Sabran, Françoise-Eleanor, Comtesse de. *Correspondance inédite de la Comtesse de Sabran et du Chevalier de Boufflers, 1778–1788*. Paris, 1875.

Saulx-Tavannes, Jacques, Comte de. *Mémoires de Jacques de Saulx, Comte de Tavannes*. Ed. Jean Baltazar. Paris, 1858.

Ségur, Louis-Philippe, Comte de. *Mémoires, ou Souvenirs et anecdotes*. Paris, 1824.

Sévigné, Marie de Rabutin-Chantal, Marquise de. *Lettres*. Pléiade ed. Paris, 1953.

Suard, Mme. *Essais de mémoires sur M. Suard*. In *Mémoires biographiques et littéraires*. Vol. 37. Paris, 1881.

Thon, Jacques-Auguste de. *Mémoires de Jacques-Auguste de Thon*. Rotterdam, 1711.

Tilly, Comte Alexandre de. *Mémoires . . . pour servir à l'histoire des moeurs de la fin du dix-huitième siècle*. Paris, 1830.

Turgot, Anne-Robert-Jacques. *Lettres de Turgot à la duchesse d'Enville (1764–74 et 1777–80)*. Ed. Joseph Ruevet et al. Louvain and Leiden, 1976.

Vigée-Lebrun, Louise-Elizabeth. *Souvenirs de Mme. Louise-Elizabeth Vigée-Lebrun*. Paris, 1835.

Vanal, G., ed. *Journal d'un bourgeois de Caen, 1652–1733*. Caen and Paris, 1848.

Villars, Marie, Marquise de, et al. *Lettres de Mmes. de Villars, de Coulanges, de la Fayette, de Ninon de L'Enclos et de Mlle. Aisse . . .* Paris, an XIII (1805).

Villeneuve-Arifat, Aymardine-Aglaé-Louise, Marquise de. *Souvenirs d'enfance et de jeunesse (1780–92)*. Paris, 1902.

Weber, Joseph. *Mémoires de Weber, frère de lait de Marie Antoinette, Reine de France*. Ed. M.-F. Barrière, Paris, 1847.

B. Travelers' Accounts

Andrews, John. *Letters to a Young Gentleman, On His Setting Out for France. . . .* London, 1784.

———. *Remarks on the French and English Ladies in a Series of Letters. . . .* London, 1783.

Beaumont, Elie de. *Un Voyageur français en Angleterre en 1764*. Paris, 1895.

Beauregard, C. de. *Nouveaux tableaux de Paris, ou Observations sur les moeurs et usages de Parisiens au commencement du dix-neuvième siècle*. Paris, 1828.

Brice, Germain. *Description nouvelle . . . de la ville de Paris*, Paris, 1684.

Coudray, Le Chevalier du. *Anecdotes intéressantes et histoire de l'illustre voyageur pendant son séjour à Paris*. Paris, 1777.

Cradock, Fanny. *Journal de Mme. Cradock: Voyage en France (1783–1786).* Trans. O. Delphin-Balleyguier. Paris, 1896.

Craven, Elizabeth. *A Journey through Crimea to Constantinople.* Dublin, 1786. Facsimile ed. New York, 1970.

Desjobert, Louis. *Notes d'un voyage en Bretagne effectué en 1780.* Vannes, 1910.

Dezallier d'Argenville, Antoine-Nicolas. *Voyage pittoresque de Paris.* Paris, 1749.

Dubois, de. St. Gelais. *Histoire journalière de Paris, 1716.* Paris, 1717.

Fontenaym, Louis-Abel de Bonafous, Abbé de. *Le Voyageur français, ou La Connaissance de l'ancien et du nouveau monde.* Paris, 1781.

Grangier de Liverdis, Balthazar. *Journal d'un voyage de France et d'Italie.* Paris, 1667.

Guibert, Comte Jacques. *Voyages . . . de la France et en Suisse.* Paris, 1806.

Karamzine, Prince Nicolai. *Voyage en France, 1789–90.* Paris, 1885.

Knight, Philippina Deane, Lady. *Lady Knight's Letters from France and Italy, 1776–1795.* Ed. Lady Eliott-Drake. London, 1905.

La Mesangère, Pierre-Antoine Leboux de. *Le Voyageur à Paris: Tableau pittoresque et moral de cette capitale.* Paris, an V (1797).

Lamouzèle, E., ed. *Toulouse au dix-huitième siècle d'après les "Heures Perdues" de Pierre Barthes.* Toulouse, 1914.

Le Blanc, Abbé Jean-Bernard. *Lettres de M. L'Abbé Le Blanc.* Amsterdam, 1757.

Liger, Louis. *Le Voyageur fidèle, ou Le Guide des étrangers dans la ville de Paris.* Paris, 1715.

Lister, Dr. Martin. *A Journey to Paris in the Year 1698.* London, 1699.

Muralt, B. L. de. *Lettres sur les Anglois et les François et sur les voiages (1728).* Ed. Charles Gould and Charles Oldham. Paris, 1933.

Nemeitz, J. C. *Séjour de Paris, c'est à dire, Instructions fidèles pour les voiageurs de condition.* Leiden, 1727.

Noyer, Mme. du. "Ce qu'on a dit de Toulouse." *L'Aûta* (April 1928), 60–63.

Nugent, Thomas. *The Grand Tour, or a Journey through the Netherlands, Italy, Germany, France. . . .* London, 1778.

Piozzi, Hester Lynch. *Observations and Reflections Made in the Course of a Journey through France, Italy and Germany.* Ed. Herbert Banoues. Ann Arbor, 1967.

Pollnitz, Charles-Louis, Baron de. *Memoirs: Being the Observations He Made in His late Travels from Prussia through Germany, Italy, France, Flanders, Holland, England, etc.* London, 1737.

Rigby, Edward. *Dr. Rigby's Letters from France in 1789.* London, 1880.

Thiery, Luc-Vincent. *Almanach du voyageur à Paris, année 1783.* Paris, 1783.

C. Printed Household Accounts

Angot, Abbé A., ed. *Livre de raison d'un notaire du Chantrigie.* Laval, 1896.

[Anon.]. *La Famille Contard du Burgaud: Détails de la vie privée aux XVIe et XVIIe siècles en pays toulousain.* Toulouse, n.d.

[Anon.]. *Le Livre de raison d'un médecin réalmontais, 1783–1802.* N.p., n.d.

Caillet, Maurice, ed. "Le livre des dépenses de la maison de l'Archevêque Loménie de Brienne." *L'Aûta* 273 (April 1958), 51–57.

Durand, Jacques-Quentin. *Le Livre de raison de J. Q. Durand, avocat et bourgeois de Rethel au XVIIIe siècle.* Rethel, 1898.

Guimbard, Louis, ed. *Un grand bourgeois au XVIIIe siècle: Auget de Montzon, 1733–1820*. Paris, 1909.

La Belleissue-Lyman, François Michel de. *Journal historique et domestique d'un magistrat breton, 1694–1765*. St.-Brieuc, 1885.

Mesplé, Paul, ed. "Le Livre de raison de M. de Gennes." *Mémoires de l'Académie des Sciences, Inscriptions et Belles-Lettres de Toulouse*, 3: 8 (1957), 67–93.

Oger, Réné-François. *Livre de raison d'un notaire de Chantrigne (Réné-François Oger)*. Laval, 1892.

Regne, Jean, ed. *Le Livre de raison d'un bourgeois d'Armisson près Narbonne dans le premier tiers du XVIIIe siècle*. Narbonne, 1913.

Ribbe, Charles de. *Une Grande Dame dans son ménage au temps de Louis XIV, d'après le journal de la Comtesse de Rochefort (1689)*. Paris, 1889.

Taminez de Larroque, P. N., ed. *Extraits du livre de raison de Bertrand Noguères, 1649–82*. N.p., n.d.

Tollemer, A., ed. *Un Sire de Gouberville: Gentilhomme campagnard au Cotentin de 1553 à 1562*. Intro. E. Le Roy Ladurie. Paris, 1972.

V. F. "Gages des domestiques au dix-huitième siècle." *Revue de Gascogne* 20 (1925), 3–124.

D. Domestic Manuals and Guidebooks for Servants

Adamson, Mme. Aglaé. *La Maison de campagne*, Paris, 1822.

[Anon.] *Des Devoirs des serviteurs, des maîtres, des enfants, des parents, de tous les hommes envers l'Eglise et l'état*. Lyons, 1830.

[Anon.] *Devoirs généraux des domestiques de l'un et de l'autre sexe, envers Dieu et leurs maîtres et maîtresses . . . par un domestique*. Paris, 1713.

[Anon.] *Les Domestiques chrétiens, ou La Morale en action des domestiques*. Paris, 1828.

Audiger. *La Maison réglée ou L'Art de diriger la maison d'un grand seigneur et autres. . . .* Paris, 1692.

Bailleul, Jean-Charles. *Moyens de former un bon domestique, ouvrage ou l'on traite de la manière de faire le service de l'intérieur d'une maison. . . .* Paris, 1812.

Bastien, Jean-François. *La Nouvelle Maison rustique*. Paris, 1798.

Bernard dit Le Sauvage. *Epistre de Bernard dit Le Sauvage, contenant des règles pour la conduite d'un mesnage*. Published with François Barbaro, *Les Deux Livres de l'estat du mariage*. Paris, 1667.

Cambry, Abbé P. de. *Maison de prince réiglée, tant en économie, que discipline domestique*. Brussels, 1652.

Cartier-Vinchon, M. *La Parfaite Demoiselle*. 2d ed. Paris, 1825.

Collet, Philibert. *Traité des devoirs des gens du monde et surtout des chefs de famille*. Paris, 1763.

Conti, Armand de Bourbon, Prince de. *Mémoires de Msgr. le Prince de Conty touchant les obligations d'un gouverneur de province et la conduite de sa maison*. Paris, 1669.

Corail de Ste-Foy, François de. *Maison rustique abrégée*. Toulouse, n.d. (1823?).

Cousin, Gilbert. *Traité de Gilbert Cognatus ou Cousin, intitulé de l'office des serviteurs*. In François Barbaro, *Les Deux Livres de l'estat du mariage*. Paris, 1667.

Crelon, Nicolas-Joseph. *Le Bonheur domestique*. Paris, 1826.

Crespin, Sieur. *L'Oeconomie, ou Le Vray Advis pour se faire bien servir*. Paris, 1641.

Demarson, Mme. *Guide de la ménagère*. Paris, 1828.

Demolière, Mme. Henriette. *Conseils aux jeunes femmes, ou Lettres sur le bonheur domestique*. Paris, 1836.

Fleury, Claude. *Les Devoirs des maîtres et des domestiques*. In Alfred Franklin, ed., *La Vie privée d'autrefois*. Vol. 18. Paris, 1898.

Fouin, L. F. *De l'Etat des domestiques en France et des moyens propres à les moraliser*. Paris, 1837.

Froger, Curé de Mazet. *Instructions de morale, d'agriculture, d'économie pour les habitans de la campagne, ou Avis d'un homme de campagne à son fils*. Paris, 1749.

Gaçon-Dufour, Marie-Armande. *Manuel de la ménagère à la ville et à la campagne, et de la femme de basse-cour*. Paris, 1805.

______. *Recueil pratique d'économie rurale et domestique*. 3d ed. Paris, 1806.

Genlis, Stéphanie de St.-Aubin, Comtesse de. *Le La Bruyère des domestiques, précédé de considérations sur l'état de domesticité en général, et suivi d'une nouvelle*. Paris, 1828.

Grégoire, Abbé Henri-B. *De la Domesticité chez les peuples anciens et modernes*. Paris, 1814.

Lambert, Anne-Thérèse de Courcelles, Marquise de. *Avis d'une mère à sa fille*, Paris, 1811.

Le Grand d'Aussy, P. Pierre-Jean-Baptiste. *Histoire de la vie privée des françois*. Paris, 1815.

Le Prince de Beaumont, Marie. *Farmers', Mechanics', and Servants' Magazine*. New York, 1812.

Liancourt, Jeanne de Schomberg, Duchesse de. *Règlement donné par une dame de haute qualité à sa petite-fille, pour sa conduite, et pour celle de sa maison*. Paris, 1698.

[Liger, Louis]. *Le Ménage universal de la ville et des champs et le jardinière*. Brussels, 1733.

Liger, Louis. *Oeconomie générale de la campagne, ou nouvelle maison rustique*. Paris, 1700.

[Lordelot, Benigné]. *Les Devoirs de la vie domestique, par un père de famille*. Paris, 1706.

Perennes, François. *De la Domesticité avant et depuis 1789. . . .* Paris, 1844.

Serres, Olivier de, Seigneur de Pradel. *Le Théâtre d'agriculture et mesnage des champs*. Facsimile ed. Paris, 1941.

Toussaint de St. Luc, R. P. *Le Bon Laquais, ou La Vie de Jacques Cochois dit Jasmin*. Paris, 1739.

Viollet de Wagnon, Jacques. *L'Auteur laquais, ou Réponse aux objections qui ont été faites au corps de ce nom, sur la vie de Jacques Cochois. . . .* Avignon, 1750.

E. Educational Treatises and Medical Works on Child-Raising

Allety, Pons-Augustin. *Magasin des adolescents, ou Entretiens d'un gouverneur avec son élève*. Paris, 1765.

Ballexserd, Jacques. *Dissertation sur l'éducation physique des enfans, depuis leur naissance, jusqu'à l'âge de puberté*. Paris, 1762.

Baudouin, Abbé Nicolas. *De l'Education d'un jeune seigneur*. Paris, 1728.

Beneteau, Julien. *La Parfaite éducation des enfans*. Paris, 1650.

[Bouyer de St.-Gervais, Jacques]. *Conseils d'un gouverneur à un jeune seigneur*. Paris, 1727.

Brouzet. *Essai sur l'éducation médicinale des enfants et sur leurs maladies*. Paris, 1754.

Buchan, William. *Médecine domestique, ou Traité complet des moyens de se conserver en santé*. Edinburgh, 1775.

Castel de St. Pierre, Abbé Charles-Irénée. *Advantages de l'éducasion des colèges sur l'éducasion domestique*. Amsterdam, 1740.

Chamousset, Claude-Humbert Piarron de. "Mémoire politique sur les enfans." In *Oeuvres complètes*. Paris, 1787.

Coeurderoy, Claudine. *Dialogue d'une mère avec sa fille*. Paris, an X.

Combes-Brossard, J. M. *L'Ami des mères, ou Essai sur les maladies des enfans*. Paris, 1819.

Desessartz, Jean-Charles. *Traité de l'éducation corporelle des enfans en bas âge, ou Réflexions pratiques sur les moyens de procurer une meilleure constitution aux citoyens*. Paris, 1760.

Formey, Jean-Henri-Samuel. *Traité d'éducation morale, ou . . . Comment on doit gouverneur l'esprit et le coeur d'un enfant, pour le rendre heureux et utile*. Liège, 1773.

Four, Sylvestre du. *Instruction morale d'un père à son fils, qui part pour un long voyage, ou Manière aisée de former un jeune homme à toutes sortes de vertus*. Paris, 1679.

Frank, J. P. *Traité sur la manière d'élevé sainement les enfants*. Paris, an VII.

Gaudon, Jacques-Maurice. *Avis à mon fils âgé de sept ans*. Paris, an XIII.

Genlis, Comtesse de. *Lessons of a Governess to her pupils, or Journal of the Methods Adopted by Mme. de Sillery-Brulart . . . in the Education of the Children of M. D'Orléans*. . . . Dublin, 1793.

Giost, Mme. *Avis aux bonnes mères sur la manière de soigner les enfans*. . . . Paris, 1824.

Girouard, I. *Avis aux mères et aux nourrices*. . . . La Chapelle, 1804.

Guérin-Albert, Citoyenne. *Avis aux mères républicaines, ou Des Réflexions sur l'éducation des jeunes citoyennes*. N.p., n.d.

Guérin, Claude. *Méthode d'élever les enfans selon les règles de la médecine* . . . . Paris, 1675.

Guillemeau, Jacques. *De la Nourriture et gouvernement des enfans*. . . . Paris, 1609.

Le Rebours, Marie-Angélique Anel. *Avis aux mères qui veulent nourrir leurs enfans*. 3d ed. Paris, 1775.

Leroy, Alphonse. *Recherches sur les habillemens de femmes et des enfans, ou Examen de la manière dont il faut vêtir d'un et l'autre sexe*. Paris, 1772.

Maintenon, Françoise d'Aubigné, Marquise de. *Entretiens sur l'éducation des filles*. Ed. Théophile La Vallée. Paris, 1854.

Prost de Royer, Antoine-François. *Mémoire sur la conservation des enfants*. Lyons, 1778.

Raulin, Joseph. *De la Conservtion des enfans*. Paris, 1768.
Rousseau, Jean-Jacques. *Emile*. Everyman ed. London, 1911.
[Varet, Alexandre.] *De l'Education chrétienne des enfants selon les maximes de l'Ecriture Sainte*. Paris, 1666.
Verdier-Heurtin, Dr. Jean-François. *Discours et essai aphoristique sur l'allaitement et l'éducation des enfans*. Paris, an XII (1804).

F. Moral Tracts and Etiquette Books
[Anon.] *La Meschancété des filles et de leur libertinages*. Toulouse, 1662.
Callières, François de. *De la Science du monde et des connoissances utiles à la conduite de la vie*. Brussels, 1717.
Frain du Tremblay, Jean de. *Nouveaux Essais de morale, sur le luxe et les modes*. Paris, 1691.
Guerchois, Mme. de. *Avis d'un mère a son fils*. Paris, 1743.
Goussault, Abbé. *Les Conseils d'un père à ses enfants sur les divers états de la vie*. Paris, 1695.
———. *Le Portrait d'une femme honneste, raisonnable et veritablement chrétienne*. Paris, 1694.
———. *Le Portrait d'un honneste homme*. Paris, 1692.
———. *Réflexions sur les défauts ordinaires des hommes et sur les bonnes qualitez*. Paris, 1692.
Grenaille, François de. *L'Honneste fille*. Paris, 1640.
———. *L'Honneste garçon*. Paris, 1642.
———. *La Mode*. Paris, 1642.
Lattaignant, Père Jean-Charles. *Manière de réciter l'oraison dominicale dans les divers états et selon les différents situations de la vie*. Paris, 1721.
[Meusnier, Jean]. *Nouveau Traité de la civilité qui se pratique en France parmi les honnestes gens*. La Hay (?), 1731.
[Pradel, Jean du]. *Traité contre le luxe des hommes et des femmes, et contre le luxe avec lequel on élève les enfans de l'un et l'autre sexe*. Paris, 1705.

G. Cookbooks
[Anon.]. *L'Escole parfaite des officiers de bouche* . . . Paris, 1662.
Audot, Louis Eustache. *La Cuisinière de la campagne et de la ville, ou La Nouvelle Cuisine économique*. Paris, 1818.
Beauvilliers, A. *L'Art du cuisinier*. Paris, 1814.
[Bonnefors, Nicolas de]. *Les Délices de la campagne, suitte du jardinier françois*. 2d ed. Amsterdam, 1655.
Carème, M. A. *Le Maître d'Hôtel français*. Paris, 1822.
Chevrier, M. A. *Le Cuisinier national et universel*. Paris, 1836.
Emy, M. *L'Art de bien faire les glaces d'office*. . . . Paris, 1768.
Fouret. *Le Cuisinier royal*. Paris, 1822.
Gauthier. *Le Petit Cuisinier de la ville et de la campagne*, Lons-le-Saunier, 1827.
Gilliers, Chef d'office. *Le Cannameliste français, ou Nouvelle Instruction pour ceux qui désirent d'apprendre l'office*. . . . Nancy, 1768.
La Varenne, François Pierre de. *Le Cuisinier françois*. . . . Paris, 1654.
Le Cointe, Jourdan, docteur en médecine. *La Cuisine de santé, ou Moyens faciles et économiques de préparer toutes nos productions alimentaires de la manière la plus délicate et la plus salutaire*. . . . Paris, 1790.

[Liger, Louis]. *Le Ménage des champs et de la ville, ou Nouveau Cuisinier françois. . . .* Paris, 1714.

———. *Le Ménage des champs et le jardinier françois*. Paris, 1711.

Lune, Sieur Pierre de. *Le Cuisinier, où il est traité de la veritable méthode pour apprester toutes sortes de viandes, gibbier, volailles, poissons. . . .* Paris, 1656.

Marin, François. *Suite des dons de Comus, ou L'Art de la cuisine, réduit en pratique*. Paris, 1742.

[Marin, François]. *Les Dons de Comus, ou Les Délices de la table. . . .* Paris, 1739.

Massialot, François. *Le Nouveau Cuisinier royal et bourgeois . . . ouvrage très utile dons les familles, aux maîtres d'hôtel et officiers de cuisine*. Paris, 1712.

———. *Le cuisinier roial et bourgeois, qui apprend à ordonner toute sorte de repas. . . .* Paris, 1691.

[Menon]. *La Cuisinière bourgeois, suivi de l'office à l'usage de tous ceux qui se mêlent de dépenses de maisons*. Paris, 1746.

———. *Le Manuel des officiers de bouche, ou Le Précis de tous les apprets que l'on peut faire des alimens pour servir toutes les tables, depuis celles des grands seigneurs jusqu'à celles des bourgeois*. Paris, 1759.

———. *Nouveau Traité de la cuisine*. Paris, 1742.

———. *La Science du maître d'hôtel confiseur, à l'usage des officiers, avec des observations sur la connoissance et les propriétés des fruits*. Paris, 1750.

———. *La Science du maître d'hôtel cuisinier, avec des observations sur la connoissance et propriétés des alimens*. Paris, 1749.

———. *Les Soupers de la cour, ou L'Art de travailler toutes sortes d'alimens. . . .* Paris, 1755.

H. Architectural Treatises

Bullet, Pierre. *L'Architecture pratique*. Paris, 1691.

Jombert, Charles-Antoine. *Architecture moderne, ou L'Art de bien bâtir pour toutes sortes de personnes*. Paris, 1764.

Krafft, Johann Karl and Pierre Nicolas Ransonette. *Plans, coupes, élévations des plus belles maisons et des hôtels construits à Paris et dans les environs*. Facsimile ed. Paris, 1902.

Savot, Louis and François Blondel. *L'Architecture français des bâtiments particulières*. Facsimile ed. Geneva, 1973.

I. Legal Treatises and Works on the Police

Dénisart, J. B. *Collection de décisions nouvelles et de notions relatives à la jurisprudence*. Paris, 1754.

Fournel, Jean-François. *Traité de la séduction, considérée dans l'ordre judiciaire*. Paris, 1781.

Isambert, Jourdan, and Decrusey, eds. *Recueil général des anciennes lois françaises depuis l'an 420 jusqu'à la révolution de 1789*. Paris, 1822–33.

Le Maire, Jean-Baptiste-Charles. *La Police de Paris en 1770: Mémoire inédit composé par ordre de G. de Sartine sur la demande de Marie-Thérèse*. Ed. A. Gazier. Paris, 1879.

LeMoyne, Nicolas-Toussaint, pseud. Desessarts. *Dictionnaire universel de police*. Paris, 1787.

Marville, Claude-Henri Feydeau de. *Lettres de M. De Marville, lieutenant-général de police, au ministre Maurépas, 1742–47.* Ed. A. de Boislisle. Paris, 1896.

[Moranderie, Turmeau de la]. *Police sur les mendians, les vagabonds, les joueurs de profession, les intrigans, les filles prostituées, les domestiques hors de maison depuis long-tems, et les gens sans aveu.* Paris, 1764.

Prost de Royer, Antoine-François. *De l'Administration des femmes.* Geneva, Paris, and Lyons (?), 1782.

Sallé, Jacques-Antoine. *Traité des fonctions, droits et privilèges des commissaires au Châtelet de Paris.* Paris, 1759.

J. Newspapers

1. Toulouse

Affiches, annonces et avis divers de Toulouse, 1775, 1783, and 1790 in the Bibliothèque Municipale, Toulouse; 1782, 1785–89 in the Bibliothèque Nationale.

2. Bordeaux

Journal de Guienne, 1784–87, 1789 in the Bibliothèque Municipale, Bordeaux.

3. Paris

Annonces, affiches et avis divers, 1751–54 in the Bibliothèque Nationale.

Réimpression de L'Ancien Moniteur, Paris, 1840.

K. Literature

Beaumarchais, Pierre-Augustin Caron, *Le Mariage de Figaro.* Larousse ed. Paris, n.d.

Marivaux, Pierre Carlet de Chamblain de. *La Double Inconstance.* Larousse ed. Paris, n.d.

Molière, Jean-Baptiste Poquelin. *The Learned Ladies.* Trans. Richard Wilbur. New York, 1978.

______. *Tartuffe.* Trans. Donald M. Frame. New York, 1967.

Montaiglon, Anatole de, ed. *Recueil de poésies françoises des quinzième et sixième siècles.* Paris, 1855.

Montier, Mme. du. *Lettres du Mme. Du Montier à la Marquise de ____ sa fille . . . ou l'On trouve les leçons . . . d'une mère, pour servir de règle à sa fille, dans l'état du mariage. . . .* Lyons, 1756.

Nougaret, Pierre-Jean-Baptiste. *Tableau mouvant de Paris, ou Variétés amusants.* Paris, 1787.

Restif, de la Bretonne, Nicolas Edmé. *Les Contemporains.* Paris, 1930.

______. *Les Nuits de Paris.* Paris, 1930.

Richardson, Samuel. *Pamela, or Virtue Rewarded.* New York, 1958.

Rousseau, Jean-Jacques. *La Nouvelle Héloise.* In *Oeuvres complètes de Jean-Jacques Rousseau.* Vols. 4 and 5. Paris, 1909.

L. Miscellaneous

André, mulatre. *Pétition à la Convention nationale.* N.p., n.d.

[Anon.] *Les Amours, intrigues, et caballes des domestiques des grandes maisons de ce temps.* Paris, 1633. In Alfred Franklin, ed. *La Vie privée d'autrefois.* Paris, 1898.

[Anon.] *Avis à la livrée par un homme qui la porte*. N.p., 1789.
[Anon.] *La Maltôte des cuisinières, ou La Manière de bien ferrer la mule. . . .* In Alfred Franklin, ed. *La Vie privée d'autrefois*, Paris, 1898.
[Anon.] *Requête présentée par le corps des domestiques employés dans la ville de Paris, à l'Assemblée générale des representatives de la municipalité de la ville de Paris*. Paris, 1789.
Bastide, Jean-François de. *Dictionnaire des moeurs*. La Haye [Paris], 1773.
Chambon, valet de chambre. *Adresse à la Convention nationale*. N.p., n.d.
Delacroix, Jacques-Vincent. *Peinture des moeurs du siècle, ou Lettres et discours sur differens sujets*. Amsterdam (?), 1777.
Lasalle, J. Henri. *Projet d'un establissement destiné à recevoir les femmes domestiques aux époques ou elles sont sans places*. Paris, 1827.
Stewart, John Hall. *A Documentary Survey of the French Revolution*. New York, 1951.
Tallement des Reaux, Gédon. *Historiettes*. Pleiade ed. Paris, 1960.

III. Secondary Sources

A. Works on Domestic Service, Servants, and the Household

Ariès, Philippe. "Le Service domestique: Permanence et variations." *XVIIe Siècle* 32, no. 4 (October–December 1980), 415–20.
Babeau, Albert. *Les Artisans et les domestiques d'autrefois*. Paris, 1886.
Bienaymé, Gustave. "La Coût de la vie à Paris à diverses époques." Extract from the *Journal de statistique de Paris*, 1900.
Botlan, Marc. "Domesticité et domestiques à Paris dans la crise (1770–1790)." *Thèse*, Ecole des Chartes, 1976.
Broom, L., and J. H. Smith. "Bridging Occupations." *British Journal of Sociology* 14, no. 4 (December 1963), 321–34.
Coser, Lewis A. "Servants: The Obsolescence of an Occupational Role." *Social Forces* 52 (September 1973), 31–40.
Cunnington, Phillis. *Costume of Household Servants: From the Middle Ages to 1900*. London, 1974.
Cusenier, Marcel. "Les Domestiques en France." *Thèse*, Université de Paris, Faculté de Droit, 1912.
Davidoff, Leonore. "Class and Gender in Victorian England: The Diaries of Arthur J. Munby and Hannah Cullwick." *Feminist Studies* 1 (Spring 1979), 87–141.
———. "Mastered for Life: Servant and Wife in Victorian England." *Journal of Social History* 7, no. 4 (Summer 1974), 406–29.
Dessert, D. "Le Laquais financier au Grand Siècle: Mythe ou réalité?" *XVIIe Siècle* 22 (January–March 1979), 21–36.
Dubois, Rémy. *De la Condition juridique des domestiques*. Lille, 1907.
Elias, Norbert. *The Civilizing Process: The History of Manners*. Trans. Edmund Jephcott. Oxford, 1978.
Fairchilds, Cissie C. "Masters and Servants in Eighteenth Century Toulouse." *Journal of Social History* 12, no. 3 (Spring 1979), 368–93.
Girard, A. "Le Triomphe de 'La Cuisinière Bourgeois': Livres culinaires, cuisine et

société en France au dix-septième et dix-huitième siècles." *Revue d'histoire moderne et contemporaine* 24 (October–December 1977), 499–523.

Girouard, Mark, *Life in the English Country House*. New Haven, 1978.

Gutton, Jean-Pierre. *Domestiques et serviteurs dans la France de l'ancien régime*. Paris, 1981.

Hecht, J. Jean. *The Domestic Servant Class in Eighteenth Century England*. London, 1956.

Katzman, David M. *Seven Days a Week: Women and Domestic Service in Industrializing America*. New York, 1978.

Kussmaul, Ann. *Servants in Husbandry in Early Modern England*. Cambridge, 1981.

Marcoul, Bernard. "Les Domestiques à Toulouse au XVIIIe siècle." *Diplôme d'études supérieures*, Université de Toulouse, 1960.

Marshall, D. "The Domestic Servants of the Eighteenth Century." *Economica* 9, no. 25 (1929), 15–40.

Martin-Fugier, Anne. *La Place des bonnes: La Domesticité feminine à Paris en 1900*. Paris, 1979.

Maza, Sarah C. "An Anatomy of Paternalism: Masters and Servants in Eighteenth-Century French Households." *Eighteenth Century Life* 2, no. 1 (October 1981), 1–24.

———. "Domestic Service in Eighteenth Century France." Ph.D. diss., Princeton University, 1978.

McBride, Theresa. " 'As the Twig Is Bent': The Victorian Nanny." In *The Victorian Family: Structure and Stresses*. Ed. Anthony S. Wohl. New York, 1978.

———. *The Domestic Revolution*. New York, 1976.

Nicolardot, Louis. *Ménage et finance de Voltaire, avec une introduction sur les moeurs des cours et des salons au dix-huitième siècle*. Paris, 1854.

Origo, Iris. " 'The Domestic Enemy': The Eastern Slaves in Tuscany in the Fourteenth and Fifteenth Centuries." *Speculum* 30, no. 3 (July 1955), 321–66.

Rétat, Pierre, ed. *L'Attentat de Damiens: Discours sur l'événement au XVIIIe siècle*. Lyons, 1979.

Richard, H. *Du Louage de services domestiques en droit français*. Angers, 1906.

Thomson, Gladys Scott. *Life in a Noble Household, 1641–1700*. London, 1937.

Tilly, Louise A. et al. *Female Servants and Economic Development. Michigan Occasional Papers in Women's Studies*. Vol. 1 (Fall 1978).

Towner, Lawrence W. "A Fondness for Freedom: Servant Protest in Puritan Society." *William and Mary Quarterly* 19, 3d ser., no. 2 (April 1962), 201–19.

Turner, E. S. *What the Butler Saw: 250 Years of the Servant Problem*. London, 1962.

Verlinden, Charles. *L'Escalavage dans l'Europe médiévale*. Bruges, 1955.

Wheaton, Barbara. *Savoring the Past*. Philadelphia, 1983.

B. Works on the History of the Family and the Psychology of Sexual Relations and Family Life

Ariès, Philippe. *Centuries of Childhood: A Social History of Family Life*. Trans. Robert Baldick. New York, 1962.

Backer, Dorothy Anne Liot. *Precious Women*. New York, 1974.

Badinter, Elizabeth. *Mother Love: Myth and Reality*. New York, 1981.

Berlanstein, Lenard. "Illegitimacy, Concubinage, and Proletarianization in a French Town, 1760–1914." *Journal of Family History* 5, no. 4 (Winter 1980), 360–75.

Biraben, J. N. "Le Médecin et l'enfant au 18e siècle: Aperçu sur la pédiatrie au 18e siècle." *Annales de démographie historique* (1973), 215–23.

Boswell, John. *Christianity, Social Tolerance, and Homosexuality*. Chicago, 1980.

Bowlby, John. *Attachment and Loss*. Vol. 2: *Separation: Anxiety and Anger*. New York, 1973.

Corbin, Alain. *Les Filles de noce: Misère sexuelle et prostitution aux 19e et 20e siècles*. Paris, 1978.

Darrow, Margaret. "French Noblewomen and the New Domesticity, 1750–1850." *Feminist Studies* 5, no. 1 (Spring 1979), 41–65.

Davis, Natalie Zemon. "Ghosts, Kin, and Progeny: Some Features of Family Life in Early Modern France." *Daedalus* 106, no. 2 (Spring 1977), 87–114.

Depauw, Jacques. "Illicit Sexual Activity and Society in Eighteenth-Century Nantes." In *Family and Society*. Ed. Robert Forster and Orest Ranum. Baltimore, 1976.

Donzelot, Jacques. *The Policing of Families*. Trans. Robert Hurley. New York, 1979.

Duby, Georges. *Medieval Marriage: Two Models from Twelfth-Century France*. Baltimore, 1978.

Erikson, Erik. *Childhood and Society*, New York, 1963.

———. *Identity and the Life Cycle: Selected Papers*. New York, 1959.

Faderman, Lillian. *Surpassing the Love of Men*. New York, 1981.

Fairchilds, Cissie. "Female Sexual Attitudes and the Rise of Illegitimacy: A Case Study." *Journal of Interdisciplinary History* 8, no. 4 (Spring 1978), 627–67.

———. "Women and the Family in Eighteenth Century France," in *French Women and the Age of Englightenment*. Ed. Samia Spencer. Bloomington, forthcoming.

Finnegan, Frances. *Poverty and Prostitution: A Study of Victorian Prostitutes in York*. Cambridge, 1979.

Flandrin, Jean-Louis. *Les Amours paysannes*. Paris, 1975.

———. *Familles: Parenté, maison, sexualité dans l'ancienne société*. Paris, 1976.

Foucault, Michel. *The History of Sexuality*. Vol. 1. Trans. Robert Hurley. New York, 1978.

Galabert, François. "Le Recherche de la paternité à Toulouse en 1792 et les volontaires nationaux."

Gélis, J. et al. *Entrer dans la vie: Naissances et enfances dans la France traditionnelle*. Paris, 1978.

Hernandez, Dr. Ludovico. *Les Procès de sodomie au 16e, 17e, 18e siècles*. Paris, 1920.

Hunt, David. *Parents and Children in History: The Psychology of Family Life in Early Modern France*. New York, 1970.

Laget, Mireille. "Childbirth in Seventeenth- and Eighteenth-Century France: Obstetrical Practices and Collective Attitudes." In *Medicine and Society in France*. Ed. Robert Forster and Orest Ranum. Baltimore, 1980.

Laslett, Peter. *Family Life and Illicit Love in Earlier Generations*. Cambridge, 1977.

______ et al. *Bastardy and Its Comparative History*. London, 1980.

Lebrun, François. *La Vie conjugale sous l'ancien régime*. Paris, 1975.

Lottin, Alain, et al. *La Désunion du couple sous l'ancien régime: L'Exemple du Nord*. Paris, 1975.

Lougee, Carolyn C. *Le Paradis des Femmes*. Princeton, 1976.

MacFarlane, Alan. *The Family Life of Ralph Josselin*. Cambridge, 1970.

Marvick, Elizabeth Wirth. "Nature versus Nurture: Patterns and Trends in Seventeenth Century French Child-Rearing." In *The History of Childhood*. Ed. Lloyd de Mause. New York, 1974.

______. Personal communication. March 14, 1981.

Miller, Christian. "A Scottish Childhood: The Castle." *The New Yorker* (November 12, 1979), 100–180.

Morel, Marie-France. "City and Country in Eighteenth-Century Medical Discussions about Early Childhood." In *Medicine and Society in France*. Ed. Robert Forster and Orest Ranum. Baltimore, 1980.

Murtin, M.-Cl. "Les Abandons d'enfants à Bourg et dans le département de l'Ain à la fin du 18e siècle et dans la première moitié du 19e." *Cahiers d'histoire* 102 (1965) 135–69.

Parent-Duchâlet, Dr. Alexandre. *De la Prostitution dans la ville de Paris*. Paris, 1857.

Phan, Marie-Claude. "Les Déclarations de grossesse en France (XVIe–XVIIIe siècles): Essai institutionel." *Revue d'histoire moderne et contemporaine* 17 (1975), 61–88.

Phillips, Roderick. *Family Breakdown in Late Eighteenth-Century France: Divorces in Rouen, 1792–1893*. Oxford, 1980.

Quaife, G. R. *Wanton Wenches and Wayward Wives*. New Brunswick, 1979.

Shorter, Edward. "Female Emancipation, Birth Control, and Fertility in European History." *American Historical Review* 78 (1975), 605–40.

______. "Illegitimacy, Sexual Revolution, and Social Change in Modern Europe." *Journal of Interdisciplinary History* 2 (1971), 257–72.

______. *The Making of the Modern Family*. New York, 1975.

______. "Sexual Change and Illegitimacy: The European Experience." In *Modern European Social History*. Ed. Robert J. Bezucha. Lexington, Mass., 1972.

Slater, Miriam. "The Weightiest Business: Marriage in an Upper-Gentry Family in Seventeenth Century England." *Past and Present* 72 (August 1976), 25–54.

Smith, Bonnie L. *Ladies of the Leisure Class*. Princeton, 1981.

Stone, Lawrence. *The Family, Sex, and Marriage in England, 1500–1800*. New York, 1977.

Stone, M. H., and C. J. Kestenbaum. "Maternal Deprivation in Children of the Wealthy." *History of Childhood Quarterly* 2 (1974), 78–96.

Sussman, George D. "The End of the Wet-Nursing Business in France, 1874–1914." In *Family and Sexuality in French History*. Ed. Robert Wheaton and Tamara K. Hareven. Philadelphia, 1980.

______. "Three Histories of Infant Nursing in Eighteenth-Century France." Paper presented at the Berkshire Conference on Women's History, Northampton, Mass., 1979.

Tilly, Louise A., Joan W. Scott, and Miriam Cohen. "Women's Work and European Fertility Patterns." *Journal of Interdisciplinary History* 6 (1976), 447–76.

Traer, James F. *Marriage and the Family in Eighteenth Century France*. Ithaca, 1980.

Trumbach, Randolph. "London's Sodomites: Homosexual Behavior and Western Culture in the Eighteenth Century." *Journal of Social History* 7, no. 1 (Fall 1977), 1–33.

———. *The Rise of the Egalitarian Family*. New York, 1978.

Vann, Richard. "Wills and the Family in an English Town." *Journal of Family History* 4, no. 4 (Winter 1979), 346–68.

Walkowitz, Judith. "The Making of an Outcast Group: Prostitutes and Working Women in Nineteenth Century Plymouth and Southampton." In *A Widening Sphere: Changing Roles of Victorian Women*. Ed. Martha Vicinus. Bloomington, 1977.

Wheaton, Robert. "Affinity and Descent in Seventeenth-Century Bordeaux." In *Family and Sexuality in French History*. Ed. Robert Wheaton and Tamara K. Hareven. Philadelphia, 1976.

C. Works on the General Social and Cultural History of France

Allen, James Smith. "The *Cabinets de Lecture* in Paris, 1800–1850." Paper presented at the American Historical Association, Washington, 1980.

Ariès, Philippe. *The Hour of Our Death*. Trans. Helen Weaver. New York, 1981.

Bitton, Davis. *The French Nobility in Crisis, 1560–1640*. Stanford, 1969.

Bollême, Genevieve. *La Bibliothèque bleue: Littérature populaire en France du XVIIe au XIXe siècles*. Paris, 1971.

Chartier, R. et al. *L'Education en France du XVIe du XVIIIe siècles*. Paris, 1976.

Châtelain, Abel. *Les migrants temporains en France de 1800 à 1914*. Villeneuve d'Arcq, 1976.

Chaussinand-Nogaret, Guy. *La Noblesse au XVIIIe siècle: De la Féodalité aux lumières*. Paris, 1976.

Chevalier, Louis. *Labouring Classes and Dangerous Classes in Paris during the First Half of the Nineteenth Century*. Trans. Frank Jellinek. London, 1973.

Chisick, Harvey. *The Limits of Reform in the Enlightenment: Attitudes toward the Education of the Lower Classes in Eighteenth Century France*. Princeton, 1981.

Cobban, Alfred. *The Social Interpretation of the French Revolution*. Cambridge, 1964.

Cohen, William B. *The French Encounter with Africans*. Bloomington, 1980.

Coste, Jean Paul. *La Ville d'Aix en 1695: Structure urbaine et société*. Aix, 1970.

Darnton, Robert. "The High Enlightenment and the Low-Life of Literature in Pre-Revolutionary France." *Past and Present* 51 (May 1971), 81–115.

———. "Work and Culture in an Eighteenth-Century Printing Shop." Paper presented at the Library of Congress, 1980.

Davis, Natalie Zemon. *Society and Culture in Early Modern France*. Stanford, 1975.

Dubois, Dom. "Cartes des diocèses de France des origines à la Révolution." *Annales E. S. C.* (1965), 680–91.

Fairchilds, Cissie C. *Poverty and Charity in Aix-en-Provence, 1640–1789*. Baltimore, 1976.

Forster, Robert. *Merchants, Landlords, Magistrates: The Depont Family in Eighteenth-Century France*. Baltimore, 1980.

______. "The Survival of the Nobility." *Past and Present* 37 (July 1967), 71–86.
Foucault, Michel. *Histoire de la folie à l'âge classique*. Paris, 1961.
Furet, François and Jacques Ozouf. *Lire et écrire*. Paris, 1977.
______, and W. Sachs. "La Croissance de l'alphabétisation en France, XVIIIe–XIXe siècles." *Annales E. S. C.,* 29, no. 3 (May–June, 1974), 714–37.
Garden, Maurice. *Lyon et les lyonnais au 18e siècle*. Paris, 1970.
Goubert, Jean-Pierre. "The Art of Healing: Learned Medicine and Popular Medicine in the France of 1790." In *Medicine and Society in France*. Ed. Robert Forster and Orest Ranum. Baltimore, 1980.
Greer, Donald. *The Incidence of the Emigration during the French Revolution*. Cambridge, 1951.
______. *The Incidence of the Terror during the French Revolution*. Cambridge, 1935.
Gutton, Jean-Pierre. *La Société et les pauvres: L'Exemple de la généralité de Lyon*. Paris, 1970.
Hélias, Pierre-Jakez. *The Horse of Pride: Life in a Breton Village*. Trans. June Guicharnaud. New Haven, 1978.
Hufton, Olwen H. *The Poor of Eighteenth-Century France, 1750–1789*. Oxford, 1974.
Kaplow, Jeffry. *Elbeuf during the Revolutionary Period: History and Social Structure*. Baltimore, 1964.
Kors, Alan Charles. *D'Hôlbach's Coterie: An Enlightenment in Paris*. Princeton, 1976.
Ladurie, Emmanuel Leroy. *Montaillou: The Promised Land of Error*. Trans. Barbara Bray. New York, 1978.
Marion, Marcel. *Les Impôts directs sous l'ancien régime*. Facsimile ed. Geneva, 1974.
Mauzi, Robert. *L'Idée du bonheur dans la littérature et la pensée française au XVIIIe siècle*. Paris, 1960.
McManners, John. *Death and the Enlightenment*. Oxford, 1981.
Michelet, Jules. *Histoire de France au dix-huitième siècle*. In *Oeuvres de J. Michelet*. Vol. 18. Paris, 1886.
Newman, Edgar Leon. "*L'Ouvrière: Elle souffre et se plaint rarement:* The Politics and Spirit of the French Women Worker Poets of the July Monarchy, 1830–1848." Paper.
Parent, F. "Les *Cabinets de lecture* à Paris sous la Restauration." *Annales E. S. C.* 34, no. 5 (September–October 1979), 1016–38.
Ranum, Orest. *Artisans of Glory: Writers and Historical Thought in Seventeenth Century France*. Chapel Hill, 1980.
______. *Richelieu and the Councillors of Louis XIII*. Oxford, 1963.
Roche, Daniel. "Talent, Reason, and Sacrifice: The Physician during the Enlightenment." In *Medicine and Society in France*. Ed. Robert Forster and Orest Ranum. Baltimore, 1980.
Rothkrug, Lionel. *Opposition to Louis XIV*. Princeton, 1965.
Rudé, George. *The Crowd in the French Revolution*. Oxford, 1959.
Sennett, Richard. *The Fall of the Public Man*. New York, 1977.
Solomon, Howard M. *Public Welfare, Science and Propaganda in Seventeenth Century France: The Innovations of Théophraste Rénaudot*. Princeton, 1972.

Vanel, G. *Une Grande ville au dix-septième et dix-huitième siècles: La Vie privèe à Caen: Les Usages, la société, les salons*. Caen, 1912.

Vovelle, Michel. *Piété baroque et déchristianisation*. Paris, 1973.

______. "Le Tournant des mentalités en France, 1750–89: La Sensibilité prérévolutionnaire." *Social History* 5 (May 1977), 605–29.

Woloch, Isser. *The French Veteran from the Revolution to the Restoration*. Chapel Hill, 1979.

Zeldin, Theodore. *France, 1848–1945*. Oxford, 1973 & 1977.

D. Works on the History and Social Structure of Toulouse, Bordeaux, and Paris

1. Toulouse

Berlanstein, Lenard. *The Barristers of Toulouse*. Baltimore, 1975.

Castan, Nicole. "La Criminalité familiale dans le resort du Parlement de Toulouse (1690–1730)." In A. Abbiateci et al. *Crimes et criminalité en France: 17e–18e siècles*. Paris, 1971.

______. *Justice et répression en Languedoc à l'epoque des lumières*. Paris, 1980.

Castan Yves. *Honnêteté et relations sociales en Languedoc, 1715–1780*. Paris, 1974.

______. "Mentalités rurales et urbaines à la fin de l'Ancien Régime sous le ressort du Parlement de Toulouse d'après les sacs à procès criminels (1730–1790)." In A. Abbiateci et al. *Crimes et criminalité en France: 17e–18e siècles*. Paris, 1971.

Coppolani, J. "Bilan démographique de Toulouse de 1789 à 1815." *Contributions a l'histoire démographique de la Révolution française* (1965), 221–34.

Forster, Robert. *The Nobility of Toulouse*. Baltimore, 1960.

Frêche, Georges. *Toulouse et la région Midi-Pyrénées au siècle des lumières (vers 1670–1789)*. Paris, 1974.

Higgs, David. "Lower-Class Royalism in Toulouse, 1789–1820." Paper.

Rives, Jean. "L'Evolution démographique de Toulouse au 18e siècle." *Bulletin d'histoire économique et sociale de la Révolution française* (1968), 85–146.

Sentou, Jean. *Fortunes et groupes sociaux à Toulouse sous la Révolution, 1789–1799*. Toulouse, 1969.

2. Bordeaux

Butel, Paul. *Les Négociants bordelais: L'Europe et les îles au XVIIIe siècle*. Paris, 1974.

______, and Jean-Pierre Poussou. *La Vie quotidienne à Bordeaux au 18e siècle*. Paris, 1980.

Corbin, Alain. *Archaisme et modernité en Limousin au XIXe siècle, 1845–1880*. Paris, 1975.

Forrest, Alan. *Society and Politics in Revolutionary Bordeaux*. Oxford, 1975.

Nicolai, Alexandre. *Essai statistique sur le clergé, les communautés réligieuses, la noblesse . . . à Bordeaux au 18e siècle*. Paris and Bordeaux, 1909.

Poussou, Jean Pierre. "Les Structures démographiques et sociales." In *Bordeaux au dix-huitième siècle*. Ed. Pariset. Bordeaux, 1968.

Pariset, F.-G., ed. *Bordeaux au dix-huitième siècle*. Bordeaux, 1968.

3. Paris

Cobb, Richard. *Death in Paris*. Oxford, 1978.

______. *Paris and Its Provinces, 1792–1802*. Oxford, 1975.

Descimon, R., and J. Nagle. "Espace et fonctions sociales: Les Quartiers de Paris du Moyen Age au XVIIIe siècle." *Annales: E. S. C.* 34, no. 5 (September–October 1979), 956–83.

Daumard, Adeline, and François Furet. *Structures et relations sociales à Paris au milieu du XVIIIe siècle*. Paris, 1961.

Farge, Arlette. *Vivre dans la rue à Paris au dix-huitième siècle*. Paris, 1979.

______, and A. Zysberg. "Les Théâtres de la violence à Paris au XVIIIe siècle." *Annales E. S. C.* 34, no. 5 (September–October 1979), 984–1016.

Isherwood, Robert M. "Entertainment in the Parisian Fairs in the Eighteenth Century." *Journal of Modern History* 53, no. 1 (March 1981), 24–48.

Kaplow, Jeffry. *The Names of Kings: The Parisian Laboring Poor in the Eighteenth Century*. New York, 1972.

Mousnier, Roland. *Paris au XVIIe siècle*. Paris, n.d.

"Petrovitch, Porphyre." "Recherches sur la criminalité à Paris dans la seconde moitié du XVIIIe siècle." In A. Abbiateci et al. *Crimes et criminalité en France: 17e–18e siècles*. Paris, 1971.

Ranum, Orest. *Paris in the Age of Absolutism*. New York, 1968.

Reinhard, Marcel, ed. *Contributions a l'histoire démographique de la Révolution française*. 2d and 3d series. Paris, 1965 and 1970.

Roche, Daniel. *Le Peuple de Paris*. Paris, 1981.

Williams, Alan. *The Police of Paris, 1718–1789*. Baton-Rouge, 1979.

Wills, Antoinette. "Criminal Life and Criminal Justice during the French Revolution: The Six Provisional Criminal Courts of Paris, 1791–92." Ph.D. diss., University of Washington, 1975.

E. Works on the History of Art, Architecture, Literature, and Music

Braham, Allan. *The Architecture of the French Enlightenment*. Berkeley, 1980.

Dacier, Emile. *La Gravure en France au dix-huitième siècle: La Gravure de genre et de moeurs*. Paris and Brussels, 1925.

Demers, Maria Ribaric. *Le Valet et la soubrette de Molière à la Révolution*. Paris, n.d.

Dimier, Louis. *Les Peintures françaises du dix-huitième siècle*. Paris and Brussels, 1928.

Emelina, Jean (Michel Leman). *Les Valets et les servantes dans le théâtre comique en France de 1610 à 1700*. Cannes and Grenoble, 1975.

Florisoone, Michel. *La Peinture française: Le Dix-huitième siècle*. Paris, 1948.

Fried, Michael. *Absorption and Theatricality: Painting and the Beholder in the Age of Diderot*. Berkeley, 1980.

Gallet, Michel. *Stately Mansions: Eighteenth-Century Paris Architecture*. New York, 1972.

Rocheblane, S. *French Painting in the XVIIIth Century*. Trans. George Frederic Lee. London, 1937.

Rosenberg, Pierre. *The Age of Louis XV: French Painting, 1710–44*. Toledo, 1975.

______. *Chardin, 1699–1779*. Bloomington, 1979.

Tick, Judith. "Musician and Mécène: Some Observations on Patronage in Late 18th Century France." *International Review of the Aesthetics and Sociology of Music* 4 (1973), 245–56.

Van Eerde, John Andrews. "The Role of the Valet in French Comedy between 1630 and 1789 as a Reflection of Social History." Ph.D. diss., Johns Hopkins University, 1953.

Watt, Ian. *The Rise of the Novel*. Berkeley, 1957.

Weber, William. "Musical Taste in Eighteenth-Century France." *Past and Present* 89 (November 1980), 58–85.

F. Miscellaneous

Bailyn, Bernard. *The Ideological Origins of the American Revolution*. Cambridge, Mass., 1967.

Billington, James H. *Fire in the Minds of Men*. New York, 1980.

Brunschwig, Henri. *Enlightenment and Romanticism in Eighteenth Century Prussia*. Trans. Frank Jellink. Chicago, 1974.

Burke, Peter. *Popular Culture in Early Modern Europe*. New York, 1978.

Eisenstein, Elizabeth L. *The Printing Press as an Agent of Change*. Cambridge, 1980.

Ettesvold, Paul M. *The Eighteenth-Century Woman*. New York, 1982.

Genovese, Eugene D. *Roll, Jordan, Roll: The World the Slaves Made*. New York, 1972.

Gilbert, Sandra M., and Susan Gubar. *The Madwoman in the Attic*. New Haven, 1979.

Herold, J. Christopher. *Mistress to an Age: A Life of Madame de Stael*. New York, 1958.

Hollander, Anne. *Seeing through Clothes*. New York, 1976.

Lurie, Alison, "From Rags to Rags." *New York Review of Books* (December 7, 1978), 24–26.

MacPherson, C. B. *The Political Theory of Possessive Individualism*. Oxford, 1962.

Mansel, Philip. "Monarchy, Uniform and the Rise of the *Frac*, 1760–1830" *Past and Present* 96 (August 1982), 103–32.

May, Gita. *Madame Roland and the Age of Revolution*. New York, 1970.

Raeff, Marc. *Origins of the Russian Intelligensia: The Eighteenth-Century Nobility*. New York, 1966.

Roelker, Nancy Lyman. *Queen of Navarre: Jeanne d'Albret, 1528–1572*. Cambridge, Mass., 1968.

Schochet, Gordon J. *Patriarchalism in Political Thought*. New York, 1975.

Shammas, Carole. "The Domestic Environment in Early Modern England and America." *Journal of Social History* 14, no. 1 (Fall 1980), 1–24.

Sharlin, Allan. "Natural Decrease in Early Modern Cities: A Reconsideration." *Past and Present* 79 (May 1978), 126–38.

Stampp, Kenneth M. *The Peculiar Institution: Slavery in the Ante-Bellum South*. New York, 1968.

Stearns, Peter N. *Old Age in European Society: The Case of France*. New York, 1976.

Steckel, Richard H. "Miscegenation and the American Slave Schedules." *Journal of Interdisciplinary History* 40, no. 2 (Autumn 1980), 251–63.

Thompson, E. P. "The Crime of Anonymity." In Douglas Hay et al. *Albion's Fatal Tree: Crime and Society in Eighteenth-Century England.* New York, 1975.

______. "Patrician Society and Plebeian Culture." *Journal of Social History* 7, no. 4 (Summer 1974), 382–405.

Zehr, Howard. *Crime and the Development of Modern Society.* London, 1976.

Index

About the Author

Cissie Fairchilds teaches history at Syracuse University. She is the author of POVERTY AND CHARITY IN AIX-EN-PROVENCE, 1640-1789 (also published by Johns Hopkins).

The Johns Hopkins University Press
Domestic Enemies

This book was set in Caslon display and Times Roman text type by the Oberlin Printing Company from a design by Susan P. Fillion. It was printed on S. D. Warren's 50-lb. Sebago Eggshell Cream paper and bound in Holliston Roxite by the Maple Press Company.